Handbook on Women in Business and Management

Edited by

Diana Bilimoria and Sandy Kristin Piderit

Case Western Reserve University, USA

Edward Elgar

Cheltenham, UK • Northampton, MA, USA

Published by
Edward Elgar Publishing Limited
Glensanda House
Montpellier Parade
Cheltenham
Glos GL50 1UA
UK

Edward Elgar Publishing, Inc.
William Pratt House
9 Dewey Court
Northampton
Massachusetts 01060
USA

A catalogue record for this book
is available from the British Library

Library of Congress Cataloguing in Publication Data
Handbook on women in business and management / edited by Diana Bilimoria and Sandy Kristin Piderit.
    p. cm.
Includes bibliographical references and index.
1. Women executives—Handbooks, manuals, etc. 2. Businesswomen—Handbooks, manuals, etc. I. Bilimoria, Diana, 1960– II. Piderit, Sandy Kristin, 1969–

HD6054.3.H36 2006
658.40082—dc22

2006015865

ISBN 978 1 84542 432 9 (cased)

Printed and bound in Great Britain by MPG Books Ltd, Bodmin, Cornwall

Contents

Figures and tables

Contributors

Nancy J. Adler is Professor of International Management at McGill University in Montreal, Canada. She conducts research and consults on global leadership, cross-cultural management, and women as global leaders and managers. She has authored more than 100 articles, produced the film, *A Portable Life*, and published four books, *International Dimensions of Organizational Behavior* (now in its 5th edition, with over half a million copies in print in various languages), *Women in Management Worldwide*, *Competitive Frontiers: Women Managers in a Global Economy*, and *From Boston to Beijing: Managing with a Worldview*. Dr Adler consults with global companies and government organizations on projects worldwide. Among numerous other awards, Dr Adler has been honored as a Fellow of the Academy of Management, the Academy of International Business, and the Royal Society of Canada. Canada has honored Professor Adler as one of the country's top university teachers. Nancy is also an artist working primarily in watercolor and ink.

Joy E. Beatty received her Ph.D. in Organization Studies from Boston College in 2004. She is currently an Assistant Professor of Organizational Behavior at the University of Michigan – Dearborn. Her primary research areas are diversity, careers, and management education. Her current diversity research explores how chronic illness and other hidden social identities such as disability and sexual preference influence people's experience at work. Her work has been published in *Academy of Management Review*, *Academy of Management Learning and Education*, *Organizational Dynamics*, *Women in Management Review*, *Journal of Management Inquiry*, and *Employee Responsibilities and Rights Journal*. She serves on the editorial board of *Academy of Management Learning and Education*.

Diana Bilimoria is Associate Professor of Organizational Behavior at the Department of Organizational Behavior, Weatherhead School of Management, Case Western Reserve University. She received her Ph.D. in Business Administration from The University of Michigan. She is a Co-Investigator on a five-year award from the National Science Foundation to advance women faculty in the sciences and engineering. She served as the Editor of the *Journal of Management Education* during 1997–2000. Her research focuses on gender and diversity in leadership and governance, and university transformation. She has published several articles and book chapters in leading journals and edited volumes such as *Academy of Management Journal* and *Advances in Strategic Management*. She serves as an organizational consultant and management educator for private, public and non-profit organizations. She has received awards for doctoral teaching and professional leadership and service. She has served on the editorial boards of *Academy of Management Learning and Education*, *Equal Opportunities International*, *Journal of Leadership and Organizational Studies*, *Journal of Management Education*, and *Journal of Managerial Issues*.

Kristina A. Bourne is Assistant Professor in Management at the University of Wisconsin in Eau Claire. She recently received her Ph.D. in Organization Studies at the University of Massachusetts in Amherst, after completing an MBA and Women's Studies Graduate Certificate there in 2000. Her dissertation explores the social construction of 'work–family balance' in the lives of women business owners. Drawing from socialist feminism, she examines empirically the practical accomplishment of separating life into public and private spheres. Her current research interests include feminist theories, gender, work–family, entrepreneurship, and qualitative research methodologies. She has also worked on a collaborative research project focusing on part-time work arrangements and family-friendly workplace policies and practices, resulting in a publication in *Organizational Dynamics* and *Multi-Level Issues in Organizational Behavior Processes*. In addition, she has presented her work at the Academy of Management meetings and the Organizational Behavior Teaching Conference. In 2005, as a doctoral candidate, she received the Outstanding Teaching Assistant College Award from the Isenberg School of Management at the University of Massachusetts in Amherst.

Ronald J. Burke (Ph.D., University of Michigan) is Professor of Organizational Behavior, Schulich School of Business, York University in Toronto, Canada. His current research interests include work and health, women in science, technology, engineering and mathematics, and using behavioral science knowledge to build more effective organizations. He has consulted with a variety of private and public sector organizations in these areas.

Marta B. Calás is Professor of Organization Studies and International Management at the Department of Management, Isenberg School of Management, and Adjunct Professor of Women's Studies, at the Women's Studies Program, University of Massachusetts, Amherst. Her scholarly work draws from poststructuralism, cultural studies, feminist postmodernism and postcolonial/transnational theorizing to interrogate and re-theorize areas of organizational scholarship such as globalization, leadership, business ethics and information technology. She and Linda Smircich recently completed a chapter, 'From the "woman's point of view" ten years later: towards a feminist organization studies' for the forthcoming second edition of the *Handbook of Organization Studies*, edited by Clegg, Hardy, Nord and Lawrence. She is part of the founding editorial team of *Organization: The Critical Journal of Organization, Theory and Society.*

Cary L. Cooper is Professor of Organizational Psychology and Health, Lancaster University Management School and Pro Vice Chancellor (External Relations) at Lancaster University. He is the author of over 100 books (on occupational stress, women at work and industrial and organizational psychology), has written over 400 scholarly articles for academic journals, and is a frequent contributor to national newspapers, TV and radio. He is currently Founding Editor of the *Journal of Organizational Behavior* and Co-Editor of the medical journal *Stress and Health* (formerly *Stress Medicine*). Professor Cooper is the immediate past President of the British Academy of Management. He is a Fellow of the Academy of Management (having also won the 1998 Distinguished Service Award) and in 2001 he was awarded a CBE in the Queen's Birthday Honours List for his contribution to organizational health. He holds Honorary Doctorates from Aston University, Heriot-Watt University, Middlesex University, and Wolverhampton University; and an Honorary Fellowship of the Faculty of Occupational Medicine of the Royal College of Physicians.

Marilyn J. Davidson is Professor of Work Psychology; Head of the Organisational Psychology Group and the Co-Director of the Centre for Diversity and Work Psychology at Manchester Business School, the University of Manchester. Her research interests include equal opportunities, diversity management, women in management, female entrepreneurs and gender issues in occupational stress. She has published over 150 academic articles and 19 books. She is Fellow of the Royal Society of Arts, a fellow of the British Psychological Society, a Chartered Psychologist, a member of the Division of Occupational Psychology (British Psychological Society – BPS) and a member of the Division of Psychology of Women section (BPS). She has also acted as a consultant for numerous private and public sector organizations.

Linda M. Dunn-Jensen received her Ph.D. from the Management and Organizations Department at New York University. She earned an MSIR from Loyola University and a BS from Marquette University. Linda's research interests are workplace visibility, time compression and women in management. More specifically, she explores how the changing nature of work and expectations about appropriate work hours have multiplied the challenges people face in the workplace and how these challenges have complicated the ways people integrate their work and non-work lives. In her dissertation, 'Unmasking face time: the implications of visibility norms in the workplaces', Linda explores the contextual and individual factors that influence employees to spend additional time at the workplace beyond what is necessary for their workload. She describes this behavior as engaging in 'face time'. Her teaching areas are organizational behavior and organizational theory.

Alice H. Eagly is Professor of Psychology and Faculty Fellow in the Institute for Policy Research at Northwestern University. She has also held faculty positions at Michigan State University, University of Massachusetts in Amherst, and Purdue University. Her research and writing pertain mainly to the study of gender and of attitudes. One of her special interests is the study of gender and leadership. She has written two books, *Sex Differences in Social Behavior: A Social Role Interpretation* and *The Psychology of Attitudes*, and edited four volumes. She served as President of the Midwestern Psychological Association and the Society of Personality and Social Psychology and Chair of the Board of Scientific Affairs of the American Psychological Association. Her awards include the Distinguished Scientist Award of the Society for Experimental Social Psychology, the Donald Campbell Award for Distinguished Contribution to Social Psychology, and the Carolyn Wood Sherif Award of the Society for the Psychology of Women for contributions as a scholar, teacher, mentor and leader.

Caroline Gatrell is a Teaching Fellow at Lancaster University Management School. Her work focuses on motherhood, management and employment. Caroline is engaged in examining the relationship between the maternal body and paid work, and this research will be published in her forthcoming book on Women's Work. In her empirical research Caroline has explored parenting and work practices, with a focus on understanding demographic changes and shifting attitudes towards careers and child care. Aspects of this research have been recently published in her book *Hard Labour: The Sociology of Parenthood* (2005, Open University Press).

Lindsey Godwin is a Ph.D. candidate in Organizational Behavior at the Weatherhead School of Management, Case Western Reserve University where she is currently working on her dissertation. She holds a MS in Conflict Analysis and Resolution from George Mason University and a BA in Psychology and Sociology from Ohio Wesleyan University. She currently works as a Research Associate for the Case Weatherhead Center for Business as Agent of World Benefit (BAWB) where she is the co-editor of the Interactive Working Paper Series for BAWB and is involved with the Center's work to integrate sustainability and social responsibility into the management school curriculum. Her research interests include exploring women's career advancement, leadership development, moral imagination in organizational decision-making, and morality in business education. Her work has been published in *Entrepreneurship Theory and Practice, Information & Organization, Advances in Interdisciplinary Studies of Work Teams*, and presented at the Annual Academy of Management Meeting, the Babson-Kauffman Entrepreneurship Research Conference, the Institute for Behavioral and Applied Management Conference, and the International Conference on Knowledge, Culture and Change in Organizations.

Laura M. Graves is Associate Professor of Management at the Graduate School of Management at Clark University. She is an internationally recognized scholar on diversity issues in the workplace. Her work focuses on topics such as balancing work and family, preventing sex bias in employee selection, and managing diverse teams. Her recent book, *Women and Men in Management* (3rd edn. 2003, Sage, coauthored with Gary N. Powell), considers how gender influences individuals' experiences in organizations. Her research has appeared in leading academic journals, including *Academy of Management Review*, *Journal of Applied Psychology*, *Journal of Organizational Behavior*, *Human Relations*, and *Personnel Psychology*. She holds a doctorate in social psychology from the University of Connecticut.

Douglas T. (Tim) Hall is the Morton H. and Charlotte Friedman Professor of Management in the School of Management at Boston University. He received his graduate degrees from the Sloan School of Management at MIT and his undergraduate degree from the School of Engineering at Yale University. He has held faculty positions at Yale, York, Michigan State and Northwestern Universities, as well as visiting positions at Columbia, Minnesota, and the US Military Academy at West Point. Tim is the author of *Careers In and Out of Organizations* (Sage Publications, 2002). He is the co-author of *The Career is Dead – Long Live the Career: A Relational Approach to Careers, Careers in Organizations, Organizational Climates and Careers, The Two-Career Couple, Experiences in Management and Organizational Behavior, Career Development in Organizations, Human Resource Management: Strategy Design and Implementation*, and *Handbook of Career Theory*. He is a recipient of the American Psychological Association's James McKeen Cattell Award (now called the Ghiselli Award) for research design, the American Society for Training and Development's Walter Storey Professional Practice Award, and the Academy of Management's Everett C. Hughes Award for Careers Research. He is a Fellow of the American Psychological Association, the Society for Industrial and Organizational Psychology, and of the Academy of Management. He has served on the editorial boards of ten scholarly journals.

Margaret M. Hopkins is an Assistant Professor of Management at the University of Toledo, teaching courses in the areas of leadership and organizational behavior. She has published on the topics of women entrepreneurship, leadership in a crisis, and executive coaching. Her research interests include leadership and leadership development, gender and diversity, and executive coaching. She has taught courses in the Executive Education programs and the MBA program at the Weatherhead School of Management, Case Western Reserve University (including Leadership Assessment & Development and Organizational Behavior) as well as leadership courses in the Masters in Management Program at Ursuline College. She also has an organizational development consulting practice with a specialization in the area of executive coaching. Margaret recently served as the Chair and the Vice Chair of the Board of Education for the Cleveland Municipal School District. Margaret holds a Ph.D. in Organizational Behavior from the Weatherhead School of Management, Case Western Reserve University, a Master of Science Degree in Organizational Development from Case Western Reserve University, and a BS in Psychology from Boston College.

Mary C. Johannesen-Schmidt received MA and Ph.D. degrees in social psychology from Northwestern University, a MAT from the University of Chicago, and a BA from Haverford College. Currently she is an Assistant Professor of Psychology at Oakton Community College, where she teaches Introduction to Psychology and Social Psychology and has been awarded the Ray Hartstein Award for Excellence in Teaching. She also conducts teaching and training seminars for college faculty and academic administrators. Her research and publications focus on gender similarities and differences, particularly in preferred mate characteristics and leadership styles. She was awarded the Annual Prize for Psychological Research on Women and Gender from the American Psychological Association and the Society for the Psychology of Women.

Alison M. Konrad joined the Richard Ivey School of Business, University of Western Ontario in 2003 as a Professor of Organizational Behavior and holder of the Corus Entertainment Chair in Women in Management. She is the 2003–07 Editor of *Group and Organization Management*, a ranked journal in the fields of management and applied psychology. She is a past Associate Editor of the journal, *Gender, Work and Organization* and a past editorial board member for the *Academy of Management Review*. She has published over 40 articles and chapters on topics relating to workplace diversity in outlets such as the *Academy of Management Journal*, *Administrative Science Quarterly*, *Gender, Work and Organization*, *Group and Organization Management*, *Human Relations*, the *Journal of Organizational Behavior*, *Psychological Bulletin*, *Sex Roles*, and the *Strategic Management Journal*. She is co-editor of the *Handbook of Workplace Diversity* (Sage, 2005) and author of *Cases in Gender & Diversity in Organizations* (Sage, 2005). Professor Konrad chaired the Academy of Management's Gender and Diversity in Organizations Division in 1996–97. She was President of the Eastern Academy of Management in 1997–98 and was named a Fellow of that association in 2004. Her current work focuses on organizational diversity and inclusivity initiatives, job retention among former welfare clients, and the links between individual preferences and career outcomes for women and men.

Mireia Las Heras is currently teaching at Boston University while she finishes her Doctoral Studies also at Boston University, in the School of Management. She studied Industrial Engineering at the Polytechnic School of Catalonia, specializing on Industrial Organization, in Barcelona, Spain. After graduation she managed different educational institutions in Spain and served on the board of a number of charities. She studied her MBA at IESE Business School. She has taught Organizational Behavior at IESE, and researched in the work–family arena. She started her doctoral studies in September 2004. Currently Las Heras is involved in an international project on career management, which seeks to discover the different meanings of career success. She is also working on other projects that focus on the dynamism of career success and its interplay with work and family integration.

Deborah A. O'Neil is currently a Visiting Professor in the Department of Management, College of Business Administration at Bowling Green State University in Bowling Green, Ohio. She is also a Senior Lecturer at the Weatherhead School of Management, Case Western Reserve University in Cleveland, Ohio, and a Professorial Lecturer with the American University in Washington, DC. She teaches classes in organization development and analysis, organizational behavior and leadership. She has published articles on women's career development, the use of coaching behaviors in management education, and the importance of emotional intelligence in developing leadership skills for life. Her research is focused on career-in-life development, women leaders, and the positive impact of coaching and mentoring relationships. She holds a doctorate in Organizational Behavior from Case Western Reserve University.

Sandy Kristin Piderit has taught organizational behavior at Case Western Reserve University since 1998. She earned her Ph.D. at the University of Michigan, and conducts research on the relational dynamics of organizational and social change processes. Her past work ranges from theoretical work on resistance and other responses to change (published in the *Academy of Management Review*), to studies of middle managers as issue sellers (published in *Administrative Science Quarterly* and the *Journal of Management Studies*), to an ongoing action research project studying community members engaged in transformative cooperation. Her other edited volume in press is *A Handbook of Transformative Cooperation: New Designs and Dynamics*.

Gary N. Powell is Professor of Management and Ackerman Scholar in the School of Business at the University of Connecticut. He is co-author with Laura M. Graves of *Women and Men in Management* (3rd edn., 2003, Sage), editor *of Handbook of Gender and Work* (1999, Sage), and author of *Managing a Diverse Workforce: Learning Activities,* (2nd edn., 2004, Sage). He is an internationally recognized scholar and educator on gender and diversity issues in the workplace. He has served as Chair of the Women in Management (now Gender and Diversity in Organizations) Division of the Academy of Management, and received both the Janet Chusmir Service Award for his contributions to the division and the Sage Scholarship Award for his contributions to research on gender in organizations. He has published over 90 articles in journals such as *Academy of Management Journal, Academy of Management Review, Journal of Applied Psychology,* and *Organizational Behavior and Human Decision Processes* and has presented over 100 papers at professional conferences. He has served on the Board of Governors of the Academy of Management and is a Past President and Fellow of the Eastern Academy of Management. He has also served on the Editorial Board of *Academy of Management Review, Academy of Management Executive, Journal of Management,* and *Journal of Management Studies.* He holds a doctorate in organizational behavior from the University of Massachusetts.

Val Singh is Reader in Organisational Behaviour, and Deputy Director of the Centre for Women Business Leaders at Cranfield School of Management where she gained her doctorate, after a major change of career in midlife. Her research includes the annual *Female FTSE Index* *and Report* on companies with women directors (which has been presented at Downing Street) co-authored with Professor Susan Vinnicombe, and similar studies on ethnicity of directors for the Department of Trade & Industry. Other projects include corporate promotion of gender and ethnic diversity management; corporate governance and diversity; social construction of leadership; work–life balance; mentoring; role models; networking; commitment and impression management. She is Gender Section Editor of the *Journal of Business Ethics*, Associate Editor of *Gender Work & Organization*, and has published widely, including in *Long Range Planning*, *Corporate Governance: An International Review*, *Journal of Business Ethics*, *Gender Work & Organization*, *Women in Management Review*. She has written the Masterclass in Corporate Governance and Diversity for the *Financial Times*, and is a regular speaker and workshop leader on women's careers and diversity on boards at international events and conferences. She has been a judge of the UK National Business Awards since 2003.

Linda Smircich is Professor of Organization Studies at the Isenberg School of Management at the University of Massachusetts at Amherst. Her scholarly writing applies cultural, critical and feminist perspectives for understanding organizational issues and for reframing research. She and Marta B. Calás recently completed a chapter, 'From the "Woman's Point of View" Ten Years Later: Towards a Feminist Organization Studies' for the forthcoming second edition of the *Handbook of Organization Studies*, edited by Clegg, Hardy, Nord & Lawrence. She is part of the founding editorial team of *Organization: The Critical Journal of Organization, Theory and Society*.

Linda K. Stroh is a Loyola University Faculty Scholar and Professor at the Graduate School of Business, Loyola University Chicago. Dr Stroh received her Ph.D. from Northwestern University. She has taught and published over 100 articles and books on issues related to domestic and international organizational behavior issues. Linda's work can be found in journals such as *Strategic Management Journal*, *Journal of Applied Psychology*, *Academy of Management Journal* and various others. Dr Stroh is co-author of four books, *Globalizing People Through International Assignments*, *Organizational Behavior: A Management Challenge*, *International Assignments: An Integration of Strategy, Research & Practice*, and *The Basic Principles of Consulting*. Dr Stroh was honored at the 2000 Academy of Management Meeting with the Sage publications research scholar award. She was also named the Graduate Faculty Member of the Year at Loyola University, Chicago (2000). *The Wall Street Journal*, the *New York Times*, the *Washington Post*, the *Chicago Tribune*, *Fortune*, *Newsweek*, *US News and World Report* and *Business Week*, as well as various other news and popular press outlets have cited Dr Stroh's work. Professor Stroh's research has also been featured several times on NBC's *Nightly News* and CNN. Linda currently serves on the editorial review board for the *Journal of Applied Psychology*, *Journal of World Business* and *Journal of Leadership and Organizational Studies*.

Siri Terjesen is a post-doctoral Research Fellow at Queensland University of Technology in Brisbane, Australia and the Max Planck Institute of Economics in Jena, Germany, and a Lecturer at the London School of Economics and Political Science's summer school program. Siri completed a Ph.D. at Cranfield School of Management, a Master's in International Business as a Fulbright Scholar to the Norwegian School of Economics and Business Administration and BSc from the University of Richmond. Prior to her graduate studies, Siri worked in strategy consulting in the US and Europe. Siri is the author of several book chapters and her papers have been published in various journals, including *Strategic Management Journal*, *Small Business Economics*, *Venture Capital* and *European Business Forum*. In addition to gender, Siri's research interests include international entrepreneurship and new venture formation and financing.

Susan Vinnicombe is Professor of Organisational Behaviour and Diversity Management, Director of the Centre for Women Business Leaders and an executive member of the board of Cranfield School of Management. She directs the trailblazing executive program for senior women managers and directors, 'Women as Leaders'. In addition, she runs customized programs for women executives, which have won three national awards. Susan's particular research interests are women's leadership styles, the issues involved in women developing their managerial careers and gender diversity on corporate boards. Her research center is unique in the UK with its focus on women leaders, and the annual Female FTSE 100 Index is regarded as the UK's premier research resource on women directors. Susan has written eight books and numerous articles. Her most recent books are *Working in Organizations* (with A. Kakabadse and J. Bank, Gower, 2004) and *Women with Attitude: Lessons for Career Management*, (with John Bank, Routledge, 2003). She is on the editorial board of *Group and Organization Management*, *Women in Management Review* and *Leadership*. Susan was awarded an OBE for her services to diversity in the Queen's New Year's Honour List on 31 December, 2004.

Helen M. Woolnough is a Research Fellow at the Centre for Diversity and Work Psychology, Manchester Business School, the University of Manchester, UK. Her research interests include mentoring, diversity management, mental health nursing and female entrepreneurs. Prior to joining the University of Manchester she coordinated a wide variety of research projects for the National Health service in England, many of which have resulted in radical and creative new ideas and program development and delivery. Helen has published numerous articles. She is also a Leadership Effective Analysis (LEA) facilitator.

Deborah Dahlen Zelechowski has been a Senior Executive at Robert Morris College of Illinois for the last 15 years. While Chief Academic Officer, the college earned a number of national recognitions for educating minority students. She also spearheaded a model of student-centered practitioner-focused education that touts exceptional graduation and job placement rates. As Senior Vice President of Institutional Advancement she develops innovative programs with community partners that support the advancement of the institution. Some of the newest programs include culinary, surgical technology and nursing. Recently she earned an Executive Doctorate of Management from Case Western Reserve University where she conducted extensive research on women inside directors in *Fortune* 1000 companies. Her extensive background as an officer of an educational institution and research expertise on women inside directors (termed in the UK 'executive directors') provides a unique blend of real-world and academic experience.

Introduction: research on women in business and management

Diana Bilimoria and Sandy Kristin Piderit

The purposes of this *handbook* are to provide a forum for presentation of the current state of knowledge about women in business and management and to specify the directions for future research that will be most constructive for advancing the representation, treatment, quality of life and success of women who work in these fields. In this sense, we hope that the *Handbook on Women in Business and Management* will serve as a reference for recent advances in research and theory, informing both scholars and those with a general interest in the subject.

From the early days of inquiry into women and work (a collation of early research appeared in Larwood et al.'s (1986) Volume 1 of their *Women and Work* edited series) the topic of women in business and management has continued to garner interest by research scholars. A few specialized academic journals are devoted entirely to this and related topics of gender and work (for example, *Equal Opportunities International, Gender, Work and Organization, Sex Roles, Women in Management Review*), with special issues of these and other journals (for example, *British Journal of Management, Journal of Organization Change Management*), past and upcoming, focused on pertinent sub-topics such as women's career advancement, women and leadership, work–life integration, women corporate directors, and the gendering of work and organization. Within the past two decades, published research on women in business and management has mushroomed; several books and textbooks (for example, Padavic and Reskin, 2002; Parker, 2005; Powell and Graves, 2003; Smith, 2000; Vinnicombe and Colwill, 1995; Wirth, 2001) and edited volumes (for example, Burke and Mattis, 2005; Burke and Nelson, 2002; Ely et al., 2003; Davidson and Burke, 2000, 2004; Powell, 1999; Riger, 2000) compiling the research have been published in recent years.

Concurrent with the large volume of ongoing knowledge creation, dissemination venues for research on women in business and management have expanded. Most leading schools of business and management offer MBA and executive education coursework on topics relevant to the careers and effectiveness of women leaders, managers and executives, exposing tens of thousands of students annually to research findings about women in business and management. A vibrant and growing segment of the popular trade publications market pertains specifically to women's life and career development concerns within organizational workplaces (for example, Babcock and Laschever, 2003; Frankel, 2004; Kolb et al., 2004; Stanny, 2004). Finally, the subject of women in business and management has grown extremely popular within the general media and business press, with articles, surveys and report cards of various kinds appearing regularly in the public domain (for example *Harvard Business Review*, 2005; Catalyst, 2002, 2003a and b, 2005; *Working Mother*, 2005).

Yet, despite decades of ongoing inquiry, numerous outlets for knowledge creation, and widespread public interest, research on women in business and management remains a specialized field of study that appears not yet to have reached widespread mainstream acceptance as a scholarly field of inquiry within business and management disciplines. Our search of six leading business and general management academic journals (*Academy of Management Executive, Academy of Management Journal, Academy of Management Learning and Education, Academy of Management Review, Administrative Science Quarterly*, and *Strategic Management Journal*) revealed that of the 60 special issues, special sections, or special topic forums appearing in these journals over the last two decades, not one pertained specifically to the topics of women or gender in business and management. Similarly, while individual articles addressing these topics have been scattered throughout many of these six leading management journals, their proportions remain disturbingly low. A search of the keywords 'women', 'gender', 'sex' or 'diversity' in article titles, abstracts or subjects revealed that only 76 (out of a total of 2753) articles on these topics were published in these six leading business and management journals during the 10-year period from January 1996 to January 2006. That is, only 2.76 per cent of the articles published in the last 10 years in top academic business and management journals specifically related to *women* in business and management. Taken together, these statistics about special issues and individual articles published in the field's premier journals point to the failure of top-quality academic publication outlets to recognize and invite inquiry into this important issue, and suggest that scholars must rise to the challenge of improving their future research and theorizing about women in business and management so as to better qualify for publication in these top journals.

It appears that the statistics of published research on this subject oddly mirror the stark realities of the numbers of women in business and management: many in the larger field but few at the top. In 2002, when the percentage of women in the labor force was 59.2, women constituted

46 per cent of the total US labor force and 38 per cent of the managerial and professional work force (US Department of Labor, 2004). Of the net new entrants into the workforce between 1994 and 2005, 62 per cent were projected to be women (Hudson Institute, 1997). Yet, the most up-to-date statistics indicate that women constitute only 15.7 per cent of *Fortune* 500 corporate officers (Catalyst, 2002), 13.6 per cent of *Fortune* 500 directors (Catalyst, 2003a), 11 per cent of corporate officers and 9 per cent of corporate directors of high-tech *Fortune* 500 firms (Catalyst, 2003b), and 9.9 per cent of *Fortune* 500 corporate officers in line jobs (Catalyst, 2002). Women hold only 7.9 per cent of *Fortune* 500 influential titles such as Chair, CEO, Vice-Chair, President, Chief Operating Officer, Senior Executive Vice-President and Executive Vice-President and are only 7.1 per cent of *Fortune* 500 Chief Financial Officers and only 5.2 per cent of *Fortune* 500 individuals who are their company's five most highly compensated officers (Catalyst, 2002). Only 3 per cent of corporate board directors (Catalyst, 2003a) and 1.6 per cent of *Fortune* 500 officers (Catalyst, 2002) are women of color. And most tellingly, only 1.4 per cent of *Fortune* 500 CEOs are women (USA Today, 2005).

It appears, thus, that the institutional inclusion of research on women in top business and management academic journals mirrors the prevailing gendered practices of our larger society. From the numbers cited above, we draw the unsettling conclusion that only token research on women appears at the premier levels of academic publication in business and general management. This is particularly troubling because business and management research and scholarship has the potential to lead in the betterment of the world of work, proactively charting courses that construct and communicate more effective solutions to everyday workplace realities. Without this progressive aspiration and function, scholarly research limits its vitality and usefulness for the real world, and falls short of its potential as the herald of constructive business and management change.

Simply said, to date our top-level academic research journals generally have not been proactive in addressing the realities facing women in business and management. We hope that this *handbook* serves as a call inviting future scholarship of the kind that improves the societal and work conditions and experiences of women in business and management. But at the same time, we would like to acknowledge that our hope is that the insights simultaneously offer the foundations for improved societal and organizational structures, policies and relational practices affecting *all* in business and management. Thus, by enhancing the knowledge base that improves the work and life situations of women, we hope this collection provides guidance that elevates the societal and organizational systems for all.

We organize the chapters in this compilation into four broad parts relevant to research on women in business and management. The first part describes the societal roles and contexts facing women in these fields. In this part, the authors identify different aspects of the pervasive gendering of work and organizations, expose the covert and subtle roles of assumptions, expectations and beliefs that constrain women in the workforce, and provide directions for a more liberating scholarship that has the potential to catalyze change.

In their chapter, Linda Dunn-Jensen and Linda Stroh address major myths and stereotypes, pervasive in the popular media, about women in the workforce. They provide research evidence to counter the prevailing myths that women are opting out of top-level jobs in greater numbers than men, women are not as willing as men to work hard for top spots in organizations, women are too passive to claim their just rewards in organizations, women don't want power, and women find there are more psychological and social rewards for staying home. They call for future research at the level of the underlying assumptions made about both women and work, to uncover the factors that perpetuate the media's adherence to inaccurate myths and stereotypes about women.

The chapter by Joy Beatty addresses the pervasive role of woman as 'other' in organizations and the process of women's identity creation in light of their symbolic outsider status in organizational life. Addressing women's invisible social identities and hidden stigmas in the workplace, she identifies three powerful assumptions engendering women as the other: organizations are genderless, organizations are bodyless, and organizations are sexless. She describes the main mechanisms by which women cope with this otherness (blending in to meet others' expectations or internalizing self-discipline and control), exploring the personal costs to women from either strategy of managing hidden stigmatized identities.

Caroline Gattrell and Cary Cooper's chapter proposes that the main causes of the stress experienced by women in business and management are structural and institutional; social attitudes and misplaced assumptions about the low work-orientation of women managers heighten their stress levels. These authors offer a social explanation for the continued existence of the glass ceiling by discussing the historical expectation that women should be mothers and homemakers, not work-orientated careerists. Their call to future research is not to narrowly determine the causes of stress for women in business and management (as these are well documented), but rather to find ways of constructing new social relations that promote and encourage working women.

In the fourth chapter of the first part, Marta Calás, Linda Smircich and Kristina Bourne call on future research on women's entrepreneurship to be more grounded in applications of feminist theory: to produce more relevant knowledge for a more just society, away from situations of women's and others' subordination. Their chapter portrays research on gender and entrepreneurship as fertile for imagining these social change possibilities. Relying on metaphoric illustration and feminist theorizing, they raise important questions for future research that address both who the woman entrepreneur is (and what kind of issues can be raised about her) and the gendering of entrepreneurship (addressing how knowledge production about women's entrepreneurship can catalyze improved social relations).

The second part of the *handbook* concerns research on specific career and work–life issues of women in business and management. In this part, the authors review research findings, recognize the complex intertwining and subtle nuances of women's careers and lives, caution against treating women or their careers as monolithic, and identify the shape and direction of future research on women's career and life development that takes into account their multiple responsibilities and commitments.

In his chapter on women's career advancement, Ron Burke provides an extensive review of influences on the career development and retention of professional and managerial women (including models of career development, work and career experiences, developmental jobs, developmental relationships, and opting-out). Highlighting a gap in the literature, his article also explores organizational initiatives most supportive of women's career development, particularly work–family balancing practices, alternative work arrangements, and talent development. Burke's article calls for future scholarship that recognizes the complexity of women's work lives, and which takes into consideration career changes as women age and change with multiple life roles.

In Chapter 6, Margaret Hopkins and Deborah O'Neil explore changing definitions of women's careers and career success. Paying attention to how women's careers and lives are confluent, they examine the myriad ways by which women perceive personal and professional success. Calling for research that acknowledges and celebrates the complexities of women's lives in contemporary society and that moves beyond traditional gendered constructions of career success, these authors challenge future scholarship to take on a more positive approach to women's careers and career success: to study what women are moving toward as opposed to what women are leaving, to understand how women self-determine and not passively accept their careers, to explore women's own definitions and experience of success in addition to those that are societally or organizationally mandated, and to identify the contributions made and not just the costs incurred by women's careers in business and management.

Helen Woolnough and Marilyn Davidson's chapter on mentoring as a career development tool addresses the roles of gender as well as race and ethnicity in formal and informal mentoring. They review research that describes the impact of gender and race/ethnicity on the availability, selection, type, amount and benefits of mentoring. In a valuable discussion of new alternative forms of mentoring such as peer mentoring, group mentoring and online mentoring, the authors call on future research to study these newer forms of mentoring. In raising awareness of the roles of women and black and ethnic minorities in mentoring relationships, the authors invite future research to question current workforce practices of demographically homogenous relationships, and preferences for informal and traditional dyadic mentoring.

The final two chapters of Part 2, by Mireia Las Heras and Tim Hall and by Sandy Piderit, address the quality of work–life in contemporary organizations. Both articles call for future research on work–life to promote newer constructions of integration and harmonization, which move away from traditional decomposition of work and life into separate entities. Both articles propound the well-being and satisfaction of the individual as the main career outcomes, not the objective success criteria (for example, salary, rank and promotions) so frequently utilized in the mainstream literature on career development. Drawing on the first years of career development, the Las Heras and Hall chapter suggests that integration of work and non-work is an outcome of adult development; that a person's growing self-awareness about extrinsic and intrinsic career goals can lead to psychological development and identity integration. Piderit's chapter cautions scholars not to perpetuate the view of work–life issues as problems that can be solved at the individual level with better choices, and calls for future research to open up societal assumptions regarding work–life quality.

Part 3 of the *handbook*, 'Organizational processes affecting women in business and management', tackles the organizational and human resource policies and practices, both positive and negative, which influence the effectiveness and success of women in organizations. In the first chapter of this part, Laura Graves and Gary Powell review theories and research evidence regarding the effects of sex, sex similarity, and sex diversity in ongoing mixed-sex teams. They consider how key factors associated with the contexts and situations in which mixed-sex teams operate may influence the nature and extent of each type of effect. These authors recommend a comprehensive future research program that examines the influence of a wide array of situational factors (for example, whether the context emphasizes or de-emphasizes sex, the team's overall demographic composition, the team's longevity, the gender orientation and structure of the team's task, the gender composition of the larger organization and its top management, and the organization's culture) on individual-level and team-level effects.

Chapter 11, by Diana Bilimoria, Lindsey Godwin and Deborah Zelechowski, draws attention to the subtle organizational processes and practices that facilitate or hinder women's career success and advancement in business and management. Building the case for why women's career advancement is uniquely different from men's in organizations, these authors develop a framework for women's career advancement that includes the characteristics, skills and networks of individuals (personal influence) and the friendliness of the environment (social inclusion). Overall, they recommend that future research take into account the myriad organizational situations of women in business and management, and call for finer-grained understanding to emerge about how women's career advancement patterns differ in these situations.

Chapter 12, by Alison Konrad, addresses how diversity-related practices (of recruitment, selection, training and development, career progression and retention) in organizations can promote women's careers in business and management. Like the other two chapters in this part, Konrad urges future scholarship to be more cognizant about diversity among women. She reviews the empirical literature on the types of human resource management practices with career outcomes for women, the factors linked with higher adoption levels of diversity-related practices, and the relationship between diversity and organizational performance. Her recommendations for future research call for research to examine the strategic effects of diversity and diversity training, and to consider their impacts on a wide variety of women.

Part 4 of the *handbook* pertains specifically to the role of women as leaders in business and management. The three chapters in this part all draw attention to the many opportunities and challenges facing women in leadership positions. They raise questions about how research can spur the creation of better societal and organizational policies and practices for the advancement to and success of women in leadership roles in business and management.

Alice Eagly and Mary C. Johannesen-Schmidt's chapter provides an extensive review of the literature on leadership styles, addressing questions such as: why would we expect women's and men's leadership styles to be similar or different? How do women and men compare on task-oriented and interpersonally oriented leadership styles, on autocratic versus democratic styles, and on transformational, transactional and laissez-faire styles? Their review concludes that the preponderance of evidence suggests small, but possibly consequential, differences in how women and men lead: women lead with an especially collaborative, interactive, participative style and that this style produces female advantage.

Val Singh, Sue Vinnicombe and Siri Terjesen's chapter addresses the international representation of women at the highest levels of corporate leadership and governance: women corporate board directors. Their in-depth review covers the statistics on women corporate directors and the varied approaches used in countries such as the USA, UK and Scandinavia to address the issue of lack of female representation on corporate boards: liberal, coercive and consensus methods. The authors call on future research to build the business case for women corporate directors more thoroughly, especially with regard to their impact directly on board performance, and indirectly on corporate performance.

The final chapter of this part and the *handbook*, by Nancy Adler, pertains to women ascending to international leadership roles. Her forward-looking review suggests that the scarcity of women at the top is no longer an option for business and management, especially for engendering the necessary global and societal improvements to create a world worthy of bequeathing to future generations. In this regard, she exposes the myths that women don't want international careers, that foreigners' prejudice makes it impossible for women to succeed internationally, and that dual-career marriages create insurmountable obstacles for women working abroad. Her essay holds that the traditional masculine-dominated American style of organizing is losing ground in the global workplace, that women are well equipped to take on the leadership of global institutions, and that corporations worldwide would do well to understand that the most effective leadership comes from both women and men.

References

Babcock L. and S. Laschever (2003), *Women Don't Ask: Negotiation and the Gender Divide*, Princeton, NJ: Princeton University Press.

Burke, R.J. and M.C. Mattis (eds) (2005), *Supporting Women's Career Advancement: Challenges and Opportunities*, Cheltenham, UK and Northampton, MA: Edward Elgar.

Burke, R.J. and D.L. Nelson (eds) (2002), *Advancing Women's Careers*, Oxford, UK: Blackwell Publishing.

Catalyst (2002), 'Census of women corporate officers and top earners', www.catalyst.org/files/fact/COTE%20Factsheet%202002updated.pdf.

Catalyst (2003a), 'Census of women board directors', www.catalyst.org/files/fact/WBD03factsheetfinal.pdf.

Catalyst (2003b), 'Bit by bit: Catalyst's guide to advancing women in high tech companies', www.catalyst.org/files/fact/BitbyBitfactsheetfinal.pdf.

Catalyst (2005), 'Women "take care", men "take charge": stereotyping of US business leaders exposed', catalystwomen.org/files/full/Women%20Take%20Care%20Men%20Take%20Charge.pdf.

Davidson, M.J. and R.J. Burke (eds) (2000), *Women in Management: Current Research Issues Volume II*, London: Sage.

Davidson, M.J. and R.J. Burke (eds) (2004), *Women in Management Worldwide: Facts, Figures, and Analysis*, Aldershot, Hants, England; Burlington, VT: Ashgate.

Ely, R.J., E.G. Foldy, M.A. Scully and the Center for Gender in Organizations, Simmons School of Management (eds) (2003), *Reader in Gender, Work, and Organization*, Malden, MA: Blackwell Publishing.

Frankel, L.P. (2004), *Nice Girls Don't Get the Corner Office: 101 Unconscious Mistakes That Women Make that Sabotage their Careers*, New York: Warner Business Books.

Harvard Business Review (2005), *Harvard Business Review on Women in Business*, Boston, MA: Harvard Business School Publishing.

Hudson Institute (1997), *Workforce 2020: Work and Workers in the 21st Century*, Washington, DC: Hudson Institute.

Kolb, D.M., J. Williams and C. Frohlinger (2004), *Her Place at the Table: A Woman's Guide to Negotiating Five Key Challenges to Leadership Success*, San Francisco: Jossey-Bass.

Larwood, L., A. Stromberg and B. Gutek (eds) (1986), *Women and Work*, Newbury Park, CA: Sage.

Padavic, I. and B. Reskin (2002), *Women and Men at Work*, 2nd edn, Thousand Oaks, CA: Sage, Pine Forge Press.

Parker, P.S. (2005), *Race, Gender and Leadership: Re-envisioning Organizational Leadership from the Perspectives of African American Women Executives*, Mahwah, NJ: Lawrence Erlbaum.

Powell. G.N. (ed.) (1999), *Handbook of Gender and Work*, Thousand Oaks, CA: Sage.

Powell, G.N. and L.M. Graves (2003), *Women and Men in Management*, 3rd edn, Thousand Oaks, CA: Sage.

Riger, S. (ed.) (2000), *Transforming Psychology: Gender in Theory and Practice*, Oxford and New York: Oxford University Press.

Smith, D.M. (2000), *Women at Work: Leadership for the Next Century*, Upper Saddle River, NJ: Prentice Hall.

Stanny, B. (2004), *Secrets of Six-Figure Women: Surprising Strategies to Up Your Earnings and Change Your Life*, New York: HarperBusiness.

USA Today (22 December 2005), Not-so-good year for female CEOs, www.usatoday.com/money/companies/management/2005-12-22-women-ceos-usat_x.htm.

US Department of Labor (2004), Bureau of Labor Statistics, www.dol.gov/wb/stats/main.htm.

Vinnicombe, S. and N.L. Colwill (1995), *The Essence of Women in Management*, London and New York: Prentice Hall.

Wirth, L. (2001), *Breaking through the Glass Ceiling: Women in Management*, Geneva: International Labour Office.

Working Mother (2005), '100 best companies for working mothers', Working Mother Media Inc., New York, www.workingmother.com/100BEST_2005.html.

PART 1

SOCIETAL ROLES AND CONTEXTS OF WOMEN IN BUSINESS AND MANAGEMENT

1 Myths in the media: how the news media portray women in the workforce

*Linda M. Dunn-Jensen and Linda K. Stroh**

One of the most significant changes to the workforce in the twentieth century has been the unprecedented number of women joining the labor market. According to the US Bureau of Labor Statistics, by the year 2008 women will constitute 48 per cent of the labor force, up from 46 per cent in 1998 (Fullerton and Toossi, 2001). Even with these growing numbers of women in the workforce, women have been unable to make successful inroads into top management levels of corporate leadership. For example, according to the US Bureau of Labor Statistics (2004), approximately 50 per cent of women hold managerial jobs, but these jobs are mostly at lower and middle levels of management. A number of women have been able to climb to the top levels of corporations, but the rate of change has not kept pace with the changes occurring in the pipeline. For example, the number of women pursuing graduate degrees has increased in the last decade. In 1995, over 50 per cent of Master's degrees were awarded to women (Glass Ceiling Commission, 1995); by 2001, over 58 per cent of Master's degrees were awarded to women (US Department of Education, 2002). Yet, in the *Fortune* 500, women filled only 15.7 per cent of the corporate officer positions in 2002 (Catalyst, 2002). Many ask the question, why is it that women are not in more leadership positions in corporate America?

In 1986, an article appeared in *The Wall Street Journal* that discussed an invisible barrier, called 'the glass ceiling' (Hymowitz and Schellhardt, 1986), which seemingly blocked women from advancing to senior leadership roles. Since then, efforts have been made by scholars and corporations to identify particular barriers and biases that have hindered the career advancement of women. In 1989, the US Department of Labor decided to investigate the glass ceiling phenomenon. The Glass Ceiling Commission was established to identify barriers and also to recommend strategies to eliminate discrimination at the highest levels of the organization.

The Glass Ceiling Commission found that women in both the public and private sector were underrepresented at senior levels, and in some cases underutilized (Glass Ceiling Commission, 1995). It is clear that the government's attention to the glass ceiling problem prompted many changes in corporate America; however, as we look to the future, it is important not only to assess progress, but also to continue the discussion about barriers and potential solutions, since barriers do still exist (Davidson and Burke, 2004). Morrison and Von Glinow (1990) identify three broad classes of theoretical explanations for the differential attainment of men and women; 1) women's deficiencies as managers, 2) structural discrimination and 3) bias and stereotyping by the dominant group. Considerable research related to women's deficiencies theory has not supported the idea that there are significant differences between men and women's abilities to manage (see Eagly et al., 1995 for a review). There has also been considerable research related to structural discrimination theory that provides support in explaining the differences between men and women with regard to managerial success (Etzkowitz et al., 2000; Rosser, 2004). While much has also been written about the effects of negative stereotypes, few have examined the role that the news media and more specifically the business press play in fostering (maybe even creating) negative stereotypes of females in the workplace (Krefting, 2002).

The mass media and business press

Mass media have an influential role in creating and reinforcing a particular worldview that shapes the perspectives and beliefs that individuals have about the world (Meyers, 1999). News media shape our perspectives by using frames to convey the messages they produce. In other words, 'news stories are structured or "framed" in ways that convey value-laded messages' (Norris, 1997: 10). In fact, Norris (1997) asserts that media use a gendered frame to 'simplify, prioritize, and structure the narrative flow of events when covering women and men in public life' (p. 10). Thus, the mass media influence the construction and reproduction of gender identities (Meyers, 1999).

While this ongoing discourse has been examined in the mass media, recent research has begun to examine this discourse in the business press (Fondas, 1997; Krefting, 2002). Recent research has found the business press also perpetuates a gendered frame in reporting on leadership in organizations. For example, Fondas (1997) posits that contemporary management advice books identify feminine qualities as important management skills for future leaders; however, Fondas (1997) notes that the authors of these books are unwilling to acknowledge that the values that they are offering in their advice are of a feminine nature. Thus, according to Fondas (1997), these feminine qualities are being co-opted into the male manager prototype.

When reporting is done on women in leadership roles, the business press sometimes provides a fractured portrayal of women versus men. For example, in her study of coverage of men and women executives in *The Wall Street Journal*, Krefting (2002) found that identities of high profile women were not valorized in their positions as management executives. Reporting of women executives reflected the tensions between personality dimensions of competence and likeability or the tension that existed for these executives between work and home. Thus, business press articles such as these create and sustain 'a profound ambivalence about women and work' (Thomas, 1999). Because the business press has a strong effect on people's views of women in management, we seek to contribute to this growing body of literature by examining propositions related to the business press and the articles that ensue.

The problem

Recent discourse in the popular press would suggest that there are a variety of reasons why women are not in leadership positions. Belkin (2003), in her controversial article entitled 'Q: Why don't more women choose to get to the top? A: They choose not to', suggested that women are 'opting-out'. In other words, women are not in leadership positions because they are choosing to leave their high-powered jobs and become full-time parents. Another article, by Tischler (2004), entitled, 'Where are the women?: So what happened?' asserts that women are not willing to work as hard as men for top spots. These articles caught the attention of Mainiero and Sullivan (2005) who suggest the popular press presents women in such a fashion that:

> A reader would assume that women are failing to achieve the top posts in their Fortune 500 firms because: 1) highly educated women are leaving the workforce, thus reducing the number of female contenders for top positions, 2) women aren't willing to work as hard as men for the top spots, 3) women are too timid or too passive to claim their reward, 4) women don't want power and 5) women find there are more psychological and social rewards for staying home (p. 106).

We are curious about the accuracy of the media's claims. In this chapter, we examine the five propositions presented in the popular press, as noted by Mainiero and Sullivan (2005). We begin our chapter by presenting the popular press propositions and argument. Next, we examine recent empirical research that tests the assertions made in the popular press and assess the accuracy of the popular press claims. In the final discussion section of this chapter, we discuss the implications of the mass media's portrayal of women in management. We discuss whether this portrayal is a myth or reality, and question whether the news media have tainted public opinion of women in management. Our primary focus in this chapter is to address the broader question: Do the news media perpetuate a skewed and unwarranted negative public impression of women in the workplace that fosters a mistaken belief that 1) women are leaving top-level jobs in greater numbers than men and that 2) women no longer want demanding, challenging jobs?

Are women 'opting-out'?

Proposition 1: The news media claim that highly educated women are leaving the workforce, thus reducing the number of female contenders for top-level jobs. Does scholarly research support the news media's claim?

Recently, there has been a debate in the media that suggests that women are voluntarily leaving the workforce, thus reducing the number of female contenders for leadership positions in organizations. This debate was prompted by Lisa Belkin, in her article in the *New York Times Magazine* entitled, 'Q: Why don't more women choose to get to the top? A: They choose not to'. In her article, Belkin (2003) claims that women are 'opting-out' of the workforce. This term is used to describe the phenomenon in which highly educated successful women are giving up or curtailing their careers to become full-time parents. This article suggests that a majority of highly educated women are leaving the workforce to become full-time parents. However, we argue that this claim may not be accurate because it is not based on a systematic and rigorous methodology. We found that this claim is based on limited sampling and interviews of a few highly educated privileged women who have made the choice to leave their careers to raise their family. Nevertheless, the term 'opting-out' has become commonplace in the media. For example, an article by Wallis (2004) on the cover of *Time* magazine, March 2004, was entitled, 'The case for staying home: why more young moms are opting out of the rat race' and another recent article in the *Chicago Tribune* (Kleiman, 2005), was entitled 'Opting out, dropping out or forced out?' These articles suggest several reasons for the 'opting out' revolution. However, in a review of scholarly research, we found several of these assertions are not supported by scholarly research.

The news media claim that highly educated women are leaving the workforce. However, we did not find support for that claim. For example, a survey in a large multinational financial services organization (Lyness and Judiesch, 2001) found that female managers' voluntary turnover rates were slightly lower than those of male managers. In addition, highly educated female managers were less likely to resign than female managers with less education. Thus, highly educated and successful women may not be 'opting-out' of the workforce to a greater extent than men, or more than less successful women. However, women may be opting out of their current organizations for greater opportunities.

In a review of recent research, several articles suggest that women are not leaving the workforce to become full-time parents but are leaving their current organizations to seek other career opportunities or self-employment. In their article, Miller and Wheeler (1992) found that age, meaningful work and promotional opportunities were significant predictors for women in their intention to leave their organizations. In fact, promotional opportunities are an important consideration for women leaving their current organizations. For example, in a sample of both managerial and professional men and women, Mano-Negrin (2003) found that women's turnover decisions were associated with their perceived perceptions of career opportunities. Furthermore, in their study of 615 managers from *Fortune* 500 corporations, Stroh et al. (1996) found that female managers' intentions to leave were based on a perceived lack of career opportunities within their organizations, not on family reasons. In other words, women were leaving organizations for the same reason men have been known to leave – the lack of opportunity within their organization.

To find better career and work opportunities, many highly educated women are also leaving organizations to pursue self-employment opportunities. This trend has been growing over the last 20 years. In a study by Rosen et al. (1989), with 245 managerial and professional men and women, the most frequent reason given for women leaving an organization was the acceptance of a similar position in another organization. Starting a new business was ranked significantly lower. However, in 2000, according to the National Foundation for Women Business Owners (NFWBO), there are now over 10.6 million women-owned businesses in the US. Therefore, women leaving corporate America to become entrepreneurs is a significant trend in the US.

There are several reasons why women become entrepreneurs. For example, in their study of 129 women executives and professionals who left large organizations to become entrepreneurs, Buttner and Moore (1997) found that entrepreneurs rated the desires for challenge and self-determination as the most influential reasons to leave corporate America. Buttner and Moore (1997) also found that frustration about blocks to career advancement were also cited as reasons for making this career move. In fact, women's perceived lack of opportunity in their current organization is an important factor in women seeking self-employment. In addition, Mallon and Cohen (2001) found in their study of managerial and professional women's transition from careers with organizations to self-employment, that 85 per cent of the women interviewed cited their change to self-employment was triggered by dissatisfaction and disillusionment with their current organization. Contrary to Belkin's proposition of 'opting out', Mallon and Cohen (2001) found that not one participant cited the need to balance work and family as the sole reason for leaving their organization.

In a review of scholarly research, we find partial support to the news media claims that highly educated women are leaving the workforce, thus reducing the number of contenders for top-level jobs. We would agree that the number of women contenders for top-level jobs is shrinking, but we would assert that women are not leaving the workforce per se, but are likely to leave corporate America. Research has found that women-owned businesses are the fastest growing segment of new business start-ups (Mattis, 2004). In a recent study conducted by the National Foundation for Women Business Owners (1998), in a sample of 650 women business owners, over 30 per cent of these women had held positions in senior and middle management in corporate America prior to starting their own businesses. Thus, this trend is likely to reduce the number of contenders for top-level jobs. In addition, we did not find scholarly research to support the primary reason offered by the media on why women are 'opting out' – to become full-time parents. We found support that some women are leaving the workforce to become full-time parents but, there are also several other reasons of personal aspirations and organizational influences that affect women's decisions to leave their large organizations – maybe reasons that are much stronger than those presented in the news media.

Are women as committed?

Proposition 2: The news media claim that women aren't willing to work as hard as men for top spots. Does the scholarly research support these news media claims?

This proposition suggests that women are not as willing as men to work hard for top spots in organizations. In fact, in her article in *Fast Company*, 'Where are the women? So what happened?' Tischler (2004) suggests that women remain underrepresented in top management because they are unwilling to compete as hard as men in the workplace. Tischler (2004) asserts that 1) men put in more hours at work than women, 2) men are more willing to relocate than women, 3) men are more committed to organizations than women and 4) men aspire to top positions more than women. Let's examine each of these claims separately and review what the scholarly research says about each of Tischler's claims.

Proposition 2a: Men put in more hours at work than women. Does the scholarly research support the news media claims?

We found equivocal results in scholarly research about Tischler's (2004) assertion that men put in more hours than women. Recent research suggests that in the aggregate, men may work longer hours than women but there is a large percentage of women who work as many hours as men. For example, Brett and Stroh (2003) found that proportionally, more men (28.6 per cent) than women (11 per cent) worked 61 or more hours per week. In fact, men averaged 56.4 hours per week and women averaged 51.5 hours per week. However, when examining the sample of women who worked at least 35 hours per week, the percentage of women who worked 61 or more hours per week was 38 per cent. Proportionally, not all women were working the same hours as men but there was still a large portion of women working 61 or more hours per week. Similarly, in her study with lawyers, Wallace (1999) found that male lawyers worked on average (50.04) hours per week and female lawyers worked (45.60) hours per week. Although the female lawyers were working fewer hours than their male counterparts, the women were still working over 9 hours a day. In two separate studies of professional men and women, Gutek and her colleagues found no differences in the number of hours worked per week. In fact, in a study with 209 senior managers, women on average worked 52.6 hours while the men worked 51.3 hours (Gutek et al., 1991).

This group of studies suggests that while some women may be not working the same number of hours as men, there are clearly many women working as hard as men (if we use only number of hours worked as a measure of how hard men and women work). Therefore, there is partial support for this media claim.

Proposition 2b: Men are more willing to relocate than women. Does the scholarly research support the news media claims?

We found little support for Tischler's (2004) media claim that men are more willing to relocate than women. Research has found that developmental experiences are critical to career success to facilitate career advancement (Lyness and Thompson, 2000). In a global economy, international assignments are critical in the career path to top management in organizations (Stroh et al., 2005). Lyness and Thompson (2000) found that both men and women executives reported that developmental assignments were instrumental in their career advancement. Yet, research finds that women were less likely to be offered developmental assignments (Stroh et al., 2000; Varma and Stroh, 2001). One claim made to explain why women are offered fewer developmental assignments than men is that women are less interested in pursuing international assignments. However, again, research has not supported this claim.

In her research with MBA students, Adler (1984) found no differences between men's and women's preparation or interest in pursuing international careers. Similarly, Varma and Stroh (2001) found that when offered international assignments, there were no significant differences in women and men's international assignment acceptance rates (90 per cent, females; 92 per cent males). Therefore, if women are interested in pursuing international assignments and, when offered international assignments women accept these assignments at the same rate as men, maybe women are less likely to actually have developmental assignments because they are not offered the opportunity by the organization. In fact, Varma and Stroh (2001) found that out of 44 participating organizations in their sample, the average number of international assignments for men was over 10 times as high as the average for women. Data from the Stroh et al. study (2000) shows that the low number of women who pursue an international assignment may be because women are offered fewer opportunities by organizations (Stroh et al., 2000).

As a reminder, research has shown that developmental assignments are important for career advancement. Women may not be considered for top-level positions because they do not have the international experience. And, research shows that women are as willing to relocate internationally as men but women are not offered the opportunity for an international assignment as often as men (Stroh et al., 2005). This is not to say that all women are willing to take an international assignment, but rather, when offered, women accept international assignments as often as men.

Proposition 2c: Men are more committed to organizations than women. Does the scholarly research support the news media claims?

Tischler (2004) also claims that men are more committed to their organizations than women. Yet we found little to support this news media claim. For example, in a meta-analysis of organizational commitment, Mathieu and Zajac (1990) found a small relationship between gender and organizational commitment. In fact, Mathieu and Zaja (1990) found women to be more committed to organizations than men. In a study of men and women Ph.D. students, Ellemers and his colleagues found no difference in self-reporting level of commitments (Ellemers et al., 2004). These studies suggest that women are as committed or even more committed than men to organizations. These finding are confirmed even when women work part-time jobs (Thorsteinson, 2003). This group of studies disconfirms the media's claim that men are more committed to organizations than women. In fact, these findings suggest that men and women do not have a difference in their commitment to their organizations.

Proposition 2d: Men aspire to top management positions more than women. Does the scholarly research support the news media claims?

Finally, Tischler (2004) also claims that men aspire to higher management levels than women. Interestingly, we found little support for this claim in scholarly works for women early in their career; however, we did find support for this claim for women in mid-career who had lowered their aspirations. For example, in a survey of 571 professional and managerial women, Merrill-Sands et al. (2005) found that 75 per cent of the women wanted to have a leadership role in their organization and that 47 per cent aspired to be in the position of the CEO. Furthermore, Merrill-Sands et al. (2005) found no differences in aspirations to top management position between women with or without children. In an interview study with 30 middle women managers, Wentling (1996) found that 83 per cent of these women aspired to top management positions and 17 per cent aspired to upper-middle management. In a study comparing men and women, Powell and Butterfield (2003) found that 81 per cent of men versus 67 per cent of women were more likely to aspire to top management positions. Yet there is some evidence that women's levels of aspirations may lessen over time.

For example, Powell and Butterfield (2003) found that the proportion of female undergraduate business students who had aspirations to top management positions had increased from 49 per cent in 1976–1977 to 73 per cent in 1999. On the other hand, the proportion of female part-time graduate business students who aspired to top management positions had decreased from 72 per cent in 1976–1977 to 59 per cent in 1999. Studies of career satisfaction of MBAs early in their career, found that women have satisfaction levels equal to or greater than men. However, by mid-career, Schneer and Reitman (1994) find that women had lower career satisfaction then men even though they found no gender differences for the importance of work between the women and men in the study. This research by Schneer and Reitman (1994) suggests that women may become disillusioned with their careers due to the organizational barriers they perceive as impediments to career opportunities.

Recent research is equivocal about the news media claim that men aspire to top management positions more than women. While women begin their careers with similar career aspirations to men, upon entering the mid-career stage women become disillusioned and their expectations are altered. These results suggest that the claim made in the media may need further clarification. This group of studies suggests that women early in their career may aspire to top management positions while women in mid-career may lower their aspirations. Thus, grouping all women into one category may be overshadowing the subtleties of this claim.

Are women too passive?

Proposition 3: The news media claim women are too timid or too passive to claim their reward? Does the scholarly research support the news media claims?

This proposition suggests that women are too timid or too passive to claim their rewards. In a recent article entitled 'Women fall behind when they don't hone negotiation skills' the author suggests that women are uncomfortable negotiating better salaries and job assignments (Lublin, 2003). In her article entitled, 'Women still find it hard to say, "Let's Make a Deal"', Gardner (2003) asserts that women dread the prospect of negotiation. We did find some support for this claim in scholarly research. In their recent book, *Women Don't Ask: Negotiation and the Gender Divide*, Babcock and Leschever (2003) found that men were twice as likely as women to ask for what they wanted and four times more likely to negotiate than women. This would suggest that women are not engaging in behaviors to claim opportunities. Why then, might women be engaging in self-limiting behaviors?

Bandura (1977) argues that individuals who do not believe that they are capable of completing a task are more likely to pursue less challenging tasks. Furthermore, research has shown that women may lack confidence in pursuing non-traditional tasks (McMahan, 1982). This lack of confidence may hinder women's pursuit of leadership roles. In fact, Dickerson and Taylor (2000) found that women who scored lower on task-specific self-esteem were more likely to choose a follower role than a leadership role. Thus, low task-specific self-esteem becomes self-limiting (Dickerson and Taylor, 2000: p. 206). Although we found that some women may engage in self-limiting behavior we assert that there is also a secondary factor that may further explain the claim by the news media. We suggest that other people may also be projecting limiting evaluations on women.

In their recent study, Heilman and Haynes (in press) suggest that attributional rationalization, when a successful performance outcome is attributed to someone other than a female team member, may have negative implications for women. They found that in a mixed-sex dyad, if the team had a successful outcome, but the evaluation was based on team performance rather than individual performance, the male team member was given more credit than the female team member. Thus, women may also be at a disadvantage when evaluated against their male counterparts.

Research also suggests that women are perceived as less effective leaders and that men are perceived as better decision makers (Rizzo and Mendez, 1990). However, these perceptions are often based on stereotypes.

For example, in a study with undergraduate students (n=702), Deal and Stevenson (1998) found that male and female students have substantially different perceptions of female managers. Male participants had a much more negative view of women managers, describing them as bitter, passive, having a strong need for social acceptance, timid and uncertain. The female participants had a much more positive view of female managers, describing them as competent, creative, desirous of responsibility, self-reliant, having a strong need for achievement, and well informed. This finding might suggest that male respondents in this study have negative stereotypes of women. These societal stereotypes (Steele, 1997) have implications for women's performance and aspirations of leadership.

According to the theory of stereotype threat (Steele, 1997), when an individual has the potential to be the target of a negative group stereotype, that individual may fear that he or she may be reduced to the stereotype, thus finding themselves in a self-threatening situation. This threat of stereotyping may then lead to lower performance. For example, when a woman is performing a male-oriented task in the presence of males, in her attempt not to perform the task 'as a woman' she inadvertently may under-perform. Stereotyping can also have implications for women's aspirations of leadership.

In their study, Davies et al. (2005) found that female participants exposed to gender-stereotypic commercials were more likely to volunteer for a subordinate's role over a leadership role. This was found to be true even when the leadership role was portrayed to rely heavily on interpersonal and communication skills. This exposure to stereotypical commercials undermined the leadership aspirations of the women. A second study found that when an identity-safe environment is created, women are then 'able to concentrate on fulfilling their potential rather than worry about fulfilling a negative stereotype' (Davies et al., 2005: 285). Thus, stereotyping may have an effect on how women pursue their career advancement. Stereotyping may also have an effect on how others evaluate women's performance.

Women who engage in counterstereotypical behavior may suffer from a backlash effect (Rudman, 1998). Heilman and Haynes (in press) found that women needed to rank in the top twentieth percentile to be considered on a par with the average males' performance. Thus, women need to engage in behaviors that convey their competence. However, Rudman (1998) did find that women who engaged in self-promotion were more likely to increase perceptions of their competence, but at the expense of social rejection. This tension between looking competent and experiencing social inclusion has implications for women's behaviors.

Recent research supports the media claim that women may be too timid or passive to claim their rewards, especially within a negotiation setting.

However, we would argue that this claim is only part of the story. We have also shown several research articles that provide empirical support that stereotyping has negative implications for women. Thus, we argue that the media's claim that women may be too timid or passive to claim their rewards is too simplistic an explanation. We would argue that understanding the role of stereotyping, stereotype threat and backlash are also important to examining this claim. And, it is an important reminder that biased media reporting can affect stereotypical beliefs about women.

Do women want power?

Proposition 4: The news media claim women don't want power. Does the scholarly research support the news media claims?

The news media claim that women don't want power. In her article entitled, 'Power: Do women really want it?' Sellers (2003) suggests that women lack power in business because they do not want power. In fact, in her interviews with women from *Fortune*'s list of the top 50 most powerful women, these powerful women suggested that they were uncomfortable with power. For example, 'Power, says Meg Whitman, has a negative connotation' (Sellers, 2003) and 'Power is in your face and aggressive. I'm not like that, says another newcomer, Jenny Ming' (Sellers, 2003). Cleaver (2004a), in her article entitled, 'The P word; though they possess it, many high-ranking women seem reluctant to call it what it is: power', suggests that women are not uncomfortable having and using power, but prefer using a different descriptor than the term power. Are women uncomfortable with power?

Recent scholarly research suggests that women are comfortable with power. Merrill-Sands et al. (2005) found that 80 per cent of their respondents were comfortable with, respected and liked what they could accomplish with power. But, these respondents perceived differences in behaviors between men and women exerting power. The respondents saw men as exerting control over others while women were seen as working with others to achieve results. This would suggest that women use referent power (French and Raven, 1959) more than other types of power such as expert or legitimate power (French and Raven, 1959). Thus, women are more likely to acquire power through building relationships and achieving results rather than more 'traditional' strategies of developing positional power, expanding span of control to build 'turf' and networking with more powerful people (Merrill-Sands et al., 2005).

Women may want power but organizational structural factors may also limit women's power resources. Women may have less power because they tend to occupy female-type occupations. For example, in the management field, women tend to be in staff functions rather than line positions, which may be associated with less influence in the organization (Ragins and Sundstrom, 1989). Furthermore, Ragins and Sundstrom (1989) found that when women receive promotions within an organization they are less likely to achieve higher ranks in these promotions. In fact, Tsui and Gutek (1984) found that female managers were promoted more often than their male counterparts but remained at lower ranks. Thus, women may experience barriers in their ability to gain power. Tsui and Gutek (1984) assert that men's ability to acquire power contains fewer obstacles that are derived from their gender and may actually contain sources of support unavailable to their female counterparts. Thus, women may be less likely to gain access to interpersonal and organizational resources due to structural barriers.

The news media claim that women do not want power; however, the scholarly research does not support this claim. As suggested by Wade (2001), both men and women have the necessary skills to exert power and influence but gender-linked stereotypes, roles and social norms constrain women from pursuing and asking for resources and rewards for themselves. Research has found that men possess higher amounts of expert and legitimate power than women, and women possess higher amounts of referent power than men (Carli, 1999). Thus, we would argue that women want power – keeping in mind that women's power might be demonstrated differently from men's.

Are there more rewards for staying at home?

Proposition 5: The news media claim women find there are more psychological and social rewards for staying home. Does the scholarly research support the news media claims?

In her article entitled, 'The case for staying home: why more young moms are opting out of the rat race', Wallis (2004) suggests that mothers are choosing to leave the workforce to become full-time parents because they find staying at home more psychologically and socially rewarding. Lewis (1998), in her article entitled, 'Homeward bound: many are trading in long hours, little satisfaction for family time, peace of mind', also argues that women are leaving the workforce to stay at home. We found mixed support for this claim. For example, in her provocative book, *Maternal Desire*, de Marneffe (2004) asserts that the public discourse rarely takes into account that mothers have an embodied, aching desire to nurture their children. In fact, she suggests that mothers often see nurturing children as an extension of their authentic self. Not only may women be staying at home to fulfill their maternal desires, but they are choosing to be full-time parents to lower the stress in their lives because they feel that they are shortchanging their children. For example, Luo and Chen (2000) found that women who worked 50- to 60-hour weeks were unhappier with their parent–child interactions than women who worked a reduced hour schedule. Not only are women unhappy with their relationships with their children but they also feel guilty about working long hours. In a recent study, Ivarsson and Ekehammar (2001) found managerial women used a self-blame coping mechanism more than non-managerial women. Self-blame coping mechanisms have been associated with job anxiety and depression, which could lead to long-term stress-related health problems. Thus, the authors suggest that managerial women might have feelings of guilt due to reduced involvement in their family. Thus, some women do receive psychological and social rewards from being at home.

On the other hand, other women choose to have both a family and a career. Brett and Stroh (2003) found that female managers who worked long hours were more satisfied with their family lives than those who worked shorter hours. One reason for this satisfaction is that these women had husbands who contributed to childcare and had substantial support in paid help. Although these women were satisfied with their family life, they did feel more alienated from their families. However, work and family does not always need to conflict. In fact, recent research has found work and family can enhance one another. For example, Ross and Mirowsky (1995) found in a study comparing employed and non-employed mothers that employed mothers had a higher level of satisfaction, self-esteem and less depression than non-employed mothers.

Why is it that some women experience more psychological and social rewards from staying at home while other women experience more psychological and social rewards from having a career and yet other women experience these rewards from having both a family and career? The differences between these findings might depend on the strategy used to balance work and family and how that strategy is aligned with aspirations. In a recent in-depth interview study with 10 senior financial executives, Gersick and Kram (2002) found these women used three different strategies to incorporate a sense of efficacy in motherhood and satisfying career involvement. These three patterns were delegation, sequencing and full-tilt career and family.

Women who assigned much of the mothering role to others such as family members or full-time childcare highlight the first pattern, delegation. These women maintained a high level of involvement in their careers and were satisfied with this arrangement. The second pattern, sequencing, involves women who alternated their investment in career and parenting. They were more likely to postpone motherhood, and once they did have children they reduced their work involvement. This allowed them to satisfy their need to be with their children but also kept them engaged in their career. The third strategy of full-tilt career and family was not as effective. These women aimed to keep high involvement in both their career and their family. This, however, generally caused conflict because of the impossibility of achieving high involvement in both domains of their life, leaving them feeling that they were unable to fulfill either role well and lowering their sense of well-being. Regardless of the strategy used, these women found that parenthood enhanced their abilities as leaders. More importantly, by using one of these three strategies, these women were able to integrate both motherhood and working in an engaging meaningful career (Gersick and Kram, 2002). This group of scholarly works provides mixed support for the news media claim that women find there are more psychological and social rewards gained by staying at home. Indeed, some women find being a full-time parent rewarding, while other women find that integrating motherhood and career is more rewarding. Thus, we would argue that when women have choices regarding integrating their career and motherhood that there are several different paths women may choose.

Discussion

In this chapter, we set out to evaluate the accuracy of the news media's claims that foster negative stereotypes of women in the workplace. We considered five media claims that were proposed by Mainiero and Sullivan (2005) as popular press representations of why women were not reaching top levels in their organizations. For many of the propositions set forth, we found little support in scholarly works or mixed findings to support the media claims. Thus, we believe that our investigation does in fact suggest that at best, the news media have negatively tainted public opinion of women in organizations. For example, in 1997, Brenda Barnes, after 22 years at PepisCo, a high power executive in line for a CEO position, left PepsiCo to become a stay-at-home mother. The print media, and also network TV, kept this story alive for many weeks. Many stories in the news media perpetuated the debate about the tension between motherhood and career. For example, articles found during that time period include: 'Who's news: top PepsiCo executive picks family over job' (Deogun, 1997), 'Woman's resignation from top Pepsi post rekindles debates' (Shellenbarger, 1997), 'A disastrous loss for feminists' (Osias, 1997) and 'What to teach our daughters' (Hartmann, 1998). However, after six years, Brenda Barnes went back to work as CEO of Sara Lee. Although Barnes's return did not garner the same media intensity as her departure, there were several articles about her return. In a positive manner, several articles were written that were more business focused about Barnes's return, such as 'Sara Lee President "Brings

Experience": Barnes a former top Pepsi exec' (Schmeltzer, 2004) or 'Sara Lee: former PepsiCo executive hired' (Sluis, 2004) or 'Barnes is back with plan for Sara Lee' (Berk, 2004). However, there were also several articles that again perpetuated the tension between motherhood and career. For example, 'A Bellwether working mom returns to the office: executive's re-entry shows how times are changing: "more ammo to negotiate"' (Shellenbarger, 2004), 'Brenda's back: others won't be so lucky' (Tischler, 2005) and 'The consequences of sequencing: for women who've stepped off the career ladder to stay at home: with their kids, the return to work isn't as smooth as they thought it would be' (Cleaver, 2004b). Had Brenda Barnes been a male, there is little doubt that the return to the workforce would not have been portrayed in this negative light. Thus, high profile women executives continue to be treated not just as executives but also as a small sample which the media can use to make claims about women in organizations. Thus, the far-reaching arm of the media can cast a long dark shadow over other women in top-level positions in the corporate world, making success much more difficult for them.

A recent speech by Deborah Merrill-Sands, the Dean of Simmons School of Management, highlights three important implications of these claims made in the news media and demonstrates the negative effect the media can have on women in the workplace. First, Merrill-Sands argued that claims made in the popular press are based on anecdotal data rather than statistically sound data. Consistent with Merrill-Sands' claim, we did indeed find that many of the news articles are based on anecdotal findings. For example, in the news media writings, often there was a limited sample, with no comparison group of men and no controls to validate the claims. Secondly, Merrill-Sands argued that claims made in the popular press continue to perpetuate gender stereotypes, thus curtailing opportunities for women. Meyers (1999) argues that the mass media are influential in creating and reinforcing a worldview – a worldview that can be harmful to women in the workplace. This information provided by the news media influences the information people recall in making observations about the world. In fact, Tversky and Kahneman (1974) argue that most people will recall the vivid, emotional claims made in the media rather than the scholarly research that may disconfirm the media claims. Thus, because of this bias, people continue to believe the perpetuated stereotypical claims made in the media, even in the face of real hard data that dispute the emotional claims. Finally, Merrill-Sands argued that claims made in the popular press take the responsibility for change from organizations and put the responsibility on individual women. With this article, we encourage the news media to share in that responsibility as well. In particular, we make the following three suggestions to the news media. First, we recommend that reporters not rely only on anecdotal evidence for reporting their stories. Second, we recommend that reporters do not over-sensationalize their stories but offer a more balanced point of view. Third, we recommend that reporters acknowledge the whole story, not just the part of the story that makes 'good' reading.

Directions for future research

Future research can help broaden our understanding of a more accurate picture of women in the workplace. One area that may be worthwhile to understand is the underlying organizational assumptions regarding working hours. In this chapter, we found equivocal results regarding the differences between actual hours worked between men and women. While the focus of research on actual hours worked is a worthy area of study, we urge scholars to also explore assumptions about working hours. Williams (2000) in her book, *Unbending Gender*, asserts that an assumption regarding work hours, which she refers to as the 'executive schedule', places women at a disadvantage. In her recent work, Dunn-Jensen (2005) suggests that the lack of perceived time availability had negative career implications for women. Do men and women have different levels of temporal resources available to them? Are assumptions about work hours resulting in negative career implications for women? Are there differences across occupations or industries or countries regarding assumptions about work hours?

Future research can add to our understanding about differences between the careers of men and women. In their recent article on kaleidoscope careers, Mainiero and Sullivan (2005) suggest that decisions regarding women's careers are heavily influenced by relationships with others. They further assert that women will focus on different career issues depending on their life stage. This new career model may add insight into the provocative finding that women's aspirations and career satisfaction may lessen over time but the importance of their work will not (Powell and Butterfield, 2003; Schneer and Reitman, 1994). What, then, happens to women's career aspirations and career satisfaction when women enter the late career stage?

Additionally, future research could explore the growth of women-owned businesses. Is it possible that this trend is lowering the pool of potential applicants for top-level positions? Are these entrepreneurs gaining the flexibility that they are looking for? How do they define career success and are they attaining that success? Does this group of entrepreneurs have access to capital markets? How do mentorship and social networks apply to this group of women? As research suggests, this rapidly growing segment of the workforce outside of traditional organizations will have important implications for women in the workplace.

The globalization of the workplace may also be worthy of exploration. Is the discourse of how women are portrayed in the news media similar or different across countries? What impact does this discourse have on women's ability to achieve positions in top management? Furthermore, does the career model presented by Mainiero and Sullivan (2005) apply to women beyond the United States? Future research investigating topics of career development, power, organizational commitment and work and family across countries may be a crucial step in the effort to understand why women are not in top management positions worldwide.

Conclusion

In this chapter, our goal was to join the discourse of how women are portrayed in the news media. We wanted to understand the accuracy of claims in the news media when addressing the question of why it is that women are not in leadership positions in corporate America. In reviewing the empirical research, we found that there is evidence that the news media's claims are in fact, at times, a negatively skewed portrayal of women in the workplace. We encourage the news media to offer a more balanced view of organizational life.

Note

* We thank Diana Bilimoria, Elizabeth Boyle and Sandy Piderit for their helpful comments and suggestions.

References

Adler, N.J. (1984), 'Women do not want international careers: and other myths about international management', *Organizational Dynamics*, **13**, 66–79.

Babcock, L.C. and S. Laschever (2003), *Women Don't Ask: Negotiation and the Gender Divide*, Princeton, NJ: Princeton University Press.

Bandura, A. (1977), 'Self-efficacy: toward a unifying theory of behavioral change', *Psychological Review*, **84**, 191–25.

Belkin, L. (2003), 'Why don't more women choose to get to the top? A: They choose not to', *New York Times Magazine*, 26 October, pp. 42–47, 58, 85.

Berk, C.C. (2004), 'Barnes is back with plan for Sara Lee', *Wall Street Journal*, 10 November, p. 1.

Brett, J.M. and L.K. Stroh. (2003), 'Working 61 plus hours a week: why do managers do it?', *Journal of Applied Psychology*, **88**, 67–78.

Buttner, E.H. and D.P. Moore (1997), 'Women's organizational exodus to entrepreneurship: self-reported motivations and correlates with success', *Journal of Small Business Management*, **35**, 34–46.

Carli, L. (1999), 'Gender, interpersonal power and social influence', *Journal of Social Issues*, **55**, 81–99.

Catalyst (2002), *Catalyst Census of Women Corporate Officers and Top Earners*, New York: Catalyst.

Cleaver, J. (2004a), 'The P word: Though they possess it, many high-ranking women seem reluctant to call it what it is: Power', *Chicago Tribune*, 21 January, p. 1.

Cleaver, J. (2004b), 'The consequences of sequencing: for women who've stepped off the career ladder to stay at home with their kids, the return to work isn't as smooth as they thought it would be', *Chicago Tribune*, 19 May, p. 1.

Davidson, M.J. and R.J. Burke (2004), *Women in Management Worldwide: Facts, Figures and Analysis*, Aldershot, UK: Ashgate Publishing Limited.

Davies, P.G., S.J. Spencer and C.M. Steele (2005), 'Clearing the air: identity safety moderates the effects of stereotype threat on women's leadership aspirations', *Journal of Personality and Social Psychology*, **88**, 276–87.

Deal, J.J. and M.A. Stevenson (1998), 'Perceptions of female and male managers in the 1990s: Plus ça change...', *Sex Roles*, **38**, 287–300.

De Marneffe, D. (2004), *Maternal Desire: On Children, Love and the Inner Life*, New York: Little, Brown and Company.

Deogun, N. (1997), 'Who's news: top PepsiCo executive picks family over job', *Wall Street Journal*, 24 September, p. B1.

Dickerson, A. and M.A. Taylor (2000), 'Self-limiting behavior in women: self-esteem and self-efficacy as predictors', *Group & Organization Management*, **25**, 191–210.

Dunn-Jensen, L.M. (2005), 'Being busy, looking busy...Who has time? When perceived time availability has career implications', Presented at the 21st EGOS Colloquium, Berlin, Germany.

Eagly, A.H., S.J. Karau and M.G. Makhijani (1995), 'Gender and the effectiveness of leaders: A meta-analysis', *Psychological Bulletin*, **117**, 125–45.

Ellemers, N., H. van den Heuvel, D. de Gilder, A. Maass and A. Bonvini (2004), 'The underrepresentation of women in science: Differential commitment or the queen bee syndrome?', *British Journal of Social Psychology*, **43**, 315–38.

Etzkowitz, H., C. Kemelgor and B. Uzzi (2000), *Athena Unbound: The Advancement of Women in Science and Technology*, Cambridge, UK: Cambridge University Press.

Fondas, N. (1997), 'Feminization unveiled: management qualities in contemporary writings', *Academy of Management Review*, **22**, 257–82.

French, J. and B. Raven (1959), 'The bases of social power', in D. Cartwright (ed.), *Studies in Social Power*, Ann Arbor, MI: Institute for Social Research, pp. 150–67.

Fullerton Jr., H.J. and M. Toossi (2001), 'Labor force projections to 2010: steady growth and changing composition', *Monthly Labor Review*, **124**, 21–38.

Gardner, M. (2003), 'Women still find it hard to say, "Let's make a deal"', *Christian Science Monitor*, 3 September, p. 14.

Gersick, C.J. and K.E. Kram (2002), 'High-achieving women at midlife: an exploratory study', *Journal of Management Inquiry*, **11**, 104–27.

Glass Ceiling Commission (1995), *A Solid Investment: Making Full Use of the Nation's Human Capital*, Washington DC: US Department of Labor.

Gutek, B.A., S. Searle and L. Klepa (1991), 'Rational versus gender role explanations for work–family conflict', *Journal of Applied Psychology*, **76**, 560–68.

Hartmann, S. (1998), 'What to teach our daughters', *New York Times*, 1 March, p. 14.

Heilman, M.E. and M.C. Haynes (in press), 'No credit where credit is due: attributional rationalization of women's success in male/female teams', *Journal of Applied Psychology*, **90**, 905–16.

Hymowitz, C. and T.D. Schellhardt (1986), 'The glass ceiling: why women can't seem to break the invisible barrier that blocks them from top jobs', *Wall Street Journal*, 24 March, pp. 1D, 4D–5D.

Ivarsson, S.M. and B. Ekehammar (2001), 'Women's entry into management: comparing women managers and non-managers', *Journal of Managerial Psychology*, **16**, 301–14.

Keltner, D., D.H. Gruenfeld and C. Anderson (2003), 'Power, approach and inhibition', *Psychological Review*, **110**, 265–84.

Kleiman, C. (2005), 'Opting out, dropping out, or forced out? *Chicago Tribune* online edition, www.chicagotribune.com/classified/jobs/columnists/chi-0504260254apr26,1,3068721. column?coll=chi-navrailbusiness-nav.

Krefting, L.A. (2002), 'Re-presenting women executives: valorization and devalorization in US business press', *Women in Management Review*, **17**, 104–19.

Lewis, D. (1998), 'Homeward bound: many are trading in long hours, little satisfaction for family time, peace of mind', *Boston Globe*, 29 March, p. C1.

Lublin, J.S. (2003), 'Women fall behind when they don't hone negotiation skills', *Wall Street Journal*, 4 November, p. B1.

Luo, Y. and Q. Chen (2000), 'What matters more, jobs or children?', Sloan Center, University of Chicago, working paper, August.

Lyness, K.S. and M.K. Judiesch (2001), 'Are female managers quitters? The relationships of gender, promotions, and family leaves of absence to voluntary turnover', *Journal of Applied Psychology*, **86**, 1167–78.

Lyness, K.S. and D.E. Thompson (2000), 'Climbing the corporate ladder: do female and male executives follow the same route?', *Journal of Applied Psychology*, **85**, 86–101.

Mainiero, L.A. and S.E. Sullivan (2005), 'Kaleidoscope careers: An alternate explanation for the "opt-out" revolution', *Academy of Management Executive*, **19**, 106–23.

Major, V.S., K.J. Klein and M.G. Ehrhart (2002), 'Work time, work interference with family, and psychological distress', *Journal of Applied Psychology*, **87**, 427–36.

Mallon, M. and L. Cohen (2001), 'Time for a change? Women's accounts of the move from organizational careers to self-employment', *British Journal of Management*, **12**, 217–30.

Mano-Negrin, R. (2003), 'Gender-related opportunities and turnover: the case of medical sector employees', *Gender, Work and Organization*, **10**, 342–60.

Mathieu, J.E., and D.M. Zajac (1990), 'A review and meta-analysis of the antecedents, correlates, and consequences of organizational commitment', *Psychological Bulletin*, **108**, 171–94.

Mattis, M.C. (2004), 'Women entrepreneurs: out from under the glass ceiling', *Women in Management Review*, **19**, 154–63.

McMahan, I.D. (1982), 'Expectancy of success on sex-linked tasks', *Sex Roles*, **8**, 949–58.

Merrill-Sands, D., J. Kickul and C. Ingols (2005), 'Women pursuing leadership and power: challenging the myth of the "opt-out" revolution', *GDO Insights, No. 20*, Boston, MA: Simmons School of Management.

Meyers, M. (1999), 'Introduction', in M. Meyers (ed.) *Mediated Women: Representations in Popular Culture*, Cresskill, NJ: Hampton Press, pp. 3–22.

Miller, J.G. and K.G. Wheeler (1992), 'Unraveling the mysteries of gender differences in intentions to leave the organization', *Journal of Organizational Behavior*, **13**, 465–78.

Morrison, A.M. and M. Von Glinow (1990), 'Women and minorities in management', *American Psychologist*, **45**, 200–208.

The National Foundation for Women Business Owners (1998), http://www.nfwbo.org.

Norris, P. (1997), 'Introduction: women, media and politics', in P. Norris (ed.), *Women, Media and Politics*, New York: Oxford University Press, pp. 1–18.

Osias, R. (1997), 'A disastrous loss for feminists', *New York Times*, 19 October, p. 14.

Powell, G.N. and D.A. Butterfield (2003), 'Gender, gender identity and aspirations to top management', *Women in Management Review*, **18**, 88–96.

Ragins, B.R. and E. Sundstrom (1989), 'Gender and power in organizations', *Psychological Bulletin*, **105**, 51–88.

Rizzo, A. and C. Mendez (1990), *The Integration of Women in Management*, New York: Quorum Books.

Rosen, B., M. Miguel and E. Peirce (1989), 'Stemming the exodus of women managers', *Human Resource Management*, **28**, 475–91.

Ross, C.E. and J. Mirowsky (1995), 'Does employment affect health?', *Journal of Health and Social Behavior*, **36**, 230–43.

Rosser, S.V. (2004), *The Science Glass Ceiling: Academic Women Scientists and the Struggle to Succeed*, New York: Routledge.

Rudman, L.A. (1998), 'Self-promotion as a risk factor for women: the costs and benefits of counterstereotypical impression management', *Journal of Personality and Social Psychology*, **74**, 629–45.

Schmeltzer, J. (2004), 'Sara Lee President "brings experience": Barnes a former top Pepsi Exec', *Chicago Tribune*, 4 May, p. 1.

Schneer, J.A. and F. Reitman (1994), 'The importance of gender in mid-career: a longitudinal study of MBAs', *Journal of Organizational Behavior*, **15**, 199–207.

Sellers, P. (2003), 'Power: do women really want it?', *Fortune*, 13 October, **148**, 80.

Shellenbarger, S. (1997), 'Woman's resignation from top Pepsi post rekindles debates', *Wall Street Journal*, 8 October, p. B1.

Shellenbarger, S. (2004), 'A Bellwether working mom returns to the office: executive's re-entry shows how times are changing: "More Ammo to Negotiate"', *Wall Street Journal*, 4 May, p. D1.

Shore, L.M., K. Barksdale and T.H. Shore (1995), 'Managerial perceptions of employee commitment to the organization', *Academy of Management Journal*, **38**, 1593–615.

Sluis, W. (2004), 'Sara Lee: former PepsiCo executive hired', *Chicago Tribune*, 9 May, p. 3.

Steele, C.M. (1997), 'A threat in the air: how stereotypes shape intellectual identity and performance', *American Psychologist*, **52**, 613–29.

Stroh, L.K., J.M. Brett and A.H. Reilly (1996), 'Family structure, glass ceiling, and traditional explanation for the differential rate of turnover of female and male managers', *Journal of Vocational Behavior*, **49**, 99–118.

Stroh, L.K., A. Varma and S.J. Valy-Durbin (2000), 'Why are women left at home: are they unwilling to go on international assignments', *Journal of World Business*, **35**, 241–55.

Stroh, L.K., J.S. Black, M.E. Mendenhall and H.B. Gregersen (2005), *International Assignments: An Integration of Strategy, Research, & Practice*, Mahwah, NJ: Lawrence Erlbaum Associates.

Thomas, P. (1999), 'Gender confusion: America has long shown profound ambivalence about women and work', *Wall Street Journal*, 11 January, p. 30.

Thorsteinson, T.J. (2003), 'Job attitudes of part-time versus full-time workers: a meta-analytic review', *Journal of Occupational and Organizational Psychology*, **76**, 151–77.

Tischler, L. (2004), 'Where are the women? So what happened?', *Fast Company*, February, **79**, 52–60.

Tischler, L. (2005), 'Brenda's back: others won't be so lucky', *Fast Company*, June, p. 23.

Tsui, A.S. and B.A. Gutek (1984), 'A role set analysis of gender differences in performance, affective relationships, and career success of industrial middle managers', *Academy of Management Journal*, **27**, 619–35.

Tversky, A. and D. Kahneman (1974), 'Judgment under uncertainty: heuristics and biases', *Science*, **185**, 1124–31.

US Bureau of Labor Statistics (2004), *Current Population Survey*, Washington, DC: US Census Bureau.

US Department of Education, National Center for Educational Statistics, (2002), *Digest of Education Statistics*, Washington, DC: Government Printing Office.

Varma, A. and L.K. Stroh (2001), 'Different perspectives on selection for international assignments: the impact of LMX and gender', *Cross Cultural Management*, **8**, 85–97.

Vescio, T.K., S.J. Gervais, M. Snyder and A. Hoover (2005), 'Power and the creation of patronizing environments: the stereotype-based behaviors of the powerful and their effects on female performance in masculine domains', *Journal of Personality and Social Psychology*, **88**, 658–72.

Wade, M.E. (2001), 'Women and salary negotiation: the costs of self-advocacy', *Psychology of Women Quarterly*, **25**, 65–76.

Wallace, J.E. (1999), 'Work-to-nonwork conflict among married male and female lawyers', *Journal of Organizational Behavior*, **20**, 797–816.

Wallis, C. (2004), 'The case for staying home: why more young moms are opting out of the rat race', *Time*, 22 March, pp. 52–58.

Wentling, R.M. (1996), 'A study of the career development and aspirations of women in middle management', *Human Resource Development Quarterly*, **7**, 253–70.

Williams, J. (2000), *Unbending Gender: Why Family and Work Conflict and What to Do About It*, Oxford, New York: Oxford University Press.

2 Women and invisible social identities: women as the Other in organizations

Joy E. Beatty

Over the last century women's participation in the workforce has increased, their employment in white collar and managerial jobs has increased, and the sex gap in pay has decreased (Powell and Graves, 2003). All these suggest that women have made significant strides in decreasing discrimination in employment. Despite this, gender differences still play a role in our daily worklives. Gender differences are revealed in commonly held stereotypes about personal attributes and behaviors. The original differences in gender stereotypes found by Broverman et al. (1972), that men are instrumental and women are expressive, are held by both men and women, have been consistent across time (Deaux and LaFrance, 1998) and are shared across cultures (Williams and Best, 1990). These persistent beliefs shape expectations about role performance, as people are expected to behave consistently with gender stereotypes.

Despite the improvements women have experienced in employment statistics, the workplace is still a primary domain for the enactment of these gender stereotypes. Women are often stereotyped as emotional, nurturing and communal, a stereotype that is not highly relevant to performance in the task and achievement oriented environment of the workplace (Carli and Eagly, 1999; Heilman, 1995). Men are seen as more assertive, independent, competitive and analytical. This stereotype leads people to consider men to be better suited for tasks involving reasoning and problem solving, which are core processes of management. Recent studies have shown that good managers are still perceived as higher in stereotypically masculine traits than stereotypically feminine traits (Powell et al., 2002).

One's gender is a highly salient and visible category of social identity which triggers such stereotypes. This visible social identity is built upon a foundation of characteristics that are to varying degrees invisible and undiscussable. Social norms about sex roles and organizational practices built upon them operate implicitly to give women's presence in the workplace a quality of the Other.

Postcolonial theorists use the term 'the Other' as the repository of all the characteristics which are opposite of the core privileged moral, ethical and aesthetic attributes which define their own self-image (Prasad, 1997). Both colonizers and the Other rely on this dichotomy to form their identities. The cultural attitude is that the Other is inferior, yet this masks a more complicated and ambivalent set of reactions. The Other is both undesirable and desirable, weak and threatening, needing to be controlled and impossible to control (Prasad, 1997). The idea of the Other is a fitting metaphor for women's experiences of organizations. The structure of organizational life which casts women as the Other defines the options for women's self-expression, and to some extent women must internalize the view of themselves as Other.

Social identities are associated with certain stereotypes which can influence others' perceptions. As Morgan Roberts (2005: 689) points out, 'merely belonging to a negatively stereotyped social identity group can create an image discrepancy if stereotypes are inconsistent with one's desired professional image.' All social actors regardless of gender have impression management concerns. For example, in the workplace most people desire that others perceive them as committed and competent. But the situation for women is more complicated because the social meanings ascribed to women's stereotypical traits and behaviors, such as weakness and passivity, can be stigmatizing for women in the workplace environment. Women are the 'visitors' who are required to fit in with the culture that they did not create. In addition to meeting external standards, women must reconcile these standards with their self-image and desire for authenticity. This is identity work that requires them to distance themselves from stereotypically feminine behaviors and attitudes, proving to others that they are not what they appear at first to be, while at the same time being authentically 'feminine' in their own way. As such, women face an identity management situation that is similar to that experienced by other groups with invisible or ambiguous social identities.

In this chapter, I discuss the nature of invisible social identities and apply this idea to women's social identities in the workplace. I draw upon ideas from feminist, identity and stigma research to explain how and why women are cast as the Other. Additionally I draw upon studies of the practices women use to convey the proper social image, to manage the invisible aspects of being a woman in the workplace, and their feelings about doing so. This chapter contributes to our understanding of women's experience of work by highlighting the difficulties they experience in maintaining a credible and authentic identity.

Invisible social identities

Invisible social identities occur when people have personal characteristics which are invisible or ambiguous and are also potentially stigmatizing in certain contexts (Clair et al., 2005). Stigma arises when people have characteristics that vary from normal expectations that are negatively valenced or devalued by others. There are many types of invisible social identities that are recognized as potentially stigmatizing. Race (in the case of mixed race people), sexual preference (for non-heterosexuals), mental or chronic illnesses, religion, socioeconomic status, and prior experiences (such as a criminal record or abortion) are all invisible characteristics that may form the basis for a devalued and stigmatized social identity.

Stigma theory suggests that visibility of an individual's mark significantly influences social interaction and coping strategies. Concealable marks are considered less stigmatizing (Jones et al., 1984), as long as people make the effort and are successful at keeping them concealed. Why then are invisible differences problematic in social interaction? The central issue is the identity formation process that occurs as people's identities are confirmed or disconfirmed in social interaction. Identity formation relies on a 'logic of visibility' (Schlossberg, 2001: 1) which includes both our vision for ourselves and our vision of others. Visible features provide a comforting certainty: what is seen is known, and visible knowledge trumps other kinds of knowledge. In contrast, invisibility creates ambiguities in the social classification process that can interfere with normal social interaction (Schlossberg, 2001).

When people with invisible identities pass in social interactions, which they do every time they enter the public domain without announcing their identity, social relationships occur based on misconceptions about their identities (Clair et al., 2005). When the invisible identity is a potentially stigmatizing one, there is a subtext of risk of being discovered, and always uncertainty. Studying visible stigma, Crocker et al. (1991) referred to the 'attributional ambiguity' which occurs because stigmatized people must infer the meaning of both positive and negative evaluations they receive from others and decipher if and how their stigma influenced those evaluations. This ambiguity or uncertainty applies even more to people with invisible differences, who must also infer if their stigma is actually known to others.

Goffman (1963) wrote that people with invisible marks must constantly attend to the personal information they reveal through both words and actions in order to keep their secret concealed. This is the key difference between visible and invisible stigma which leads to different personal and social adaptation processes. Maintaining and performing one's desired social identity becomes more difficult because of the effort required for information management. People may feel pleasure, pride, or even shame about keeping their secret (Schlossberg, 2001). These reactions, whether positive or negative, will tinge the individual's identity with anxiety and heightened attention. As Smart and Wegner (2000) note, 'concealing a stigma leads to an inner turmoil that is remarkable for its intensity and its capacity for absorbing an individual's mental life' (p. 221). This is because attempts at secrecy typically activate a set of cognitive processes that lead to obsessive thinking about the secret which constantly interferes with one's mental abilities (Lane and Wegner, 1995). In empirical research Frable, Blackstone and Sherbaum (1990) found that people with invisible differences compensate for their differences when they interact with 'normal' people and are more mindful in their interactions. For example, people with concealable marks recalled detailed information about the situation and often took their partner's perspective, doing more of the work to make the relationship flow.

Research on the experiences of people with a variety of concealable stigmas has found that these people experience negative self-perceptions that result in anxiety and depression. People with concealable stigma have lower self-esteem than both people with conspicuous stigma and a control group of people without stigma (Frable, Platt and Hoey, 1998). Similarly people with invisible illness conditions also experience more emotional problems than those with visible manifestations of illness (Ireys et al., 1994). Repressing potentially stigmatizing information about the self requires physiological effort that detracts from normal biological functions and is associated with higher levels of physical illness (Pennebaker, 1989; Tardy, 2000). There are also psychological effects as the individual experiences a fragmented sense of self and a loss of authenticity that comes from keeping portions of themselves hidden (Moorhead, 1999).

The effects of invisible stigma influence social dynamics and, potentially, organizational performance. Relationships that were formed under normal assumptions may be damaged if the stigma is revealed, not only from the negative reaction to the stigma (similar to the reactions to visible stigma) but also from the feelings of betrayal that the relationship was formed under false pretenses. Knowing this risk, people with invisible social identities may live with the fear of being unmasked or 'found in a lie'.

The social relationships that underpin effective group performance are often based on reciprocal disclosure of personal information (Herek, 1996), so concealing information can impede group processes. Although hidden differences may not affect an individual's task-related capability to perform the job, once a stigmatized identity becomes known or suspected it can indirectly decrease group performance. This is because relationship-oriented attributes trigger stereotypes that influence cognitive framing, social interaction, communication patterns and decision making (Jackson and Joshi, 2001), all of which in turn shape group development.

Note that many of the issues identified here as problematic for people with invisible identities only occur if the identity is disclosed, technically making it no longer invisible. This is why the interface between invisibility and visibility and the actions and behaviors people take to maintain that interface is especially interesting to researchers.

The hidden elements of women's social identities

Gender is usually considered a visible difference because gender is enacted, and society has a pattern of practices and expectations that make this enactment visible. The strength of these visible gender norms is intense because they form the requisite foundation for social interaction. Anyone who has ever dressed their baby girl in blue clothes has probably experienced the difficulties in social interaction that occur when visible signals do not follow normative gender expectations. Once we arrive at adulthood with years of gender socialization, gender enactment becomes more sophisticated and nuanced than the choice of blue or pink clothing. Further, our expectations for others' signaling behavior and our ability to interpret more subtle and less visible cues become highly developed. Enacting gender becomes a rich performance with both visible and invisible cues.

Underlying the visible 'fact' of gender is a variety of gendered attributes and behaviors which are less visible. The characteristics associated with women arise from women's ways of seeing the world, and from the symbolism and cultural meanings ascribed to women's bodies and biology. Many of the differences associated with women conflict with organizational values and ideology and are therefore devalued in the workplace. This devalued status is consistent with the definition of stigma. Women are aware of their differences and make efforts to manage the identity they convey. This often means that they attempt to 'blend in' with the dominant organizational culture by hiding their differences. This is similar to the passing strategies used by people with other types of invisible social identities (Clair et al., 2005).

This section will discuss women's implicit differences which contribute to their Otherness and the ways that these factors conflict with traditional organizational ideology. The behaviors women practice to manage their identities and their reactions to being the Other will be addressed in the following sections.

Women as Other in the organizational context

Women in the workplace are subject to stigma based on a combination of visible and invisible differences because their presence challenges three core assumptions of the workplace. These assumptions, stated in the simplest terms, are that organizations by design are genderless, bodyless and sexless. The concepts of gender, body and sexuality are all related to the fact of embodiment and are simply glossed over in organizational life. Each assumption includes both visible features and the invisible subtext associated with them. These shape the social context of organizations in cultural and symbolic ways that create a sense of Otherness for women.

Assumption 1: organizations are genderless

The context and processes of organizations are gendered, based on male experiences and norms which symbolically marginalize or devalue attributes associated with women (Ferguson, 1984; Mumby and Putnam, 1992). Kanter (1977: 43) says the masculine ethic of rationality elevates the traits assumed to belong to men, such as 'analytic abilities to abstract and plan, a capacity to set aside personal and emotional considerations in the interests of task accomplishment, and cognitive superiority in problem-solving and decision making.' Organizational hierarchy and competition are also considered to be part of the masculine ethic. Referring to society in general, Bem (1981) has adopted the term androcentrism, which she defines as the privileging of male experience and the 'otherizing' of female experience. The male experience is defined as the standard or norm, while the female experience is a sex-specific deviation. Using discourse analysis, Swan (1994: 106) illustrates this idea in the way we speak of managers. She notes that when we wish to distinguish between managers of different genders, we refer to 'managers' and 'women managers': 'The concept of "man managers" makes little sense.' Because work is associated with men and men's bodies, women and women's bodies become poignant markers or signifiers of otherness (Birke and Best, 1982; Martin, 1989).

Researchers have offered explanations for women's otherness and the preferencing of traditionally male perspectives based on historic Western cultural values. They note that Western society is divided into public and private spheres, and the social order values reason and rationality. The public space is supposed to be rational and orderly, while the private space is for meeting natural and bodily needs for leisure, intimacy and sex. Bureaucratic organizations are seen as the demonstration of pure rationality, with rules and procedures in place to eliminate the taint of emotion and irrationality (Clegg, 1990). Men are seen as intrinsically involved in the public world, while women are more involved in the private world, associated with the family domain where natural and bodily functions take place (Martin, 1989). Feminine virtues of empathy, capacity for nurturance, and self-sacrifice are set against the assertive and competitive values necessary for success in business (Bender, 1997).

This logic of this private/public difference is the basis of the gender stereotypes of men being instrumental and women being expressive. The expression of emotion is a gendered concept that must be controlled and hidden in organizations. In particular, women's emotional expressiveness is especially out of place in organizational life. Swan (1994) offers the example of crying as stereotypically feminine behavior that is problematic in organizations. Crying is seen as 'natural' for women, as a sign of their sensitivity and weakness.

The relationship between the public and private domains is valenced, favoring the public domain. As Tretheway (1999: 426) notes, 'historically, discourses of professionalism have privileged formal terms such as male, public, mind, and rational over their informal opposites – female, private, body, and emotional.' The informal terms are subordinated as less important to organizational life. While on the surface organizations aspire to be gender neutral, the underlying culture and ideology gives preference to the instrumental and public sides and symbolically to men's ways of being.

Assumption 2: organizations are bodyless
Women's bodies are also markers of otherness in organizations. An emphasis on order and rationality excludes physical bodies, both male and female. Organizations are structured such that bodies are seemingly removed or missing. As Jaggar and Bordo (1989: 4) note, 'the body has been cast as the chief enemy of objectivity', formed in opposition to the mind. Thus organizations must eliminate or control the influence of passion and instinct which may interfere with rationality, specifically the effects of lower-order bodily behaviors on rationality (Brewis and Sinclair, 2000). Obviously bodies cannot be 'eliminated' in a literal sense, but organizations can minimize their effect by ignoring them. On a symbolic level, women in the workplace are deviant because their very presence makes bodies salient, which threatens control and order.

While organizational ideology seeks to neutralize or make invisible bodies of any kind, the unique features of women's bodies make it especially difficult to ignore corporeality. Women are valued by men for their beauty, which is associated with youth and reproductive capacity. Women must balance the tensions between being attractive, but not so attractive as to be dismissed as sex objects (Nicolson, 1996). Women's bodies and biology contain implicit and powerful invisible differences which are inconsistent with traditional organizational ideology. These differences are most evident surrounding issues of reproduction and women's illnesses.

Reproduction   Physical issues women experience because of their reproductive systems are inconsistent with workplace values of discipline and consistency. For example, the behavior changes and mood swings that some women experience during their menstrual cycle are inconsistent with the Western ideals of remaining constant, ever productive, and not changing one's mind (Lorber, 1997). Women are seen as victims of their fluctuating hormones which represent a loss of discipline and control of their bodies and render them periodically unreliable and incapable of sensible decision-making (Martin, 1989).

In popular culture, women's biology and illnesses or conditions associated with reproduction make women unreliable employees (Lorber, 1997). The perception of monthly inefficiency and unreliability has been used historically as justification to keep women out of the workforce during times of high unemployment (Birke and Best, 1982), and generally out of jobs that require responsibility and mental effort (Lorber, 1993). Feminists argue that it is in this way that biology is used as a justification for women's subordination (Martin, 1989).

Historically in most societies there has been taboo associated with women's monthly cycles, with menstruation seen as pathological. One view sees menstruation as associated with demonic forces which, if not properly contained, can wreak havoc on the world. Another cultural view (not held in Western culture) sees menstruating women as sacred. Both views see menstruation as something that disturbs the usual social order and must be contained, often by separating menstruating women from other people (Birke and Best, 1982). In the scientific explanations offered by the Western medical perspective, menstruation is an illness to be controlled. Consistent with this illness view, many cultures have viewed menstruation as a source of contagion (Lorber, 1997).

Menstruation is likely to be invisible most of the time, and women make significant efforts to conceal it. Yet concealing menstruation can be challenging due to the practical difficulties of managing it throughout the day. Some women experience shame and embarrassment in coping with menstruation at work, perceiving it as messy and dirty (Martin, 1989).

The ultimate reproductive issue, pregnancy, is particularly interesting because it has a predictable cycle that moves from invisibility to visibility. In its visible state it becomes a public good, open to public comment. It displays a woman's identity as a sexual being. Even when a woman is not pregnant, the potential of motherhood is present as an invisible identity. Employers perceive the demands of child-rearing as a potential conflict of interest that diverts women's focus and availability for work. Research by Homans (1987) showed that the selection and promotion of women reflected the widely held beliefs that women will leave work to have children and that pregnancy is therefore a liability for employers. Since this study is almost 20 years old, it would be interesting to see if this view is still prevalent in the present work environment. Clearly this underlying perception would shape the employment opportunities of any woman of reproductive age.

On a related point, should a working mother continue to breastfeed after returning to work, this practice can create tension between (male) work ideology, motherhood and sexuality (Stearns, 1999). Both motherhood and sexuality are out of place and can be stigmatizing in organizational life.

Women's illnesses and conditions   Also regarding the particular nature of women's bodies, some women experience illnesses that are unique to women, and they are often invisible conditions. Examples include breast and uterine cancer, infertility, and other diseases of the reproductive tract. Invisible illness causes a number of impression management issues for both men and women (Beatty, 2004). People with some invisible illnesses worry that illness may damage their career success because others may perceive them as less committed or available to perform their work. Other people may assume that people with illness lack the stamina for rigorous work assignments, or that they will eventually have to leave the organization due to either the impairment of the illness or the complicated maintenance regimen it requires. Being able-bodied is the normative assumption in the workplace (Pinder, 1995), and one must be seen as a physically competent actor by supervisors, colleagues and clients. Because illness can threaten one's image of competency or reliability, it poses a possible barrier to career advancement.

The above issues apply to anyone with a chronic illness, but women have additional difficulties regarding illness. One concern is that their illness claims may not be taken seriously because their claims may be trivialized and seen as imaginary or psychosomatic (Jackson, 1992; Ware, 1999). They may be given a psychiatric label, which is deeply discrediting. Women with invisible symptoms are caught in the odd position of trying to make their symptoms socially visible and real to maintain credibility, both in medical encounters and in the workplace (Beatty, 2004; Werner et al., 2004). They strive to achieve the sick role to obtain the rights this role affords, even though their condition might allow them otherwise to pass. In the workplace, women fear that if they fail to achieve credibility they will be stigmatized as 'slackers' with poor work ethics, and that others will believe they are using their perceived illness to be relieved of undesirable tasks (Beatty, 2004).

Imaginary illnesses or hysteria have historically been a women's diagnosis. In fact the word comes from *hystera*, the Greek word for uterus (Showalter, 1997). Classical healers believed that many women's illnesses were caused by the uterus traveling around the body, causing symptoms in its wake. After anatomists showed that the uterus did not migrate, these illnesses were assumed to be a manifestation of woman's weak and delicate nature. Classic psychoanalysts believed women's propensity for hysterical illness was due to Oedipal conflicts, as women transfer their desires from the mother to the father. More modern psychoanalysts such as Janine Chasseguet-Smirgel

(1994) hypothesize that women's propensity to turn emotions into physical manifestations is related to their diffuse sexuality (Showalter, 1997). In contrast to men, with a single visible sex organ, women's entire body is seen as sex organ, making women's identity maintenance much more complex. This discussion of hysteria illustrates that even in illness, women's sexual bodies are always present and potentially problematic. It is ironic that the problems are seen as belonging to the woman, when one could argue they instead rest with the audience's interpretation of her and her body; it is the onlookers and analysts thinking about her sex life, not necessarily the woman herself. The other feature to note is that by attributing a woman's illness to hysteria, her sexuality has been made a public tool to be used against her. A diagnosis of hysteria trivializes women's illness claims, as the implication is that her illness is really a manifestation of unresolved sexual issues.

The other problem with women's illnesses is that they are stigmatizing and may be difficult to discuss at all in a public setting. For example, breast cancer is stigmatizing because, in addition to being life threatening, it affects the breast which is a major symbol of sexuality in our society (Bloom and Kessler, 1994). Infertility is stigmatizing because of the norms and cultural pressures around married couples reproducing (Whiteford and Gonzalez, 1994). Menopause, which is not technically an illness (but is often treated as one), is discrediting because it signals the end of women's reproductive capacity. Reproductive capacity is an important cultural symbol of women's value in society. These conditions are discrediting to a woman's femininity because they interfere with stereotypical norms of sex roles surrounding reproduction and sexuality. Talking about illness, especially women's illness, is an undiscussable private topic that, if revealed, can damage a woman's social identity.

Empirical research with women shows that women have internalized the norms of avoiding talking about illness because they do not want to be seen as 'whiners and complainers' (Werner et al., 2004). This suggests, as will be discussed below, that they have adopted a strategy of self-discipline to fit in with others' expectations. Illness research has shown that social and emotional support, specifically being able to discuss one's troubles with another person, are essential to cope effectively with illness (Pennebaker, 1997). For stigmatizing women's illnesses, getting this kind of social support is more difficult. Women who have 'women's illnesses' experience the double stigma of having an illness and having a woman's illness which makes visible her body, her sexuality, and her otherness.

Assumption 3: organizations are sexless
The presence of women in organizations makes sex and sexual differences visible. As has been discussed above, organizations have been designed to

either eliminate or control sex because it interferes with rational production. Burrell (1984: 98) suggests that historically 'the suppression of sexuality is one of the first tasks bureaucracy sets for itself.' He offers several possible historical explanations for the explicit exclusion of sex in organizations. As the civilizing processes of society increased, people began to feel shame and embarrassment around sexual activities which may have been a normal part of the day prior to industrialization. Sexual activities were also constrained by religious ideology that sought to elevate man above the baser animal instincts. With the development of rationality as a valued world view, sexuality was seen as non-rational and emotional, and it needed to be suppressed to maintain efficiency. Capitalist ideology relied on control of time and the body, so energies and time spent in sexual relations were seen as wasteful. Taken together, Burrell suggests that the developing social norms and cultural ideologies pushed sexual behavior more firmly to the private domain. In each example, the elimination is mediated by organizations or organizational practices (Hearn and Parkin, 1995).

The organizational rationale for eliminating sexuality is based in part on the work-related problems it causes. Sexuality and romantic relationships in the workplace can lead to a long list of troubles that organizations would prefer to avoid such as: work disruption that interferes with productivity (Powell, 2001); decreased morale of co-workers, which can arise due to perceptions that the lower status employee in the relationship has special access or is receiving job-related rewards (Jones, 1999); moral distress for co-workers if the romantic situation violates their moral principles about adultery or homosexuality (Jones, 1999; Powell, 2001); and potential sexual harassment and accompanying lawsuits when the relationship ends (Pierce and Aguinis, 2001).

Overt sexuality is taboo in most organizations. Anthropologist Margaret Mead actually suggested we should have a taboo on sexual relationships within organizations that operate like incest taboos in the family (Mead, 1980: 55). This taboo would say 'You don't make passes at or sleep with the people you work with'. Incest taboos in the family insure that children can learn to trust in a sexually safe environment. By comparison, incest taboos in the workplace would assure that men and women are able to work together on an equal basis without fear of sexual exploitation.

As Mead recommended, some organizations have tried to create strong norms to limit workplace romance. Some explicitly ban certain kinds of sexual relationships. For example, adultery and homosexuality are formally banned in the military. Others have policies that prohibit direct reporting relationships between members of a romantic couple, in an effort to address the perceptions that sexual favors offer unfair career advantages.

Effectively prohibiting workplace romances is impossible. When they do occur and become public, women suffer more of the negative consequences because they are often in the lower power and status job positions (Pierce et al., 1996). Women are evaluated more negatively than men because others assume that the lower-status female is using her sexual relationship with the higher-status male to get preferable job treatment (Anderson and Fisher, 1991; Mainiero, 1989). In his empirical study of the motives people have for pursuing workplace romances, Quinn (1977) called these kinds of relationships utilitarian, with the male most often pursuing ego gratification and the female seeking job-related goals.

Women also have the most negative reactions to others' office romances (Mainiero, 1989; Powell, 2001). Women may interpret workplace romances as threatening to their own reputation because they are concerned about the perpetuation of the perception that women rise in the organization because of their sexual activity and not their competence (Crary, 1987). When Mainiero (1989) asked women executives about their perceptions of workplace romance, two-thirds of her respondents expressed concern about the risks to career, work performance and professional relationships, suggesting negative outcomes are common in romantic relationships. Yet when asked about actual cases they had observed, negative effects occurred less frequently. For example, in only 10 per cent of the cases were the people in the office romance 'more difficult to get along with', and 23 per cent were less productive. Mainiero proposed that women exaggerated the risks because they feared the negative consequences: 'Many women believe that falling in love with a colleague destroys a woman's already tenuous credibility' (p. 121). Allowing oneself to become intimately involved with an office colleague is considered 'unprofessional', so some women in Mainiero's sample regulated their own behaviors to avoid this risk. Following a similar logic, feminist scholars such as Tancred-Sheriff (1989) believe that most romantic relationships in the workplace could be classified as sexual harassment because they serve as instruments of men's domination and control of women.

Although sex is unacknowledged in organizations, it is always present below the surface. Many social contexts that are associated with organizational life introduce sexual differences. For example, activities like visits to bars, sporting events, men's bathrooms, and even strip bars are either sex-segregated or predominantly male. If women attend these events, they are obliged to fit in with the overtly sexual environment which in extreme cases objectifies women (Sheppard, 1989).

It is ironic that the undiscussable nature of sex in the workplace makes it all the more present. Women are the flashpoint illuminating sexuality because they are seen as the walking embodiment of sexuality (Schultz, 2003). Sex becomes the lens through which everything is interpreted, even when the situation or behavior has nothing to do with sex. For example, in workplace relationships between men and women, women's actions are often interpreted by men to be sexual, even when the women intend only to be friendly (Abbey, 1982). This over-sexualized interpretation is similar to the distorted focus on homosexual sex that gays and lesbians experience. As Herek (1996) notes, although sexual activity comprises only a very small portion of an individual's life, homosexuals are seen almost entirely through the lens of sex.

When sex does enter the workplace, it may be framed negatively as sexual harassment. Harassment laws provide the justification for the exclusion of sexuality. They may be perceived as support for women by ensuring women's safety and comfort in the organization, or more cynically for the purposes of increasing managerial efficiencies by formally prohibiting sex at work. Schultz (2003) notes that organizations are quick to categorize all intimate relationships as potential harassment suits, and that they use this body of law to increase their control over employees' lives. These laws also provide justification for increasing surveillance of employee behavior. Others note that sexual activities in the workplace can be seen as a form of resistance to organizational control (Burrell, 1984; Hearn and Parkin, 1995). Whether seen as proscribed harassment or subversive resistance, either view underscores that sex is something that is out of place in organizational life.

Gender management: how women cope with otherness
The above discussion illustrates how the presence of women and women's bodies in organizations violates key ideological assumptions of organizational life. These cultural and organizational values and assumptions affect the environment in which women create and maintain their identities. How does all this hidden subtext of otherness affect women in the workplace? These features of organizational life require women to perform 'gender management', treating gender as a managed status (Sheppard, 1989). Much like other invisible identities such as sexual preference or disability, women use impression management strategies to project and maintain their desired selves. Women may aim to 'pass' or 'out' this identity to their co-workers. This concept of 'outing' oneself may seem odd for a visible identity. However, the analogy rests on the fact that claiming a female identity in a male-dominated culture requires one to make the implicit taken for granted differences explicit.

As with other hidden identities, women's identity management strategies must address the ambiguity of their role and constantly incorporate the perceived perceptions of others. Sheppard (1989) has offered two versions of identity management strategies women use, called blending in and claiming a rightful place. These strategies are at opposite ends of a continuum.

Blending in is similar to passing, and attempts to conform to the prevailing expectations and comfort levels of male co-workers. In contrast, women who adopt the strategy of claiming their rightful place are less reluctant to challenge prevailing gender assumptions and less likely to accommodate the perceived need to make male colleagues comfortable. In empirical work Sheppard found claiming a rightful place to be a less common strategy, with most women blending in.

At its core, the concept of blending in requires that women exercise control and self-discipline. The specific differences of women's bodies and ways of being make this challenging. Tretheway (1999) notes that women's bodies are excessively sexual because the female body has a tendency to overflow, and to display messages that were not intended. The metaphor of overflowing can describe pregnancy, menstruation, emotional displays, or wardrobe malfunctions. Being aware of their otherness in organizations and the difficulties it presents, working women walk a fine line presenting themselves as both competent and feminine. The female body is a liability for their professional identity (Trethewey, 1999), and their ability to participate fully in the organization system depends on careful self-presentation. Women managers must maintain credibility as a serious manager while, at the same time, meeting feminine stereotypes (Sheppard, 1989).

Blending in to meet others' expectations
As women entered the professional workforce in greater numbers in the 1970s and 80s, they received well-intentioned advice on how to hide their sexuality and bodily differences. The most well-known book in this genre was *The Woman's Dress for Success Book* by John Molloy (1977). Molloy recommended that women's business dress should be modeled after men's traditional suits. During this period women wore dark or neutral colored tailored suits, light-colored blouses, and some neck detail like a scarf (the infamous 'floppy bow') to mimic the man's tie. Big shoulder pads helped create a more masculine look, and, as one writer noted, helped to diminish the emphasis on a woman's bust. Indeed, we see this kind of reasoning employed consistently. A brief visit to the archives of popular books illustrates a similar kind of focus on women's sexuality and bodies as a barrier to 'blending in' in the modern organization. The recurring themes are self-discipline and control, as women are advised to blend in to the male work world as seamlessly as possible.

Sheppard (1989) offers several poignant examples from these books. For example Molloy (1977) advises that women wear bras that hold their breasts in place and hide their nipples. He notes that dressing for success in business and dressing to be sexually attractive are mutually exclusive. Proper self-presentation should also be conveyed in one's choice of office art. Subsequently he recommends women avoid displaying overly feminine art in favor of neutral art, which is also part of a strategy to avoid displaying one's differences.

Another advice-giver, Jeanette Scollard (1983: 81), suggests that when leaving a business group to go to the bathroom, women should say that they have to make a phone call: 'She never refers to her bodily habits, her gender, or any personal need'. Scollard also cautions that a woman should never be seen purchasing sanitary supplies in the women's bathroom since this could lead to a manager's behavior being attributed to her menstrual cycle. A final important tip is that women should not take more than six weeks of maternity leave because men interpret this time as 'goof-off time' (Scollard, 1983: 158).

Sheppard (1989) notes that the advice-givers encourage women to trade their feminine sexuality for the more highly valued characteristic of power. Power can be available to them if they make an effort to control their sexuality. Yet a woman must be careful not to eliminate all hint of sexuality. If she becomes completely asexual then she risks being seen as a lesbian or a prude, which are also devalued positions.

Internalizing self-discipline and control

While one may question whether these historical texts portray an accurate picture of today's organizational life for women, more recent empirical research shows that women's self-presentation in the workplace still requires careful balance between displaying competence and femininity. To achieve this balance, working women use a variety of strategies to attend to and control their verbal and non-verbal communication, emotional displays, bodies and sexuality. These strategies optimize the power that women have and allow them to assimilate to the male culture of organizations.

Women adopt communication styles that demonstrate a non-threatening competence. Overt displays of directness, authority or competency by women can result in rejection because these violate stereotypical norms of female behavior. Research has shown that women who are perceived as modest evoke more favorable reactions than assertive women (Wosinska et al., 1996), consistent with gender role stereotypes. Women create the impression of modesty and non-aggression through their communication behaviors. For example, women use more tentative speech when communicating with men, using tag questions, disclaimers, and hedging statements (Carli, 1990; Tannen, 1990). This is functional for women because studies support that men are more influenced by women speaking tentatively than women speaking assertively. Although speech behaviors also make women appear less competent, women may use these strategies as a subtle form of influence.

Women also use non-verbal behaviors such as a forward-leaning body, smiling, eye-contact, and non-intrusive hand gestures to convey both competence and sociability. Sociability has been shown to improve the influence of both men and women, but its effects are more pronounced for women (Carli et al., 1995). Sociability reduces the threat of women's dominant or competent behaviors, and is more consistent with gender role norms for women. Tretheway (1999) has found that women use comportment behaviors, such as eye-contact, crossed or not crossed legs, the way they walk or sit, and a firm handshake to convey a feminized power. Similarly, Sheppard (1989) describes how one of her participants is careful to avoid male presentation styles and behaviors such as pacing or putting her hands in her pockets because she perceives that her male co-workers find this style too assertive. Comportment is a performance that must simultaneously demonstrate grace, constraint and competency, and this performance requires some degree of conscious thought.

These verbal and non-verbal communication strategies are well-suited to women's power base which is more likely to come from relationships. Carli (1999) suggests that women possess higher levels of referent power than men do. People generally evaluate women more favorably than men, and like them more. Thus women use indirect influence strategies that build on their referent power. Gender norms dictate the wisdom of indirect influence and a focus on relationships. Women who violate these gender norms may be punished in the workplace for their perceived lack of gender-appropriate interpersonal skills (Rudman and Glick, 1999).

A second area of control occurs with emotional displays. Emotional displays significantly shape the way people are evaluated by others. Emotion has historically been associated with irrationality, immaturity and extreme subjectivity (Shields, 1987); it is dangerous, irrational and physical. The expression of emotion is stereotypically associated with women. Emotional displays are considered a sign of weakness, as a character defect and a sign of the 'intrapsychic disorganization' (Lutz, 1991: 70). Being called 'emotional' is usually not a compliment.

Emotional displays are governed by display rules which are shaped by gender norms. There is a double standard affecting the displays of certain emotions for men and women. One example is the display of anger. The expression of anger by men is seen as a sign of deeply held convictions and is considered more appropriate than displays of anger by women. Women's anger is perceived as overreacting or 'bitchy' and implies personal instability (Hochschild, 1983). It is also less likely to be seen as appropriate (Shields, 1987). Another emotional display that is considered highly gendered is crying. Empirical work with professional women shows that women control both anger and crying to avoid male disapproval (Swan,

1994; Tretheway, 1999). There is an irony in that women who often work in positions that require emotional labor in the service of the organization are at the same time devalued for their tendency to become too emotional and therefore irrational.

A third area of control and impression management occurs with women's bodies. Women demonstrate control by maintaining fit bodies (Tretheway, 1999). The rationale is that women who can discipline their bodies appropriately can be trusted with professional responsibilities. Further, a fit body signals endurance and an ability to complete tasks on behalf of the organization without her body becoming an undue constraint. Overweight women are stigmatized for their perceived lack of control. Their weight is attributed to internal failings and personal weakness. The parameters for women's weight and body shape are more constraining than are men's parameters, perhaps because women must meet standards of attractiveness that men do not have to meet (Kimle and Damhorst, 1997).

Personal appearance is an important image management tool, as evidenced by the number of books that tell women what to wear for maximum professional impact. The issue of women's clothing speaks to both body and sexuality. Empirical studies have shown that women invest a lot of care in the way they dress for work in order to establish credibility (c.f., Kimle and Damhorst, 1997; Sheppard, 1989; Tretheway, 1999). Tretheway's (1999) participants said that revealing the body causes women to be seen as sexual instead of professional beings, thereby destroying their credibility. The choices women made about their necklines, hemlines, fit of clothing (tailored but not too tight), hair color, amount of makeup, and jewelry were all important for professional presentation.

In contrast to the *Dress for Success* era in which women had a narrow range of fashion choices which mimicked men's styles, the present era affords women more flexibility in self-presentation. While this is seen as a general improvement, a byproduct of increasing freedom is the difficulty of choosing the right clothes. Women's choices are more varied than men's, so the choices are interpreted as more meaningful of a woman's character or identity. As Kimle and Damhorst (1997: 63) note, 'women's appearances are more laden with information', and there is a greater risk of miscommunication. Since there is not a standard woman's business uniform, women must work harder by making active choices about their self presentation.

Studies on women's work clothing have also found that some women spend a lot of effort to dress in a way that reduces their visibility, so they do not stand out as different. Kimle and Damhorst (1997) found that the higher women were in the corporate hierarchy, the more conservatively they dressed. Their study participants felt it was important to distinguish themselves from the clerical women who tend to dress in a more visibly feminine style which they perceived as reducing their credibility. On a similar note Nicolson (1996) suggests that as women rise in organizational rank, they make increasing efforts to make their sexuality invisible. In contrast, women in lower occupational ranks may have to use their sexuality as a source of power in a structure that allows them few other options.

Outcomes of self-discipline

When gender management is effective, women experience the personal satisfaction of organizational success and career progress. Yet achieving this success does come at a price. Sheppard (1989) has found that women have feelings of ambivalence about their identity management situation. While it gives women a positive feeling of accomplishment when they realize they are succeeding in the world of male status and power, it is also uncomfortable to feel the liabilities of being a visitor or outsider to this world.

Information management behaviors take a lot of effort and can be emotionally taxing, which can lead women to feel fatigue and stress. Women in Marshall's (1995) study felt tired from the continued pressures of managing themselves and the images they presented. Establishing and maintaining credibility, and overcoming negative stereotypes required constant effort. The same study found that some women experienced stress from the cognitive dissonance of maintaining incongruous inner and outer selves; these women felt inauthentic. Further, they did not like who they had become in order to survive and be successful in organizational life. These women made intense efforts to keep these negative emotions under control. In some cases this fatigue and stress prompted women to change careers or leave the workforce all together, as the game just wasn't enjoyable any more.

Ironically, if a woman has truly succeeded at blending in and making herself invisible, it is also possible that her achievements may also be invisible, which can actually diminish her feelings of career success (Sheppard, 1989). Sheppard also notes that impression management behaviors may lead women to feel isolated and marginalized in the workplace. This is similar to the experiences of other groups with hidden identity markers such as gay and lesbian or illness identities. Some researchers in these areas suggest that concealing one's stigmatized identity leads to a bifurcated self and associated decreased self-esteem, stress, and feelings of being disconnected (Beatty and Joffe, 2006; Frable et al., 1998; Herek, 1996).

The self-help books would lead us to believe that gender management always works, but this is not the case. Women's efforts at control and self-discipline may fail and allow female attributes and behaviors such as biological differences or emotional displays to show. When this happens, for example in the case of crying, women may feel ashamed or embarrassed by their demonstration of 'unprofessional' behaviors (Swan, 1994). Sometimes women's efforts at gender management fail when their actions are seen as overly feminine or sexual. For example, a gesture that was intended to be friendly may be perceived as a sexual come on, or a woman's clothing may be considered too frilly. Failed impression management attempts over time may have career repercussions. When women are seen as 'not fitting in' for being too feminine, they may be passed over for promotions and important developmental job assignments. A loss of credibility can also threaten a woman's self-esteem (Tretheway, 1999).

The cause of these problems of self presentation is due at least in part to the social expectations which constrain the range of acceptable workplace behaviors and give preference to the male-generated norms. However, to point this out is to risk being called an uppity woman or a feminist. Marshall (1995) found that the feminist label was shunned by professional women because of its association with confrontation and antagonism: being militant or disruptive was not seen as helpful to one's career advancement. The ideology and norms are implicit and undiscussable, so women approach the problem of 'fitting in' as a personal project (Sheppard, 1989). Failures to fit in are also personal, and women are likely to take personal responsibility for triggering the wrong interpretation.

Conclusion

This chapter has examined gender as a performance that women enact, looking at the practices women use to accomplish gender and identity. Giddens (1991) has suggested that the kind of reflexivity and self-analysis presented here is a requirement of the postmodern identity, and he places special emphasis on the body. Observation of one's own and others' bodies is the basis for identity for everyone; identity creation is work for both men and women.

This discussion has focused specifically on women's identity creation because of their symbolic outsider status in organizational life. Women's ability to form their own identities is constrained because organizational discourse supports male images and behaviors. The issues I identify deal with pervasive gender stereotypes and symbolic aspects of womanhood such as reproduction, motherhood and sexuality, issues which are also fundamentally linked to women's bodies and biology. These features contribute to women's otherness, which is presented as a problematic master status to be managed.

As noted at the beginning of this chapter, the Other is seen as simultaneously weak and threatening, as needing to be controlled and unable to be controlled. Research on women's identity in the workplace highlights the importance of control on many levels. It also highlights the fact that women have internalized the 'panoptical gaze of the male connoisseur' (Tretheway, 1999: 425) and the view of themselves as the Other. Women have accepted the idea that they are the ones who must apply self-discipline to blend in to the organizational environment, which they accomplish by controlling their body and sexuality. This disciplined self-presentation is the hallmark of identity management, making women's self-presentation strategies an interesting illustration of the challenges of managing hidden stigmatized identities.

References

Abbey, A. (1982), 'Sex differences in attribution of friendly behavior: do males misperceive females' friendliness?', *Journal of Personality and Social Psychology*, **42**(5), 830–38.

Anderson, C.J. and C. Fisher (1991), 'Male–female relationship in the workplace: perceived motivations in office romance', *Sex Roles*, **25**, 163–80.

Beatty, J.E. (2004), 'Chronic Illness as invisible diversity: disclosing and coping with illness in the workplace', unpublished dissertation, Boston College, Boston, MA.

Beatty, J.E. and R. Joffe (2006), 'An overlooked dimension of diversity: the career effects of chronic illness', *Organizational Dynamics*, **35**, 182–95.

Bem, S. (1981), 'Gender schema theory: A cognitive account of sex-typing', *Psychological Review*, **88**, 354–64.

Bender, E. (1997), 'Malice in Wonderland: American working-girl scenarios', in O.F. Williams (ed.), *The Moral Imagination*, Notre Dame, IN: University of Notre Dame Press, pp. 53–70.

Birke, L.I. and S. Best (1982), 'Changing minds: women, biology, and the menstrual cycle', in R. Hubbard, M.S. Henifin and B. Fried (eds), *Biological Woman: The Convenient Myth*, Cambridge, MA: Schenkman Publishing, pp. 161–84.

Bloom, K.R. and L. Kessler (1994), 'Emotional support following cancer: a test of the stigma and social activity hypothesis', *Journal of Health and Social Behavior*, **35**, 118–33.

Brewis, J. and J. Sinclair (2000), 'Exploring embodiment: women, biology, and work', in J. Hassard, R. Holliday and H. Willmott (eds), *Body and Organization*, London: Sage, pp. 192–214.

Broverman, I.K., S.R. Vogel, D.M. Broverman, F.E. Clarkson and P.S. Rosenkrantz (1972), 'Sex role stereotypes: a current appraisal', *Journal of Social Issues*, **28**(2), 59–78.

Burrell, G. (1984), 'Sex and organizational analysis', *Organization Studies*, **5**(2), 97–118.

Carli, L.L. (1990). 'Gender, language, and influence', *Journal of Personality and Social Psychology*, **59**, 941–51.

Carli, L.L. (1999), 'Gender, interpersonal power, and social influence', *Journal of Social Issues*, **55**, 81–94.

Carli, L.L. and A.H. Eagly (1999), 'Gender effects in social influence and emergent leadership', in G.N. Powell (ed.), *Handbook of Gender and Work*, Thousand Oaks, CA: Sage, pp. 203–22.

Carli, L.L., S. LaFleur, and C.C. Loeber (1995), 'Nonverbal behavior, gender, and influence', *Journal of Personality and Social Psychology*, **68**, 1030–41.

Chasseguet-Smirgel, J. (1994), 'The femininity of the analyst in professional practice', *International Journal of Psycho-Analysis*, **65**, 169–78.

Clair, J.A., J.E. Beatty and T.L. MacLean (2005), 'Out of sight but not out of mind: managing invisible social identities in the workplace', *Academy of Management Review*, **30**, 78–95.

Clegg, S. (1990), *Modern Organizations: Organization Studies in the Postmodern World*, London: Sage.

Crary, M. (1987), 'Managing attraction and intimacy at work', *Organizational Dynamics*, **15**(4), 27–41.

Crocker, J., K. Voelkl, M. Testa and B.M. Major (1991), 'Social stigma: affective consequences of attributional ambiguity', *Journal of Personality and Social Psychology*, **60**, 218–28.

Deaux, K. and M. LaFrance (1998), 'Gender', in D.T. Gilbert, T. Fiske and G. Lindzey (eds), *The Handbook of Social Psychology*, Boston: McGraw Hill, pp. 788–827.

Ferguson, K. (1984), *The Feminist Case Against Bureaucracy,* Philadelphia: Temple University Press.

Frable, D., T. Blackstone and C. Sherbaum (1990), 'Marginal and mindful: deviants in social interaction', *Journal of Personality and Social Psychology*, **59**, 140–49.

Frable, D., L. Platt and S. Hoey (1998), 'Concealable stigmas and positive self-perceptions: feeling better around similar others', *Journal of Personality and Social Psychology*, **74**, 909–22.

Giddens, A. (1991), *Modernity and Self Identity*, Cambridge: Polity Press.

Goffman, E. (1963), *Stigma: Notes on the Management of Spoiled Identity*, Englewood Cliffs, NJ: Prentice Hall.

Hearn, J. and W. Parkin (1995), *'Sex' at 'Work': The Power and Paradox of Organisation Sexuality*, New York: St. Martin's Press.

Heilman, M.E. (1995), 'Sex stereotypes and their effects in the workplace: what we know and we don't know', *Journal of Social Behavior and Personality*, **10**(6), 3–26.

Herek, G.M. (1996), 'Why tell if you are not asked? Self-disclosure, intergroup contact, and heterosexuals' attitudes toward lesbians and gay men', in G.M. Herek, J.B. Jobe and R.M.Carney (eds), *Out in Force: Sexual Orientation and the Military*, Chicago: University of Chicago Press, pp. 197–225.

Hochschild, A.R. (1983), *The Managed Heart*, Berkeley, CA: University of California Press.

Homans, H. (1987), 'Man-made myths: The reality of being a woman scientist in the NHS', in A. Spencer and D. Podmore (eds), *In a Man's World: Essays on Women in Male-Dominated Professions*, London: Tavistock, pp. 87–112.

Ireys, H.T., S.S. Gross, L.A. Werthamer-Larsson and K.B. Kolodner (1994), 'Self-esteem of young adults with chronic health conditions: appraising the effects of perceived impact', *Journal of Developmental and Behavioral Pediatrics*, **15**, 409–15.

Jackson, J.E. (1992), 'After a while no one believes you: real and unreal pain', in M.J.D.V. Good, P.E. Brodwin, B.J. Good and A. Kleinman (eds), *Pain As Human Experience: An Anthropological Perspective,* Berkeley: University of California Press, pp. 138–68.

Jackson, S.E. and A. Joshi (2001), 'Research on domestic and international diversity management in organizations: a merger that works?', in N. Anderson, D.S. Ones, H.K. Sinangil and C. Viswesvaran (eds), *Handbook of Industrial, Work, and Organizational Psychology,* London: Sage, pp. 206–31.

Jaggar, A.M. and S.R. Bordo (eds) (1989), *Gender/Body/Knowledge: Feminist Reconstructions of Being and Knowing*, New Brunswick, NJ: Rutgers University Press.

Jones, E.E., A. Farina, A.H. Hastorf, H. Markus, D.T. Miller and R.A. Scott (1984), *Social Stigma: The Psychology of Market Relationships*, New York: W.H. Freeman.

Jones, G.E. (1999), 'Hierarchical workplace romance: an experimental examination of team member perceptions', *Journal of Organizational Behavior*, **20**, 1057–72.

Kanter, R.M. (1977), *Men and Women of the Corporation*, New York: Basic Books.

Kimle, P.A. and M.L. Damhorst (1997), 'A grounded theory model of the ideal business image for women', *Symbolic Interaction*, **21**, 45–68.

Lane, J.D. and D.M. Wegner (1995), 'The cognitive consequences of secrecy', *Journal of Personality and Social Psychology*, **69**, 1–17.

Lorber, J. (1993), 'Believing is seeing: biology as ideology', *Gender and Society*, **7**, 568–81.

Lorber, J. (1997), *Gender and the Social Construction of Illness*, Thousand Oaks, CA: Sage.

Lutz, C.A. (1991), 'Engendered emotion: gender, power, and the rhetoric of emotional control in American discourse', in C.A. Lutz and L. Abu-Lughod (eds), *Language and the Politics of Emotion*, Cambridge: Cambridge University Press, pp. 69–91.

Mainiero, L.A. (1989), *Office Romance: Love, Power, and Sex in the Workplace,* New York: Rawson Associates.

Marshall, J. (1995), *Women Managers Moving On: Exploring Career and Life Choices,* London: Routledge.

Martin, E. (1989), *The Woman in the Body: A Cultural Analysis of Reproduction*, Milton Keynes: Open University Press.

Mead, M. (1980), 'A proposal: we need taboos on sex at work', in D.A. Neugarten and J.M. Shafritz (eds), *Sexuality in Organizations*, Oak Park, IL: Moore Publishing, pp. 53–6.

Molloy, J.T. (1977), *The Woman's Dress for Success Book*, New York: Warner Books.

Moorhead, C. (1999), 'Queering identities: the roles of integrity and belonging in becoming ourselves', *Journal of Gay, Lesbian, and Bisexual Identity*, **4**, 327–43.

Morgan Roberts, L. (2005), 'Changing faces: professional image construction in diverse organizational settings', *Academy of Management Review*, **30**, 685–711.

Mumby, D.K. and L.L. Putnam (1992), 'The politics of emotion: a feminist reading of bounded rationality', *Academy of Management Review*, **17**, 465–86.

Nicolson, P. (1996), *Gender, Power, and Organisation: A Psychological Perspective*, London: Routledge.

Pennebaker, J.W. (1989), 'Confession, inhibition and disease', in L. Berkowitz (ed.), *Advances in Experimental Social Psychology*, New York: Academic Press, pp. 211–44.

Pennebaker, J.W. (1997), *Opening Up: The Healing Power of Expressing Emotions,* New York: Guilford.

Pierce, C.A. and H. Aguinis (2001), 'A framework for investigating the link between workplace romance and sexual harassment', *Group and Organization Management*, **26**, 206–29.

Pierce, C.A., D. Byrne and H. Aguinis (1996), 'Attraction in organizations: a model of workplace romance', *Journal of Organizational Behavior*, **17**, 5–32.

Pinder, R. (1995), 'Bringing back the body without the blame?: the experience of ill and disabled people at work', *Sociology of Health and Illness*, **17**, 605–31.

Powell, G.N. (2001), 'Workplace romances between senior-level executives and lower-level employees: an issue of work disruption and gender', *Human Relations*, **54**, 1519–44.

Powell, G.N. and L.M. Graves (2003), *Women and Men in Management*, Thousand Oaks, CA: Sage.

Powell, G.N., D.A. Butterfield and J.D. Parent (2002), 'Gender and managerial stereotypes: Have the times changed?', *Journal of Management*, **28**, 177–93.

Prasad, A. (1997), 'The colonizing consciousness and representations of the other: a postcolonial critique of the discourse of oil', in P. Prasad, A.J. Mills, M. Elmes and A. Prasad (eds), *Managing the Organizational Melting Pot: Dilemmas of Workplace Diversity*, Thousand Oaks, CA: Sage, pp. 285–311.

Quinn, R. (1977), 'Coping with Cupid: the formation, impact and management of romantic relations in organizations', *Administrative Science Quarterly*, **22**, 30–45.

Rudman, L.A. and P. Glick (1999), 'Feminized management and backlash toward agentic women: the hidden cost to women of a kinder, gentler image of middle managers', *Journal of Personality and Social Psychology*, **77**, 1004–10.

Schlossberg, L. (2001), 'Introduction: rites of passing', in M.C. Sanchez and L. Schlossberg (eds), *Passing: Identity and Interpretation in Sexuality, Race, and Religion*, New York: New York University Press, pp. 1–12.

Schultz, V. (2003), 'The sanitized workplace', *Yale Law Journal*, **112**(206), 2063–193.

Scollard, J.R. (1983), *No-nonsense Management Tips for Women*, New York: Pocket Books.

Sheppard, D.L. (1989), 'Organizations, power, and sexuality: the image and self-image of women managers', in J. Hearn, D.L. Sheppard, P. Tancred-Sheriff and G. Burrell (eds), *The Sexuality of Organization*. London: Sage.

Shields, S.A. (1987), 'Women, men, and the dilemma of emotion', in P. Shaver and C. Hendrick (eds), *Sex and Gender*, Newbury Park, CA: Sage, pp. 229–50.

Showalter, E. (1997), *Hystories: Hysterical Epidemics and Modern Culture*, New York: Columbia University Press.

Smart, L. and D.M. Wegner (2000), 'The hidden costs of hidden stigma', in T.F. Heatherton, R.E. Kleck, M.R. Hebl and J.G. Hull (eds), *The Social Psychology of Stigma*, New York: Guilford Press, pp. 220–41.

Stearns, C.A. (1999), 'Breastfeeding and the good maternal body', *Gender and Society*, **13**, 308–25.

Swan, E. (1994), 'Managing emotion', in M. Tanton (ed.), *Women in Management: A Developing Presence*, London: Routledge, pp. 89–109.

Tancred-Sheriff, P. (1989), 'Gender, sexuality, and the labour process', in J. Hearn, D.L. Sheppard, P. Tancred-Sheriff and G. Burrell (eds), *The Sexuality of Organization*, London: Sage, pp. 45–55.

Tannen, D. (1990), *You Just Don't Understand: Women and Men in Conversation*, New York: Ballantine.

Tardy, C.H. (2000), 'Self-disclosure and health: revisiting Sydney Jourard's hypothesis', in S. Petronio (ed.), *Balancing the Secrets of Private Disclosures*, Mahwah, NJ: Lawrence Erlbaum Associates.

Tretheway, A. (1999), 'Disciplined bodies: women's embodied identities at work', *Organization Studies*, **20**, 423–50.

Ware, N.C. (1999), 'Toward a model of social course in chronic illness: the example of chronic fatigue syndrome', *Culture, Medicine, and Psychiatry*, **23**, 303–31.

Werner, A., L.W. Isaksen and K. Malterud (2004), '"I am not the kind of woman who complains of everything": illness stories on self and shame in women with chronic pain', *Social Science and Medicine*, **59**, 1035–45.

Whiteford, L.M. and L. Gonzalez (1994), 'Stigma: the burden of infertility', *Social Science and Medicine*, **40**, 27–36.

Williams, J.E. and D.L. Best (1990), *Measuring Sex Stereotypes: A Multination Study*, Thousand Oaks, CA: Sage.

Wosinska, W., A.J. Dabul, R. Whetstone-Dion and R.B. Cialdini (1996), 'Self-presentational responses to success in the organization: the costs and benefits of modesty', *Basic and Applied Social Psychology*, **18**, 229–42.

3   (No) cracks in the glass ceiling: women managers, stress and the barriers to success

Caroline Gatrell and Cary L. Cooper

Introduction

Why, one might ask, should women managers be stressed? In these days of 'equal opportunities', is it not the case that women 'have it all'? It is certainly true that the number of women in all occupations has risen sharply over the past 30 years. And it is particularly the case that, for well-qualified women managers, opportunities to participate in paid employment are greater now than they were in previous decades. For the past 30 years, anti-discrimination and equal pay legislation has been in place to protect and encourage women in employment, and state-run and funded organizations have been set up to support working women: in the USA, the Department of Labor Women's Bureau, and in the UK, the Equal Opportunities Commission (EOC), soon to become a single commission on equality and human rights.

In the press and media, women are often portrayed as having 'won' the battle for equality at the expense of men, and of supposedly 'male' values. The UK BBC television reporter Michael Buerk, who has been described as 'the most important journalist of the post-war period' recently sparked off a furious debate by suggesting that 'women increasingly set the agenda in business ... and in society at large, [and] women's values are now considered superior to men's values.' (Gibson, 2005). Buerk argues that men have been emasculated by women's rise up the corporate and political ladder and asserts that there is a need to reverse this trend.

While some writers and broadcasters have refuted these claims, others have been quick to support such views. Writing in the British *Daily Mail*, Ruth Dudley Edwards suggests: 'I cannot see how any fair-minded person can argue with Mr Buerk's assertion that men ...are out of fashion and that society now values the female.' Dudley Edwards goes so far as to suggest that examination systems have been unfairly re-engineered to favour female scholars, thus 'cheating' those examinees (by inference boys) who 'can rise to the occasion and perform well under pressure' (Dudley Edwards, 2005: 14).

If, as Buerk and Dudley Edwards claim, women are doing so well in society that men are now disadvantaged, what do women managers have to be stressed about? We suggest that there are several important reasons why women in business and management might feel stressed. Citing some well established statistics, we argue that the idea of women's rise through the business and corporate ranks at the expense of male executives is mythical because, while it is true that there are more women managers now than there were 20 years ago, it is also the case that women remain persistently absent from top corporate jobs across Europe and America (Vinnicombe and Bank 2003; *The Economist* 2005). The gender pay gap remains high: at just under 20 per cent in the UK for full-time women workers and up to 40 per cent for part-timers (EOC, 2005), and at around 28 per cent for full-time female workers in the USA (Padavic and Reskin, 2002).

In the light of these figures, we argue that concerns about women taking over the business and management agenda are unfounded. We contend that women managers, no matter how well-qualified and hard working, continue to be excluded from senior and executive roles due to discriminatory attitudes on the part of employers. We also suggest that the exclusion of women managers from top-level roles has a negative impact on their well-being. This is because women experience a greater level of workplace stress than men due to structural factors such as barriers to promotion which are placed in front of women, but not in front of men (Davidson and Cooper, 1992; Roxburgh, 1996; Desmarais and Alksnis, 2005). Structural factors are important because, while we acknowledge that stress is *experienced* at an individual level (and that the individual may act to alleviate it: Cooper and Cartwright 1997), the main *causes* of stress for women in management are structural and institutional, and significant changes in business and social practice will be required if the situation is to improve (Fielden and Cooper, 2001). We therefore attempt to provide a social explanation for the continued existence of the 'glass ceiling' by discussing the historical expectation that women should be mothers and homemakers, not work-orientated careerists. We consider the problem of discrimination faced by women managers and we explore how social attitudes and misplaced assumptions about the low work-orientation of women managers heighten stress levels. Finally, we consider how far women managers may experience stress due to a multiplicity of roles.

The continued existence of the 'glass ceiling'

A recent report in *The Economist* (2005) notes that, despite the American Government's specially appointed Glass Ceiling Commission (established in 1995 to bring down the barriers that prevented women from reaching the top of the corporate ladder), women account for 46.5 per cent of America's workforce but for less then 8 per cent of its top managers. This figure has altered very little since 1995 when the commission was set up. In the UK, the situation is similar: while 44 per cent of the workforce is female, very few women command positions on corporate boards. In 2001, only 5 per cent of FTSE 100 companies had more than 20 per cent female directors on their boards, while 43 per cent had no female directors at all (Vinnicombe and Bank, 2003). And in 2002, only 61 per cent of the top 100 companies included a female director on their boards – a figure which was down from 64 per cent in 1999 (Singh and Vinnicombe, 2004). Even where some improvements can be seen in the numbers of women on corporate boards, the numbers of female executives remain tiny. For example, between 2000 and 2004 the total number of female executive directors of FTSE 100 companies rose from 11 to 17. However, in comparison with the number of men in such posts (400 male executive directors) even the improved figure could be regarded as negligible (*The Economist*, 2005: 67). As *The Economist* points out,

> The glass ceiling ...is proving particularly persistent. The corporate ladder remains stubbornly male and the few women who reach it are paid significantly less than the men whom they join there... [This is despite the] so called 'diversity programmes,' aimed at promoting minorities as well as women, which are as common as diversity on the board is rare. (*The Economist*, 2005: 67–68)

Social resistance to women in managers – a source of stress

The social resistance to women in professional and management roles is widely recognized as a significant source of stress and demotivation for senior women (Cooper and Davidson, 1982; Davidson and Cooper, 1992; Nelson and Burke, 2000; Eagly and Karau, 2002, Desmarais and Alksnis 2005). Although discrimination goes against both the spirit and the letter of the law, many women managers still find themselves fighting discriminatory practices in organizations. Thus, while both male and female senior managers may experience stress due to long hours cultures, short-term contracts or work overload, women managers face additional stress-related problems due to their gender. In the context of stress which is related to discrimination and the 'glass ceiling', women managers are likely to experience the frustrations of tokenism, the 'maternal wall' and exclusion from male networks (and may thereby find their path to promotion is blocked).

As if this were not enough, women managers may also be seen as failing to perform their social and gendered role 'properly' because ambition and success are regarded as appropriate characteristics for men, but not for women, to possess (Nelson and Quick, 1985; Davidson and Cooper, 1992;

Desmarais and Alksnis, 2005). Women managers may be openly criticized for failing to perform 'womanhood' in accordance with social expectations. Women leaders are often accused of (and censured for) adopting male behaviours, and childless women without male partners may be labelled as being 'not quite normal' (Cooper and Davidson, 1982: 134). Conversely, female managers who are also mothers, and who have male partners who are employed, are often accused of selfish behaviour, and of failing their children by undertaking paid work (Gatrell, 2005). Women both with, and without, children are pressured into 'proving' themselves by taking on unreasonable workloads.

In what follows, we will consider each of these sources of stress in some detail. Before doing so, however, we will consider why it is that so many career women continue to face resistance in the workplace, despite the passage of 30 years since the anti-discrimination laws. It is interesting (and disheartening) to observe that the causes of stress among women managers discussed in this chapter were identified over 25 years ago, since when they have changed relatively little. In our view, this is due to unchanged and critical social approaches towards senior female managers. As long ago as 1982, Cooper and Davidson highlighted the issues discussed here as problematic, reflecting that: 'discrimination appears to be still a major potential cause of stress faced by women in the workforce' (1982: 110). These authors observed that women were denied promotion because of assumptions that they were not work-oriented and that women who did obtain senior roles were both highly visible, and open to criticism if they exhibited characteristics which are more generally associated with 'male' behaviours. Ten years later, Davidson and Cooper (1992) undertook a re-evaluation of the causes of stress for women managers and recognized that they appeared to be dealing with many of the same issues which had concerned them ten years earlier. They observed that 'discrimination [against women] can lead to stress and disillusionment' (1992: 119) and reflected that the 'overriding barrier which undoubtedly restricts the application of equal opportunity policy is the discriminatory attitudes of managers and employers, often linked to assumptions that [women] possess characteristics which would make them unsuitable for employment/promotion' (1992: 165). Davidson and Cooper also noted (1992: 104–5) that: 'women have to be perceived as being more competent than their male counterparts' in order to progress, but that 'very competent, professional women' continued, nevertheless, to be seen as 'threatening' by male colleagues.

In 2005, very similar problems were identified by Desmarais and Alksnis, who note that discrimination continues to place additional stress on women managers and argue (p. 466) that 'women experience a set of work stressors that are …associated with traditional gendered expectations; their work efforts, competence and commitment are evaluated increasingly negatively the more they deviate from the traditional gender script for women'.

Arguably, it is in this last statement that the explanation for discriminatory practices against women managers (and the resulting stress this causes) can be found. The continued existence of the glass ceiling and the reluctance on the part of employers to promote women to executive positions accords with the concept of 'role congruity' (Eagly and Karau, 2002; Desmarais and Alksnis, 2005) in which it is argued that 'organizations and the people within them continue to hold the implicit assumption that the ideal worker is a white man who is employed full time' and 'The idea persists that women should be responsible for [the home]...We believe that all working women are violating the normative assumptions of the role of women to some degree' Desmarais and Alksnis (2005: 459). This reveals why influencers in the community such as Michael Buerk continue to argue that women's contribution to the political and the business agenda is emasculating and should be resisted, attitudes which accord with the idea that women may be criticized for aspiring to leadership roles (Eagly and Karau, 2002; Desmarais and Alksnis, 2005).

The social role of women – an historical view

It has been suggested that a consideration of history may be useful in enhancing the understanding of contemporary issues (Parsons and Rose, 2005). For this reason (and before we go on to consider in more detail the negative impact of the glass ceiling on the well-being of women managers) we consider the position of women in society prior to, and post, the equal opportunities legislation in the mid-1970s. We suggest that our analysis helps explain (but not to validate) the reasons *why* many organizations are reluctant to allow women access to promotion at executive level, preferring, in most cases, to appoint only men.

'Woman' and home
Women who seek careers in management are battling with deeply ingrained traditions and preconceptions about what the role of women, and especially mothers, should be. The social role of 'woman' in Western society has long been associated with the home, and with homemaking. In the UK, writing in 1856, the Victorian poet Coventry Patmore constructed the British ideal of the 'gentle', 'sweet' and 'virtuous' woman in his poem 'The Angel in the House' (Patmore, 1856: 169). This was a very popular but also highly political work about a self-effacing wife who achieved perfection by devoting herself to her home and her husband. 'The Angel in the House' became the catchphrase for those who opposed women's claim to independence

(in the form of women's suffrage and the women's property act), and who held the viewpoint that 'a woman's place was in the home' (Anstruther, 1992: 7). 'The Angel in the House' became symbolic of a social ideal of unselfish femininity which has, historically, been a constraint to ambitious career women and remains so to the present day (Woolf, 1979; Oakley, 1993; Gatrell, 2005).

In the post-war years, an image of 'ideal' womanhood, popular in the 1950s and 1960s, was constructed by the American sociologist Talcott Parsons (Parsons and Bales, 1956). Parsons' work was influential in both Britain and the USA because it offered policy makers a seductive picture of family life in which heterosexual men and women would marry and produce children and would divide labour along gendered lines. Husbands were expected to go out to work and wives were supposed to do housework, shop and raise children (Parsons and Bales, 1956). Parsons stated:

> The role of housewife is still the ... predominant one for the married woman with small children...the adult feminine role is anchored ... in the internal affairs of the family as wife, mother and manager in the household, while the role of the adult male is ... anchored in the occupational world, in his job (Parsons and Bales, 1956: 14–15)

Parsons has been criticized for failing to acknowledge that many families in America in the 1950s and 1960s did not fit this middle class, heterosexual ideal (Bernardes, 1997). However, the Parsonian image of 'mother in the home' predominated in popular culture between 1950 and 1970 (Gagg, 1961; Conil, undated). In order to conform to this image, women were supposed to behave in a 'sweet and gentle' manner, to become mothers and to give up paid work following childbirth. As recently as 1980, the St Michael [Marks and Spencer] 'Complete Book of Babycare', urged women to recognize that: 'A child needs his [sic] mother.... Sadly, there is an idea in circulation that to be a mother and a housewife is to be a second-rate citizen; that worthwhile work and opportunities ... exist only outside the family. Nothing is further from the truth. A mother who [stays at home] is performing the most worthwhile job that life has to offer' (Nash, 1980: 161).

The 'correct' way of performing the role of wife and mother was thus socially defined, and this did not include going out to work or exhibiting work-orientated, ambitious behaviour, as these characteristics were associated only with men (Rich, 1977).

Women and the labour market
Until the 1980s, the 'Parsonian' image of maternal, home based and unpaid labour was accurately reflected in labour market trends, partly because British and American post-war governments dissuaded women from

joining the labour market, requiring jobs to be freed up for ex-service men (Rowbotham, 1997). The number of mothers in the labour market remained low until the end of the 1970s. For example, as late as 1979, in the UK, only 24 per cent of all mothers returned to work within 11 months of the birth of their first child (Pullinger and Summerfield, 1998).

By 1998, however, a major social change had taken place in the labour markets in the UK and the USA. Partly as a result of the anti-discrimination laws which were passed in the 1970s, and partly due to other social factors such as reduction in birth rates, rising divorce rates and the increasing number of women doing university degrees, the percentage of mothers who maintained continuous employment had risen sharply – to 55 per cent in the UK. In particular, there was a sharp rise in the number of women with pre-school children who remained in paid work, and at the vanguard of this change were those mothers who were qualified to degree level or over, and who were in managerial or professional roles. Seventy-six per cent of these women maintained continuous employment following childbirth (Thair and Risdon, 1999). As Macran et al. (1996: 285) observe, 'the trend to more employment among mothers with young children is not a uniform experience, but socially selective. As higher education became more common, so did combining it with both motherhood and employment'. (It should be noted, however, that for women with no qualifications the situation looks less promising – only 27 per cent of women with no qualifications returned to work after giving birth, which might suggest that their opportunities are even more sharply circumscribed than those of women with degrees).

Given the rising rate of women's employment and the changes in legislation, which outlawed discrimination and required equality of pay for men and women in equivalent jobs, it might be supposed that the idea of mothers engaging in paid work would be more acceptable now than it was in the 1950s–1970s. Arguably, however, although social change has occurred rapidly (especially for the highly educated women in professional roles referred to above), current discourse and literature has been slow to keep pace and in some significant quarters has resisted women's employment.

Discrimination and stress – the present day

From 1975 onwards, following the enactment of the Equal Rights laws in the UK and the USA, employed women were supposed to receive the same treatment in the workplace as did their male counterparts. However, until this date, in both Britain and America, it was legal to discriminate against women and to pay them less than men for doing equivalent jobs. Some organizations introduced a 'marriage bar', forcing women to leave their employment on marriage, and others made it company policy to dismiss women who were pregnant (Rowbotham, 1997). In 1982, seven years after the legislation had been enacted, Cooper and Davidson observed that: 'for working women, discrimination is a prominent occupational stress factor and indeed every participant in one study of American women executives reported having been discriminated against in some way throughout her career'(p. 110). Today, over 30 years since the Equal Opportunities legislation, explicit discrimination against women managers remains problematic. Women managers often find their route to executive status blocked, while equivalent male colleagues appear to be knocking at an open door. Top American businesswomen attribute difficulties of achieving promotion at executive level to the 'pervasive stereotyping of women's capacity for leadership' suggesting that 'everyone is unconsciously biased and there is strong evidence that men are biased against promoting women inside companies' (*The Economist*, 2005: 68). This is partly due to the exclusion of women from male social networks which may be key in influencing men's career progress, and to which women have no access (Davidson and Cooper, 1992; *The Economist*, 2005).

Discrimination is an acknowledged source of stress for women managers (Cooper and Davidson, 1982), and the experience of being discriminated against may itself contribute to women's lack of career progress, because women managers who feel stressed about unfair treatment find it difficult to maintain their full potential (Larwood and Wood, 1979; Cooper and Davidson, 1982). Furthermore, if a female manager is seen by others to be experiencing discrimination, she will be perceived as 'unsuccessful' and will not, therefore, be respected by colleagues. As a result, those working under her will feel dissatisfied and will doubt her abilities – this proving a source of stress for both parties (Larwood and Wood, 1979). Conversely, however, if a female manager is seen by senior colleagues as thriving and capable, her performance will be enhanced and those working for her will feel confident about her abilities to lead her team and 'any doubts they have about working for her will disappear' (Cooper and Davidson, 1982).

Discrimination against women managers on grounds of their female status is a well documented occurrence. Each year both the Equal Opportunities Commission in the UK and the Women's Bureau in the USA report a significant number of discrimination cases which women have successfully brought against their employers. Arguably, however, this is only the tip of the iceberg. In order to claim discrimination and seek compensation, the onus is on the woman herself to prove that she was treated unjustly. In professions where the number of women is small, they may feel very exposed, and anxious about the affect their claim may have on future career prospects (Gatrell and Turnbull, 2003). Thus, using the equal opportunities legislation to try and eradicate discrimination may have very limited appeal to individuals who believe they have been dealt with inequitably. Many women, therefore, simply accept and put up with unfair treatment, rather then fight their corner (Fielden and Cooper, 2001; Galinsky et al., 1993).

It is worth noting here, that the difficulties experienced by white, able-bodied women managers are likely to be even worse for black and ethnic minority women, who may experience unfair treatment not only because of their gender, but also in relation to their ethnic background. In their research on women's professional identities, Bell and Nkomo (2001) acknowledge the existence of the glass ceiling as a barrier to promotion for all women, but suggest that black women are also faced with a 'concrete wall', meaning that wherever they turn, their career progression is limited. This is reflected in the gender pay gap, which affects women of colour more severely than it does white women. For example in the USA in 1998, as a proportion of men's wages, white women earned 73 per cent, African-American women 63 per cent and Hispanic-American women only 53 per cent (Seager, 2005).

It is also worth observing that (unsurprisingly) employers who discriminate against female managers will find that these employees are unhappy, dissatisfied and stressed (Cooper and Davidson, 1982). Those who are educated to degree level or over have highly transferable skills and are likely to seek employment elsewhere because they see the possibility of negotiating improved terms and conditions with new employers (Gatrell, 2005). This leaves unsupportive employers with the costs of recruiting new staff. However, women managers who perceive their organizations to be supportive are more likely to be able to cope with their multiple roles (even if hours are long) and report less work stress, fewer psychosomatic problems and less intention to leave (Burke, 2001).

Tokenism and stress
The above historical analysis of anti-discrimination policies in the context of social attitudes towards women's social role, provides a reason for (but does not justify), why women managers are at risk of experiencing narrow-minded and intolerant reactions on the part of others (Eagly and Karau, 2002; Desmarais and Alksnis, 2005). As women managers progress to executive levels they are increasingly likely to experience the stress associated with 'tokenism, where [women] are the first of their gender to enter [a particular role, which leaves them] …feeling isolated and excluded … they often experience stereotyping and discrimination from the majority group which creates a more stressful workplace environment' (Desmarais and Alksnis, 2005: 463). Being a 'token woman' not only means a lack of female peer support, but also entails working in an environment which provides few role models of women in executive positions. It is asserted by Davidson and Cooper (1992) that female role models in higher managerial positions

act as important influences in terms of career aspirations for other women. Given the small number of female role models at senior levels, many women find themselves with little apparent alternative other than to 'adapt to the organizational culture by taking on male attitudes and values' which can lead to their feeling 'marginalized', and 'isolated and alone' (Fielden and Cooper, 2001: 5). For women who reach executive status in organizations with predominantly male senior personnel, their position as a lone female in a male environment makes it difficult to relate to either male, or female colleagues (Marshall, 1995).

Stress and social resistance to women's work-orientation

Thus, women who 'defy the traditional female gender path by taking on leadership roles' at work may find themselves excluded and criticized, which makes their situation stressful because society believes '...that all working women are violating the normative assumptions of the role of women... simply by choosing to be employed' (Desmarais and Alksnis, 2005: 459). Arguably, women managers are failing to meet social expectations about the gender-based roles which are generally considered appropriate, and this is sufficient to cause them problems. In particular, women without a male partner may find themselves under scrutiny, especially if they have no children. Davidson and Cooper (1992: 134) observe that 'career orientated women who choose not to marry ... experience ... adverse pressure associated with being labelled as an "oddity", both at work and socially'. Furthermore, women who exhibit characteristics associated with male managers may, instead of being praised for their decisiveness and their ability to 'pursue their objectives in a vigorous manner' be labelled 'bossy' or 'nagging', where a male manager would be more likely to be praised for his 'leadership qualities' (Cooper and Davidson, 1982: 36). This is due to 'inconsistency between the predominantly communal qualities that perceivers associate with women and the predominantly agentic qualities they believe are required to succeed as a leader' (Eagly and Karau, 2002: 575).

Women who do achieve very senior positions may be accused of being 'Queen Bees' – protective of their own position and unhelpful and unsupportive to other women trying to climb their way up. Arguably, in order to succeed, women managers may adopt traditionally male behaviours and, if they do manage to infiltrate male networks and gain promotion, will go to some lengths to exclude other women (Mavin, 2006). This may be so – but it is worth noting that 'Queen Bee' syndrome only exists because of the lack of women in senior positions. Were women to be more equally represented at executive level, then the possibility of lone female executives playing (or being accused of playing) the role of 'Queen Bee' would cease to exist.

Discrimination and women's 'maternal bodies'
A further aspect of work stress which is experienced by women managers is their exclusion from senior positions and promotion opportunities due to the 'maternal wall' (Williams, 1999; Desmarais and Alksnis, 2005) This accords with the assertions of Gatrell (2005) that discrimination against women who combine motherhood and career is explicit and widespread. Gatrell's research indicated that women's jobs were downgraded and their opportunities for promotion blocked once they became mothers, especially if they wished to change working practices in order to accommodate family commitments. Research participant 'Jayne', a Lead Electronic Engineer who returned to her job on a part-time basis reported:

> I was shocked, I found that I wasn't given the same respect as when I was a childless full-time worker. I began to realise what was happening when they were doing the annual pay rounds and I didn't get my pay review. I haven't had a personal development review since I started working part time and I wasn't given the same responsibility in the big projects that all the other Lead Engineers were getting. Something new and exciting would come along and they'd get it, not me. I wouldn't get anything. (Gatrell, 2005: 192)

Motherhood, career and work-orientation
Assumptions that career mothers are uncommitted to their paid work are often misplaced and may, understandably, be the cause of high levels of workplace stress (Cooper and Davidson, 1982). Nevertheless, despite evidence to the contrary, working mothers are often presumed to experience reduced commitment to their paid work. (Cooper and Davidson, 1982; Davidson and Cooper, 1992; Gatrell, 2005). This perception of employed mothers reinforces the social assumption that they are less work-oriented than fathers, which is a serious source of stress for women with a high work-orientation (Fielden and Cooper, 2002; Desmarais and Alksnis, 2005). The argument about mothers' lack of commitment to paid work is often presented as an explanation for their lack of promotion because it provides employers with a pretext for laying the blame for discriminatory practices at the woman's door (i.e. women do not really want promotion), rather than taking action about the low number of women in senior positions (Adler, 1993). Collinson (2000) illustrates this phenomenon in his description of a situation in which 'Jane', a pregnant employee who had consistently achieved an 'A' in her performance reviews sought promotion within her own company. Jane's organization espoused a strong commitment to equal opportunities. Nevertheless, the promotion was refused on the basis that Jane was not 'fully committed' and had 'allowed personal issues to interfere with her work' (Collinson, 2000: 175). In this way, despite evidence to the contrary (Jane's performance reviews were excellent and she had applied for

a more senior role) Jane's employer inferred that, due to her pregnant status she could not, or should not be committed to progressing her career.

The idea that mothers are not work-oriented is supported by the research of James Tooley (2002) and Catherine Hakim (1996a, 1996b, 2000). Although feminist writers have, over the years, attempted to refute Hakim's views (Ginn et al., 1996), the influential nature of Hakim's work cannot be underestimated – she has, for example undertaken work with the UK Institute of Directors, advising on policy issues (Malthouse, 1997). Hakim is vociferous in her argument that women lose interest in careers once they have children. She suggests that women are divided into three categories – home centred (20 per cent), work centred (20 per cent) and adaptive (60 per cent). Work centred women are described as 'childless', and adaptive women are defined as those with children who seek to earn money, but who are not driven by ambition and commitment to their profession (Hakim, 2000: 140). Hakim's work is discussed in the press and media, where Hakim herself has been featured as claiming: 'You can have one child and be a kind of nominal mother [then] you can concentrate on your career. But once you have two children or more [you will]... want work that is interesting [but] fits in with your children' (Moorhead, 2004). This way of looking at things suggests further evidence of the conflicting pressures of role (in)congruity (Eagly and Karau, 2002). The 'working mother' is constructed both as a 'nominal' mother who is failing to perform her maternal role appropriately and an uncommitted, unambitious employee, when in fact she may be deeply committed both to her children *and* to her paid work: 'the working women ... might be defined as an imperfect worker, an unsuitable mother, or both' (Desmarais and Alksnis, 2005: 459; see also Dobson and Chittenden 2002).

James Tooley (2002) takes the argument about mothers' low work-orientation a step further. He argues that women have been duped into believing that female satisfaction may be found through paid work and careers, but asserts that women are mistaken in this assumption. Tooley argues that any attempt to pursue career goals will make women unhappy because satisfaction, for them, should lie in being at home and raising children. Tooley warns women who seek a career that they may do so 'at the expense of [obtaining] a man and future family,' (p. 11). He suggests that wise women should limit their career progress and curb their ambition, otherwise they may risk 'undermining the romance [for a man] of being a provider' (p. 19), thus 'pricing [themselves] out of the [marriage] market' (p. 20) because prospective husbands will regard their success as unattractive and insulting to ideals of masculinity. A woman who seeks a career may, therefore, find herself alone, like Bridget Jones, 'drowning her sorrows in glass after glass of Chardonnay...her inner voice crying out for relief from her independence'(p. 3). Tooley criticizes the Women's Rights Movement and raises the question as to whether 'Betty Frieden sits by guiltily, not yet quite able to withdraw her feminist prescriptions, even though she knows they are likely to lead to unhappiness?' (p. 11). He does not acknowledge that many women may be genuinely work-oriented, as are many men, nor does he address the issues faced by single, divorced or lesbian women, who may not wish to be supported by a male partner.

Child-free status and discrimination

The 'maternal wall' restricts in particular the career opportunities available to women who have children. Unfortunately for women managers, however, being without children does not necessarily offer protection against discrimination because the 'maternal wall' affects all women who are considered to be of an age where they *might* potentially have a child in the future. Thus, in career terms, a woman may be punished for having a 'maternal body' even if she never has a child. Cockburn (2002: 180), in keeping with the arguments of Williams (1999) and Desmarais and Alksnis (2005), asserts that 'even if the woman in question is celibate or childless she is seen and represented as one of the maternal sex. Much of the argument surrounding Equal Opportunities …circles about the question: can women ever be equal given their different relation to reproduction?'

Arguably, as women make their way up the corporate ladder, their maternal bodies and their reproductive capacity will be sufficient to disadvantage them. In the UK the Institute of Directors has argued that many employers are resentful of mothers' rights and are often reluctant to employ women of childbearing age (that is from 16–49) for this reason (Malthouse, 1997). And Padavic and Reskin (2002: 49) suggest that employers in America are guilty of 'statistical discrimination' – preferring not to give jobs to women because motherhood might make them more 'costly' than men.

In summary, therefore, employers may discriminate against women managers who are also mothers, assuming a lack of work-orientation on the woman's part once she has children. However, they may also discriminate against women managers without children, because such women are still regarded as 'maternal bodies' whose reproductive status might mean that a child is born at some future date. The impact of such discriminatory behaviour on the part of employers and organizations has been to inhibit the career progress of the majority of women managers, so that minimal progress has been made towards achieving a better balance of women at senior and Board level. This is a source of stress for women managers who are more likely than men to blame themselves for lack of promotion, seeking individual reasons for failure to succeed at executive level, rather than relating this to social and historical structures. As Fielden and Cooper (2001: 11) suggest: 'very little has been done to eliminate [institutional] sources of stress without which real change cannot be achieved. Organisational culture, societal attitudes and a reluctance to see beyond the status quo have combined to prevent the success of women in management'.

Work-life balance and family responsibilities

The impact of working long hours in the workplace has been well documented (Worrall and Cooper, 1999; Swan and Cooper, 2005). In 1999, in their research on working patterns and working hours, Worrall and Cooper observed that one in five managers thought that the number of hours they worked was unacceptable but felt they had no choice but to comply with employer requirements. Worrall and Cooper argue that the pressure of work in contemporary organizations is the main driver for causing (male and female) managers to work excessive hours and suggest that cost-cutting and de-layering may be to blame. The writers also note that working long hours over extended periods adversely affects the health and morale of managers. In particular, it is noteworthy that, of those managers who worked over 50 hours, 64 per cent considered that this workload actually reduced their productivity levels (Worrall and Cooper, 1999). Furthermore, long hours cultures can have a negative impact on managers' personal lives – relationships with partners and children may suffer.

The working patterns research was concerned, in the main, with hours worked in the context of managers' paid employment against a backdrop of longer hours and increased levels of job insecurity (see also Lewis and Cooper, 1999; Cooper et al., 2001). For most workers, however, the concept of 'labour' does not encompass only the number of hours spent in paid work, but the amount of time that is also required to keep a household running and care for dependent family members. As we have noted earlier, housework and the raising of children have historically been associated with women, as have elder care and sick care (Finch and Mason, 1993). As the number of women in paid work has grown, so have the workloads of many women (Lewis and Cooper, 1999). Initially, organizations and governments failed to shoulder much of the responsibility for the increasing likelihood that women would be bearing the dual burdens of paid employment and unpaid household labour. This was because policy makers tended to construct these issues as individual problems for families to manage by themselves, not structural issues for organizations to address (Lewis and Cooper, 1999). During the 1970s and 1980s assumptions that women were (or should be) responsible for domestic and child care work, underpinned much of the research on women's labour. Issues under investigation tended to focus on the impact of women's employment on family lives – on husbands, children and on women's health, these studies only serving to substantiate the underlying presumption that employed women were 'deviating from their expected roles, with possible negative consequences for all' (Lewis and Cooper, 1999: 382). In the 1990s it became more common for research about long hours cultures and the balance between paid and unpaid labour to consider the position of both women and men, especially in the context of heterosexual couples where both partners were working. Many of these studies (Delphy and Leonard, 1992; Dryden, 1999; Maushart, 2002) show that, no matter how many hours she works, and no matter how senior she may be, a woman in a heterosexual relationship will probably find herself undertaking the lion's share of domestic and caring labour within the household. Even if this means outsourcing domestic chores (which is more likely to be an option for women managers than for those in lower paid work), the responsibility for organizing this, and funding it, is likely to remain with the woman (Gregson and Lowe, 1994). The female partner in a heterosexual relationship may also be expected to provide practical support to her husband/partner in his paid work, especially if he has a managerial career. This will encompass not only domestic duties such as the maintenance of his business attire, but accompanying him to official 'functions' and moving home (or staying put) to support his career, often at the expense of her own (Delphy and Leonard, 1992; Maushart, 2002).

Multiple roles and stress

Interestingly, however, assumptions that women managers are unable to cope with multiple roles may be inaccurate. While some research has demonstrated that women who are overworked may suffer stress and ill-health as a result, other research indicates that women are good at multi-tasking. While they may resent time spent on repetitive domestic chores, many mothers value time spent with their children. As a consequence, it is argued that women may find satisfaction in multiple roles, and the combination of motherhood and employment often has positive effects on their well-being (Crosby, 1987; Barnett, 2004).

However, the energy invested in child care and employment does mean that the time available for women managers to spend on themselves is limited, and it may also put strain on the marital relationship/partnership (Sullivan, 1997; Gatrell, 2005) Arguably, time pressures faced by women managers who are combining paid work with family and domestic responsibilities can result in behaviour patterns often associated with 'Type A' behaviour: time consciousness, aggressiveness, competitiveness and overt ambition. This kind of 'hard driving' behaviour has been identified as a predictor of stress (Fielden and Cooper, 2001) and this fits in with research that married working women with children may be at a higher risk of coronary heart disease than men or single women (Fielden and Cooper 2001).

It is also argued, however, that the pressures placed on individual women managers as a result of family life appear to be caused less by the burden of household and child care responsibilities (which they shoulder in addition to their paid work) and more by the negative attitudes toward married and co-habiting women managers that persist among social institutions and employers (Davidson and Cooper, 1992). For example, while heterosexual, committed relationships (and especially marriage) benefit men's careers, employers regard married women with suspicion, fearing that husbands and children may be a demand that competes with commitment to employment. As Fielden and Cooper (2001: 10) observe: 'female managers are not only deprived of the benefits of having a wife but are also condemned for having a husband, [which may impact negatively] on the well-being of female managers.'

Women managers 'doing' work and family in their own way
For some women it may be that their situation differs from the traditional notions about both parenthood and heterosexuality, and this may impact on our understanding of work-orientation and stress for both women and men in management. For example, Dunne (1999), in her work on women in lesbian relationships, notes that female couples who co-habit are careful to share out household tasks as fairly as possible, especially if they have previously been in heterosexual relationships where male partners assumed little responsibility. And Hochschild (1997), in her study of heterosexual parents and employment has argued that work-orientation may be very strong for both women and men, who may therefore both regard paid work as a refuge from the stresses associated with home and family.

Beck and Beck-Gernsheim (1995), while acknowledging that heterosexual career women are often expected to defer to the work-orientation of male partners, also observe an increased propensity for men (especially post-divorce) to seek an active – if not central – role in children's lives. And Smart and Neale (1999), while observing that some divorced men make little effort to maintain relationships with children from previous relationships, also acknowledge a growing number of fathers who experience a drop in work-orientation post-divorce. This group of men are prepared to downshift their paid work and make sacrifices regarding careers, because they wish to co-parent. Given that the number of lone parents in the UK has increased (from 8 per cent in 1971 to 27 per cent in 2005: Swan and Cooper, 2005: 5) it is also important to remember that some working parents will be combining paid work with child care in a single parent household. Arguably, therefore, an increasing number of women and men who combine paid work with childrearing 'do' parenting in a way which does not fit in with preconceived and gendered notions about commitment to employment and family. Thus, while the decision to have children does not automatically signal a reduction in women's commitment to paid work, a strong work-orientation does not necessarily mean that either women *or* men also wish to spend every waking hour in the office. In this context, Anderson et al. (2002) argue that lack of managerial support and negative career consequences may lead to stress which affects family lives, and that unhappy home lives may also lead to stress and absences from the workplace. Interestingly, Anderson et al. observed no significant differences between women and men in terms of the observed relationships. As Swan and Cooper (2005) note, half of parents (by which they mean mothers *and* fathers) are unhappy with their work/family balance and would prefer a culture of greater flexibility in their working arrangements. Arguably, therefore, while assumptions about the low work-orientations of women managers are outdated and inaccurate, beliefs about the high-work low-family orientations of male managers and executives may also need to be questioned, as both men and women may seek a balance between work and personal time (Swan and Cooper, 2005).

Conclusion

In our concluding section, we revisit our original question: why should women managers be stressed? In our view, there are many reasons why women managers and professionals might feel stressed, as they attempt to progress their careers in a climate of opprobrium and discouragement. It is a matter for concern that these pressures are not acknowledged in the arguments of influential writers and journalists such as Tooley, Hakim and Buerk. We acknowledge that causes of stress among women managers might include the lower salaries they earn relative to men in equivalent positions, the conflicting pressures of managing multiple roles, and the very long hours that some women are obliged to work, when the hours devoted to paid work are added to the amount of time spent on unpaid labour.

We have suggested, however, that these issues (challenging though they are) are not the main causes of stress among women managers and professionals. Arguably, the most significant source of stress among women managers is the negative attitude of others towards working women, and the barriers placed in front of women as they try to progress their careers. This is exacerbated by the assumption that women may be less committed to their jobs than their male counterparts and by the belief, on the part of employers and professional bodies, that this justifies discriminatory behaviour. We have observed that women managers experience stress and frustration when they are perceived as 'maternal bodies' who cannot, or should not hold senior roles, (regardless of whether or not they have children), as a result of which they are excluded from important networks and their routes to executive positions are blocked. We have also asserted that women managers find it stressful to aim for executive positions when they have few female role models to follow, and when they know that the higher they climb, the more isolated they will be.

Additionally, we have acknowledged that the social explanation for discriminatory beliefs and behaviours may be better understood within the context of the historical image of women as homemakers and men as economic providers. However, we do not regard history as providing an excuse for the discriminatory and outdated practices that disadvantage women managers in today's society. We have also made the point that gendered assumptions about the strong work-orientation of male managers may be rather simplistic. For example some men – while they may enjoy their paid work – are also seeking a better work-family integration, and not all employed women and men who parent are doing so in the context of heterosexual coupledom.

Arguably, we are now at a point where individual women managers have only a limited opportunity to change their own circumstances, and this social constraint is a major source of stress for women managers. It is accepted that there may be steps that individual women managers can take to manage stress and to improve their personal situation. These are identified by Cooper and Davidson (1982), Davidson and Cooper (1992), Cooper and Cartwright (1997), Nelson and Burke (2000) and Barling et al. (2005). These authors suggest individual strategies for coping with stress such as exercise, meditation and learning to be assertive.

However, we would suggest that individual coping strategies can have only limited value in the long term. While stress management is important for each woman who is dealing with the pressures of trying to progress her career in the context of a discriminatory and exclusionary environment, this should not detract from the point that fundamental changes in organizational attitudes to women managers are still required. If women are to achieve the equality of opportunity that was promised them in the 1970s when the anti-discrimination laws were first enacted, then a transformation in the treatment of, and behaviour towards, employed women is required. Such a change will require not only continued improvements to social policy, but a shift in social attitudes, with employers, professional bodies and other key influencers regarding women's paid work as 'normative', and positive, rather than a negative deviation from women's historical social role as homemaker.

As a result, we suggest that further, policy-related research is needed. This is not in the narrow sense of discovering what *causes* stress among women managers, since this has already been well documented. Rather, we argue the need for further research in relation to seeking imaginative ways of changing social approaches to women managers, with the aim that the promotion and encouragement of working women – as opposed to discrimination and exclusion – should become the 'norm'.

References

Adler, N.J. (1993), 'Competitive frontiers: women managers in the triad', *International Studies of Management and Organization*, **23** (2), 3–23.

Anderson, S.E., B.S. Coffey and T. Byerly (2002), 'Formal organizational initiative and informal workplace practices: links to work–family conflict and job-related outcomes', *Journal of Management*, **28** (6), 787–810.

Anstruther, I. (1992), *Coventry Patmore's Angel: A study of Coventry Patmore, his wife Emily and 'The Angel in the House'*, London: Haggerston Press.

Barling, J., K. Kelloway and M. Frone (2005), *Handbook of Work Stress*, Thousand Oaks, CA: Sage.

Barnett, R. (2004), 'Women and multiple roles: myths and reality', *Harvard Review of Psychiatry*, **12** (3), 158–64.

Beck U. and E. Beck-Gernsheim (1995), *The Normal Chaos of Love*, Cambridge: Polity Press.

Bell, E. and S. Nkomo (2001), *Our Separate Ways: Black and White Women and the Struggle for Professional Identity*, Boston, MA: Harvard University Press.

Bernandes, J. (1997), *Family Studies: An Introduction*, London: Routledge.

Burke, R.J. (2001), 'Organizational values, work experiences and satisfactions among managerial and professional women', *The Journal of Management Development*, **20** (4), 346–54.

Cockburn, C. (2002), 'Resisting equal opportunities: the issue of maternity', in S. Jackson and S. Scott (eds), *Gender: A Sociological Reader*, London: Routledge, pp. 180–91.

Collinson, D. (2000), 'Strategies of resistance: power, knowledge and subjectivity in the workplace', in K. Grint (ed.), *Work and Society: A Reader*, Cambridge: Polity Press, pp. 163–98.

Conil, J. (n.d.), *The Good Neighbour Cookery Book* (Tips from Mrs Smith), Bovril.

Cooper, C.L. and S. Cartwright (1997), *Managing Workplace Stress*, Thousand Oaks, CA: Sage.

Cooper, C.L. and M. Davidson (1982), *High Pressure: Working Lives of Women Managers*, Glasgow: Fontana.

Cooper, C.L, P. Dewe and M.P. O'Driscoll (2001), *Organizational Stress: A Review and Critique of Theory, Research and Applications*, London: Sage.

Crosby, F.J. (ed.) (1987), *Spouse, Parent, Worker: Gender and Multiple Roles*, New Haven: Yale University Press.

Davidson, M.J. and C.L. Cooper (1992), *Shattering the Glass Ceiling: The Woman Manager*, London: Paul Chapman Publishing.

Davies, H., H. Joshi and R. Peronaci (2000), 'Forgone income and motherhood: what do recent British data tell us?', *Population Studies*, **54**, 293–305.

Delphy, C. and D. Leonard (1992), *Familiar Exploitation: a New Analysis of Marriage in Contemporary Western Societies*, Oxford: Polity Press.

Desmarais, S. and C. Alksnis (2005), 'Gender issues', in J. Barling, K. Kelloway and M. Frone (eds), *Handbook of Work Stress*, Thousand Oaks, CA: Sage.

Dex, S., H. Joshi, S. Macran and A. McCulloch (1998), 'Women's employment transitions around childbearing', *Oxford Bulletin of Economics and Statistics*, **60**, 79.

Dobson, R. and M. Chittenden (2002), 'Working mothers' children lag behind in tests', *The Sunday Times*, 28 July, p. 10.

Dryden, C. (1999), *Being Married, Doing Gender*, London: Routledge.

Dudley Edwards, R. (2005), 'Feminisation and why he's no Buerk!' *Daily Mail*, 19 August, p. 14.

Dunne, G. (1999), 'A passion for "sameness?" Sexuality and gender accountability', in E. Silva and C. Smart (eds), *The New Family?*, London: Sage, pp. 66–82.

Eagly, A.H. and S.J. Karau (2002), 'Role congruity theory of prejudice toward female leaders', *Psychological Review*, **109** (3), 573–98.

Economist, The (2005) 'Special report: women in business, the conundrum of the glass ceiling', 23 July, pp. 67–69.

Equal Opportunities Commission (EOC) (2005), *Sex and Power, Who Runs Britain*, Manchester: Equal Opportunities Commission

Fielden, S. and C.L. Cooper (2001), 'Women managers and stress: a critical analysis', *Equal Opportunities International*, **20** (1), 3–16.

Fielden, S. and C.L. Cooper (2002), 'Managerial stress: are women more at risk?', in D.L. Nelson and R.J. Burke (eds), *Gender, Work Stress and Health*, Washington, DC: American Psychological Association, pp. 19–34.

Finch, J. and J. Mason (1993), *Negotiating Family Responsibilities*, London and New York: Tavistock/Routledge.

Gagg, M.E. (1961), *Helping at Home*, A Ladybird Learning to Read Book, Loughborough: Ladybird.

Galinsky, E., J. Bond and D.E. Friedman (1993), *The National Study of the Changing Workforce*, New York: Families and Work Institute.

Gatrell, C. (2005), *Hard Labour: The Sociology of Parenthood*, Maidenhead: Open University Press.

Gatrell, C. and S. Turnbull (2003), *Your MBA with Distinction, Developing a Systematic Approach to Succeeding in Your Business Degree*, Harlow: FT Prentice Hall.

Gibson, O. (2005), 'The Guardian Profile: Michael Buerk', *The Guardian*, 19 August.

Ginn, J., S. Arber, J. Brannen, A. Dale, S. Dex, P. Elias, P., Moss, J. Pahl, C. Roberts and J. Rubery (1996), 'Feminist fallacies: a reply to Hakim on women's employment', *British Journal of Sociology*, **47**, 167–74.

Gregson, N. and M. Lowe (1994), *Servicing the Middle Classes: Class Gender and Waged Domestic Labour in Contemporary Britain*, London and New York: Routledge.

Hakim, C. (1996a), *Key Issues in Women's Work*, London: Athlone.

Hakim, C. (1996b), 'The sexual division of labour and women's heterogeneity', *British Journal of Sociology*, **47**, 178–88.

Hakim, C. (2000), *Work–Lifestyle Choices in the 21st Century: Preference Theory*, Oxford: Oxford University Press.

Hochschild, A. (1997), *The Time Bind: When Work Becomes Home and Home Becomes Work*, New York: Henry Holt.

Larwood, L. and M.M. Wood (1979), *Women in Management*, London: Lexington Books.

Lewis, S and C.L. Cooper (1999), 'The work–family agenda in changing contexts', *Journal of Occupational Health Psychology*, **4** (4), 382–93.

Macran, S., H. Joshi and S. Dex (1996), 'Employment after childbearing: a survival analysis', *Work, Employment and Society*, **10**, 273–96.

Malthouse, T-J. (1997), *Childcare, Business and Social Change*, London: Institute of Directors.

Marshall, J. (1995), 'Working at senior management and board level: some of the issues for women', *Women in Management Review*, **10** (3), 21–25.

Maushart, S. (2002), *Wifework: What Marriage Really Means for Women*, London: Bloomsbury.

Mavin, S. (2006), 'Expectations of women in leadership and management – advancement through solidarity?' in D. McTavish and K. Miller (eds) *Women in Leadership and Management*, Cheltenham, UK and Northampton, MA, USA: Edward Elgar, pp. 71–88.

Moorhead, J. (2004), 'For decades we've been told that Sweden is a great place to be a working parent but we've been duped', *The Guardian*, 22 September, pp. 10–11.

Nash, B. (1980), St Michael: *The Complete Book of Babycare*, London: Octopus Books.

Nelson, D.L. and R.J. Burke (2000), 'Women, work stress and health', in M.J. Davidson and R.J. Burke (eds), *Women in Management: Current Research Issues*, Volume II, London: Sage.

Nelson, D.L. and J.C. Quick (1985), 'Professional women: are distress and disease inevitable?', *Academy of Management Review*, **10**, 206–18.

Oakley, A. (1993), *Essays on Women, Medicine and Health*, Edinburgh: Edinburgh University Press.

Padavic, I. and B. Reskin (2002), *Women and Men at Work*, Thousand Oaks, CA: Sage.

Parsons, M. and M. Rose (2005), 'Teaching innovation through innovative teaching', unpublished working paper, Lancaster University Management School, Lancaster, UK.

Parsons, T. (1971), 'The normal American family', in B. Adams and T. Weirath (eds), *Readings on the Sociology of the Family*, Chicago, IL: Markham, pp. 53–66.

Parsons, T. and R. Bales (1956), *Family and Socialization and Interaction Process*, London: Routledge and Kegan Paul.

Patmore, C. (1856), *The Angel in the House*, London: Boston Ticknor and Fields.

Pullinger, J. and C. Summerfield (1998), *Social Focus on Women and Men*, Office for National Statistics, London: The Stationery Office.

Rich, A. (1977), *Of Woman Born: Motherhood as Experience and Institution*, London: Virago.

Rowbotham, S. (1997), *A Century of Women: The History of Women in Britain and the United States*, London: Penguin.

Roxburgh, S. (1996), 'Gender differences in work and well-being: effects of exposure and vulnerability', *Journal of Health and Social Behaviour*, **37**: 265–77.

Seager, J. (2005), *The Atlas of Women in the World*, London: Earthscan.

Singh, V. and S. Vinnicombe (2004), 'Why so few women directors in top UK boardrooms? Evidence and theoretical explanations', *Corporate Governance*, **12** (4), 479–88.

Smart, C. and B. Neale (1999), *Family Fragments?*, Cambridge: Polity Press.

Sullivan, O. (1997), 'Time waits for no (wo)man: an investigation of the gendered experience of domestic time', *Sociology*, **31**, 221–39.

Swan, J. and C.L. Cooper (2005), *Time, Health and the Family: What Working Families Want*, London: Working Families.

Thair, T. and A. Risdon (1999), 'Women in the labour market?, results from the Spring 1998 Labour Force Survey, *Labour Market Trends*, London: Office for National Statistics, **107**, 103–28.

Tooley, J. (2002), *The Miseducation of Women*, London: Continuum.

Vinnicombe, S. and J. Bank (2003), *Women with Attitude: Lessons for Career Management*, London: Routledge.

Williams, J. (1999), *Unbending Gender: Why Work and Family Conflict and What to Do About It*, New York: Oxford University Press.

Woolf, V. (1979), *Women and Writing*, London: Women's Press.

Worrall, L. and C.L. Cooper (1999), 'Working patterns and working hours: their impact on UK managers', *Leadership and Organization Development Journal*, **20** (1), 6–10.

4 Knowing Lisa? Feminist analyses of 'gender and entrepreneurship'

Marta B. Calás, Linda Smircich and
Kristina A. Bourne

At 7:45 am, Lisa enters through the back door of the bakery she founded five years ago. She has Tiffany, her 7-year-old daughter, in tow. She strides through the bustling workspace, saying hello to the several bakers and the pastry chef who've been at work for hours. She tells Tiffany to unzip her coat and sit at the table. She checks in with the front counter staff and sees a long line building up. She calls out that she'll be there to help in a few minutes.

Meanwhile, Lisa has been thinking of a way for Tiffany to practice writing correctly spelled words before her school bus comes in half an hour. She had planned to help her practice on a white board at home last night, but ran out of time when discussions with a regional grocery chain about becoming their supplier spilled way over time. She returns with a baking tray filled with cornmeal and places it in front of her daughter. Her attention is diverted as the fax machine starts sputtering with details of a large order. She needs to tell Lee, her life partner, that a special delivery is due to arrive this morning and that space has to be made for it. But just as she's remembering this, Lee enters and says, 'I'm so glad you're here. I've got to tell you about this call I just had from someone from the university. She's studying women entrepreneurs and wants to study the business....'

During this conversation, Lisa stops and yells across the workspace, 'Tiffany, how do you spell "bright"?' and Tiffany fingers the letters in the cornmeal, reads them back to Lisa and Lee, and shakes the pan, ready for the next word Lisa shouts outs.

Women entrepreneurs have been the subject of research and writing in the academic and popular press for more than two decades. Given the considerable contributions women who start their own businesses have been making to their local and national economies in the US and in the rest of the world, such interest is not surprising. But, who, and what, is 'a woman entrepreneur'? Who and what is Lisa? Our question points *not* to a need for more precise definitions and measurable constructs. Rather, the question is motivated by a concern that much of the research has been limiting, theoretically and methodologically, regarding who counts as 'a woman entrepreneur', as well as what kind of questions and issues can be raised about her.

The contribution we hope to make in this chapter is an epistemological one, guided by insights from feminist theorizing. In particular, we share Greer and Greene's (2003: 1) view that future research on women in entrepreneurship would benefit from grounding 'in more complete applications of feminist theory'. While there is already an emerging body of work that can be labeled 'feminist perspectives on entrepreneurship' (for example, Ahl, 2004; Bird and Brush, 2002; Bruni et al., 2004a; 2004b; Carter and Williams, 2003; Fischer, Reuber and Dyke, 1993; Greer and Greene, 2003; Hurley, 1999; Mirchandani, 1999), it is now scattered in different places. One of our interests is to bring together aspects of this work for consideration. Beyond that, however, our main interest is to show that the work done so far, although important, is not enough, and that much more needs to be done and can be done.

Explicitly, this chapter is an attempt to encourage a more inclusive theory and research on gender and entrepreneurship through a *clearer* understanding of feminist epistemologies. Further, consistent with its feminist aims, this chapter is also an attempt to portray 'gender and entrepreneurship' as a critical area of activity for imagining possibilities for social change. For this purpose, we introduce insights from feminist theorizing and their 'applications' in organization studies (for example, Calás and Smircich, 1996; 2006; Greer and Greene, 2003; Halford and Leonard, 2001).

Feminist theorizing is critical and always political, oriented towards social change for a more just society away from situations of women's and others' subordination, and starting from a position that considers *all forms of knowledge*, implicitly or explicitly, as *furthering the interests of some and not others*. A feminist epistemological standpoint 'shifts the question from how to eliminate politics from science to two different questions: which politics advance and which obstruct the growth of knowledge; and, for whom (for which groups) does such politics advance or obstruct knowledge' (Harding, 2004: 30–31).

However, the degree of critique and the nature of the politics vary across different feminist theoretical perspectives, leading to knowledge that, when applied to organization studies, ranges from concerns with reforming organizations, to more dramatic views about transforming organizations *and* society, and to transforming our prior understandings of what constitutes knowledge/theory/practice in organization studies (Calás and Smircich, 1996; 2006). Those differences also account for how research results are translated into institutional practices and public policy, and how issues of social inequality are confronted more broadly. The central concept in feminist theorizing through which these issues are articulated is *gender* but, as we discuss below, the meaning of this concept has developed much beyond 'women's issues', and differs according to the various feminist theoretical strands (Ahmed, 2000; Jaggar, 1983).

Our discussion is organized under two main sections: the first considers feminist theories leading to questions about 'the woman entrepreneur' while the second addresses feminist theories leading to questions about 'gendering entrepreneurship' and beyond. We show how and why the majority of gender and entrepreneurship research has been formulated under the premises of particular feminist perspectives in contrast to others. At the end of each section, we return to Lisa to *illustrate research questions* that can be asked about her according to the premises of different feminist theoretical approaches and to *consider appropriate methodologies* for answering such questions.

Our hope is that as we expand the possibilities for knowing Lisa we will also be expanding the conceptual space where 'women entrepreneurs' currently reside. We conclude with further considerations on Lisa's life and the importance of such entrepreneurial lives in relationship to others in the contemporary world. We suggest that the feminist theoretical tendencies leading towards 'gendering entrepreneurship' offer the most promising avenues towards new conversations about entrepreneurship and gender, both for knowledge production and, potentially, for social change.

The woman entrepreneur

The feminist theoretical tendencies we discuss first – Liberal, Radical and Psychoanalytic – have in common a fundamental ontological assumption: that women's disadvantages result from *their condition as women*. Arguments are centered on her 'sameness' or her 'difference' (from man) with the expectation that the two sexes may come to share common or separate spaces in society, in either case without oppression or subordination (Calás and Smircich, 2006).

The earliest feminist theory, Liberal feminism, was at its inception concerned with inequality between 'the sexes', that is, between two categories of persons ('males' and 'females') denoted by biological characteristics. Later on, Liberal, Radical and Psychoanalytic theorizing distinguished between biologically based 'sex', and 'gender' as a product of socialization and experience. Yet, these theories differ over what aspects of experience are most important in constituting gender. For instance, Liberal feminism focuses on socialization into sex/gender roles; Radical feminism addresses cultural practices that value men's experiences over women's; Psychoanalytic feminism is concerned with experiences acquired in early developmental relations with parents. However, black 'womanists' criticize all these by questioning which 'women's experiences' are constitutive of 'gender'.

Liberal feminist theory and the woman entrepreneur

Liberal feminism's roots are in nineteenth century liberal political theory, which envisions a good or just society as one allowing *all people* to exercise autonomy and fulfill themselves through a system of individual rights, based on a conception of abstract individualism independent of social context. Behind these arguments is the ideal of a universal humanity where, underneath it all, human beings are equal.

Yet, despite liberal political thought's lofty aims, white women, as well as women and men of color, had a long road to travel before their rights as people were to be considered. Participation in the public sphere of social life was based on the right to ownership of private property, sustained in turn by a formulation of *the people* that was coded, from its inception, as 'propertied white male'. *Equal rights*, thus, became the dominant aim of first wave Liberal feminism, sometimes also participating in movements for the emancipation of slaves.

Consistent with these assumptions, the second wave women's movement in the 1960s stressed equality, advocating equal access and equal representation in public life for women without stressing sex differences (for example, Friedan, 1963). But by the 1980s, Friedan (1981), among others, began to question the avoidance of talk about difference, arguing it treated women as 'male clones.' In her view, 'equality' must be reconceptualized to take into consideration 'that women are the ones who have the babies' (Friedan, in Tong, 1998: 30). Thus, Liberal feminism gradually made a transition from themes of '*sameness*' in the 1960s and 70s to themes of '*difference*' in the 1980s and 1990s, noting that sex, a matter of chromosomes and anatomy, has been conflated with gender, a cultural construct defining what is seen as appropriately 'masculine' or 'feminine'.

Organizational research grounded explicitly in assumptions of Liberal feminist theory, considers men and women as equally capable, rational, human beings. Any difference in their performance in roles such as leader, manager or entrepreneur would require explanation with reference to *conditions in society or organizations that limit the equal rights of women.* Thus, identifying these conditions would be of particular interest to a Liberal feminist perspective on entrepreneurship.

The entrepreneurship literature was written initially by men, and about men's activities and experiences (for example, Moore, 2004; Reed, 1996). Gradually, as a consequence of the women's movement and the rising numbers of women in economic roles, research attention turned to women as business owners. A good example of this can be gleaned in research addressing whether 'the glass ceiling' in corporations has fueled the increased number of women starting their own businesses (for example, Moore et al., 1992; Moore and Buttner, 1997; Weiler and Bernasek, 2001).

However, most of this research is *not* feminist in orientation. Rather, it has focused on comparisons between female and male entrepreneurs in terms of their characteristics, traits, attitudes and behaviors, which seemed to pose the question, in the words of one study, whether entrepreneurial women and men were 'two different species?' (Cowling and Taylor, 2001). Topics of research have varied, but they often included demographics and background (for example, Hisrich and Brush, 1984); psychological make-up and personality (for example, Fagenson, 1993); motivation to start a business (for example, Buttner et al., 1997); firm characteristics (for example, Rosa et al., 1994); management practice and strategies (for example, Chaganti, 1986), networking (for example, Aldrich et al., 1989); sources of financing (for example, Greene et al., 1999); and performance (for example, Kalleberg and Leicht, 1991).

Nonetheless, Fischer et al. (1993), observing that much research on women entrepreneurs was non-theoretical, explicitly derived their research hypotheses through Liberal feminist theory. They hypothesized that women would be less successful than men because they are less likely to have access to valuable opportunities, less likely to obtain the relevant formal education, and less likely to have relevant experience that would help them in running their own businesses. Their findings suggested that in seeking to account for performance differences between businesses run by men and women (particularly in terms of size) researchers should focus on 'relevant opportunities other than experience or education that are systematically less available to women and that impeded them from starting large firms or growing their firms rapidly.' (Fischer et al., 1993: 165). Thus, from a Liberal feminist perspective, the beginning assumption of women's equality would lead to further questioning about what accounts for women's differential access to resources (for example, Carter et al., 1997; Brush et al., 2004).

In sum, the women and entrepreneurship literature in search of equality of opportunities for women can be seen as congruent with aims of Liberal feminism. Still, this literature is timid in addressing the persistence of systemic conditions disadvantaging women. Little is likely to change insofar as research on the situation of women entrepreneurs focuses on women's cognitive, behavioral or demographic differences in relationship to men without questioning the dominant institutions, and the practices of men *and* women in these institutions, as complicit in maintaining the current social and economic system.

Further, which women are represented in this research and which ignored? As black ('womanists') feminists have argued, Liberal feminism of the second wave of American women's movement represented only the interests of white, middle class, heterosexual women under the guise of representing all women (for example, Combahee River Collective, 1977), and organizational research has not been an innocent bystander in these issues (for example, Nkomo, 1992; Bell and Nkomo, 2001). With few exceptions, research on women entrepreneurs is mostly mute on representations of women of color. The typical woman represented in this research seems to be white and middle class. In fact, when race is explicitly addressed, often under the label of 'minorities', it seems to be under the premise that non-white women are less likely to become successful entrepreneurs because they are less likely than white women to have access to resources (for example, Moore, 2004).

However, historical analyses have shown that all kinds of women in the US, despite disadvantages of race and class or perhaps because of this, have been business founders and entrepreneurs more often than acknowledged. Black women, in particular, were able to start and run several companies, often against all odds, making important contributions to the development of US businesses (Kwolek-Folland, 1998; Peiss, 1998). These women, often coming from poor or socially marginal backgrounds, also created jobs for other women, became involved in political activities for equal rights and against discrimination, and made economic contributions to their communities. Their actions were consistent with the aims of Liberal feminism.

To underscore, the equity aims in Liberal feminism require political engagement to reform institutions. Yet, the organizational literature, including the gender and entrepreneurship literature focusing on issues of 'women's access to…', seldom addresses the politics of the situation. In a quest for 'neutrality and objectivity', researchers, including some claiming a commitment to feminist theories (for example Carter and Williams, 2003), may miss identifying activities of those who, acting beyond the extant economic and social dominant institutions, are attempting to change their circumstances and even those of their communities.

Radical feminist theory and the woman entrepreneur

Feminism of 'sameness' in the US Liberal tradition eventually spawned several types of feminisms of 'difference', including a Liberal feminism of 'difference' intending to account for differences in socialization between men and women but continuing to focus on equality of rights as well as the complementarities of the sexes (for example, Evans, 1995). Quite distinct from this, Radical feminism, the most notable feminism of 'difference', emerged from women's dissatisfaction with the sexism of the supposedly emancipatory movements of New Left politics, the civil rights and the anti-Vietnam war movements of the 1960s, and what they considered conservative or elitist trends in Liberal feminism (Willis, 1975).

Radical feminism takes the subordination of women as its starting point: gender is a system of male domination, a fundamental organizing principle of patriarchal society, at the root of all other systems of oppression. What are seen by Liberal feminists as problems of rights within what is supposed to be a gender-neutral system, are seen here as a more general condition of the social system, as the consequence of male gender privilege and power in a society where the male and the masculine define the norm (Jaggar, 1983).

Earlier Radical feminism emphasized that in a patriarchal sex/gender system, 'femininity', including women's reproductive and sexual roles, was at the center of women's oppression. By the late 1970s many of these arguments were rethought through *Radical-cultural feminism*, suggesting that it is possible for women to regain a sense of wholeness and connectedness to the 'authentic feminine' outside of patriarchy through a female counter culture (Tong, 1998). Thus, Radical feminism is 'women centered', envisioning a new social order where women are not subordinated to men, proposing alternative and often separatist, social, political, economic, and cultural arrangements that challenge the structural conditions of a male dominated society. They have put into practice organizational forms reflecting avowed feminist values, such as equality, community, participation, and an integration of form and content (Brown, 1992; Ferree and Martin, 1995).

Numerous case studies have detailed feminist organizations and their practices (for example, Ashcraft, 2001; Baines and Wheelock, 2000; Balka, 1997; Colgan and Ledwith, 2000; Koen, 1984; Ferree and Martin, 1995; McBride, 2001; Riger, 1994). Many of these organizations embrace the goals and values of Radical feminism combined with attention to issues of hierarchy and organization structure similar to those found in theories of anarchy and in collectivist organizations (Iannello, 1992), and they often have an explicit agenda to invert the values of capitalist masculinist organization (P.Y. Martin, 1990).

Struggles are nonetheless documented where 'the rhetoric of equality, the collective decision-making structure, and the explicit goals of women's and community empowerment' confront differences in work styles and sexuality, class, race and ethnicity conflicts (Morgen, 1994: 681; also Ostrander, 1999). The identification of a shared set of core values informing organizing activity in the women's movement does not mean that their enactment is unproblematic or indisputable (Brown, 1992; Cholmeley, 1991).

Curiously, the 'women entrepreneurs' literature has mostly ignored the widespread existence of such feminist organizations that could surely be considered entrepreneurial in nature (Greer and Greene, 2003). This is noteworthy, but perhaps not surprising. Their strong political commitments and aspirations for social change mark these organizations as outside the frame of reference of what is typically thought of as 'entrepreneurship', at least in the US. For instance, Goffee and Scase (1985) identified the existence of 'radical proprietors' in the UK who see entrepreneurship as an avenue to enact feminist values in contrast to the dominant values of society. In reviewing this book Dexter (1985) suggested that radical proprietors are perhaps more common in the UK than in the US. Yet, given the ongoing documentation of the existence of feminist organizations in the US in the sociology literature since at least the 1970s, what seems more common is that US management scholars are unable or unwilling to recognize these organizations as entrepreneurial. That is, separatism in Radical feminist activities, and therefore organizations, has often been connected with a sexual politics in which lesbianism plays a part (for example, Baker, 1982), and thus, non-recognition of feminist organizations as entrepreneurial also reflects the absence of a critical orientation and uneasiness with issues of sexuality in US organization and management theory and research more generally.

Radical feminist analyses would further reflect on this situation. Analyses may argue that neglect of Radical feminist organizations in entrepreneurship research is evidence that knowledge practices enacted in the academic community are also embedded in a patriarchal system whose values determine what is defined as 'entrepreneurial activities and success', such as evaluating organizations' long-term survival but not their impact on their participants' lives over time (Staggenborg, 1995). Accounting for Radical feminist organizations in the 'women and entrepreneurship' research would thus require inquiring about them differently. It would include evaluating their success also in terms of actualizing feminist values and improving specific needs and conditions of women and others in society despite what may often seem to be insurmountable obstacles.

An almost ironic variation on these issues is demonstrated in Florida's (2002) popularly acclaimed research on regional development, where he argues that there is a 'creative class' that accounts for the emergence of communities in the US where social and economic well-being go hand in hand. A hallmark of these communities is tolerance of diversity including alternative lifestyles, that is, the social acceptance of gay and lesbians who, as members of the 'creative class', develop cultural and other business organizations that eventually improve the life of the community more generally.

Psychoanalytic feminist theorizing and the woman entrepreneur
Freud's theories of sexuality, and its application to women's *problems* in psychoanalytic practice, became objects of critique by Liberal and Radical feminists during the late 1960s and early 1970s. At this time, new Psychoanalytic feminist theorizing also went beyond these critiques (Mitchell, 1974). Two strands are identified within this feminist theoretical tendency: the original *Psychoanalytic* (Freudian) *feminism* and *Gender-*

cultural feminism (Tong, 1998). The former is often associated with the work of object-relations theorists who explore the implications of mother–child relations for psychosexual development (for example Chodorow, 1978; Dinnerstein, 1977), while Gender-cultural feminism focuses instead on psychomoral development (for example Gilligan, 1982; Miller, 1976; Noddings, 1984). Both strands are oriented toward changing gender relations and structural conditions, such as the patriarchal family and educational systems that produce unequal gender development as well as disdain for certain values associated with female development (for example, Flax, 1990).

Gender-cultural feminism, in particular, entered organization studies mostly through such notions as 'women's ways of knowing', an ethics of care, and relational development theory toward fully developing the self as a self-in-relationship (Belenky et al., 1986; Gilligan, 1982; Miller, 1976; Noddings, 1984). These ideas were adopted in the women in management literature to further various claims, including that women's unique sex-role socialization and different character traits, such as an ethics of care, were not deficiencies, but advantages for corporate effectiveness (for example, Helgesen, 1990; Liedtka, 1999; Rosener, 1990).

The 'women and entrepreneurship' literature has also incorporated several of these ideas. Bird and Brush (2002) articulated a feminine model of organization creation, noting that knowledge of entrepreneurship has been limited by its reliance on male-derived theories. They developed an archetypal feminine or 'creatrix' process of organizing, discussing gender maturity (an individual characteristic) and gender balance (an organizational quality) as additional dimensions through which it is possible to understand new venture creation. In another example, Buttner (2001) considered Miller's relational theory to classify the way women entrepreneurs managed employees and worked with clients.

Research focused on the relationship between family and work also looms large in this literature. For instance, Brush (1992) introduced the notion 'integrated perspective', forwarding that women entrepreneurs' business relationships are integrated with family, societal and personal relationships. Brush (1997) also proposed that women may be able to draw on their relational skills (that 'naturally' arise out of their role in the family) to overcome their lack of business education and/or experience. Others, such as Carter and Allen (1997) affirm that a limiting factor to the size of women's businesses is their deliberate choice emphasizing family in relation to work.

Despite these arguments, empirical support for 'women's differences' is not always easy to find. For instance, Chell and Baines (1998) found little evidence for Brush's assertions regarding women's and men's distinctive orientations to their businesses, while Buttner, Holly and Moore (1997) found that managing family and career was not the most highly reported reason women gave for their 'organizational exodus to entrepreneurship'. As documented by Hopkins and Bilimoria (2004), there is no reason to believe that because of socialization 'women's differences' would rise to the surface and be enacted by individual women entrepreneurs.

That is, these 'women's differences' arguments are supported by an assumption that women and men are attached, a priori, to different modes of thinking and sets of values that are 'naturally' activated in the context of their everyday life. However, women and men's actions occur in the context of a society where, in the main, gender relations have not changed nor have the values underpinning their major institutions, business and entrepreneurship included.

A feminist critique of these arguments would contend that an interest in 'women's differences', as expressed in entrepreneurship and organizational research, does nothing other than promote women's further exploitation in a patriarchal society. This critique would further remark that most Psychoanalytic and Gender-cultural feminist theoretical premises address women's differences *as problematic* insofar as they are the product of specific developmental conditions that eventually disadvantage women. The devaluation of these differences is inscribed in social institutions, including the family, schools and all organizations. If anything is going to change, both women *and men* must *develop* by valuing the others' differences and acquiring the others' values. This will change gender relations in society and, eventually, change the patriarchal structure of all social institutions. It is the *gender relations* that must be *changed* in order ultimately to effect social change.

For instance, Chodorow's arguments articulated needed changes in the patriarchal family with the intention of changing the conditions of women and men in private *and* public life. One without the other would not achieve needed social changes. The patriarchal family, and the role of mothering within it, inscribe in the unconscious of *both* sexes gendering patterns that affect the development of sex/gender relations and lead to female subordination in all other institutions in society. In Chodorow's views, changing parenting arrangements to dual parenting, where *both* parents function as nurturers in the household *and* as independent human beings working side by side in public life, will break down sexual divisions.

Misinterpretations of Gender-cultural and Psychoanalytic feminist theories in the women and entrepreneurship literature, as noted above, are also noticeable in the ways this literature has employed the notion 'social feminism'. The original work by Black (1989) developed from various historical case studies of women's organizing, taking insights from what today would be known as Radical-cultural feminism and Gender-cultural feminism. Black is intent on distinguishing Social feminism from 'equity feminism' (that is, Liberal feminism of equality). She views equity feminism as assimilationist when women ask for equality in extant institutions. Social feminism in the short run may be separatist, women creating their own organizations, but eventually it is transformative of existing social institutions. In these new institutions, men would have lost the exclusive power of decision-making. According to Black's Social feminism, the family, not as a settled institution but as conflictual, and full of contradictions that must be constantly negotiated, is the concrete model and metaphor for the new social order, and the basis for critique of the patriarchal public realm.

Most 'women and entrepreneurship' studies, invoking the term 'social feminism' as an assumed theoretical lens are, however, composed of little more than 'women's difference' arguments, conflating various 'gender differences' perspectives minus their critical edge. A primary interest of this research is to understand the extent to which women and men have different values, motivations and desires, and the impact these differences may have on their businesses, but there is little intent to call into question the social and economic system *sustaining dominant views* of business and their purposes.

For example, Fischer et al. (1993), in their study reviewed above under Liberal feminism, claim to compare Liberal and Social feminist perspectives to explore sex differences in small firm success. Despite citing Black, this work is mostly a comparison of women and men's instrumental aims in the context of a social system that promotes such aims, which shows a general misunderstanding of feminist 'gender differences' perspectives, and, in particular, of Social feminism. Under these research premises, significant differences between men and women are unlikely to appear – that is, it is the wrong question. If truly inspired by Social feminism, research would attempt *understanding* activities of women entrepreneurs to assess whether through these activities *other than instrumental values become possible.*

Ironically, Fischer et al.'s comparative research found that women were more motivated than men by financial reasons (making the business more profitable or valuable) and equally as motivated as men by lifestyle motives (achieving a balance between work and family). Not surprisingly, others attempting to explain entrepreneurial firms' growth or growth intentions based on comparing women's and men's differences have invoked Social feminism without much success in finding such avowed differences (for example, Carter and Williams, 2003; Cliff, 1998).

Altogether, feminist critiques would notice the contradictions embedded in these arguments. They would point out, for instance, that Radical-cultural feminist organizations were explicitly created to counter patriarchal social structures, and therefore had a separatist political aim from inception, but Psychoanalytic and Gender-cultural feminist theories showed that changing the patriarchal society would require other kinds of changes. They would argue that the devaluation of women, which women even do to themselves as members of a patriarchal society, is ingrained in men's and women's psyches and reproduced in the social institutions where men and women co-exist.

By contrast, research on women entrepreneurs, and women in organizations more generally, mythologize and essentialize 'women's differences' while, paradoxically, harnessing those differences in order to reproduce the values of a patriarchal society. Further, while in appearance interested in changing institutions (for example, 'women's way of leading'), once these ideas are exploited under the instrumental rationality of traditional (that is, patriarchal) organizational parlance and research, the possibilities for critical change become annulled in the rush to another quick fix for the bottom line.

'The woman entrepreneur' through feminist epistemologies

Most 'women and entrepreneurship' literature, despite its apparent variety, fails to recognize that there are strong political implications even to Liberal feminism. Conventional 'women entrepreneurs' research, in particular from the US, partakes at best of a weak Liberal feminist sensibility, but often seems anti-feminist in its inability to forward a critique of much of what disadvantages women and also some men. It obscures the fact that many of the aims of capitalist societies predefine successful activities in modes that reproduce patriarchal arrangements, where the values of instrumental rationality are dominant *regardless of sex of the bodies* that make the decisions. Altogether, this literature seems to be so wedded to the status quo that it is unable to ask for what and for whom are 'entrepreneurial activities' good? Who benefits, and in which ways, from these activities and who does not? What needs to change?

Researching Lisa: Feminist analyses of women entrepreneurs

In reading Lisa's story at the beginning of this chapter, a feminist researcher would ask different questions, depending on the theoretical perspective informing her research. For instance, if informed by **Liberal** feminist theory, equal rights and opportunities would be the dominant feature, and documenting whether Lisa, and others like her, are in fact treated fairly by, for example, suppliers, financial backers, and even customers would be the focus. Documentation would typically be based on quantitative data using comparisons by sex, but if differences were found, questions would be further asked not about the 'Lisas' of this world but about suppliers, financial institutions and customers whose perceptions and behaviors may be at the root of inequalities. Further research would address broader social and structural issues that might disadvantage entrepreneurial women but also successes that might have been attained; for instance, whether increased numbers of women in positions such as financial officers had been instrumental in reducing barriers to credit for women entrepreneurs.

However, research from a **Radical** feminist perspective would be more incisive in finding out which women are advantaged and which are disadvantaged and in which ways, and what to do to remedy their situation. Consciousness-raising would be part of the researcher's role, not simply observing and asking questions but also creating a relationship with Lisa for considering organizational approaches and ownership structures that would also benefit the situation of other women, such as her employees. The aim is to consciously create 'a women's entrepreneurial culture' which reconfigures patriarchal structures of inequality, and the researcher's role is part of this aim. **Psychoanalytic-cultural** feminist theorizing would be more concerned with the formation of patriarchal ideologies and how relationships between women and men, in private and public life, contribute to reiterate or limit these ideologies. Research might be approached in clinical fashion, including case studies, to document how entrepreneurial activities may or may not promote different types of relationships between partners, given the assumed freedom from prescribed norms allowed by the entrepreneurial situation. Do Lisa and Lee share the burdens of work and family equally? What roles does Lisa take in dealing with Tiffany in contrast to Lee? Does Lisa's approach contest or foster the reproduction of gender differences?

In summary, we insist that Liberal, Radical and Psychoanalytic feminist theoretical perspectives, if fully articulated, can make important contributions to the study of gender and entrepreneurship. Yet, at a minimum, this research must recognize and convey that even attaining basic feminist goals of equality might imply very fundamental changes, not small corrections in what is taken to be, ultimately, a rational and just system and a desired state of affairs – that is, organizational, managerial, and entrepreneurial 'rationality', their goals and values, within specific modalities of capitalism. Further, in our view, women entrepreneurs could be *retheorized* as agents of social change if their activities are framed in research as exemplars of a new social system: the starting point of a psychic and material transformation where together women *and* men would be capable of creating a better society *for all*.

Gendering entrepreneurship

Socialist, Poststructuralist/Postmodern, and Transnational/(Post)colonial feminist theoretical tendencies, and contemporary trends emerging from their blending and interweaving share an aim to complicate notions of 'gender' as primarily referring to specifically sexed bodies. As they see it, gender(ing) as social(ly) system(ic) *is a process and a practice*, produced and reproduced through relations of power among differently positioned members of society, including relations emerging from historical processes, dominant discourses and institutions, and dominant epistemological arguments, all of which become naturalized as *the way it is* (Calás and Smircich, 2006).

Compared to Liberal, Radical and Psychoanalytic feminist theories, the notion of *gender* is more distanced from that of 'personal experience' in all of these perspectives. Socialist feminist theory understands gender(ing) as a process embedded in power relations and particular historical *material* conditions, including practices of masculinity as well as identities formed in the intersectionalities of gender, race, class, sexuality and other categories of social oppression. More recently, both Poststructuralist and Transnational feminist approaches, and other approaches to gender that have emerged in the wake of various 'posts', such as 'queer theory', problematize the notion of 'experience'. They critique investing 'sex' and 'gender' with stability as analytical categories, noting that subjectivity and identity are constructed linguistically, historically, culturally and politically, and are therefore flexible and multiple.

According to these theoretical tendencies, feminist projects focusing simply on the existence of oppression and discrimination miss how these conditions are *effects of multiply related processes*, which contribute to their reproduction. Critique and rethinking in order to change these conditions should start from analyzing the complex structuring of social, economic, cultural *and* knowledge relations, as relations of power, in which gendered (and other) identities and subjectivities are thus formed, and which in turn produce, resist or reproduce the social system. There is a dearth of entrepreneurship literature under these perspectives but, as we argue below, today these theoretical tendencies are the most promising avenues for new research and theorizing regarding gender and entrepreneurship that might truly effect social change.

Gendering entrepreneurship through Socialist feminist theorizing

Socialist feminism is a confluence of Marxist, Radical and Psychoanalytic feminism resulting from Marxist feminists' dissatisfaction during the 1970s with the tendency of traditional Marxism to dismiss women's oppression as not nearly as important as workers' oppression (Ferguson, 1998; Holmstrom, 2002). Socialist feminists critique Liberal feminism as totally inadequate for explaining the subordinate position of women in the economy. The capitalist economy is *not* best described through such concepts as market forces, exchange patterns, supply and demand, as liberal and neoliberal economic theory posits; rather, the capitalist economy should be analyzed by focusing on *relations of inequality and power*. They also critique Radical and Psychoanalytic feminisms because they exhibit universalizing tendencies, assuming (Western) patriarchal conditions as normative with limited regard for culture or historical circumstances. Further, Radical feminism is criticized as naive for suggesting that there could be a separate 'women's culture' under patriarchy *and* capitalism.

Socialist feminist theorists have also been particularly concerned with epistemological issues: not only what is to be known, but also how knowledge is constituted and for what purposes. Theoretical developments such as *standpoint theory* (for example, Harding, 2004), *institutional ethnography* (Smith, 1987), and analyses of *intersectionalities*, aiming to understand subjectivities formed *as simultaneous processes and outcomes* in the intersections of race, class, gender, sexuality, and so on, (for example, Crenshaw, 1991; Glenn, 1999; Hurtado 1989), stand out among these. These theoretical tendencies also address what Hearn (2004) calls critical studies of men and masculinities, a range of studies that address men in the context of gendered power relations (for example, Connell, 1995).

The sexual division of labor, referred to variously as the *gendered division of labor*, the *sex structuring of organizations*, and *occupational sex segregation* is an important starting point in Socialist feminist analyses. As a basic characteristic of capitalist society, it affects men as well as women in unequal, and persistent, sex-based patterns in employment, observable across multiple industries and situations (for example, Acker and Van Houten, 1974; Reskin and Roos, 1990).

Joan Acker's work has served as a theoretical foundation for much contemporary 'gendered organization' scholarship (Britton, 2000; Martin and Collinson, 2002). As conceptualized by Acker, (for example, 1990; 2004) persistent structuring of organizations along gender lines is reproduced in a number of ways through the interrelation of gendered practices with a gender substructure of organization. Gendering, racing, sexualizing of organizations occur through ordinary, daily procedures and decisions that segregate, manage, control and construct hierarchies in which gender, class and race are involved (for example, Tolich and Briar, 1999), and through symbols, images and ideologies that legitimate inequalities and differences (for example, Bell and Nkomo, 2001; Gherardi, 1995; Ward, 2004). Symbolic processes are also associated with work activities leading to gendered jobs, for images of the ideal organization member, the top manager, and the organizational hero tend to be those of forceful masculinity (for example, Prokos and Padavic, 2002). Further, gender structuring, embodiment and embeddedness are produced through social interactions that enact dominance and submission (for example, Cockburn, 1991; Martin, 2003).

While not abundant, there is some entrepreneurship literature using these approaches. For instance, Mirchandani (1999) demonstrates the processes through which *knowledge* about entrepreneurship *becomes* gendered. She suggests that 'looking at the entrepreneurial work of women or of racial and ethnic minorities would provide insight into the gendered, racialized, and class-based processes which shape entrepreneurial activity' (1999: 233). Other work that *genders* entrepreneurship under these premises is Bruni et al. (2004a). Similar to Acker's work, their ethnography of men and women entrepreneurs uses an approach that considers gender as situated practices in the enactment of entrepreneurship through codes of gendered identities.

The persistent structuring of organizations along gender lines is also supported and sustained by the gendered *substructure* of organizations, for example, the practices related to the 'extra-organizational reproduction of members' (Acker, 1994: 118). That is, women are the 'hidden providers' in the economy (Stoller, 1993: 153), for the physical and social reproduction of employees happens outside the workplace and is done primarily by women, most of it as unpaid work (Folbre, 1994). Yet, much organizational research starts by assuming the separation of 'work and family' and fails to recognize the material effects of the link between domestic and reproductive lives and work, under the premise that procreation, sexuality, and caring are outside of work boundaries.

Some gender and entrepreneurship literature critically addresses the latter arguments. For example, Marlow (1997) considers that women are still burdened by the 'double shift' – one at work and one at home – making the integration of outside work and domestic responsibility more of a necessity than a choice. Other scholars working from this perspective maintain that concepts such as 'patriarchy', 'the politics of the family' and 'gender divisions of labor', as well as 'power relations' structured through the links of 'market and non-market activities', are missing from the analysis of women's experiences of entrepreneurship (Allen and Truman, 1993; Baines and Wheelock, 2000; Chell and Baines, 1998; Marlow and Strange, 1993).

Altogether, from a Socialist feminist perspective, doing 'organization', 'management' and 'entrepreneurship', whether *practicing* or *theorizing* (that is, 'doing knowledge') about these, imply 'doing gender' (Benschop and Brouns, 2003; Bruni et al., 2004a; West and Zimmerman, 1987). It is with this 'doing' that critical analyses must begin for understanding the making of a society that we, as academics or practitioners, may want to change. As a reflective point, starting from our own research practices, what must we do such that these analytical approaches are no longer concealed, or perhaps misunderstood in gender and entrepreneurship research?

Deconstructing entrepreneurship: Poststructuralist/Postmodern feminist theorizing

The move towards Poststructuralist/Postmodern theorizing in the humanities and the social sciences is captured by the phrase the 'linguistic turn', due to its usual association with Ferdinand de Saussure's structural linguistics, and later underpinning the works of poststructuralist theorists such as Derrida, Foucault, Irigaray, Lacan and Lyotard, among others. A core insight is that the relationship between signifier and signified is contingent – that is, the sign we use to signify anything is only meaningful because we are able to *differentiate* it from another sign rather than because it *names* any essential object or concept. Language as a system of differences is *constitutive* of the things we can think/know rather than simply *representative* of them. From this perspective, the possibility of universal and generalizable knowledge based on fixed and stable language, which grounded much of the Enlightenment (that is, modern) epistemologies, was called into question.

The interrogation of modern knowledge by Poststructuralist/Postmodern theorizing entered feminist theorizing during the 1980s, becoming more clearly articulated, as well as contested, during the 1990s. Some feminist theorists expressed ambivalence toward Poststructuralist approaches, considering it risky for women to abandon modern epistemological projects, yet advocates asserted that 'postmodern-feminist theory would replace unitary notions of woman and feminine gender identity with plural and complexly constructed conceptions of social identity, treating gender as one relevant strand among others, attending also to class, race, ethnicity, age, ...' (Fraser and Nicholson, 1988: 393). New conceptualizations included notions such as *positionality* (Alcoff, 1988), and the imagery of the *cyborg*, capable of mobilizing political action through 'affinity, not identity' (Haraway, 1985: 73).

As with scholarship inspired by Socialist feminism, applications of feminist Poststructuralism to organization studies proliferated from the mid-1990s. Concurrently, debate has continued over its value and implications (for example Calás and Smircich, 1999). Several feminist deconstructive analyses of the production of traditional organizational concepts, theories and practices have been published (for example, J. Martin, 1990; Mumby and Putnam 1992; Runté and Mills 2004). Others have examined the dualisms through which knowing and practicing gender and organizing occur (for example, Baxter and Hughes, 2004). Demonstrations of the power/knowledge relations and discursive practices that constitute 'identities' and 'selves' and define gendered subjectivities have been produced (for example, Brewis, 2001).

With the exception of Helene Ahl's (2004) book and Bruni et al. (2004b), we did not find other works inspired by these theoretical perspectives within the gender and entrepreneurship literature. Yet, these works can serve as paradigmatic cases for future endeavors. For instance, Bruni et al. examine how the literature on entrepreneurship, as a discursive social practice, produces the entrepreneur subject through hegemonic masculinities in which women must then recognize themselves. Further, Ahl, in an extended study through discourse analysis, asks: how is the female entrepreneur constructed in the research literature? How does this literature reproduce the conditions that give way to gender inequalities? Her research finds that even when celebrating women entrepreneurs, the celebratory arguments actually work to reposition women in a secondary social place, casting them as 'Other'.

Collectively Poststructuralist feminist inquiry demonstrates that the *texts and language* producing 'organizational knowledge' are not naive or innocent, but rather engaged in a *politics of representation* that can and does gender organizations. The works cited above, more generally, share an interest in complicating the claims of organizational 'knowledge' by pointing to the contradictions in their representations. By attending to the performative nature of texts, such writings cast suspicion on the proclaimed objectivity and universality of organizational knowledge, unveiling the assumptions embedded in much of these claims, and showing the possibility of 'other voices' that can demonstrate how it might be otherwise.

Globalizing entrepreneurship: Transnational/(Post)colonial feminist theorizing

Transnational/(Post)colonial feminisms, while not monolithic, include several critics who challenge Western feminist theorizations of gender and gender relations as furthering the images and social experiences of privileged women (and men) in the 'First World'. These arguments, emerging mostly after the mid-1980s and early 1990s, go beyond those raised by black and other race theorists who questioned the white, middle class, heterosexist, representations of gender in feminist theorizing. They interrogate, for instance, the function of 'the nation' in gendering and racializing 'others' through specific, patriarchal, heterosexist, political projects *between and within* different countries, (for example, Collins, 1998; Monhanram, 1998). Analyses consider the heterogeneity of citizenship in its current global dimensions with notions such as *transversal* politics instead of identity politics, and the possibility of feminist projects that cut across differences without assimilation (for example, Yuval-Davis, 1997).

Issues of representation appear often in these analyses but so do questions of power and identity, justice and ethics in practices of globalization (for example, Spivak, 1999). Transnational/(Post)colonial analyses, thus, go beyond the deconstruction of Western texts. They show the production of knowledge at the (Western) center to be a form of self-fashioning, widely implicated in the constitution and legitimation of imperialism and colonialism (for example, Harding, 1998; Kaplan et al., 1999; Mohanty, 1991). In Kaplan and Grewal's (1999) words, what is needed is 'a feminist analysis that refuses to choose among economic, cultural and political concerns' and instead engages in critical practices linking 'our understanding of postmodernity, global economic structures, problematics of nationalism, issues of race and imperialism, critiques of global feminism, and emergent patriarchies' (1999: 358).

Altogether, Transnational/(Post)colonial feminist approaches portray and emphasize the agency of 'the other', and articulate the *multiple relationships* between the 'local' and the 'global' with notions such as one-third world (privileged people *all over* the world)/two-third world (*the rest* of the people all over the world) rather than using the invidious first-world/third–world distinction, which disguises worldwide poverty and inequality (for example, Mohanty, 2003). More importantly, these approaches also make visible how *transnational practices of research* can further empower or exploit those who they claim to represent (for example, Visweswaran, 1994).

While at first blush these arguments may seem more significant regarding large organizations, where globalization underpins most managerial activities today, we aim to show their immediate relevance to gendering entrepreneurship. Notably, Acker (2004) articulates three interrelated areas for analysis where gender, capitalism and globalization appear to be uniquely intertwined with organization practices. For instance, global decision-making is coded 'masculine' in specific ways and the men, but also the few women, who make decisions under this code, are immediate beneficiaries of most of the wealth and power thus produced, including transnational institutions fostering globalization policies, *and* academic domains creating theories about them (for example, business management and organization; economics). At the same time, these decisions produce cultural and economic dislocations affecting gender/race/class relations between *and* within particular local arenas and at global levels, where most other people in the world go about their lives.

Acker's analyses also remind us that corporate practices, at local and global levels, claim non-responsibility for the reproduction of human life, creating a distinction between production as monetary economy and reproduction as non-monetary. These practices may create first, at the local level, a gendered system supported by the unpaid reproductive work of women (caring work, household work) as well as by the lower paid women's work in the for-profit economy, which sometimes is also homework (Mohanty, 1997). These activities at the local level, naturalized in the name of capitalist accumulation, become further naturalized as a globalization process when production is continuously moved from location to location in search of the cheapest labor, which is often women's labor.

These global processes, thus, cannot be interpreted only from the perspective of their gendering effects in western societies, such as when women in the US are displaced from their jobs as these are moved to a cheaper region. Rather these processes need to be examined relationally, (that is, the function of women's labor globally), and also in their differential local effects and implications (for example, Chio, 1996; Méndez and Wolff, 2001; Mohanty, 2003).

Finally, Acker notes that relations between capitalist production and globalization today prosper in more complex ways than simply moving production to a 'low wage country', be it physically or through virtual offshoring of services. In particular, patterns of immigration and transmigration from third-world and other less affluent regions to rich Euro-American countries and other affluent areas, occur as members of the one-third world, both men and women often subject to work intensification, require services from members of the two-thirds world (housework, cleaning work, caring work) so that they can go about their business. These services contribute to the naturalization of work intensification and to further privatization of economies, as public services for families and workers continue to recede, as a matter of course, under neoliberal state policies (for example, Adib and Guerrier, 2003).

As can be observed, these relational analyses critically interrogate conditions that foster the exploitation of a majority of people *all over the world* (often women but not only women). They question the *patterns of relationships* that further this exploitation by making it seem 'inevitable for the progress of the global economy'. At the same time, the analyses reveal possibilities for resistance, alternatives to these processes and the agency of those often imagined by the privileged as incapable of bettering their own lot.

While there is no literature on entrepreneurship drawing on these feminist perspectives, there is at least a topical area in this context where the notion of 'women entrepreneurs' has been problematically insinuated: Moore (2004), in her review of literature on women's entrepreneurial careers, observed microenterprises as part of the international dimension of entrepreneurship. However, these activities, carried out mostly by women in the two-thirds world, can hardly be analyzed under premises of contemporary one-third world entrepreneurship literature, and even less as part of a literature on 'entrepreneurial careers'. In fact, classifying these activities under such premises homogenizes them within categories devised under one-third world notions of 'how the entrepreneurship world works' which would only contribute to obscuring the benefits as well as the limits and disadvantages of these programs.

For instance, Eversole (2004) critically positions 'microenterprise' as an activity that under tenets of capitalist development may end up disadvantaging those it intends to help out. She asks at the outset, 'What hope for decreasing poverty and improving livelihoods do microbusinesses offer? In particular, what is the role of women microentrepreneurs, whose incomes have been understood to contribute a great deal to the well-being of poor households?' (2004: 124). Thus, under premises of Transnational feminist analyses the question is not whether microenterprise producers are or are not entrepreneurs with careers, but how to frame the study of such enterprises when they have been created by 'the colonizer's knowledge' under particular Western premises for 'economic development', including the Grameen Bank as much as the World Bank (for example Dalgic, 2005).

Transnational feminist analyses would be likely to notice that 'entrepreneurship' has become a favored mantra for economic development wherever there is poverty, unemployment or underemployment, and other economic maladies that nations do not seem to be able to resolve. That is, 'entrepreneurship' works under Western neoliberal economic recipes that are intended to apply universally, whether in the inner cities of the US or the rural areas of Bangladesh. A Transnational feminist analysis would further focus on how 'entrepreneurship' functions in advantaging or disadvantaging groups of people globally who, now connected through the prescribed and likely experimental policies of powerful international organizations, may or may not attain the intended outcomes of these policies.

'Gendering entrepreneurship' through feminist epistemologies

The three theoretical perspectives in this section, Socialist, Poststructuralist/ Postmodern and Transnational/(Post)colonial are today closely related. These feminist tendencies critically examine social and economic structuring, subjectivities, sexualities and transnational processes as simultaneously implicated in *knowledge production* that naturalizes *as knowledge* the continuity of relations of oppression and subordination for many, not only women. While the materialism of early socialist feminism was subject to much critique for its economic reductionism, the move toward more cultural analyses, eventually culminating in varieties of postmodern feminisms, has now been rendered suspect as extreme in its focus on language and signification. At present there is again a broader positive reassessment of the material for feminist theorizing, brought about by Transnational feminist projects and by concepts such as 'materiality' and 'materialization' claiming to obtain a better integration of material and symbolic gendered practices (for example, Butler, 1993). According to Holmstrom (2002: 8), 'The brutal economic realities of globalization make it impossible to ignore class, and feminists are now asking on a global level the kind of big questions they asked at a societal level in the 1970s'.

Researching Lisa: Gendering entrepreneurship

While Lisa's story at the start of this chapter may seem far removed from questions of transnationalism and globalization, a researcher embedded in these 'gendering' approaches would immediately wonder about the reasons that made Lisa decide to found her bakery. Is it possible that she was working at a corporation when her job was moved to India? Did needing to contribute to the family household impel her to start this business? But, what made her go that route? What were images of 'female entrepreneurs' that were available to her? How does she perform 'entrepreneurship' in relationship to these? How does she do 'mothering' in relationship to these? What are the everyday/everynight practices allowing her to be an entrepreneur, for instance when she has Tiffany doing her spelling exercise on the cornmeal at work rather than the prior evening at home? And who are her employees? Where do they come from? What do they get paid?

Research of this nature may be done through ethnographic approaches, following the trajectories of Lisa's life, but many other sources of data would be important. For instance, analyses of historical relations of domination and subordination among countries need to be performed when considering why certain forms of employment (and the employees in those jobs) are lower paid than others. What naturalizes these jobs as low-paying? And how do entrepreneurs, who are also employers, contribute to this naturalization?

In summary, feminist theoretical tendencies gendering entrepreneurship theory and research would help reconsider 'entrepreneurship' not as 'the engine of economic development' that so many nations claim it to be, and instead observe it today as perhaps a remedy of last resort in exhausted capitalist economies when their traditional economic prescriptions and institutions no longer seem to work. These analyses might help to return the burden of creating economic opportunities and non-exploitative jobs to the hands of those who have the most power to do so: powerful economic actors, who might have disassociated from their (for example, corporate; public) responsibilities by also promoting 'the benefits of flexible employment' and the 'possibilities for individual success' emanating from mythical 'entrepreneurship'. In short, these considerations reveal the urgency of doing relational analyses regarding for whom and for what purposes entrepreneurship activities are good.

Further, 'gendering entrepreneurship' as analytical lens may help articulate explicitly what many assumptions underpinning 'women and entrepreneurship' research have often concealed: for instance, that lack of economic means in the family may be the primary reason for women starting a new business, rather than evading 'the glass ceiling' or attaining 'work–family balance'; that gender, sexual and racial discrimination, and the structural conditions that reproduce these problems may be a better explanation for lack of entrepreneurial success than any 'sex or gender difference'; that 'sex/gender differences' are the effect and not the cause of these same structural and discursive circumstances; and, that 'women's ways of...' may contribute to further exploitation and devaluation of women's entrepreneurial activities, by advancing a 'femininity' constructed under the 'masculine gaze' as a generic managerial tool. In short, these few examples would, we hope, suggest other critical questions that in our view need to be asked if 'gender and entrepreneurship' research were to offer *relevant knowledge* for a more just society, away from situations of women's and others' subordination.

References

Acker, J. (1990), 'Hierarchies, jobs, bodies: a theory of gendered organizations', *Gender & Society*, **4**(2), 139–58.
Acker, J. (1994), 'The gender regime of Swedish banks', *Scandanavian Journal of Management*, **10**(2), 117–30.
Acker J. (2004), 'Gender, capitalism and globalization', *Critical Sociology*, **30**(1), 17–41.
Acker, J. and D.R.Van Houten (1974), 'Differential recruitment and control: the sex structuring of organizations', *Administrative Science Quarterly*, **19**(2), 152–63.
Adib, A. and Y. Guerrier (2003), 'The interlocking of gender with nationality, race, ethnicity and class: the narratives of women in hotel work', *Gender, Work & Organization*, **10**(4), 413–32.
Ahl, H.J. (2004), *The Scientific Reproduction of Gender Inequality: A Discourse Analysis of Research Texts on Women's Entrepreneurship*, Frederiksberg: Copenhagen Business School.
Ahmed, S. (2000), 'Whose counting?' *Feminist Theory*, **1**(1), 97–103.
Alcoff, L.M. (1988), 'Cultural feminism versus post structuralism: the identity crisis in feminist theory', *Signs*, **13**(3), 405–36.
Aldrich, J., P.R. Reese and P. Dubini (1989), 'Women on the verge of a break-through: networking among entrepreneurs in the United States and Italy', *Entrepreneurship and Regional Development*, **1**, 339–56.
Allen, S. and C. Truman (1993), *Women in Business: Perspectives on Women Entrepreneurs*, New York: Routledge.
Ashcraft, K.L. (2001). 'Organized dissonance: feminist bureaucracy as hybrid form', *Academy of Management Journal*, **44**(6), 1301–22.
Baines, S. and J. Wheelock (2000), 'Work and employment in small business: perpetuating and challenging gender traditions', *Gender, Work & Organizations*, **7**(1), 45–56.
Baker, A.J. (1982), 'The problem of authority in radical movement groups: a case study of lesbian-feminist organization', *Journal of Applied Behavioral Science*, **18**(2), 323–41.
Balka, E. (1997), 'Participatory design in women's organizations: the social world of organizational structure and the gendered nature of experience', *Gender, Work & Organization*, **4**(2), 99–115.
Baxter, L. and C. Hughes (2004), 'Tongue sandwiches and bagel days: sex, food and mind/body dualism', *Gender, Work & Organization*, **11**(4), 363–80.
Belenky, M.F., B.M. Clinchy, N.R. Goldberger and J.M. Tarule, (eds) (1997/86), *Women's Ways of Knowing: The Development of Self, Voice and Mind. Tenth Anniversary Edition*, New York: Basic Books.
Bell, E.L.J. and S.M. Nkomo, (2001), *Our Separate Ways: Black and White Women and the Struggle for Professional Identity*, Boston, MA: Harvard Business School Press.
Benschop, Y. and M. Brouns (2003). 'Crumbling ivory towers: academic organizing and its gender effects', *Gender, Work & Organization*, **10**(2), 194–212.
Bird, B. and C. Brush (2002), 'A gendered perspective on organizational creation', *Entrepreneurship Theory & Practice*, Spring, pp. 41–65.
Black, N. (1989), *Social Feminism*, Ithaca, NY: Cornell University Press.
Brewis, J. (2001), 'Foucault, politics and organizations: (re)-constructing sexual harassment', *Gender, Work & Organization*, **8**(1), 37–60.

Britton, D.M. (2000), 'The epistemology of the gendered organization', *Gender & Society*, **14**(3), 418–34.

Brown, H. (1992), *Women Organizing*, London: Routledge.

Bruni, A., S. Gherardi and B. Poggio (2004a), 'Doing gender, doing entrepreneurship: an ethnographic account of intertwined practices', *Gender, Work & Organization*, **11**(4), 406–29.

Bruni, A., S. Gherardi and B. Poggio (2004b), 'Entrepreneur-mentality, gender and the study of women entrepreneurs', *Journal of Organizational Change Management*, **17**(3), 256–69.

Brush, C.G. (1992), 'Research on women business owners: past trends, a new perspective and future directions', *Entrepreneurship Theory and Practice*, **16**(4), 5–31.

Brush, C.G. (1997), 'Women-owned businesses: Obstacles and opportunities', *Journal of Developmental Entrepreneurship*, **2**(1), 1–24.

Brush, C., N. Carter, E. Gatewood, P. Greene and M. Hart (2004), *Clearing the Hurdles: Women Building High Growth Businesses*, London: Financial Times/Prentice Hall Books.

Butler J. (1992), 'Gender', in E. Wright (ed.), *Feminism and Psychoanalysis: A Critical Dictionary*, Oxford: Blackwell, pp. 140–45.

Butler, J. (1993), *Bodies That Matter: On the Discursive Limits of 'Sex'*, NY: Routledge.

Buttner, E.H. (2001), 'Examining female entrepreneurs' management style: an application of a relational frame', *Journal of Business Ethics*, **29**(3), 253–70.

Buttner, E. Holly and D.P. Moore (1997), 'Women's organizational exodus to entrepreneurship: self-reported motivations and correlates with success', *Journal of Small Business Management*, **35**(1), 34–46.

Calás M.B. and L. Smircich (1991), 'Voicing seduction to silence leadership', *Organization Studies*, **2**(4), 567–602.

Calás, M.B. and L. Smircich (1996), 'From "the woman's point of view": feminist approaches to organization studies', in S. Clegg, C. Hardy and W. Nord (eds), *Handbook of Organization Studies*, London: Sage, pp. 218–57.

Calás, M.B. and L. Smircich, (1999), 'Past postmodernism? Reflections and tentative directions', *Academy of Management Review*, **24**(4), 649–71.

Calás, M.B. and L. Smircich (2006, forthcoming), 'From "the woman's point of view" ten years later: towards a feminist organization studies', in S. Clegg, C. Hardy and W. Nord (eds), *Handbook of Organization Studies*, London: Sage.

Carter, N. and K.R. Allen (1997), 'Size determinants of women-owned businesses: choice or barrier to resources', *Entrepreneurship & Regional Development*, **9**, 211–20.

Carter, N. and M. Williams (2003), 'Comparing social feminism and liberal feminism', in J.E. Butler (ed.), *New Perspectives on Women Entrepreneurs*, Charlotte, NC: Information Age Publishing, pp. 25–50.

Carter, N., M. Williams and P. D. Reynolds (1997), 'Discontinuance among new firms in retail: the influence of initial resources, strategy, and gender', *Journal of Business Venturing*, **12**, 125–45.

Chaganti, R. (1986), 'Management in women-owned enterprises', *Journal of Small Business Management*, **24**(4), 19–29.

Chanter, T. (1998), 'Postmodern subjectivity', in A.M. Jaggar and I.M. Young (eds), *A Companion to Feminist Philosophy*, Malden, MA: Blackwell, pp. 263–71.

Chell, E. and S. Baines (1998), 'Does gender affect business "performance"? A study of microbusinesses in business services in the UK', *Entrepreneurship and Regional Development*, **10**, 117–35.

Chio, V.C.M. (1996), 'Boundaries and visibilities: anthropologizing women and work in the international economic arena', *Organization*, **3**(4), 627–40.

Chodorow, N. (1978), *The Reproduction of Mothering*, Berkeley, CA: University of California Press.

Cholmeley, J. (1991), 'A feminist business in a capitalist world', in N. Redclift and M.T. Sinclair (eds), *Working Women, International Perspectives on Labour and Gender Ideology*, London: Routledge, pp. 213–32.

Cliff, J.E. (1998), 'Does one size fit all? Exploring the relationship between attitudes towards growth, gender, and business size', *Journal of Business Venturing*, **13**, 523–43.

Cockburn, C. (1991), *In the Way of Women*, Ithaca, NY: ILR Press.

Colgan, F. and S. Ledwith (2000), 'Diversity, identities and strategies of women trade union activists', *Gender, Work & Organization*, **7**(4), 242–57.

Collins, P. H. (1998), 'It's all in the family: intersections of gender, race, and nation', *Hypatia*, **13**(3), 62–82.

Combahee River Collective (1977), 'A black feminist statement', in W. Kolmar and F. Bartkowski (eds), *Feminist Theory: A Reader*, Mountainview, CA: Mayfield, pp. 272–7.

Connell, R.W. (1995), *Masculinities*, Berkeley, CA: University of California Press.

Cowling, M. and M. Taylor (2001), 'Entrepreneurial women and men: Two different species?', *Small Business Economics*, May, **16**(3), 167–75.

Crenshaw, K. (1991), 'Mapping the margins: intersectionality, identity politics, and violence against women of color', *Stanford Law Review*, **43**(6), 1241–70.

Crompton, R. (ed.). (1999), *Restructuring Gender Relations and Employment*, Oxford: Oxford University Press.

Dalgic, U. (2005), 'Social capital, gender, and microfinance: the World Bank in the 1990s', paper presented at RC19 Annual Conference, International Sociological Association, Evanston, IL, USA.

Dexter, C. (1985), 'Book review: women in charge: the experiences of female entrepreneurs by Robert Goffee and Richard Scase', *Contemporary Sociology*, **16**(2), 179–80.

Dinnerstein, D. (1977), *The Mermaid and the Minotaur: Sexual Arrangements and Human Malaise*, New York: Harper.

Evans, J. (1995), *Feminist Theory Today*, London: Sage.

Eversole, R. (2004), 'Change makers? Women's microenterprises in a Bolivian city', *Gender, Work and Organization*, **11**(2), 123–42.

Fagenson, E. (1993), 'Personal value systems of men and women: entrepreneurs versus managers', *Journal of Business Venturing*, **8**(5), 409–30.

Ferguson, A. (1998), 'Socialism', in A. Jaggar and I.M. Young (eds), *A Companion to Feminist Philosophy*, Malden, MA: Blackwell, pp. 520–9.

Ferree, M.M. and P.Y. Martin (eds) (1995), *Feminist Organizations: Harvest of the New Women's Movement*, Philadelphia, PA: Temple University Press.

Fischer, E., A.R. Reuber and L.S. Dyke (1993), 'A theoretical overview and extension of research on sex, gender, and entrepreneurship', *Journal of Business Venturing*, **8**(2), 151–68.

Flax, J. (1990), *Thinking Fragments: Psychoanalysis, Feminism, and Postmodernism in the Contemporary West*, Berkeley, CA: University of California Press.

Florida, R. (2002), *The Rise of the Creative Class*, New York: Basic Books.

Folbre, N. (1994), *Who Pays for the Kids?: Gender and the Structures of Constraint*, London: Routledge.

Fraser, N. and L. Nicholson (1988), 'Social criticism without philosophy: an encounter between feminism and postmodernism', *Theory, Culture and Society*, **5**(2 & 3), 373–94.

Friedan, B. (1963), *The Feminine Mystique*, New York: Dell.

Friedan, B. (1981), *The Second Stage*, New York: Summit Books.

Gherardi, S. (1995), *Gender, Symbolism and Organizational Culture*, London: Sage.

Gherardi, S. (2003), 'Feminist theory and organization theory: a dialogue on new bases', in H. Tsoukas and C. Knudsen (eds), *The Oxford Handbook of Organization Theory*, Oxford: Oxford University Press, pp. 210–36.

Gilligan, C. (1982), *In a Different Voice*, Cambridge, MA: Harvard University Press.

Glenn, E.N. (1999), 'The social construction and institutionalization of gender and race: an integrative framework', in M.M. Ferree, J. Lorber and B.B. Hess (eds), *Revisioning Gender*, Thousand Oaks, CA: Sage.

Goffee, R. and R. Scase (1985), *Women in Charge: The Experiences of Female Entrepreneurs*, London: George Allen and Unwin Publishers.

Greene, P.G., C.G. Brush, M.M. Hart and P. Saparito (1999), 'Exploration of the venture capital industry: is gender an issue?', in P.D. Reynolds, W.D. Bygrave, S. Manigart, C.M. Madson, G.D. Meyer, H.J. Sapienza and K.G. Shaver (eds), *Frontiers of Entrepreneurship Research*, Babson Park, MA: Babson College, pp. 168–81.

Greer, M.J. and P.G. Greene (2003), 'Feminist theory and the study of entrepreneurship', in J.E. Butler (ed.), *New Perspectives on Women Entrepreneurs*, Charlotte, NC: Information Age Publishing, pp. 1–24.

Halford, S. and P. Leonard (2001), *Gender, Power and Organizations: An Introduction*, London: Palgrave.

Haraway, D. (1985), 'A manifesto for cyborgs: science, technology, and socialist feminism in the 1980s', *Socialist Review*, **80**, 65–107.

Harding, S. (1998), *Is Science Multicultural? Postcolonialisms, Feminisms, and Epistemologies*, Bloomington, IN: Indiana University Press.

Harding, S. (2004), 'A socially relevant philosophy of science? Resources from standpoint theory's controversiality', *Hypatia*, **19**(1), 25–47.

Hearn, J. (2004), 'From hegemonic masculinity to the hegemony of men', *Feminist Theory*, **5**(1), 49–72.

Helgesen, S. (1990), *The Female Advantage: Women's Ways of Leadership*, New York: Doubleday.

Hisrich, R.D. and C.G. Brush (1984), 'The woman entrepreneur: management skills and business problems', *Journal of Small Business Management*, **22**(1), 30–37.

Holmstrom, N. (ed.) (2002), *The Socialist Feminist Project: A Contemporary Reader in Theory and Politics*, New York: Monthly Review Press.

Hopkins, M.M. and D. Bilimoria (2004), 'Care and justice orientations in workplace ethical dilemmas of women business', *Group & Organization Management*, **28**(4), 495–517.

Hurley, A.E. (1999), 'Incorporating feminist theories into sociological theories of entrepreneurship', *Women in Management Review*, **14**(2), 54–62.

Hurtado, A. (1989), 'Relating to privilege: seduction and rejection in the subordination of white women and women of color', *Signs*, **14**(4), 833–55.

Iannello, K. (1992), *Decisions without Hierarchy: Feminist Interventions in Organization Theory and Practice*, London: Routledge.

Jaggar, A. (1983), *Feminist Politics and Human Nature*, Totowa, NJ: Rowman & Allanheld.

Kalleberg, A.L. and K.T. Leicht, (1991), 'Gender and organizational performance: determinants of small business survival and success', *Academy of Management Journal*, **34**(1), 136–61.

Kaplan, C. and I. Grewal (1999), 'Transnational feminist cultural studies: beyond the Marxism/poststructuralism/feminism divides', in C. Kaplan, N. Alarcón and M. Moallem (eds), *Between Woman and Nation: Nationalisms, Transnational Feminisms and the State*, Durham, NC: Duke University Press, pp. 349–63.

Kaplan, C., N. Alarcón and M. Moallem (eds) (1999), *Between Woman and Nation: Nationalisms, Transnational Feminisms and the State*, Durham, NC: Duke University Press.

Koedt, A., E. Levine and A. Rapone (eds) (1973), *Radical Feminism*, New York: Quadrangle Books.

Koen, S. (1984), 'Feminist workplaces: alternative models for the organization of work', Ph.D. dissertation, Union for Experimenting Colleges, University of Michigan Dissertation Information Service.

Kwolek-Folland, A. (1998), *Incorporating Women: A History of Women and Business in the United States*, New York: Twayne Publishers.

Liedtka, J. (1999), 'Linking competitive advantage with communities of practice', *Journal of Management Inquiry*, **8**(1), 5–16.

Lutz, H. (2002), 'At your service madam! The globalization of domestic service', *Feminist Review*, **70**(1), 89–104.

Lyotard, J.F. (1984), *The Postmodern Condition: A Report on Knowledge*, Minneapolis, MN: University of Minnesota Press.

McBride, A. (2001), 'Making it work: supporting group representation in a liberal democratic organization', *Gender, Work and Organization*, **8**(4), 411–29.

Marlow, S. (1997), 'Self-employed women – new opportunities, old challenges?', *Entrepreneurship and Regional Development*, **19**(3), 199–210.

Marlow, S. and A. Strange (1993), 'Female entrepreneurs: success by whose standards?', *Leicester Business Occasional Paper*, **11**, 1–16.

Martin, J. (1990), 'Deconstructing organizational taboos: the suppression of gender conflict in organizations', *Organization Science*, **1**(4), 339–59.

Martin, P.Y. (1990), 'Rethinking feminist organization', *Gender and Society*, **4**(2), 182–206.

Martin, P.Y. (2003), '"Said and done" versus "saying and doing": gendering practices, practicing gender at work', *Gender & Society*, **17**(3), 342–66.

Martin, P.Y. and D. Collinson (2002), 'Over the pond and across the water: developing the field of "gendered organizations"', *Gender, Work & Organization*, **9**, 244–65.

Méndez, J.B. and D.L. Wolff (2001), 'Where feminist theory meets feminist practice: border-crossing in a transnational academic feminist organization', *Organization*, **8**(4), 723–50.

Meyerson, D.E. (1998), 'Feeling stressed and burned out: a feminist reading and re-visioning of stress-based emotions within medicine and organization science', *Organization Science*, Jan/Feb, **9**(1), 103–18.

Miller, J.B. (1976), *Toward a New Psychology of Women*, Boston, MA: Beacon.

Mirchandani, K. (1999), 'Feminist insight on gendered work: new directions in research on women and entrepreneurship', *Gender, Work & Organization*, **6**(4), 224–35.

Mitchell, J. (1974), *Psychoanalysis and Feminism*, New York: Vintage Books.

Mohanty, C.T. (1991), 'Under western eyes: feminist scholarship and colonial discourses', in C.T. Mohanty, A. Russo and L. Torres (eds), *Third World Women and the Politics of Feminism*, Bloomington, IN: Indiana University Press, pp. 51–80.

Mohanty, C.T. (1997), 'Women workers and capitalist scripts: ideologies of domination, common interests, and the politics of solidarity', in J. Alexander and C.T. Mohanty (eds), *Feminist Genealogies, Colonial Legacies, Democratic Futures*, New York: Routledge, pp. 3–29.

Mohanty, C.T. (2003), *Feminism Without Borders: Decolonizing Theory, Practicing Solidarity*, Durham, NC: Duke University Press.

Monhanram, R. (1998), '(In)visible bodies? Immigrant bodies and constructions of nationhood in Aotearoa/New Zealand', in R. Du Plessis and L. Alice (eds), *Feminist Thought in Aotearoa/New Zealand: Connections and Differences*, Auckland: Oxford University Press, pp. 21–8.

Moore, D.P. (2004), 'The entrepreneurial woman's career model: current research and a typological framework', *Equal Opportunities International*, **23**(7/8), 78–99.

Moore, D.P. and E.H. Buttner (1997), *Women Entrepreneurs: Moving Beyond the Glass Ceiling*, Thousand Oaks, CA: Sage.

Moore, D.P., E.H. Buttner and B. Rosen (1992), 'Stepping off the corporate track: the entrepreneurial alternative', in U. Sekaran and E. Leong (eds), *Womanpower: Managing in Times of Demographic Turbulence*, Newbury Park, CA: Sage, pp. 85–110.

Morgen, S. (1994), 'Personalizing personnel decisions in feminist organizational theory and practice', *Human Relations*, **47**(6), 665–83.

Mumby, D.K. and L.L. Putnam (1992), 'The politics of emotion: a feminist reading of bounded rationality', *Academy of Management Review*, **17**(3), 465–86.

Nkomo, S. (1992), '"The emperor has no clothes": rewriting "race" in organizations', *Academy of Management Review*, **17**(3), 133–50.

Noddings, N. (1984), *Caring: A Feminine Approach to Ethics and Moral Education*, Berkeley, CA: University of California Press.

Ostrander, S.A. (1999), 'Gender and race in a pro-feminist, progressive, mixed-gender, mixed race organization', *Gender & Society*, **13**(5), 628–42.

Peiss, K. (1998), *Hope in a Jar: The Making of America's Beauty Culture*, New York: Owl Books.

Prokos, A. and I. Padavic (2002), '"There oughtta be a law against bitches": masculinity lessons in police academy training', *Gender, Work & Organization*, **9**(4), 439–59.

Reed, R. (1996), 'Entrepreneurialism and paternalism in Australian management: a gender critique of the "self-made" man', in D. Collinson, and J. Hearn (eds), *Perspectives on Men, Masculinities, and Management*, Thousand Oaks, CA: Sage, pp. 99–122.

Reskin, B.F and P.A. Roos, (1990), *Job Queues, Gender Queues: Explaining Women's Inroads into Male Occupations*, Philadelphia, PA: Temple University Press.

Riger, S. (1994), 'Challenges of success: stages of growth in feminist organizations', *Feminist Studies*, **20**(2), 275–300.

Rosa, P., D. Hamilton, S. Carter and H. Burns (1994), 'The impact of gender on small business management', *International Small Business Journal*, **12**(3), 25–32.

Rosener, J.B. (1990), 'Ways women lead', *Harvard Business Review*, November–December, 119–25.

Runté, M. and A.J. Mills (2004), 'Paying the toll: a feminist post-structural critique of the discourse bridging work and family', *Culture and Organization*, **10**(3), 237–49.

Smith, D.E. (1987), *The Everyday World as Problematic: a Feminist Sociology*, Toronto: University of Toronto Press.

Spivak, G.C. (1999), *A Critique of Postcolonial Reason: Toward a History of the Vanishing Present*, Cambridge: Harvard University Press.

Staggenborg, S. (1995), 'Can feminist organizations be effective?', in M. Ferree and P.Y. Martin (eds), *Feminist Organizations: Harvest of the New Women's Movement*, Philadelphia, PA: Temple University Press, pp. 145–64.

Stoller, E.P. (1993), 'Gender and the organization of lay health care: a socialist-feminist perspective', *Journal of Aging Studies*, **7**(2), 151–70.

Tolich, M. and C. Briar (1999), 'Just checking it out: exploring the significance of informal gender divisions amongst American supermarket employees', *Gender, Work & Organization*, **6**(3), 129–33.

Tong, R.P. (1998), *Feminist Thought: A More Comprehensive Introduction*, Boulder, CO: Westview.

Visweswaran, K. (1994), *Fictions of Feminist Ethnography*, Minneapolis, MN: University of Minnesota Press.

Ward, J. (2004), 'Not all differences are created equal: multiple jeopardy in a gendered organization', *Gender & Society*, **18**(1), 82–102.

Weedon, C. (1997), *Feminist Practice & Poststructuralist Theory*, Oxford: Blackwell.

Weiler, S. and A. Bernasek (2001), 'Dodging the glass ceiling? Networks and the new wave of women entrepreneurs', *The Social Science Journal*, **38**(1), 85–105.

West, C. and D.H. Zimmerman (1987), 'Doing gender', *Gender & Society*, **1**(2) June, 125–51.

Willis, E. (1975), 'The conservatism of *Ms.*', in Redstockings (ed.), *Feminist Revolution*, New York: Random House.

Yuval-Davis, N. (1997), *Gender and Nation*, London: Sage.

PART 2

CAREER AND WORK–LIFE ISSUES OF WOMEN IN BUSINESS AND MANAGEMENT

5 Career development of managerial women: attracting and managing talent[1]

Ronald J. Burke

During the past two decades, dramatic increases in the numbers of women entering the workforce and pursuing professional and managerial careers have had a major impact on the workplace (Burke, 2005). Although armed with appropriate education, training and years of experience, managerial and professional women have not made much progress in entering the ranks of senior management (Powell, 1999). They encounter what some have termed a glass ceiling (Morrison et al., 1987) or a glass escalator (Maume, 1999). Because women are now a significant component of the workforce, their recruitment and development is increasingly seen as a bottom-line issue related to corporate success (Burke and Mattis, 2005; Schwartz, 1992).

This chapter provides a selective review of content areas reported to have positive influences on the career development and retention of professional and managerial women and considers issues raised by these findings. Specific topics covered include: models of career development, different models of career development for women and men, work experiences and career development, developmental job experiences, developmental relationships, the opt-out revolution, alternative work arrangements and organizational initiatives supporting women's advancement.

Models of career development

Most researchers have taken the position that general models of career development should fit women as well as men, particularly if women are entering the same occupations and are similar to men in abilities and ambitions. Issues of child-rearing and family have been given little attention and it has been assumed that women would have successful careers by following the male model and by sharing child and home responsibilities with their partners (Hewlett, 2002a, 2002b). For dual-career families with children, two people now attempt to do the work of two careers and one homemaker role. Earlier in this century, before the influx of women into the workforce, two people managed one career and one home. Although some work in the home can be purchased by dual-career couples, research by Hochschild (1989) indicates that in such couples, women perform 30 extra 24-hour days per year of 'second shift' work, compared to their male partners. Clearly, not all of the traditional homemaker's work can be or is purchased. The dual-career couple has much left to do, and women do the bulk of it.

This difference, as well as findings from literature on the psychology of women, indicates that career development for women is different in some respects from career development for men (Mavin, 2000; Phillips and Imkoff, 1997; Stroh and Reilly, 1999). For example, work on the early career experiences of MBA graduates by Rosen et al. (1981) and by Cox and Harquail (1991) found that career motivation and the need for challenging work were similar for men and women, but women had fewer opportunities to share ideas and receive feedback by interacting with their supervisors. Bailyn (1989) reported, in a closely matched sample of male and female engineers, that women experienced their careers very differently from men, even though in external aspects they were similar. The women engineers reported less self-confidence and a less integrated view of their work and non-work lives.

Gallos (1989) contends that career theories have typically been built on male models of success and work in which there is an assumption of the centrality of work to one's identity and the notion that maturity involves separation from others. For women, attachment to others, not separation, is an important source of both identity and maturity and their development emphasizes the centrality of relationships, attachments and caring (Sturges, 1999). These affect how women view the world around them and how they choose to live their lives (Marshall, 1995). The success of a woman's career complements, rather than replaces, close interpersonal relations. Gallos believes that women express their professional selves over a lifetime, with commitment to accomplishment and a desire for a fair treatment and rewards for their efforts, rather than the ongoing organizational affiliation and life choices that put occupational progress first. Phases of development, for women, may not have the linear and predictable character of men's, and women may use a broader range of criteria for evaluating their choices than men (Ruderman and Ohlott, 2002).

To overcome the exclusion of family in the male model of career research, Lee (1993) has argued for a new approach to understanding women's careers, which includes the diversity of women's experiences in the workforce and in the family. She proposes six alternative models of women's careers to describe the most common ways women integrate commitment to work and family over the lifespan. Some sequence work and family, one first then the other; others try to combine high commitment to both; still others choose a particular type of work or family situation that makes combining the two easier. She also discusses the costs and benefits of each model for women themselves, the family, organizations and society. These various models of women's career development show great variety and diversity. It is important to appreciate and legitimize the different patterns that characterize women's commitment to occupation and family over the lifespan. The last phrase is critical; one must consider the lifespan perspective because many women change their levels of involvement and participation in employment and family (Gordon and Whelan, 1998).

Powell and Mainiero (1992) offer an approach to the understanding of women's careers that is significantly different from traditional models of men's careers. Their approach incorporates four unique elements: (1) it includes both non-work and work issues, (2) uses both objective and subjective measures of career success, (3) includes the influence of personal organizational, and societal factors on women's choices and outcomes, and (4) does not assume that women's careers go through a predictable sequence of stages over time.

Larwood and Gutek (1987) believe that a theory of women's career development must take five factors into account. These are: career preparation – how women are brought up to view a career and whether they believe they will have one or not, opportunities available to women and whether these are similar to those available to men, marriage, a plus or at least neutral for men, but a liability for women's careers, pregnancy and child-rearing, causing many women to take career breaks, and the effects of time and age on career breaks which result in different career patterns of timing compared to men. Therefore the process of career development most likely will be different for women than for men (Tharenou et al., 1994).

In conclusion, several writers (Phillips and Imkoff, 1997; Powell and Mainiero, 1992; White, 2000) conclude that women's career and life development involve a variety of choices and constraints, with both balance, connectedness and interdependence, and achievement and separation issues coming into play.

Different models of career advancement

There is accumulating research evidence supporting the notion of different models of career advancement for women and men. Kirchmeyer (1998), in a study of 292 mid-career managers, examined potential differential effects of four types of career success determinants among women and men. The four career success determinants were human capital variables, gender roles, supportive relationships and family status variables. Both subjective and objective measures of career success were included (income, organizational level and self-reported success). She hypothesized that the effects of human capital and interpersonal support would be stronger for men, the effects of gender roles would be stronger for women, and the effects of family status would be opposite for women and men in predicting objective career success indicators. She predicted, for perceived career success, that human capital measures would have stronger effects for men, gender role would have stronger effects for women, and that interpersonal and family status measures would have similar effects for women and men. Kirchmeyer found support for all hypothesized relationships with the exceptions of the family status measure, which was found to have similar effects for women and men.

Kirchmeyer (1998) reported that men and women indicated generally similar levels on the career determinants. Men and women indicated similar perceptions of career success as well. Women did have more career interruptions, fewer children, were less likely to be married, less likely to have a non-employed spouse and earned less money. Kirchmeyer was also able to explain more variance in men's career success than in women's.

Kirchmeyer (1999) later compared the career progression of men and women mid-career managers using a longitudinal research design. The groups of men and women were selected to have similar education and experience profiles. There was evidence that women's careers unfolded differently than men's, with gaps in income and number of promotions widening over time. Kirchmeyer measured change in progression from time of MBA graduation to the present and then change over the following four years. Three career success indicators were used: income, promotion and a subjective indicator of perceived career success. Five determinants of career success indicators were considered simultaneously: human capital, individual, interpersonal, relational demography and family. Although women and men earned the same incomes in the year of graduation, women reported less income progression since MBA graduation and less income change in the four years between these two measurement periods, as well as less likelihood of promotion. Perceived success at the two measurements showed no gender differences.

Kirchmeyer found that certain determinants of managerial success affected men and women differently. Training was associated with greater income for men, and job tenure had a positive effect on perceived success only for men. Women reported a lower payoff from education and experience than did men. Having a mentor had a positive effect only on men's income progression. Children lowered women's perceptions of success at both measurement points while they increased men's perception of success. Children also tended to have a positive effect on men's income change and a negative effect on women's. Kirchmeyer concludes, along with others (Gallos, 1989; Powell & Mainiero, 1992; Tharenou, 1990), that gender-specific career models are needed – trying to understand women's careers using the traditional male model is 'a case of comparing apples and oranges'.

Tharenou et al. (1994), in a sample of Australian managers, also concluded that career models tended to be gender-specific and they explained more variance for men's career progression than for women's. Four categories of determinants of career success have been considered in most of this work. *Human capital* determinants refer to personal investments one makes to increase one's value in the workplace (education, job tenure). *Individual* determinants include personality, levels of motivation and sex roles. *Interpersonal* determinants include supportive relationships (mentors, peers). *Family* determinants include family status variables that can affect careers (marital, parental).

Tharenou (n.d.) specifically tested gender-specific models of managerial advancement using a sample of 1682 female and 1763 male Australian managers. Four categories of determinants of career advancement were considered. Individual (age, education); interpersonal (for example, interpersonal support); organizational (for example, training); and home influences (for example, children, family interference with work). Tharenou used salary and managerial level in combination to reflect managerial advancement. Her model is comprehensive, containing relationships among variables common to women and men and relationships between some measures that are hypothesized to be different between women and men.

Her results showed that gender-specific models were required. More specifically women's education was found to lead to greater managerial advancement than men's, directly and through increased training. Women's training, however, led to fewer promotions than men's. Children was shown to reduce women's work experience and increase men's, and work experiences led to more promotions but less managerial advancement of women than men. Women's promotion was found to lead to less managerial advancement than men's.

Tharenou (n.d.) provides one of the few tests of an integrated model of women's career advancement. She suggests a sequenced interaction between individual male-typed traits, level of education, work experiences and responsibilities for children, and organizational career encouragement, training and promotion. Women had lower managerial advancement than men because of their lower human capital inputs of training and work experience, structural barriers in regard to promotion and training and the multiple roles of manager and mother. Finally, Stroh et al. (1992) studied the career progression of male and female managers employed by 20 *Fortune* 500 companies. All respondents had been geographically transferred for career advancement during the two years preceding the study. Women managers lagged behind men in both salary progression and frequency of job transfers. The women 'had all the right stuff' in terms of levels of education, similar levels of family power, working in similar industries, similar career gaps or exits, and willingness to make geographic moves. But those factors were not enough to equalize salary progression and numbers of geographic moves. Having the 'right stuff' (Stroh et al., 1992) ended up being more useful for men than for women. Stroh and her colleagues conclude there is little more that women can do. The responsibility and leverage for equalizing returns/benefits from having the 'right stuff' must rest with employers (see also Powell, 1999; Tharenou and Conroy, 1994).

Sturges (1999) identified four types of managers: climbers, experts, influencers and self-realizers. She believes that women are more likely to be experts or self-realizers. Experts define career success as being good at what they do and being recognized for this, while self-realizers define success in personal terms. Men are more likely to be climbers, defining success in terms of level of pay, and influencers, who define success in terms of their organizational influence or clout.

Vinnicombe and Bank (2003) conducted extensive interviews with 19 successful executive and entrepreneurial women, 16 of whom had won the prestigious Veuve Clicquot award for outstanding women's accomplishments. Ten key factors emerged from the journeys of the executive women: confidence, self-promotion, risk taking, visibility, career acceleration, mentoring, portfolio careers, international experiences, positive role models and a management style compatible with that of male colleagues.

These women held definitions of success that differed from those typically expressed by men. In addition, they exhibited a leadership style that seemed to be different from men's, a style that was distinctive for women but effective, and perhaps even more suited to current management challenges (Rosener, 1990; Sinclair, 1998; Helgesen, 1990).

Factors influencing women's career advancement

The literature identifies both individual and situational factors as important for career development (Tharenou and Conroy, 1994). Individual factors include women's attitudes towards career advancement, work-related demographics and early socialization experiences. Women's attitudes encompass high self-efficacy, a strong desire to succeed, a salient career identity, an internal attribution of success, and positive attitudes towards mobility and relocation. Work-related demographics include education and types of work experiences. Early career socialization is reflected in parental encouragement and maternal employment.

Situational factors usually consider two types: work and family. Work situation factors would include the old boys' network – a male-dominated culture, gender bias in training and development activities and attitudes of male decision makers towards women and their advancement. Family situation factors include marital and parental status and levels of spouse support.

Metz (2003) examined the relative importance of individual, interpersonal and organizational factors for women's advancement in management in banking in Australia. She collected data from 848 women using questionnaires. She found that women's advancement was mainly linked to individual factors. Specifically, training and development and years of work experience emerged as strong predictors of women's advancement, followed by work hours, occupation type, level of education and career opportunities.

Galinsky and her associates (2004) collected data from almost 1200 women and men executives working for 10 US-based multinational organizations in a number of countries. They found that high level women did not have to give up their personal or family lives. Many women (43 per cent) wanted to rise to executive management committees. But 34 per cent of women and 21 per cent of men have lowered their career aspirations, primarily for family and personal life; women thinking that there has been little progress in breaking the glass ceiling were more likely to lower their aspirations. Women executives were more likely than men executives to have made important life decisions in order to manage both their careers and personal lives. More women had working spouses than did men. More women delayed having children or decided not to have children. While men had higher aspirations than women, women too wanted career advancement.

Moen and Sweet (2002) looked at the career development of couples working for the same organizations. They considered both direct and indirect effects of being a co-worker on career development, work experiences, and spillover. They use the term 'linked lives' to capture the experiences of couples seeking to mesh their goals in work–family and their relationship. Co-working couples are likely to be more common in the future.

Their sample consisted of 250 co-working couples and 627 non co-working couples. Co-working was more likely to occur in the early child-rearing stage and among young non-parents. Co-working couples were likely to have met on the job. Co-working couples tend to treat each partner's careers with equal consideration. For men, being part of a co-working couple was associated with greater job prestige, longer tenure and greater work commitment (that is, working long hours, having a heavy workload). For women, being part of a co-working couple was associated with higher income and greater work–family spillover. Co-working appears to have stronger relationships with men's career development and women's work–family spillover.

Ng et al. (2005) considered four categories of predictors of both objective and subjective career success; human capital, organizational sponsorship, socio-demographic status and stable individual differences. Salary level and promotion were used as objective success indicators; career satisfaction serving as the subjective career success indicator. They found that both career success indicators were related to a wide range of predictors. Human capital and socio-demographic factors had stronger relationships with objective career success; organizational sponsorship and stable individual differences were more strongly related to subjective career success.

These four categories of predictors can be subsumed into the contest viewpoint and the sponsored-mobility viewpoint. The contest view suggests that one's abilities, competencies and job performance determine career success. The sponsored-mobility view suggests that sponsorship efforts by those higher in the organization determine career success. Ng and his colleagues conclude that both were important.

But are they equally important for women and men? Ng and his colleagues examined both gender and time (date of the study) as moderators of these relationships. They found some evidence that both gender and time since the original study (an indicator of increasing numbers of women in the workforce now than previously) moderated some of the relationships, occasionally opposite to expectations. For example, the education–salary and hours worked–salary relationship was stronger for women than men (contrary to expectations), the organizational tenure–salary relationship was weaker for women than men (as expected); the gender–salary relationship became weaker over time (as expected); but time did not moderate the gender–promotion relationship.

Work experiences and career development

Some light has been shed on the types of work experiences likely to be associated with women's career development. Morrison et al. (1987), in a three-year study of top female executives, identified six factors which contributed to the women's career success. These were: help from above; a track record of achievements; a desire to succeed; an ability to manage subordinates; a willingness to take career risks; and an ability to be tough, decisive and demanding. Three derailment factors were common in explaining the failure of some female managers to achieve expected levels. These were: inability to adapt; wanting too much (for oneself or other women); and performance problems.

Furthermore, to be successful, women, more than men, needed help from above, needed to be easy to be with, and to be able to adapt. These factors related to developing good relationships with men in a male-dominated environment (see also Ragins et al., 1998). Women, more than men, were also required to take career risks, be tough, have strong desires to succeed and have an impressive presence. These factors could be argued to be necessary to overcome the traditional stereotype of women such as being risk averse, weak and afraid of success. Unfortunately, the narrow band of acceptable behavior for women contained some contradictions. The most obvious of these were: take risks but be consistently successful, be tough but easy to get along with; be ambitious but do not expect equal treatment; and take responsibility but be open to the advice of others, that is more senior men. These findings suggest that additional criteria for success were applied to women so that women had to have more assets and fewer liabilities than men.

As part of the same study, Morrison and her colleagues (1987) also examined the experiences of women who had advanced to levels of general management. They identified four critical work experiences: being accepted by their organizations, receiving support and encouragement, being given training and developmental opportunities, and being offered challenging work and visible assignments. In speculating about their future success, these career-successful women perceived that there were even more constraints and less support now than in lower-level positions. Many reported exhaustion and talked about their futures involving doing something very different from what they were currently doing. In a series of follow-up interviews, Morrison et al. (1992) obtained information from approximately one-third of their original sample and found that although some women had made progress, many were still stuck.

The literature on work experiences and career development can be organized within a framework proposed by Morrison (1992). Her model for successful career development includes three elements which interact over time to spur and sustain development. These elements are challenge, recognition and support. This model is based on research with women in managerial practice and is consistent with her earlier work with McCall and Lombardo (McCall et al., 1988), which identified three work experiences with developmental value – specific jobs, other people and hardships. These can be recast as challenge, and presence or absence of recognition and support. McCall and his associates (1988) studied the kinds of experiences that develop managers and what makes them developmental. They found that five broad categories of experience had developmental potential (challenging jobs; other people, particularly bosses; hardships; course work; off-the job experiences) but that it was also important for the individual to have learned lessons from them. Learning was made possible, but not guaranteed, by these experiences.

Morrison defines the components of her model as follows. The *Challenge* of new situations and difficult goals prompts managers to learn the lessons and skills that will help them perform well at higher levels. *Recognition* includes acknowledgement and rewards for achievement and the resources to continue achieving in the form of promotions, salary increases and awards. *Support* involves acceptance and understanding along with values that help managers incorporate their career into rich and rewarding lives. This model assumes that all three elements must be present in the same relative proportions over time – balanced – to permit and sustain development.

Morrison proposes that, for women, an imbalance typically occurs such that the level of challenge exceeds the other two components. Her research shows that aspects of assignments and day-to-day life which constitute challenge are often overlooked, recognition may be slow, and traditional support systems may fall short. Common barriers to advancement (stereotypes, prejudices, male discomfort) contribute to this imbalance, and as a consequence managerial women become exhausted, experience failure and may 'bail out' of this frustrating work situation (White et al., 1992).

An important method for preparing individuals for executive jobs is to plan a sequence of assignments that provide continued challenge, for example for changing or rotating jobs every year or two. New assignments require the learning of new or better skills, broaden one's perspective, stretch the individual to develop and also serve as 'tests', by which individuals are rewarded, and/or promoted (Mainiero, 1994).

An interesting question becomes whether or not managerial and professional women experience the same developmental job demands and learn similar skills from them. One possible explanation for the 'glass ceiling' is that women are afforded different developmental opportunities than men over the course of their careers. McCall et al. (1988) and Horgan (1989) suggest that certain types of job assignments and challenging experiences are less available to women. For example, women may be offered staff, not line jobs, and jobs that are not high profile or challenging.

Some of these suggestions were supported by Ohlott et al. (1994) when they looked at the demands of managerial jobs and factors which may complicate learning from the job. They found that women experienced very different demands from managerial jobs and they had to work harder to prove themselves, but women were also learning about managerial work from a greater variety of sources than were men. Horgan (1989) also suggests that what is learned from a given set of developmental experiences may differ between men and women.

Although some sources of challenge are common to all managers (high stakes, adverse business conditions, dealing with staff members) women may experience additional challenges such as prejudice, isolation or conflict between career and personal life, and may also face higher performance standards, more adverse conditions (resentment and hostility of male staff), more scrutiny and more 'second-shift' work (Hochschild, 1989). Despite these things, limiting challenge is dangerous for the career advancement of women, since giving women less important jobs and not considering them for key assignments blocks their advancement by denying them important business experiences. Morrison (1992) advocates not reducing the level of job challenge but reducing demands from other sources – by reducing prejudice, promoting other women, using the same performance standards – and providing commensurate recognition and support so that the critical balance of these three items is retained.

Education, training and development can be conceived of as being either or both a challenge and support. To the extent that they may provide technical training, coaching and key assignments they represent a challenge and a chance to improve/prove oneself. To the extent that they may involve training geared to women, for example assisting women with issues unique to being women in male-dominated organizations or industries, or providing career pathing or mentoring, they could be viewed as support activities. Some activities, for example mentoring, clearly involve aspects of challenge and support.

Recognition involves acknowledging and adjusting to the additional challenges faced by women in organizations because they are women. Equal performance by men and women in a male-dominated organization may mean that women have overcome more, and this must be recognized. Furthermore, when contemplating a challenge such as a new task or promotion, women may seem less keen because they are aware of the additional challenge of being a woman performing that new task. The reward system must account for this. Morrison concludes that expected rewards fall short for women when one considers additional demands and sacrifices needed. Women are more likely to have the title 'acting' and do the job before getting it than are male colleagues, and receive fewer promotions and benefits and less pay than men (Morrison and Von Glinow, 1990). The forms that recognition takes include pay, promotion, prerequisites, inclusion in decision, respect and credibility and faith (Morrison, 1992). Statistics which indicate the continuing presence of a glass ceiling are evidence that recognition in the form of promotion has not been forthcoming for women.

Support is necessary to help women cope with the additional demands, and the absence of acceptance and colleagueship contributes to the isolation and discouragement that women feel (Morrison et al., 1987). Sources of support include features of the work environment such as mentors, sponsors, information feedback and networks as well as organizational and societal support for dual-career couples. Women may face additional unique challenges because of the scarcity of female role models, difficulty in getting feedback and a lack of acceptance and support (Morrison et al., 1987).

Developmental job experiences

Some progress has also been made in identifying specific developmental properties of jobs. Ohlott et al. (1994) compared male and female managers' experiences of developmental job demands and examined managerial skills learned from them. Their findings indicated that female managers were experiencing job demands to a greater extent than were male managers and that female managers were learning more from their experiences. 106 managerial women and 146 managerial men completed the Job Challenge Profile. Women scored higher than men on six scales (lack of top management support; lack of strategic direction; conflict with boss; downsizing/reorganization; achieving goals through personal influence; and establishing personal credibility). Men scored significantly higher than women on only one scale, supportive boss. Women also scored significantly higher than men on five of the seven 'complicating factors' (for example, not part of the organization's 'old boys'' network); men scored higher on one (no one higher in the organization was looking out for their careers). Interestingly women seemed to be learning more from their experiences than were men.

Van Velsor and Hughes (1990), in an interview study of 189 managerial men and 78 managerial women, also observed that women and men learned different things. Women were focused on discovering who they were as individuals in their organizations, on finding their niche and on integrating self with their business and working environments. Men focused on the acquisition and mastery of more specific business skills. This difference in emphasis may result from women having had less organizational experience. A number of factors (greater isolation, ambiguous criteria of what a good manager is) may also contribute to the more complex working environment women face, producing more 'personal' development.

Developmental relationships

The literature on careers suggests that mentors play a crucial role in career development and that they may be even more critical to the career success of women than men (Kanter, 1977; Kram, 1985; Gibson and Cordoba,

1999; Morrison et al., 1987). The literature reports that more women than men who advance to corporate management have mentors, and women who fail to reach these levels cite the absence of mentors as critical to their failure. Persons with mentors have been found to have more organizational policy influence and access to important people and resources (Fagenson, 1989) and higher promotion rates, income and income satisfaction (Dreher and Ash, 1990).

Although mentors are critical to the success of women, there is evidence that there may be a smaller supply of mentors available to women than men (Murrell et al., 1999). Women may have trouble finding mentors because they are different from men in more senior positions, they occupy a token status, and there may be potential discomfort in cross-gender relationships (Ragins, 1989). Noe (1988) identified six potential barriers to mentoring relationships involving women. These included lack of contact with potential mentors, high visibility of women as protéges due to their small numbers (tokenism), negative stereotypes making women unattractive as protéges, behavioral differences between men and women, women's use of non-male influence strategies and cultural and organizational biases with respect to cross-gender relationships. Mentor relationships that cross gender lines must be concerned about managing actual closeness and intimacy in the relationship, as well as the perception of those things by others in the organization (Clawson and Kram, 1984).

In addition to their role in career success, mentoring relationships may have a special role in improving the quality of organizational life for women (Ibarra, 2000). The literature suggests that one of the moderating variables which may influence the effect of stress on professional women is mentoring. Mentoring relationships have the potential to alleviate her stress by increasing the protége's self-confidence, forewarning her about career stress and suggesting ways to deal with it. In addition, female mentors provide unique role models for female protéges because they can more easily relate to the stresses that young women face – discrimination, stereotyping, and family/work interface, and social isolation (Nelson and Quick, 1985).

An additional source of organizational support may be peer relationships and interpersonal networks (Eby, 1997; Higgins and Kram, 2001; Kram and Isabella, 1985). Such networks may also be a source of challenging work and recognition; however, this discussion will focus on their role in support. It has been suggested that women lack access to informal networks with male colleagues – the 'old boys'' network (Ragins and Sundstrom, 1989; Ibarra, 1993). This may result for several reasons. Women may not be aware of informal networks and their importance and potential usefulness, they may not be as skilled as men in building informal networks, and may prefer to communicate with others similar to themselves. Men, being the dominant group, may want to maintain their dominance by excluding women from informal interactions. If women are, in fact, excluded from male networks, they may be missing several ingredients important for career success such as information, resources, support, advice, influence, power, allies, mentors, sponsors and privilege (Gibson, 2004; Higgins and Thomas, 2001).

Are women 'opting out'?

Increasing attention has recently been given to 'the opt-out revolution', a term used to describe the talent loss of highly trained women, mostly working mothers, who choose not to aspire to executive level positions. Women who first entered the managerial and professional workforce about 20 years ago thought they could combine a career and family. The difficulties in doing this have caused some women to give up their careers voluntarily.

A recent *New York Times* magazine article stated that more than a third of MBA women were not working full-time, about one quarter of mothers with graduate degrees were home full-time with children, fewer women with MBAs than men remained in the full-time workforce through to mid-career, and about one quarter of women within three levels of the executive tier were not interested in the CEO job.

Mainiero and Sullivan (2005) think the most likely explanation is a shift in how careers are viewed and used by women and an increasing number of men. Recent writing in the careers field has identified the boundaryless career; individuals are no longer bound by upward advancement within a single company, or by stability and security but instead seek self-fulfillment and work–family integration. Mainiero and Sullivan argue that women have pursued boundaryless careers for some time out of necessity.

Based on their research findings obtained in three studies, Mainiero and Sullivan concluded that men and women defined their careers differently. Women rejected the notion of a linear career and standard measures of achievement. They preferred instead non-traditional paths they themselves developed in response to barriers, challenges, opportunities and career interruptions. Men were more likely to pursue traditional linear careers.

They coined the term 'Kaleidoscope career' to refer to women's career models. Women's career histories were relational. Like the kaleidoscope that creates different patterns when the tube is turned, women alter the pattern of their careers by changing the priorities given to different aspects of their lives. As women's careers are relational, each career decision is necessarily considered in terms of how it will impact their relationships with others, they considered the needs of others as part of the totality of their career. A woman's context of relationships created the terms for career decisions made. Women desired to make their career suit their lives rather than letting their career take over their lives. Women worked to create a fit of work and family that was right for them in their particular circumstances.

Hewlett and Luce (2005) also build on the 'opt-out revolution' theme. They note the large numbers of qualified women leaving their careers, particularly women working in large organizations. They undertook a study of off-ramps (opting out) and on-ramps (returning to work). They surveyed 2443 women belonging to two age groups, 41–55 and 28–40, and a smaller group of 653 men in order to make gender comparisons.

They found that of those women who do leave corporate careers, almost 40 per cent of the women's sample had voluntarily left work at some point in their careers. Both push and pull factors were operating in these opting outs. The former included unsatisfying jobs (17 per cent); the latter included having children (over 40 per cent) and eldercare (24 per cent). Women and men use the off-ramp for different reasons – family for women, repositioning their careers for men.

Women who opt out generally plan to return to work (93 per cent), primarily for financial reasons such as having their own incomes and being independent and wanting to contribute to family finances. But many (43 per cent) also indicated the enjoyment and satisfaction they obtained from their careers as important reasons for returning as well. But only 74 per cent of off-ramped women manage to re-enter the workforce, and only 40 per cent of those that return to work, work full-time. It was difficult for these talented and motivated women to find on-ramps. Women in the business sector off-ramped for slightly over one year Women who returned to work in this sector experienced a 28 per cent drop in income; 18 per cent for women in the total sample. Women who spent three or more years out of the workforce indicated a 37 per cent drop in income.

Supporting women's career development

Work–family policies and programs
Kofodimos (1995) believes that work–family programs, though well intentioned, are not working very well. Most are not widely used and their presence often creates indifference and resentment among some employees. Kofodimos thinks these programs address the symptoms rather than the fundamental causes of work–personal life conflict.

Work–family programs emerged in response to some real and pressing organizational problems. These problems included: reducing barriers to productivity such as absenteeism and turnover, growing public relations and recruitment advantages, meeting the needs of women, single parents and dual-career couples, and responding to government legislation regarding equality, daycare and parental leave.

But work and family programs encounter difficulties. These include: a lack of top management support; they are not used by career-oriented and others afraid to use them or when using them become marginalized; a resistance on the part of supervisors to use them; a perception that work–family programs are costly and have few performance benefits; there is little or perhaps no evidence that women who use them benefit from their use. Rather than resolving work–family conflict, these programs merely reduce the effects of that conflict (the symptoms).

Organizations instead need to support work–personal life balance. This involves employees addressing and changing their mastery orientation. The goal for organizations is to support and enhance life balance. This involves changing the time and energy devoted to work, adopting collaborative and caring leadership and valuing personal development as much as organizational contribution.

Kofodimos describes a variety of interventions useful in changing to a balance-supportive culture. These include assessing the level of mastery orientation in the organization and the individual and organizational costs of this, developing a statement of purpose and vision for achieving balance, providing coaching for mastery-oriented managers, and ensuring that organizational policies and practices support balance.

Alternative work arrangements

It has been suggested that providing greater flexibility in how, when and where work gets done for short periods of time may be one way that organizations can support women's career advancement (Adams, 1995; Schwartz, 1992). Part-time work arrangements are one such option that has received increasing research attention.

MacDermid et al. (2000) examined 78 cases of women professionals and managers working on a reduced workload basis (RWL) for family or personal reasons. RWL was defined as voluntarily working 90 per cent of a normal workload or less with an accompanying reduction in pay. Most of the managers and professionals were satisfied with their jobs. Most (about two thirds) felt that the quality of their performance had been maintained or improved by working a RWL, and in most cases their managers agreed. About 20 per cent of the senior managers were rated by the researchers as supportive of the RWL arrangement.

Most of the managers and about half of the professionals were satisfied with the likely career implications of the RWL arrangement. Many thought they had given up some short-term advancements but were happy with the trade-off. About one third of the sample had been promoted while working RWL.

Some factors distinguished the most and least successful RWL arrangments as well. These included: external support (least successful RWL arrangements had uninterested managers and unsupportive corporate cultures). A supportive manager was the single most important factor critical for success of the RWL. A supportive corporate culture was also in the top five factors important to RWL success. Women in less successful RWL arrangements were more concerned about their slower career progress. They were less happy with the trade-off and less sure about how to make career progress. Women in both successful and less successful RWL arrangements shared common career development concerns as well. These included missing out on professional networking, being seen as less committed, hesitating to ask for more training and having less time for professional development.

Individual characteristics emerged as the most important success factors in making RWL arrangements work. Chief among them were flexibility, a strong performance record, and high levels of hard work and commitment. Individual women shouldered tremendous responsibility for their progress under these arrangements. It was clear, however, that RWL arrangements, if properly managed, need not be a career liability.

Organizational initiatives
The last ten years have been characterized by increased research attention being dedicated to examining women in management issues, an increasing awareness of the glass ceiling in the popular press and media, and yet only slow, hardly visible change in the number of women reaching positions of executive leadership.

Breaking the glass ceiling requires three types of information. First, it is vital to understand the obstacles women face in their advancement. Second, it is helpful to understand the career strategies used by successful women. Third, it is critical that CEOs have an accurate and complete understanding of the obstacles and cultures experienced by their female employees.

Ragins et al. (1998) report findings from a national survey of *Fortune* 1000 CEO's and the highest ranking, most successful women in their companies on the barriers to advancement women faced in their firms and the key career strategies women need to pursue to advance their careers. They report vastly different perspectives between the *Fortune* 1000 CEOs and the managerial women of organizational and environmental barriers faced by women and of their companies' progress in advancing women.

How do women break the glass ceiling? Ragins et al. found that nine career strategies were central to the advancement of these successful women executives, four standing out. These were: consistently exceeding performance expectations; developing a style with which men are comfortable; seeking difficult or high visibility assignments; and having an influential mentor.

These women had to repeatedly prove their ability by exceeding performance expectations. They also had to develop a managerial style acceptable to men, that was not too masculine or feminine. They needed challenging and highly visible job assignments, such assignments providing both growth and learning challenges. Finally, mentoring was identified as an important element in the career advancement of these successful women.

The CEOs revealed considerable consensus in their views as to what prevents women from advancing. The most common was women's lack of general management or line experience, followed by women not being in the pipeline long enough. The executive women had as their first factor, male stereotyping and preconceptions, followed by exclusion from influence networks. The CEOs and executive women had significantly different views on what was holding women back. CEOs say the problem is the women themselves; women saw it as a problem of corporate culture.

This disparity may result from the fact that two environments co-exist in organizations – one for men which explains their advancement, and one for women that has subtle barriers to their advancement. This disparity is important, however, since men are powerful agents of change in most organizations, and the way in which men frame the problem will define potential solutions.

These findings have implications for both organizations and the managerial and professional women they recruit, hire, utilize and develop. Organizations must realize that managerial and professional women, like men, are not homogeneous (Goffee and Nicholson, 1994; Ruderman and Ohlott, 2002). In addition, they must be more sensitive to work and family demands which, together, may be reducing the energy and time available for a single-minded career commitment and in fact adding to the challenge faced by women. Consideration must be given to the possibility of alternative career models in which commitment and energy over one's career may follow a different pattern for employees with primary responsibility for family and children (Gordon and Whelan, 1998). For example, early career commitment when women are single and childless may shift with the as yet unshared burdens of marriage and children, but re-emerge as children become less dependent. Perhaps organizations need to envision a restructured model in which people with primary family/child responsibility contribute later in their lives what others contribute earlier. At the present time these people are women whose life expectancy is several years greater than that of men. This differential longevity would, for example, permit a different career model in which interested women resume and continue career commitment later in their lives than men.

Other initiatives by organizations to rebalance the challenge–recognition–support model must specifically address the needs of women, and remove the barriers which contribute to the imbalance. Women need active organizational assistance and support in managing their careers. It has been found (Lee, 1993) that more, and more varied, patterns exist in the careers of women than of men. Women face more choices when it comes to investments in work, investments in family, and the timing of children. Men are influenced by these choices too, but women still experience more dislocation from particular events and usually undertake more second-shift work. Women's choices need to be legitimized and assisted by organizations. It is clear that this second-shift work is not done by free choice in most cases. To say that women choose the 'mommy track' or 'choose' more flexibility over career development activities, is to avoid discussion of the environment in which this choice occurs. We do not know how women would feel about a variety of career development activities if they could make that decision in an environment of at least equally shared second-shift work. If they had the flexibility they wanted/needed and we asked them again about career development activities, how would they respond? What employees bring to the workplace is dramatically influenced by their personal circumstances. Situational characteristics are relevant in attitudes to and energy for work, and we know from the work of Hochschild (1989) and others that the situational characteristics of women with families are dramatically different from those of men. How organizations respond to these different realities will determine how successful they are in assessing what educated women have to offer at various times in their lives. Organizations with long-run views of their relationships with their employees need to consider the present and future realities of their employees' lives and respond creatively and with their employees' input (Bailyn, 1994).

More recently researchers have begun to describe and evaluate more intensive collaborative projects with organizations interested in addressing work–family concerns. These projects make an explicit link between employee's personal needs (for example, family responsibilities) and business objectives with the intention of changing work practices so that both the organization and the employees benefit (Rapaport et al., 1998). The work of Bailyn and her colleagues describes several 'collaborative action research projects' in which researchers work jointly with companies to bring about change in the work culture and the organization of work that would facilitate work–family integration in a meaningful way (Bailyn et al., 1997; Fletcher and Bailyn, 1996; Fletcher and Rapaport, 1996).

A pressing need in this regard is to document efforts by organizations to develop the talent of women managers and professionals. This will serve to identify what works and does not work, and why. In addition, the successful efforts of some organizations will provide a blueprint for others in their own efforts. Efforts by organizations in this area will be more credible to senior corporate leaders. It is also important to have successful CEOs committed to full partnership for women at senior ranks, so that they can influence others at those levels.

Conclusions

We have achieved some understanding of the challenges and obstacles women face in the workplace (and home front) as they pursue their career journeys. We have also gained a clearer sense of the types of work and career experiences that are likely to be associated with women's advancement (many of which are also likely to be associated with men's advancement as well). We have begun to document 'best practice' initiatives among corporations interested in utilizing the talents of all employees, but more attention and effort must be placed here.

A clear gap in the research literature is the limited attention paid to interventions. Although there is substantial agreement on the problems and challenges women face in the development of their careers, there are few descriptions and evaluations of initiatives designed to support the career development of professional and managerial women over the life span.

Another gap in the research is the limited knowledge of 'what happens' as women at work exhibit changes and transition as they grapple with multiple life roles. More attention has been paid to supporting women's advancement (for example, Catalyst, 1998) resulting in less attention devoted to understanding how women prepare for the variety of choices they make in navigating the challenges of organizational life and various life roles. Women's lives, even more than men's, are complex.

Note

1. Preparation of this chapter was supported in part by the Schulich School of Business, York University. Louise Coutu prepared the manuscript.

References

Adams, S.M. (1995), 'Part-time work: models that work', *Women in Management Review*, **10**, 21–30.
Bailyn, L. (1989), 'Understanding individual experience at work: comments on the theory and practice of careers', in M.B. Arthur, D.T. Hall and B.S. Lawrence (eds), *Handbook of Career Theory*, New York: Cambridge University Press, pp. 477–89.
Bailyn, L. (1994), *Breaking the Mold*, New York: The Free Press.
Bailyn, L., J.K. Fletcher and D. Kolb (1997), 'Unexpected connections: considering employees' personal lives can revitalize your business', *Sloan Management Review*, **38**, 11–20.

Burke, R.J. (2005), 'High achieving women: programs and challenges', in R.J. Burke and M.C. Mattis (eds), *Supporting Women's Career Advancement: Challenges and Opportunities*, Cheltenham, UK and Northampton, MA, USA: Edward Elgar, pp. 13–30.

Burke, R.J. and M.C. Mattis (2005), *Supporting Women's Career Advancement: Challenges and Opportunities*, Cheltenham, UK and Northampton, MA, USA: Edward Elgar.

Catalyst (1998), *Advancing Women in Business: The Catalyst Guide*, San Francisco, CA: Jossey-Bass.

Clawson, J.G. and K.E. Kram (1984), 'Managing cross-gender mentoring', *Business Horizons*, **17**, 22–32.

Cox, T.H. and C.V. Harquail (1991), 'Career paths and career success in the early career stage of male and female MBA', *Journal of Vocational Behavior*, **29**, 54–75.

Dreher, G.F. and R.A. Ash (1990), 'A comparative study of mentoring among men and women in managerial, professional and technical positions', *Journal of Applied Psychology*, **75**, 539–46.

Eby, L.T. (1997), 'Alternative forms of mentoring in changing organizational environments: a conceptual extension of the mentoring literature', *Journal of Vocational Behavior*, **51**, 125–44.

Fagenson, E.A. (1989), 'The mentor advantage: perceived career/job experiences of protégés versus non-protégés', *Journal of Organizational Behavior*, **10**, 309–20.

Fletcher, J.K. and L. Bailyn (1996), 'Challenging the last boundary: re-connecting work and family' in M.B. Arthur and D.M. Rousseau (eds), *Boundaryless Careers*, Oxford: Oxford University Press.

Fletcher, J.K. and R. Rapaport (1996), 'Work–family issues as a catalyst for change', in S. Lewis and J. Lewis (eds), *Rethinking Employment: The Work–Family Challenge*, London: Sage Publications.

Galinsky, E. et al. (2004), *Leaders in a Global Economy: A Study of Executive Women and Men*, New York: Families and Work Institute.

Gallos, J.V. (1989), 'Exploring women's development: implications for career theory, practice and research', in M.B. Arthur, D.T. Hall and B.S. Lawrence (eds), *Handbook of Career Theory*, New York: Cambridge University Press, pp. 110–32.

Gibson, D.E. (2004), 'Role models in career development: new directions for theory and research', *Journal of Vocational Behavior*, **645**, 134–56.

Gibson, D.E. and D.J. Cordoba (1999), 'Women's and men's role models: the importance of exemplars', in A.J. Murrell, F.J. Crosby, and R.J. Ely (eds), *Mentoring Dilemmas: Developmental Relationships Within Multicultural Organizations*, Mahwah, NJ: Erlbaum, pp. 121–42.

Goffee, R. and N. Nicholson (1994), 'Career development in male and female managers – convergence or collapse?', in M.J. Davidson and R.J. Burke (eds), *Women in Management*, London: Paul Chapman, pp. 80–92.

Gordon, J.R. and K.S. Whelan (1998), 'Successful professional women in mid-life: how organizations can more effectively understand and respond to the challenges', *Academy of Management Executive*, **12**, 8–24.

Helgesen, S. (1990), *The Female Advantage*, New York: Doubleday.

Hewlett, S.A. (2002a), *Creating a Life: Professional Women and the Quest for Children*, New York: Talk Miramax Books.

Hewlett, S.A. (2002b), 'Executive women and the myth of having it all', *Harvard Business Review*, **80**(4), 66–73.

Hewlett, S.A. and C.B. Luce (2005), 'Off-ramps and on-ramps: keeping talented women on the road to success', *Harvard Business Review*, March, pp. 43–54.

Higgins, M.C. and K.E. Kram (2001), 'Reconceptualizing mentoring at work: a developmental network perspective', *Academy of Management Review*, **26**, 264–88.

Higgins, M.C. and D.A. Thomas (2001), 'Constellations and careers: toward understanding the effects of multiple developmental relationships', *Journal of Organizational Behavior*, **22**, 223–42.

Hochschild, A. (1989), *The Second Shift*, New York: Avon Books.

Horgan, D.D. (1989), 'A cognitive learning perspective in women becoming expert managers', *Journal of Business and Psychology*, **3**, 299–313.

Ibarra, H. (1993), 'Personal networks of women and minorities in management', *Academy of Management Review*, **18**, 56–87.

Ibarra, H. (2000), 'Making partner: the mentor's guide to the psychological journey', *Harvard Business Review*, 147–55.

Kanter, R.M. (1977), *Men and Women of the Corporation*, New York: Basic Books.

Kirchmeyer, C. (1998), 'Determinants of managerial career success: evidence and explanation of male/female differences', *Journal of Management*, **24**, 673–92.

Kirchmeyer, C. (1999), 'Women's vs men's managerial careers: is this a case of comparing apples and oranges?', paper presented at the 1999 Annual Meeting of the Academy of Management, Chicago.

Kofodimos, J.R. (1995), *Beyond Work–Family Programs: Confronting and Resolving the Underlying Causes of Work–Personal Life Conflict*, Greensboro, NC: Center for Creative Leadership.

Kram, K.E. (1985), *Mentors in Organizations*, Chicago, IL: Scott, Foresman.

Kram, K.E. and L. Isabella (1985), 'Mentoring alternatives: the role of peer relationships in career development', *Academy of Management Journal*, **28**, 110–32.

Larwood, L. and B.A. Gutek (1987), *Towards a Theory of Women's Career Development*, Newbury Park, CA: Sage.

Lee, M.D. (1993), 'Women's involvement in professional careers and family life: themes and variations', *Business in the Contemporary World*, **5**, 106–27.

MacDermid, S.M., M.D. Lee, M. Buck and M.L. Williams (2000), 'Alternative work arrangements among professionals and managers: rethinking career development and success', *Journal of Management Development*, **20**, 305–17.

Mainiero, L.A. (1994), 'Getting anointed for advancement: the case of executive women', *Academy of Management Executive*, **8**, 53–67.

Mainiero, L.A., and S.E. Sullivan (2005), 'Kaleidoscope careers: an alternative explanation for the opt-out revolution', *Academy of Management Executive*, **19**, 106–23.

Marshall, J. (1995), *Women Managers Moving On: Exploring Career and Life Choices*, London: Routledge.

Maume, D.J. (1999), 'Glass ceilings and glass escalators', *Work and Occupations*, **26**, 483–510.

Mavin, S.I. (2000), 'Approaches to careers in management: why UK organizations should consider gender', *Career Development International*, **5**, 13–20.

McCall, M.W., M.M. Lombardo and A.M. Morrison (1988), *The Lessons of Experience*, New York: Lexington Books.

Metz, I. (2003), 'Individual, interpersonal, and organizational links to women's advancement in banks', *Women in Management Review*, **18**, 236–51.

Moen, P. and S. Sweet (2002), 'Two careers, one employer: couples working for the same corporation', *Journal of Vocational Behavior*, **61**, 466–83.

Morrison, A.M. (1992), *The New Leaders*, San Francisco, CA: Jossey-Bass.

Morrison, A.M. and M.A. Von Glinow (1990), 'Women and minorities in management', *American Psychologist*, **45**, 200–208.

Morrison, A.M., R.P. White and E. Van Velsor (1987), *Breaking the Glass Ceiling*, Reading, MA: Addison-Wesley.

Morrison, A.M., R.P. White and E. Van Velsor (1992), *Breaking the Glass Ceiling*, (2nd edn), Reading, MA: Addison-Wesley.

Murrell, A.J., F.J. Crosby and R.J. Ely (1999), *Mentoring Dilemmas: Developmental Relationships with Multi-Cultural Oganizations*, Mahwah, NJ: Lawrence Erlbaum.

Nelson, D.L. and J.D. Quick (1985), 'Professional women: are distress and disease inevitable?', *Academy of Management Review*, **10**, 206–18.

Ng, W.H., L.T. Eby, K.L. Sorensen and D.C. Feldman (2005), 'Predictors of objective and subjective career success: a meta-analysis', *Personnel Psychology*, **58**, 367–408.

Noe, R.H. (1988), 'Women and mentoring: a review and research agenda', *Academy of Management Review*, **13**, 65–78.

Ohlott, P.J., M.N. Ruderman and C.D. McCauley (1994), 'Gender differences in managers' developmental job experiences', *Academy of Management Journal*, **37**, 46–67.

Phillips, S.D. and A.R. Imkoff (1997), 'Women and career development', *Annual Review of Psychology*, **48**, 31–59.

Powell, G.N. (1999), 'Reflections on the glass ceiling: recent trends and future prospects', in G.N. Powell (ed.), *Handbook of Gender and Work*, Thousand Oaks, CA: Sage Publications, pp. 325–46.

Powell, G.N. and L.A. Mainiero (1992), 'Cross-currents in the river of time: conceptualizing the complexities of women's careers', *Journal of Management*, **18**, 215–37.

Ragins, B.R. (1989), 'Barriers to mentoring: the female manager's dilemma', *Human Relations*, **42**, 1–22.

Ragins, B.R. and E. Sundstrom (1989), 'Gender and power in organizations: a longitudinal perspective', *Psycholgical Bulletin*, **105**, 51–88.

Ragins, B.R., B. Townsend and M. Mattis (1998), 'Gender gap in the executive suite: CEOs and female executives report on breaking the glass ceiling', *Academy of Management Executive*, **12**, 28–42.

Rapaport, R., L. Bailyn, D. Kolb and J.K. Fletcher (1998), *Rethinking Life and Work*, Waltham, MA: Pegasus Communications.

Rosen, B., M.E. Templeton and K. Kinchline (1981), 'The first few years on the job: women in management', *Business Horizons*, **24**, 26–9.

Rosener, J.B. (1990), 'Ways women lead', *Harvard Business Review*, December, pp. 199–225.

Ruderman, M.N. and P.J. Ohlott (2002), *Standing at the Crossroads: Next Steps for High-Achieving Women*, San Francisco, CA: Jossey-Bass.

Schwartz, F.N. (1992), *Breaking with Tradition*, New York: Time-Warner Books.

Sinclair, A. (1998), *Doing Leadership Differently*, Melbourne: Melbourne University Press.

Stroh, L.K. and A.H. Reilly (1999), 'Gender and careers: present experiences and emerging trends', in G.N. Powell (ed.), *Handbook of Gender and Work*, Thousand Oaks, CA: Sage Publications, pp. 307–24.

Stroh, L.K., J.M. Brett and A.H. Reilly (1992), 'All the right stuff: a comparison of male and female managers', *Journal of Applied Psychology*, **77**, 251–60.

Sturges, J. (1999), 'What it means to succeed: personal conceptions of career success held by male and female managers at different ages', *British Journal of Management*, **10**, 239–52.

Tharenou, P. (1990), 'Psychological approach for investigating women's career advancement', *Australian Journal of Management*, **15**, 363–78.

Tharenou, P. (undated manuscript), 'Managerial advancement: a confirmatory test of gender-specific models', School of Business and Economics, Monash University, Melbourne, Australia.

Tharenou, P. and D. Conroy (1994), 'Men and women managers advancement: personal or situational determinants', *Applied Psychology: An International Review*, **43**, 5–31.

Tharenou, P., S. Latimer and D. Conroy (1994), 'How do you make it to the top? An examination of influences on women's and men's managerial advancement', *Academy of Management Journal*, **37**, 899–931.

Van Velsor, E. and M.W. Hughes (1990), *Gender Differences in the Development of Managers: How Women Managers Learn from Experience*, Technical Report 145, Greensboro, NC: Center for Creative Leadership.

Vinnicombe, S. and J. Bank (2003), *Women With Attitude: Lessons for Career Management*, London: Routledge.

White, B. (2000), 'Lessons from the careers of successful women', in M.J. Davidson and R.J. Burke (eds), *Women in Management*, Thousand Oaks, CA: Sage Publications, pp. 164–76.

White, B., C. Cox and C.L. Cooper (1992), *Women's Career Development: A Study of High Flyers*, Oxford: Basil Blackwell.

6 Women and success: dilemmas and opportunities

Margaret M. Hopkins and Deborah A. O'Neil

In today's changing societal and organizational environments, traditional notions of what constitutes successful careers are open to interpretation. Definitions and measurements of success abound. There are subjective and objective as well as individual and organizational measures of success (Melamed, 1995; Sturges, 1999). Subjective measures of success incorporate internal individual perspectives, a person's level of job satisfaction and sense of accomplishment. Objective ways of examining success include observable career accomplishments which can be measured by upward mobility and/or salary level. Objective success measures have been the norm for decades. However, research suggests that hierarchical constructions of career success are becoming increasingly obsolete (Sullivan, 1999). As Hall (1996, p. 1) notes 'the career as a series of upward moves with steadily increasing power, income, status and security has died.'

In this chapter we will explore whether changing definitions of success have kept pace with changing notions of careers. We will discuss what success means to women, and explore the things that hinder and facilitate women in their quest to succeed. For many women there is no strict line of demarcation between work and life and they are striving to define career success on their own terms incorporating personal, professional, internal and external measurements. Changing notions of career development reflect the fact that careers and life are no longer as distinctly separate as they were once thought. Concepts such as kaleidoscope careers (Mainiero and Sullivan, 2005), protean careers (Hall, 1976, 1996), boundaryless careers (Arthur, 1994; Arthur and Rousseau, 1996), portfolio lives (Handy, 1989) and career development as personal development (Vinnicombe and Colwill, 1995) are becoming increasingly prevalent. Derr (1986) describes a career as 'having a sense of direction that comes from the individual careerist and because it is long term, must acknowledge and respect aspects of personal life that have an impact on work life' (p. 5).

The following sections will address how women perceive success and how they integrate their careers with the other aspects of their lives. In addition critical factors that impact women and their success, recommendations for future research, and the implications for organizations as well as for women in management will be examined.

Perceptions of career success

As women continue to assume management positions, face glass ceilings or exit organizations altogether, the question of women's perspectives on success is especially germane. As Gallos (1989, p. 110) noted in her call for re-examining the traditional male notion of career success, 'implicit in women's different vision of reality is the potential for questioning present beliefs about what is essential for a creative and productive society, and how to chart a successful course to manage life's critical adult challenge – the balance between love and work.'

Women's definitions of career success encompass personal definitions and subjective elements, incorporating the multiple interactions among personal, relational and organizational factors. For example, in a study of male and female managers' perceptions of career success, Sturges (1999) identified four distinct managerial types: climbers, experts, influencers and self-realizers. Experts and self-realizers were the types associated more with women, while climbers was the type associated more with men. Influencers were fairly evenly split by gender. The experts defined career success as skill, expertise and recognition. Self-realizers described career success as achievement and development on their own terms as well as integrated, balanced personal and professional lives. In contrast climbers defined career success in terms of the more traditional, hierarchical, status-conscious organizational constructions of success, while influencers identified their ability to impact others as central to their constructions of career success.

Career success or failure can vary according to the traditional male 'corpocratic' career model or the newer female 'lifestream' career model (O'Leary, 1997). The corpocratic model is a process of linear, hierarchical progression. The lifestream model contains a more holistic framework representing the interplay between work, relationships, organizational factors and various lifestages. In the lifestream model success is measured in both personal and professional arenas in terms of degree of challenge, satisfaction and a sense of growth and development.

Research on the career choices of professional women has found that women want to make things better for others and look for opportunities to do so through their professional and personal relationships, volunteering in their communities and in their organizations (O'Neil, 2003; O'Neil and Bilimoria, 2005a). They also expect to be compensated fairly, recognized and rewarded for their work. The authors found that this was true of women of all ages, in the early, middle and later stages of their careers. Women's definitions of success and achievement rely on internal criteria such as a sense of contribution, personal fulfillment and integrity, as well as external, tangible measures such as compensation and title. Women consider themselves successful when they are engaged in work that contributes to the organizational bottom line and more.

Generation X women in technology fields (Feyerherm and Vick, 2005) define professional success as 'being valued for their involvement in the business and impact on business results,' and personal fulfillment as 'an internal feeling of joy, happiness, and contentment that comes from close connections with family and friends which energize them and encourage them to renew their sense of purpose and drive' (p. 220). An interesting finding in this study was that 70 per cent of the Generation X women sampled, linked personal fulfillment with professional success. Themes of making a difference, relationships, learning and growing, and challenge or the opportunity to excel were present in these women's definitions of both success and fulfillment, suggesting that the personal and the professional are inextricably entwined. In a Catalyst study of Generation X workers (2001), family or personal goals were rated higher than career goals, and 76 per cent of Generation Xers wanted shorter working weeks while 59 per cent sought flexible work options.

Theories of women's development propose that relational, contextual elements are critical to women's experiences (Chodorow, 1978; Gilligan, 1982; Jordan et al., 1991; Miller, 1976). These perspectives necessitate a closer examination of the impact of contextual elements on women's careers. Applying constructs from women's psychological theory to women's careers suggest that women's definitions of success are likely to involve success in connection and relation to important personal and professional others (Fletcher, 1996; Fletcher, 1999; Gallos, 1989, Jordan et al., 1991; Kram, 1996), highlighting the highly permeable boundary between women's personal and professional lives (Fletcher and Bailyn, 1996) as the findings from previous studies attest to (for example, Feyerherm and Vick, 2005; O'Neil and Bilimoria, 2005a). Bailyn (1989) proposed that careers exist in the space between the individual and the collective level of analysis. Thus the hierarchical 'organization man' (Whyte, 1956) conceptions of career development and career success would seem to be inappropriate and inadequate models for explaining many women's experiences.

Theory building and testing of women's career success continues to draw heavily on frameworks and conceptions derived from male constructions of work and careers. For example, over-reliance on measures such as income to determine women's career success offers an incomplete picture. As we have noted, women's own definitions of success may have less to do with externally defined, traditionally male, corporate criteria and may more likely rely on internal criteria such as a sense of personal achievement, integrity and balance (Sturges, 1999). Kirchmeyer's (1998, 2002) and Dann's (1995) investigations, for instance, found that although women earned lower incomes than men, they perceived their careers to be as successful. Although some recent studies have begun to employ respondents' own personal definitions of success (for example, Kirchmeyer, 1998, 2002; O'Neil and Bilimoria, 2005a; Poole and Langan-Fox, 1997), the bulk of empirical studies continue to rely predominantly on traditional (male) career outcomes and externalized definitions of success such as income, wealth accumulation and position within the corporate hierarchy. This bias toward objective success criteria may continue to disadvantage and marginalize women who are operating out of an expanded set of criteria for leading successful lives.

Theories that address the complex choices and constraints in women's career and life development, and issues of authenticity, balance and challenge (Mainiero and Sullivan, 2005), connectedness and interdependence as well as achievement and individuation are needed (Powell and Mainiero, 1992, 1993). Powell and Mainiero's conceptualization of 'cross currents in a river of time' provides a framework for viewing women's careers that takes into account non-work issues, subjective measures of success and the impact of personal, organizational and societal factors on women's choices.

Factors impacting women and success

Empirical studies examining women, career success and organizational advancement primarily fall into three broad thematic areas, identified by O'Neil and Bilimoria (2005a, 2005b) as the impact of gender stereotypes and discrimination on women's career success, work–family considerations and the resulting balancing act for women, and women's access to developmental opportunities. Additionally, a fourth theme of women 'opting out' of traditional career paths (Belkin, 2004) may be identified as having implications for women in organizations. All four themes have direct effects on women's personal and professional success. Gender stereotypes and discrimination result in negative economic, social and psychological consequences for women seeking success, resulting in a halt to their career progression and an undermining of their level of job satisfaction, for example. The second thematic area, the management of work–family considerations, has consistently rested on the shoulders of women. Women's attention to both work and family often places them at a disadvantage in the workplace, for women are more likely to experience career interruptions and consequently to be viewed as less committed to their careers. The third theme, women's access to developmental opportunities, demonstrates the career importance of these opportunities to expand work experiences, skills, competencies and networks. Women have less access to challenging work assignments than do men, which often limits their career progression as well as their career satisfaction. Finally, the fourth theme of empirical work on women and career success, that of women 'opting out' of traditional career paths, demonstrates the movement of women out of conventional organizations. The opt-out phenomenon reveals how women are attempting to define success in their own terms. As Mainiero and Sullivan (2005) suggest, understanding the reasons women leave organizations 'requires an examination of the complex interplay between non-work demands and lack of advancement opportunities for women' (p. 107).

An exploration of the current state of research on women and success in each of these four thematic areas follows, including suggestions for further investigation.

(1) Gender stereotypes and discrimination

Both men and women perceive successful managers as male. A 'think manager, think male' (Schein, 1976; 2001) stereotypical view of management was identified decades ago and still persists today (Heilman et al., 1995; Heilman et al., 1989; Karau and Eagly, 1999; Metcalfe and Altman, 2001).

Many management skills are seen through the lens of gender stereotypes and valued differently when enacted by men or by women (Butterfield and Grinnell, 1999; Merrill-Sands and Kolb, 2001). Decision makers are more likely to evaluate males more favorably than females demonstrating equivalent performance (Bartol, 1999). Alimo-Metcalfe (1995, p. 3) argued that there was an 'insidious gender bias with regard to the assessment of leadership in organizations...' In one study of the influence of sex stereotypes on perceptions of managers, successful women managers were seen as more hostile than women in general while successful male managers were seen as less hostile than men in general (Heilman et al., 1995). The belief of think manager, think male remains embedded in our society, and both men and women continue to describe successful managers as having predominantly masculine characteristics (Powell et al., 2002).

A prevalent theme emerging from research indicates that women in managerial roles believe they are expected to outperform their male counterparts in order to be perceived as successful. A Center for Creative Leadership study (Van Velsor and Hughes, 1990) of male and female leaders reported that the females were focused on establishing their credibility and on finding their niche while the males attended to mastering certain business competencies. Women executives reporting their career strategies for success indicated similar findings (Ragins et al., 1998). To consistently exceed performance expectations and to develop a style that was comfortable for men were the two most frequently cited success strategies for women. In contrast, the chief executive officers in the same study believed that the dearth of women in management was due to a lack of experience or a shortage of women in the pipeline.

The gap of career progression, one traditional measure of success, between female and male managers has been found to be sizeable. One study reported that women had done 'all the right stuff' in order to advance themselves, following a traditional male model of career advancement (Stroh et al., 1992). Yet pursuing this male model had not eliminated the discrimination against them. Women in another study, despite their superior performance on six of seven performance dimensions measured, did not receive superior ratings on their overall potential nor did they advance at a faster rate than men (Shore, 1992).

These findings suggest that additional criteria for success are applied to women vs. men. They raise the question as to whether gender bias may influence the assessments, judgments and decisions about women in the workplace. 'It seems that because women often are expected to be less effective than men in management situations, they must prove that they are more effective than men in terms of at least some performance criteria. An imagined sex difference has apparently led to some real differences in performance expectations' (Morrison et al., 1992: 54).

In summary the profile of a successful manager remains one who is dominant, rational, competitive, independent, self assured and high in achievement orientation (Fagenson, 1990; Offermann and Beil, 1992). Since the predominant characterizations of women are in contrast to these descriptions, women are at a disadvantage (Fagenson, 1990) due to persistent gender stereotypes and discrimination.

Decades of research findings have demonstrated the existence of pervasive gender stereotypes and discrimination. This profound body of knowledge has contributed to our understanding of these practices and their impact on women in the workforce. It is essential to continue exposing the traditions and habits that hinder women's ability to be successful. At the same time the primary challenge for future research agendas may be to determine the connections between this body of literature and concrete actions or policy changes. A significant value added to the existing research would be to examine ways to move the research findings closer to practical applications in organizations.

(2) Work–family considerations
In our society work–family considerations have consistently been the concern of women more so than men. The interface of work and family has been found to be more important to women and relates to both their

job satisfaction and life satisfaction (Rothbard, 2001). Rothbard (2001) found that emotion was an important mediator between work and family roles for women, and that women compensated for any negative family issues by working harder.

Women's ability to succeed in organizations while maintaining their family responsibilities and the influence of women's family structure on their career advancement and success have been focal areas of research inquiry (Friedman and Greenhaus, 2000; Hewlett, 2002; Kirchmeyer, 2002; Schneer and Reitman, 2002; Stroh et al., 1996). Women's roles and responsibilities within the family structure has been found to hold them back in their careers (Burke, 1999; 2002; Vinnicombe and Singh, 2003) and women experience more career interruptions than men (Kirchmeyer, 1998). One investigation of dual-employed couples found that women's work–family relationships were unidirectional and static, with family taking precedence, while men's were reciprocal and dynamic (Tenbrunsel et al., 1995). Both men and women have experienced enrichment between work and family roles but in opposite directions: men from work to family and women from family to work. Yet only women have experienced depletion between roles in the direction of work to family (Rothbard, 2001).

Multiple role commitment for managerial women has been found to relate positively to life satisfaction, self-esteem and self-acceptance (Ruderman et al., 2002). Women personally benefit from multiple roles and positively transfer the skills developed in their family lives to their work lives.

Nevertheless there is substantial evidence to suggest that women's multiple roles are not rewarded organizationally (Brett and Stroh, 1999; Burke, 1999, Hopkins, 2004; Kirchmeyer, 2002). Research on work–family conflict (Netemeyer et al., 1996; Osterman, 1995) and work-family culture (Thompson et al., 1999) has linked the tension inherent in occupying multiple roles as well as organizational support for work–family integration to employees' job commitment and satisfaction. Women's career satisfaction has been found to be adversely affected by work–family conflict (Martins et al., 2002) suggesting that any examination of women and work must take into account a woman's larger life context and the interaction effects of work and life variables.

Definitions of career success continue to be based on the traditional male model of continuous employment and advancement which does not adequately reflect the broader scope of women's responsibilities (Mavin, 2001; McDonald et al. 2005; Pringle and Dixon, 2003). In their study of over 2000 women professionals, Hewlett and Luce (2005) found that 58 per cent of high achieving women described women's careers as non-linear. However, as Schneer and Reitman (2002) note, organizational realities continue to be structured around the traditional 1950s family. Hewlett (2002) takes the point even farther in suggesting that women intent on motherhood must give up their careers, or that women intent on career achievements must give up motherhood because in today's organizational environments successfully embracing the two are incompatible. As Schwartz (1992, p. 4) bluntly stated at the end of the 1980s 'two facts matter to business: only women have babies and only men make the rules.'

In conclusion, responsibility for work–family considerations remains predominantly women's domain. Managerial women face both personal and professional challenges in their attempts to balance these two roles with negative psychosocial (that is job satisfaction, self esteem) and economic (that is career advancement) implications. For women to consider themselves successful, they must succeed in the areas of their lives that they value, not just those organizationally or hierarchically defined. Yet organizational systems and practices are still operating on the reality of family structures in place decades ago which do not reflect the current realities of families and work.

Future investigations of success should be theoretically conceptualized and empirically examined to reflect women's multiple perspectives and multiple measures of success. The construct of success for women needs to be more holistically defined to incorporate women's life experiences in multiple arenas. Objective and subjective measures, internal and external aspects, human capital and social capital factors each inform our understanding of success for women. Conducting research that includes all of these variables will provide a dynamic perspective of what makes women's lives satisfying, fulfilled and ultimately successful. Researchers can take direction from Poole's and Langan-Fox's (1997, p. 1) call for 'a more contextualist and life course approach to understanding women's careers, orientations and successes.' Studies pursuing personal factors, professional factors and the elements of women's careers and lives that combine to impact women's success will provide a more robust picture of success for women.

(3) Access to developmental opportunities

Of primary importance to the career success of managers are the opportunities they are provided to develop their skills and to demonstrate their abilities to others. Over two decades ago Helen Astin (1984) proposed a sociopsychological model of career choice and work behavior to make sense of women's and men's occupational choices. Astin's model had four key elements: motivation, sex-role socialization, structure of opportunity and expectations. She proposed that motivation did not differ by gender, but suggested that work expectations would because of differential socialization and structures of opportunity. While the structures of opportunity for women have expanded over the last 20 years, there remains a significant gender gap in access to important developmental opportunities such as mentoring, networking and obtaining challenging assignments (that is critical line management roles and international experience) that theorists cite as facilitators of organizational advancement and success for women (Hewlett and Luce, 2005; Linehan and Walsh, 2000; Lyness and Thompson, 2000; Ragins et al., 1998; Vinnicombe and Singh, 2003).

Mentoring is defined as an ongoing relationship with a senior colleague (Kram, 1985), an individual with advanced experience who provides support and assistance with upward mobility in an organization. Mentoring has been acknowledged as an effective developmental tool (Higgins and Kram, 2001; Kram, 1985; Ragins and Scandura, 1994), leading to positive outcomes such as career development (Kram, 1985), career progress and mobility (Dreher and Ash, 1990; Scandura, 1992), career satisfaction (Fagenson, 1989) and clarity of professional purpose (Kram, 1985). Executives often credit their professional success to the guidance of a mentor, and individuals who have mentors are often more satisfied, more highly paid and have more interpersonal competence (de Janasz et al. 2003).

Mentors can be especially important for women in organizations, as they provide advice and assistance regarding success factors in their professions (Burke and McKeen, 1990; Ragins, 1989) and how to overcome barriers to advancement (Kanter, 1977). Women cite assistance from above as the number one factor contributing to their success while men refer to their track record (Morrison et al., 1992). Mentors serve as models of behavior, demonstrating what is considered successful conduct in an organization (Dreher and Ash, 1990), and afford access to professional and social networks not readily available to women through formal channels of communication. This access allows women to exhibit their talents, skills and abilities to a wider and more influential audience.

There are two primary mentoring functions: a career-related support function that focuses on advancement and a psychosocial function that attends to enhancing a manager's sense of competence, identity and effectiveness (Kram, 1985). Particularly for women, the psychosocial function may be critical to their ability to excel in organizations that are likely to be male dominated. Given the importance of mentoring for organizational advancement, it seems reasonable to suggest that for women whose definitions of success include professional development and advancement, mentors will be important sources of guidance and support for achieving their professional and personal goals.

In addition to mentors, networking is a critical activity for women's career success and well-being. Networking provides both social support and internal visibility. Women rely on work relationships as sources of learning and development (Van Velsor and Hughes, 1990) and for instrumental and emotional support (Ibarra, 1993). Women have cited the ability to work with people they respect and have the opportunity to collaborate with others and work as part of a team as essential factors for workplace success (Hewlett and Luce, 2005). A high level of subjective career success has been positively related to the degree of networking done by employees (Nabi, 1999). However, a positive relationship between networking behaviors and promotions and salary progression was found to be more beneficial for men than for women (Forret and Dougherty, 2004).

Similar to access to mentors, women are at a disadvantage because they are often not in influential positions and have less access to individuals in influential roles, thereby limiting their networking abilities. A common strategy used by women is to develop a differentiated network that includes individuals from different social circles, one network providing social support and the other connecting to important organizational resources (Ibarra, 1993). This strategy may result in the expansion of women's networks, but there are also potential costs such as added stress and time involved in managing a differentiated network. The demographic composition of an organization affects personal networks by predetermining the alternatives available for women (Ibarra, 1997). Often the dominant group excludes women altogether and thus limits the possibilities for women managers to gain access to organizational networks that are so critical for advancement and success (Lyness and Thompson, 2000).

Obtaining challenging assignments such as important line management positions and international experience are additional key ingredients for successful organizational advancement. Yet women have a more difficult time attaining these assignments (Adler and Izraeli, 1994; Linehan and Walsh, 1999). In one study that examined the perceptions of women's obstacles to advancement held by senior women and male CEOs, vast differences were found (Ragins et al., 1998). Ninety-four per cent of the women in the study noted that seeking difficult or high visibility assignments was either a critically or fairly important career advancement strategy, and 82 per cent of the CEOs noted that a lack of key line or managerial experience was responsible for holding women back. While some of the CEOs suggested that women were less willing to make sacrifices to obtain challenging assignments, others noted the presence of more subtle forms of discrimination that resulted in men getting the training and opportunities that led to the higher level assignments.

To sum up, the experience of women has been that developmental opportunities such as access to mentors, networks and high visibility, challenging assignments are extremely useful but are either not commonly available or quite different from those offered to men (Burke and McKeen, 1994; Van Velsor and Hughes, 1990). Seeking difficult and visible assignments and having influential mentors are key success strategies identified by male managers. In contrast, female managers report that they must first exceed performance expectations in order to be noticed (Ragins et al., 1998). Since access to developmental opportunities is granted predominantly through the support of more senior managers or mentors in organizations, women are likely to be underrepresented in challenging assignments and senior managerial roles. As long as women have limited access to powerful organizational sponsors and mentors they will be seen as less organizationally successful. Lack of access to these types of professional opportunities will continue to leave women striving in vain for senior management positions.

Additional recommended areas of research inquiry include identification of the facilitators as well as the barriers to women's access to developmental opportunities. What are the antecedents that result in expanded access to critical mentors, networks and challenging assignments for women? These investigations should incorporate individual behaviors on the part of women and other key individuals in organizations such as the decision makers, as well as any contributing organizational structural factors. While existing research has focused on the barriers to women's access to developmental opportunities, there is a need for an examination of the variables that assist women as well. It is also important to continue exploring the complexities of those roadblocks women face while attempting to develop and advance their careers.

(4) Women 'opting out'

Of late, the popular press is replete with articles suggesting that highly educated, (objectively) successful women are choosing to 'opt out' (Belkin, 2004) or 'stop out' (Wallis, 2004) of organizational careers. A broad range of statistical evidence from varied research forums suggests that at any given point, from one fifth to one half of highly educated, professional women are not in the workforce (Belkin, 2004; Hewlett and Luce, 2005; Schneer and Reitman, 1995; Wallis, 2004), and that women are leaving the corporate world at twice the rate of men (Donahue, 1998). A decade ago Judi Marshall (1995) discussed this phenomenon in her book, *Women Managers Moving On*, suggesting that organizational structures and processes did not fully allow women to bring their best selves into their organizational roles. She found that this resulted in women at middle and senior levels of organizations moving on to more entrepreneurial ventures.

The primary reasons women leave organizations to start new ventures are due to a need for more challenge and self-determination, family concerns, blocks to advancement and organizational dynamics (Moore and Buttner, 1997). Women entrepreneurs have departed organizations because of a lack of flexibility, glass ceiling issues, unhappiness with their working environments and a lack of challenge (A Catalyst–National Association of Women Business Owners survey in 1998 in Moore, 2000, p. 43). According to the US Small Business Administration, there are currently 9.1 million women-owned businesses employing 27.5 million people that contribute $3.6 trillion to the economy (SBA, 2005).

Another explanation for the recent exodus of women from the organizational world is focused on issues of motherhood and child rearing. As one woman who chose to stay at home when her daughter was born explains, 'maternity provides an escape hatch that paternity does not. Having a baby provides a graceful and convenient exit' (Belkin, 2004, p. 43). There is some evidence that a younger generation of women raised by dual employed parents is choosing a different path to motherhood. They have seen the sacrifices that their parents made and they are not interested in simultaneously trying to juggle career and parenting (Story, 2005). There is some sense of a backlash on the 'women can have it all' model, that women are reverting back to the 1950s model of working only until they become wives and mothers and then exiting the workforce to raise children. Many women who leave organizational positions to raise families eventually do decide that owning their own businesses can provide them with a level of flexibility and control over their time that the organizational world cannot.

Women are also disadvantaged by societal pressures that paint feminine characteristics in opposition to career ambition (Fels, 2004). Ambition is problematic for women but not for men who see ambition as 'necessary and desirable' while women 'fear' it (Fels, 2004: 31). When women began entering the workforce in larger numbers decades ago, the same question concerning women fearing success was raised. In competitive situations women were found to fear success because of its incongruence with the traditional female role (Ward, 1978). Women 'walk away from their dreams' because of powerful cultural imperatives that do not see ambition and femininity as compatible (Fels, 2004). Any characteristics that conflict with traditional notions of femininity get downplayed or discarded resulting in women leaving their jobs, or focusing on aspects of their lives other than careers, that is, family, in order to remain more in line with societal expectations of acceptable behavior for women.

> Women who pursue careers must cope with jobs structured to accommodate the life cycles of men with wives who don't have full-time careers. And they must suffer the social pressure to fulfill more traditional, 'feminine' roles. It's a situation that still creates unnecessarily agonizing choices. Too often, when the choice must be made, women choose to downsize their ambitions or abandon them altogether (Fels, 2004: 37).

The interaction of organizational roles with gender roles poses dilemmas for women in management (Hopkins, 2004). Gender roles are socially-constructed phenomena that help as well as hinder people's ability to be successful (Eagly, 1987). Subtle messages about what is acceptable behavior for women are often sent through the lens of expected gender roles. The expected gender role for female leaders inside the organization is similar to the role they play outside the organization, taking primary responsibility for 'raising the family' and caring for others. The demands of the organizational role compel successful female managers to concentrate on ways of behaving which are incongruent with their gender-expected roles. The gender role expectations and the managerial role expectations for men are mirror images of each other, because the normative profile of managers has been predominantly characteristic of men. Women must manage the inherent tensions and contradictions between these two roles. This is a difficult balancing act for women, and only those who are able to manage it are successful according to the normative standards of success (Morrison et al., 1992).

Push and pull factors lead to women taking career off-ramps (Hewlett and Luce, 2005). Push factors are unsatisfying or meaningless jobs. Pull factors are those life circumstances that pull women away from their careers such as children, elderly parent care and personal health issues. In contrast men take off-ramps far less often and for far different reasons such as switching careers, obtaining additional training or starting businesses (Hewlett and Luce, 2005).

An alternative to the 'opt out' phenomenon, kaleidoscope careers, has been proposed by Mainiero and Sullivan (2005). They posit that women leave the workforce because of a complex set of intersecting factors that include lack of advancement opportunities, family concerns and changing generational value systems. These authors found that women did not follow traditional, linear career models but 'self-crafted careers that suited their objectives, needs and life criteria' (p. 109), 'blending and integrating rather than segregating the work and non-work facets of their lives, while striving to obtain greater job challenge and personal fulfillment' (p. 110). Context matters to women in making career decisions. At the heart of a kaleidoscope career is the 'ABC model" (p. 115) which highlights questions of authenticity, balance and challenge that shift over time and become more or less salient depending on life stage and life context. For women in early career stages, challenge would be figural, and balance and authenticity, while active, would stay in the background. For mid-career women, balance moves into the foreground, with issues of family and relationships taking precedence. Women in later career stages are more focused on issues of authenticity as balance and challenge become less relevant. The kaleidoscope career model suggests that women's definitions of career success are likely to take into consideration the complex, changing dynamics of full lives well lived over a life span.

In summary, feminists of the 1960s and 1970s struggled for decades to achieve equal opportunity in the workplace and employment choices for women. Perhaps few envisioned that the choices at the beginning of the new millennium would be those of opting or stepping out of organizational hierarchies. Clearly organizations have not provided women with the structures to support alternatives to the traditional full-time employment model of the 'organization man' (Whyte, 1956). This suggests that organizations continue to organize for work that is non-supportive and disadvantageous to women who seek to combine career and family meaningfully and successfully. If women's definitions of success encompass both the personal and the professional spheres, and organizational expectations are focused solely on professional performance, there will continue to be an exodus of talented women from the workforce. In addition, as long as organizations fail to attend to the professional aspect of women's lives, neglect to find challenging work opportunities for women and persist in allowing stereotypes and discriminatory practices, women will continue to find alternate means of fulfillment and success.

The 'opting out' course of research presents a negative image of women leaving organizations because they can't succeed in the male-dominated world. Current research indicates that women are exiting organizations for a variety of reasons. Reframing future research studies to reflect what women are moving toward, as opposed to what women are leaving, would contribute to a richer understanding of women's conceptualizations of success. How are women redefining career and life success on their own terms? What goals are women pursuing when they choose to exit traditional organizational roles? What contributions are women making in their new ventures?

Given that more and more women are leaving traditional organizations for alternative career and life directions, it is important to understand the impact of this movement on our social structures. Future research streams should consider the sociological effects of this new development in addition to the psychological effects on women. What bearing does this change have on work–life balance issues, for example? Are new organizational structures occurring as a result? Studies answering these and additional questions focusing on the macro perspective would assist our understanding of the impact these changes are having now and will continue to have on our society for decades to come.

Implications for women

Empirical research suggests that women define work and success on their own terms, more holistically, whether they work inside or outside of the corporate organizational structure. It is imperative then that women continue to offer alternative models of success and assist other women in doing the same so that organizations have examples of work lives managed differently but no less successfully. The chasm between organizational and individual success definitions can only be bridged by positive experiences of alternatives. Women can do three important things to change this dynamic. First, they must work together to lobby for organizational policies that recognize and support the multiple aspects of their lives. Second, and equally important, women in leadership positions must continue to make the case that organizations must level the career playing field not just because it is the right thing to do but because it is vital to organizational sustainability and competitiveness over the long term. Third, women must continue to seek the sponsorship of men at senior organizational levels who have the power to enact changes in policies, attitudes and behaviors throughout the organization.

The role tensions between women's professional and personal experiences may to a greater or lesser degree be experienced by all women, but we would like to make clear that the choices to reframe successful working lives to minimize these tensions are only available to the limited few with financial and relational means of support. For women with limited incomes, education and family support, choices such as opting out, working part time or starting their own businesses are likely to be out of reach. This means that many women have no choice but to manage their multiple roles the best they can and hope that their organizations support them in doing so. We propose that the organizations that figure out how to do that well will be rewarded with loyal, successful women workers.

Women's career and life needs change over the course of their lives (Mainiero and Sullivan, 2005; O'Neil and Bilimoria, 2005a) and women need to demand organizational support for these changing needs to ensure that they will always be able to offer their best talents, skills and ideas to their organizations. Women in the early stages of their careers need to demand mentoring, coaching and sponsorship in order to develop their skills and abilities and become full contributing organizational members. Women in the middle stages of their careers, a stage that Levinson (1996) suggests may be when the 'myth of the successful career woman' (p. 370) collides with societal and organizational realities resulting in a re-evaluation of life, work and relationships, need to demand flexible work arrangements and supportive management practices. Women in later career stages must demand opportunities to apply their years of experience garnered in multiple roles to mentor and develop younger workers, especially women, as a way of adding value and feeling valued. Talented women at each stage of their careers must demonstrate to their organizations the benefits of having vitally contributing organizational members at all career stages and organizational levels (O'Neil and Bilimoria, 2005a).

Implications for organizations

Much has been written about new forms of careers being protean (Hall, 1996) and boundaryless (Arthur, 1994), and yet it seems that women who have traditionally fashioned careers out of the rich fabric of their lives and composed their careers (Bateson, 1990) in ways that reflect their multiple roles and responsibilities are still viewed as less successful. Biases inherent in the organizational model of success are apparent when we examine the gendered language surrounding women's career choices. Notions that women are 'opting out' (Belkin, 2004), taking career 'off-ramps' (Hewlett and Luce, 2005), and lacking ambition (Fels, 2004) reflect a corporate or organizational framework as the only legitimate path to success. Organizations would do well to adopt the kaleidoscope view of careers and provide women with the opportunities to embrace authenticity, balance and challenge (Mainiero and Sullivan, 2005) throughout the course of their careers by recognizing that women's career and life priorities interweave in a complex pattern over the course of their working lives (O'Neil and Bilimoria, 2005a). Creative, flexible, alternative career paths for women must be framed as equally viable options for becoming successful, fully contributing organizational citizens instead of those who are less committed, less responsible and just plain less than.

Organizations would also do well to encourage intrapreneurship (Pinchot, 1985) particularly for women. In this global, highly-competitive economy, change is the essence of modern-day companies. Cultivating an innovative environment is a vital strategic priority for organizations. It is important for organizational leaders to foster a culture that promotes creativity, innovation and empowerment. Intrapreneurship leads to new knowledge, skills and opportunities for employees and results in added value for the employee as well as the organization.

Organizational intrapreneurship may be especially critical for women. One of the things we know from the data on women and work is that organizations are losing talented women. They are losing them because women want challenging developmental opportunities, they want more autonomy over their lives, and they want to feel valued for the life experience and creative problem-solving capabilities they bring to their work roles (Moore, 2000). Organizational intrapreneurship may well contribute to addressing these particular issues for women in organizations. Identified factors for supporting intrapreneurial behaviors include the support of management, autonomy on the part of the employees, and rewards or reinforcements to enhance people's innovative behavior (Hornsby et al., 1993). Thus intrapreneurship will have an effect on retaining the talents of women and expanding creativity and innovation within organizations. If organizational structures don't acknowledge women's holistic images of success and provide opportunities for them to be successful within their organizations, women will continue to exercise their talents entrepreneurially instead of intrapreneurially and become the organizational competitors of the future.

Women may find challenge and satisfaction in entrepreneurial and alternative paths but they are still deemed unsuccessful if they leave organizational life. Perhaps instead of framing the current debate from an 'opt out' perspective we should be framing it from an 'opt in' perspective. Women are opting into meaningful, challenging, more flexible opportunities via entrepreneurial ventures and potentially creating the organizational forms of the future. Given this trend, conceivably the smaller, more nimble and adaptable businesses that women are creating will indeed become the organizations of the future, outpacing and replacing the bureaucracies of old. If there are limited incentives for women to meet their holistic needs for success by working in their current organizations, the empirical evidence suggests that they will not hesitate to create their own.

Organizational reward structures that honor multiple views of success and reflect the needs of all employees are necessary to keep accomplished women invested in their organizations. Talented women are important for the organizational bottom line and organizations must not dis-incentivize those who seek to balance their professional and personal lives. Legitimizing flexible work arrangements and compensating outcomes, not face time, are ways to engender employee satisfaction and loyalty. Although work–life policies have proliferated over the last decade, there is still a nagging sense that employees who take advantage of them will be seen as less committed and less effective overall in their careers (Burke, 1999; Schwartz, 1996). Until organizations truly demonstrate their support and commitment for alternative work arrangements, women are likely to continue to be disadvantaged in traditional organizational roles.

There is substantial evidence that gender discrimination and stereotypes are still operating in current organizational contexts. Organizations must continue to check assumptions and perpetuating stereotypes around the 'think manager think male' (Schein, 1976) model of success, and the 'disappearance' (Fletcher, 1999) of the critical practice of relational work so important for organizational viability and sustainability. Courageous women will continue to call the question of discrimination but need the support of men of conscience and good faith to stand beside them in equalizing opportunities for all workers to do their best work regardless of gender. Organizations must enforce their equal employment opportunity policies in word and in deed.

Conclusions

No one would argue that the world is rapidly changing, and that definitions of success have expanded in recent decades to include a more holistic view of achievement, perhaps as a direct result of the increase of women in the workplace. What remains is for perceptions and practices to be better aligned so that multiple paths to success are available, honored and supported in the organizational world. Such a strategy would be likely to benefit all workers, not only women.

Research that acknowledges and celebrates the complexities of women's lives in contemporary society and moves beyond traditional gendered constructions of career success is critical if women's experiences are to be adequately represented in the dialogue on successful and fulfilling careers. One direction for future research is to examine the construct of success based on the current theoretical conceptualizations of the nature of careers (that is, protean, boundaryless, kaleidoscope, and so on). For example, how is success defined in the context of a protean career? What does a successful career across organizational boundaries look like? How do women in each stage of their careers operationalize Mainiero's and Sullivan's (2005) concepts of authenticity, balance and challenge and how can organizations support them in doing so? Recognition that women's career and life responsibilities ebb and flow according to life stage concerns (O'Neil and Bilimoria, 2005a) must be taken into account in any exploration of women's career success. Empirical studies of success that investigate relationships with the latest career theories will advance our understanding of these concepts and provide opportunities for all workers to succeed.

References

Adler, Nancy and Dafna N. Izraeli (eds) (1994), *Competitive Frontiers: Women Managers in a Global Economy*, Oxford: Basil Blackwell.

Alimo-Metcalfe, B. (1995), 'An investigation of female and male constructs of leadership and empowerment', *Women in Management Review*, **10**, 3–8.

Arthur, M.B. (1994), 'The boundaryless career: a new perspective for organizational inquiry', *Journal of Organizational Behavior*, **15**, 295–306.

Arthur, Michael B. and Denise M. Rousseau (1996), 'The boundaryless career as a new employment principle', in Michael B. Arthur and Denise M. Rousseau (eds), *The Boundaryless Career*, New York: Oxford University Press, pp. 3–20.

Astin, H.S. (1984), 'The meaning of work in women's lives: a sociopsychological model of career choice and work behavior', *The Counseling Psychologist*, **12**(4), 117–26.

Bailyn, Lotte (1989), 'Understanding individual experience at work: comments on the theory and practice of careers', in Michael B. Arthur, Douglas T. Hall and Barbara S. Lawrence (eds), *Handbook of Career Theory*, Cambridge: Cambridge University Press, pp. 477–89.

Bartol, Kathryn M. (1999), 'Gender influences on performance evaluations', in Gary N. Powell (ed.), *Handbook of Gender & Work*, Thousand Oaks, CA: Sage Publications, pp. 165–78.

Bateson, Mary C. (1990), *Composing a Life*, New York: Plume.

Belkin, L. (2004), 'The opt-out revolution', *New York Times Magazine*, 26 October, p. 153.

Brett, J.M. and L.K. Stroh (1999), 'Women in management: how far have we come and what needs to be done as we approach 2000?', *Journal of Management Inquiry*, **8**(4), 392–8.

Burke, R.J. (1999), 'Are families a career liability?', *Women in Management Review*, **14**(5), 159–63.

Burke, Ronald J. (2002), 'Career development of managerial women', in Ronald J. Burke and Debra L. Nelson (eds), *Advancing Women's Careers*, Malden, MA: Blackwell Publishing, pp. 139–60.

Burke, R.J. and C.A. McKeen (1990), 'Mentoring in organizations: implications for women', *Journal of Business Ethics*, **9**, 317–32.

Burke, R.J. and C.A. McKeen (1994), 'Training and development activities and career success of managerial and professional women', *Journal of Management Development*, **13**(5–6), 53–64.

Butterfield, D. Anthony and James P. Grinnell (1999), '"Re-viewing" gender, leadership, and managerial behavior: do three decades of research tell us anything?', in Gary N. Powell (ed.), *Handbook of Gender & Work*, Thousand Oaks, CA: Sage Publications, pp. 223–38.

Catalyst (2001), *The Next Generation: Today's Professionals, Tomorrow's Leaders*, New York: Catalyst.

Chodorow, Nancy (1978), *The Reproduction of Mothering*, Berkeley, CA: University of California Press.

Dann, S. (1995), 'Gender differences in self-perceived career success', *Women in Management Review*, **10**(8), 11–18.

de Janasz, S.C., S.E. Sullivan and V. Whiting (2003), 'Mentor networks and career success: lessons for turbulent times', *Academy of Management Executive*, **17**(4), 78–91.

Derr, C. Brooklyn (1986), *Managing the New Careerist*, San Francisco, CA: Jossey-Bass.

Donahue, K.B. (1998), 'Why women leave – and what corporations can do about it', *Harvard Management Update*, June, pp. 3–4.

Dreher, G.F. and R.A. Ash (1990), 'A comparative study of mentoring among men and women in managerial, professional, and technical positions', *Journal of Applied Psychology*, **75**, 539–46.

Eagly, Alice H. (1987), *Sex Differences in Social Behavior: A Social-Role Interpretation*, Hillsdale, NJ: Lawrence Erlbaum Associates.

Fagenson, E.A. (1989), 'The mentor advantage: perceived career/job experiences of protégés vs. non-protégés', *Journal of Organizational Behavior*, **10**, 309–20.

Fagenson, E.A. (1990), 'At the heart of women in management research: theoretical and methodological approaches and their biases', *Journal of Business Ethics*, **9**, 267–74.

Fels, A. (2004), 'Do women lack ambition?', *Harvard Business Review*, Boston, MA: Harvard Business School.

Feyerherm, A. and Y.H. Vick (2005), 'Generation X women in high technology: overcoming gender and generational challenges to succeed in the corporate environment', *Career Development International*, **10**(3), 216–27.

Fletcher, Joyce K. (1996), 'A relational approach to the protean worker', in Douglas T. Hall et al. (eds) *The Career is Dead, Long Live the Career*, San Francisco: Jossey-Bass, pp. 105–31.

Fletcher, Joyce K. (1999), *Disappearing Acts: Gender, Power, and Relational Practice at Work*, Cambridge, MA: The MIT Press.

Fletcher, Joyce K. and Lotte Bailyn (1996), 'Challenging the last boundary: reconnecting work and family', in Michael B. Arthur and Denise M. Rousseau (eds), *Boundaryless Careers*, Oxford: Oxford University Press, pp. 256–67.

Forret, M.L. and T.W. Dougherty (2004), 'Networking behaviors and career outcomes: differences for men and women?', *Journal of Organizational Behavior*, **25**(3), 419–37.

Friedman, Stewart D. and Jeffrey H. Greenhaus (2000), *Work and Family: Allies or Enemies? What Happens When Business Professionals Confront Life Choices?*, New York: Oxford University Press.

Gallos, Joan (1989), 'Exploring women's development: implications for career theory, practice, and research', in Michael B. Arthur, Douglas T. Hall and Barbara S. Lawrence (eds) *Handbook of Career Theory*, Cambridge: Cambridge University Press, pp. 110–32.

Gilligan, Carol (1982), *In a Different Voice: Psychological Theory and Women's Development*, Cambridge, MA: Harvard University Press.

Hall, Douglas T. (1976), *Careers in Organizations*, Santa Monica, CA: Goodyear.

Hall, Douglas T. (1996), *The Career is Dead, Long Live the Career*, San Francisco: Jossey-Bass.

Handy, Charles (1989), *The Age of Unreason*, London: Business Books.

Heilman, M., C.J. Block and R.F. Martell (1995), 'Sex stereotypes: do they influence perceptions of managers?', *Journal of Social Behavior and Personality*, **10**, 237–52.

Heilman, M.E., C.J. Block, R.F. Martell and M.C. Simon (1989), 'Has anything changed? Current characterizations of men, women, and managers', *Journal of Applied Psychology*, **74**, 935–42.

Hewlett, S.A. (2002), 'Executive women and the myth of having it all', *Harvard Business Review*, **80**(4), 66–73.

Hewlett, S.A. and C.B. Luce (2005), 'Off-ramps and on-ramps: keeping talented women on the road to success', *Harvard Business Review*, **83**(3), 43–54.

Higgins, M.C. and K.E. Kram (2001), 'Reconceptualizing mentoring at work: a developmental network perspective', *Academy of Management Review*, **26**, 264–88.

Hopkins, M.M. (2004), 'The impact of gender, emotional intelligence competencies, and styles on leadership success', Doctoral Dissertation, Case Western Reserve University, Dissertation Abstracts International, UMI 3138801.

Hornsby, J.S., D.W. Naffziger, D.F. Kuratko and R.V. Montagno (1993), 'An interactive model of the corporate entrepreneurship process', *Entrepreneurship Theory and Practice*, Winter, pp. 29–37.

Ibarra, H. (1993), 'Personal networks of women and minorities in management: a conceptual framework', *Academy of Management Review*, **18**(1), 56–81.

Ibarra, H. (1997). 'Paving an alternative route: gender differences in managerial networks', *Social Psychology Quarterly*, **60**(1), 91–102.

Jordan, Judith V., Alexandra G. Kaplan, Jean B. Miller, Irene P. Stiver and Janet L. Surrey (1991), *Women's Growth in Connection: Writings From the Stone Center*, New York: The Guilford Press.

Kanter, Rosabeth M. (1977), *Men and Women of the Corporation*, New York: Basic Books.

Karau, S.J. and A.H. Eagly (1999), 'Invited reaction: gender, social roles, and the emergence of leaders', *Human Resource Development Quarterly*, **10**, 321–7.

Kirchmeyer, C. (1998), 'Determinants of managerial career success: evidence and explanation of male/female differences', *Journal of Management*, **24**(6), 673–92.

Kirchmeyer, C. (2002), 'Change and stability in manager's gender roles', *Journal of Applied Psychology*, **87**, 929–39.

Kram, Kathy E. (1985), *Mentoring at Work: Developmental Relationships in Organizational Life*, Glenview, IL: Scott Foresman.

Kram, Kathy E. (1996), 'A relational approach to career development', in Douglas T. Hall and Associates (eds), *The Career is Dead, Long Live the Career*, San Francisco, CA: Jossey-Bass, pp. 132–57.

Levinson, Daniel J. (1996), *The Seasons of a Woman's Life*, New York: Alfred Knopf.

Linehan, M. and J.S. Walsh (1999), 'Senior female international managers: breaking the glass border', *Women in Management Review*, **14**(7), 264–72.

Linehan, M. and J.S. Walsh (2000), 'Beyond the traditional linear view of international managerial careers: a new model of the senior female career in an international context', *Journal of European Industrial Training*, **24**(2/3/4), 178–89.

Lyness, K.S. and D.E. Thompson (2000), 'Climbing the corporate ladder: do female and male executives follow the same route?', *Journal of Applied Psychology*, **85**, 86–101.

Mainiero, L.A. and S.E. Sullivan (2005), 'Kaleidoscope careers: an alternative explanation for the "opt-out" revolution', *Academy of Management Executive*, **19**(1), 106–23.

Marshall, J. (1995), *Women Managers Moving On: Exploring Career and Life Choices*, London: Routledge.

Martins, L.L., K.A. Eddleston and J.F. Veiga (2002), 'Moderators of the relationships between work–family conflict and career satisfaction', *Academy of Management Journal*, **45**(2), 399–409.

Mavin, S. (2001), 'Women's careers in theory and practice: time for change?', *Women in Management Review*, **16**(4), 183–92.

McDonald, P., K. Brown and L. Bradley (2005), 'Have traditional career paths given way to protean ones?', *Career Development International*, **10**(2), 109–29.

Melamed, T. (1995), 'Career success: The moderating effect of gender', *Journal of Vocational Behavior*, **47**, 35–60.

Merrill-Sands, D.M. and D.M. Kolb (2001), 'Women as leaders: the paradox of success', Center for Gender in Organizations Insights, Briefing Note 9, April, 1–4.

Metcalfe, Beverly and Yochanan Altman (2001), 'Leadership', in Elisabeth Wilson (ed.), *Organizational Behaviour Reassessed: The Impact of Gender*, London: Sage Publications, pp. 104–28.

Miller, Jean B. (1976), *Toward a New Psychology of Women*, Boston, MA: Beacon Press.

Moore, Dorothy P. (2000), *Careerpreneurs*, Palo Alto, CA: Davies-Black Publishing.

Moore, Dorothy P. and Holly E. Buttner (1997), *Women Entrepreneurs: Moving Beyond the Glass Ceiling*, Thousand Oaks, CA: Sage Publications.

Morrison, Ann M., Randall P. White, Ellen Van Velsor and The Center for Creative Leadership (1992), *Breaking the Glass Ceiling: Can Women Reach the Top of America's Largest Corporations?* Reading, MA: Addison-Wesley.

Nabi, G.R. (1999), 'An investigation into the differential profile of predictors of objective and subjective career success', *Career Development International*, **4**(4), 212–24.

Netemeyer, R.G., J.S. Boles and R. McMurrian (1996), 'Development and validation of work–family conflict and family–work conflict scales', *Journal of Applied Psychology*, **81**, 400–10.

Offermann, L.R. and C. Beil (1992), 'Achievement styles of women leaders and their peers', *Psychology of Women Quarterly*, **16**, 37–56.

O'Leary, J. (1997), 'Developing a new mindset: the "career ambitious" individual', *Women in Management Review*, **12**(3), 91–99.

O'Neil, D.A. (2003), 'Working in context: understanding the career-in-life experiences of women', Doctoral dissertation, Case Western Reserve University, Dissertation Abstracts International, UMI 3097354.

O'Neil, D.A. and D. Bilimoria (2005a), 'Women's career development phases: idealism, endurance, and reinvention', *Career Development International*, **10**(3), 168–89.

O'Neil, D.A. and D. Bilimoria (2005b), 'Women and careers: a critical perspective on the theory and practice of women in organizations', Working Paper Series (WP-06–05), Department of Organizational Behavior, Case Western Reserve University, Cleveland, OH.

Osterman, P. (1995), 'Work/family programs and the employment relationship', *Administration Science Quarterly*, **40**, 681–700.

Pinchot, Gifford (1985), *Intrapreneuring: Why You Don't Have To Leave the Corporation To Become an Entrepreneur*, New York: Harper and Row.

Poole, Millicent E. and Janice Langan-Fox (1997), *Australian Women and Careers*, Cambridge, UK: Cambridge University Press.

Powell, G.N. and L.A. Mainiero (1992), 'Cross-currents in the river of time: conceptualizing the complexities of women's careers', *Journal of Management*, **18**(2), 215–37.

Powell, Gary N. and Lisa A. Mainiero (1993). 'Getting ahead in career and life', in Gary N. Powell (ed.), *Women and Men in Management*, 2nd edn, Newbury Park, CA: Sage Publications, pp. 186–224.

Powell, G.N., D.A. Butterfield and J.D. Parent (2002), 'Gender and managerial stereotypes: have the times changed?', *Journal of Management*, **28**, 177–93.

Pringle, J.K. and K.M. Dixon (2003), 'Re-incarnating life in the careers of women', *Career Development International*, **8**(6), 291–300.

Ragins, B.R. (1989), 'Barriers to mentoring: the female manager's dilemma', *Human Relations*, **42**, 1–22.

Ragins, B.R. and T.A. Scandura (1994), 'Gender differences in expected outcomes of mentoring relationships', *Academy of Management Journal*, **37**(4), 957–72.

Ragins, B.R., B. Townsend and M. Mattis (1998), 'Gender gap in the executive suite: CEOs and female executives report on breaking the glass ceiling', *The Academy of Management Executive*, **12**(1), 28–42.

Rothbard, N.P. (2001), 'Enriching or depleting? The dynamics of engagement in work and family roles', *Administrative Science Quarterly*, **46**, 655–84.

Ruderman, M.N., P.J. Ohlott, K. Panzer and S.N. King (2002), 'Benefits of multiple roles for managerial women', *Academy of Management Journal*, **45**(2), 369–86.

SBA (United States Small Business Administration) (2005), www.sba.gov/advo/research/sb_econ02-03.pdf.

Scandura, T.A. (1992), 'Mentorship and career mobility: an empirical investigation', *Journal of Organizational Behavior*, **13**, 169–74.

Schein, V.E. (1976), 'Think manager, think male', *Atlanta Economic Review*, **26**, 21–24.

Schein, V.E. (2001), 'A global look at psychological barriers to women's progress in management', *Journal of Social Issues*, **57**(4), 675–88.

Schneer, J.A. and F. Reitman (1995), 'The impact of gender as managerial careers unfold', *Journal of Vocational Behavior*, **47**, 290–315.

Schneer, J.A. and F. Reitman (2002), 'Managerial life without a wife: family structure and managerial career success', *Journal of Business Ethics*, **37**, 25–38.

Schwartz, D.B. (1996), 'The impact of work–family policies on women's career development: boon or bust?', *Women in Management Review*, **11**(1), 5–19.

Schwartz, Felice N. (1992), *Breaking with Tradition*, New York: Warner Books.

Shore, T.H. (1992), 'Subtle gender bias in the assessment of managerial potential', *Sex Roles*, **27**, 499–515.

Story, L. (2005), 'Many women at elite colleges set career path to motherhood', *New York Times*, 20 September, A1 and A18.

Stroh, L.K., J.M. Brett and A.H. Reilly (1992), 'All the right stuff: a comparison of female and male managers' career progression', *Journal of Applied Psychology*, **77**, 251–60.

Stroh, L.K., J.M. Brett and A.H. Reilly (1996), 'Family structure, glass ceiling and traditional explanations for the differential rate of turnover of female and male managers', *Journal of Vocational Behavior*, **49**(1), 99–118.

Sturges, J. (1999), 'What it means to succeed: personal conceptions of career success held by male and female managers at different ages', *British Journal of Management*, **10**, 239–52.

Sullivan, S.E. (1999), 'The changing nature of careers: a review and research agenda', *Journal of Management*, **25**, 457–84.

Tenbrunsel, A.E., J.M. Brett, E. Maoz, L.K. Stroh and A.H. Reilly (1995), 'Dynamic and static work–family relationships', *Organizational Behavior and Human Decision Processes*, **63**(3), 233–46.

Thompson, C.A., L.L. Beauvais and K.S. Lyness (1999), 'When work–family benefits are not enough: the influence of work–family culture on benefit utilization, organizational attachment, and work–family conflict', *Journal of Vocational Behavior*, **54**, 392–415.

Van Velsor, Ellen and Martha W. Hughes (1990), *Gender Differences in the Development of Managers: How Women Managers Learn From Experience*, Greensboro, NC: Center for Creative Leadership.

Vinnicombe, Susan and Nina L. Colwill, (1995), *The Essence of Women in Management*, London: Prentice Hall.

Vinnicombe, S. and V. Singh (2003), 'Locks and keys to the boardroom', *Women in Management Review*, **18**(5–6), 325–34.

Wallis, C. (2004), 'The case for staying home', *Time Magazine*, 22 March, pp. 51–9.

Ward, C. (1978), 'Is there a motive to avoid success in women?', *Human Relations*, **31**(12), 1055–68.

Whyte, William H. (1956), *The Organization Man*, New York: Simon and Schuster, Inc.

7 Mentoring as a career development tool: gender, race and ethnicity implications

Helen M. Woolnough and Marilyn J. Davidson

Introduction

Mentoring is increasingly regarded as an essential career development tool that aids individual development and contributes to a successful, progressive career. Empirical research has consistently demonstrated that mentees experience an array of positive outcomes from mentoring relationships including enhanced career mobility, increased job satisfaction and increased visibility (Chao, 1997; Fagenson, 1989; Woolnough et al., 2005). As the ability to learn, grow and adapt becomes more essential to organizational effectiveness, organizations are increasingly recognizing the benefits of life-long learning through mechanisms such as mentoring (Allen and Poteet, 1999; Kram, 2004). This is even more essential considering the traditional linear career structure is increasingly being replaced by more flexible structures to meet the complex demands of a rapidly changing marketplace. These flexible structures necessitate organizational socialization and networking (Higgins and Kram, 2001) and mentors are an effective resource to facilitate and guide this greater organizational movement (Kram, 2004).

Whilst mentoring is recognized as an important career development tool for men and women, it has been suggested that mentoring relationships are particularly crucial to the career development of women in business and management. Research conducted with senior women has identified mentoring as a specific strategy employed by women to enable them to climb the corporate ladder (Davidson and Burke, 2004; Ragins, Townsend and Mattis, 1998; Vinnicombe and Singh, 2003). This has led Ragins (2002: 44) to claim that mentoring may be the 'ice pick' for breaking through the 'glass ceiling', an invisible but very real barrier, experienced by women who vie for promotion to top jobs (Davidson and Cooper, 1992). Certainly, numerous studies have shown that many women who have mentors experience greater career success and advancement, experience enhanced self-esteem and confidence, are more prepared for leadership roles and are more able to access senior members of staff through their mentor (Kram,

1985; Vance and Olsen, 2002). The mentoring relationship can provide women with insights into organizational politics and expose them to sources of information that may otherwise have been unobtainable. Mentoring for women has therefore become an increasingly important issue and has been shown to be an invaluable tool to assist women in their careers in business and management.

That is not to say that every woman who has access to a mentor experiences a successful career (Burke and McKeen, 1997). Mentoring is a complex relationship and factors including interpersonal skills, level of commitment to the mentoring relationship and organizational influences can all impact on the effectiveness of a mentoring relationship. Recent research however, has highlighted the key role that mentoring can play in women's professional advancement compared to non-mentored women and reconfirms that mentoring is a powerful relationship that can significantly impact on the careers of women in management (Woolnough et al., 2005). This chapter will review the literature relating to the role of mentoring as a career development tool for women in business and management. Firstly, the different definitions and functions of mentoring will be discussed, leading into the specific role of gender in mentoring relationships. This will be followed by reviews of the role of race and ethnicity in mentoring relationships, the benefits of mentoring for the mentor and new alternative forms of mentoring. Figure 7.1 captures the main arguments in this chapter.

Defining mentoring

Mentoring is an age-old process that derives from Greek mythology yet it is only in the past thirty years or so that mentoring has become recognized as a key strategy for individuals to evolve in their careers and for organizations to develop and retain talented employees (Allen and Poteet, 1999; Kram, 1985; Scandura, 1992; Young and Perrewe, 2000). The value of mentoring as a tool to enhance career success began to permeate largely North American business and academic circles in the early 1970s and has been subject to much discussion and debate since its popularisation (Chao, 1997; Kram, 1985; Singh et.al., 2002). In general, mentoring is described as a developmental relationship that contributes to both an individual's growth and advancement (Fagenson, 1989; Kram, 1985; Young and Perrewe, 2000). This relationship typically occurs between a junior employee and a senior employee, who is charged with facilitating the junior employee's career and personal development, to enhance their performance and progression at work (Ragins 1997; Higgins and Kram, 2001; Ragins, Cotton and Miller, 2000). Literature tends to focus on the value of mentoring relationships for the individual being mentored but early work has shown that both individuals involved benefit from the relationship (Kram and Isabella, 1985).

In her seminal work, Kram (1985) identified two broad categories of mentoring functions: career and psychosocial. Career functions relate to development behaviours that impact on professional advancement in organizations. These career functions are: sponsorship, coaching, protection, challenging assignments and exposure. Psychosocial roles relate more to the interpersonal aspect of the relationship and help form the individual's sense of ability and self worth in their role at work. These functions are acceptance and confirmation, counselling, friendship and role modelling. As individuals develop their sense of ability and self-worth, they are more prepared to accept challenging work, which may include career change.

At the time of Kram's (1985) study, mentoring in organizations was largely an informal practice and the vast majority of literature focuses on informal mentoring relationships, that is, those relationships that develop on an ad hoc basis. Either mentee or mentor may initiate this form of mentoring. A mentee may, for example, attract the attention of the mentor through their exceptional performance at work or their involvement in similar interests. Similarly, a mentee may approach a more experienced member of the organization for guidance and support (Noe, 1988).

A decade or so after mentoring relationships had grown in prominence in North America, their value began to pervade European business and academic circles. The European concept of mentoring, however, tends to differ from the traditional North American concept and this reflects inherent cultural differences and assumptions about the purpose and focus of a mentoring relationship (Clutterbuck and Ragins, 2002). Whereas the traditional North American concept of mentoring largely follows a sponsorship model, the European approach emphasizes a more facilitative relationship, focusing on growth and development for the mentee and the mentor.

Further analysis of the mentoring literature, however, reveals a more complicated picture. It appears rather simplistic to state that there is an approach to mentoring that derives from North America and a development-focused approach that shares some of the characteristics of the former but differs in terms of its assumptions about the main functions and purpose of a mentoring relationship. While there is agreement on the critical role that mentoring relationships can have on career and personal development, studies conducted by various writers from across the globe have differing perspectives. As a result, many descriptions of the nature of mentoring relationships have been produced, and definitional clarity is a problematic area (Bierema and Merriam, 2002; Ensher et al., 2003; Lane, 2004; Roberts, 2000).

Mentoring relationships have, however, been shown to differ from other strategies employed in organizations to assist employees in their career development, including coaching. Although the functions of mentoring and coaching relationships invariably overlap, they are two separate types of developmental work relationships (Benabou and Benabou, 2000). Coaching is directly concerned with the immediate improvement of performance and development of skills by a form of tutoring or instruction (Whitmore, 2003). Mentoring is, in effect, one step removed and is concerned with the longer-term acquisition of skills in a developing career (Clutterbuck and Lane, 2004; Keane and Napper, 2001).

In recognition of the benefits of mentoring identified by Kram (1985) and others, organizations are increasingly employing formal mentoring programmes in an attempt to replicate the success of informal relationships documented in academic and business literature. In the rapidly changing social and economic climate, the need for organizations to have up-to-date knowledge of the needs of the wider community is vital. Pairing mentors with talented employees is an effective and efficient way of information exchange (Benabou and Benabou, 2000).

This has important implications for the future of mentoring, as the development and process of informal and formal mentoring differs considerably. Informal mentoring relationships for example are developed by 'mutual identification', whereas in formal mentoring relationships, potential mentors and mentees are usually paired by a third party and in some cases the mentor and mentee will not have met before they are matched (Ragins et al., 2000). In addition, the length and structure of formal mentoring relationships differ from informal relationships. According to Kram (1985), informal relationships do not follow a prescribed structure and usually last between three and six years. In contrast, formal mentoring relationships involve some form of contract in terms of learning outcomes, frequency of meetings between mentor and mentee and usually last between six months and a year. Furthermore, the purpose of the relationship is often different in formal and informal relationships. Informal relationships may focus on long-term goals whereas formal relationships tend to focus more on the mentee's current position and immediate career goals (Benabou and Benabou, 2000).

Despite the problems with definitional clarity and the differences in the forms that mentoring can take, it is well established that mentoring relationships offer a number of important benefits in terms of career and personal development for mentees. Empirical research has demonstrated that the outcomes of mentoring for mentees include, that they experience faster promotion rates, increased career mobility, increased job satisfaction, higher rates of pay, and enhanced self-esteem (Chao, 1997; Dreher and

Ash, 1990, Fagenson, 1989; Koberg, et al., 1994; Kram, 1985; Whitely et al., 1991). Since work influences the quality of life in general, mentoring relationships can contribute to an overall sense of well-being (Clutterbuck and Ragins, 2002).

The role of gender in mentoring relationships

Initially, mentoring theory was developed from the results of studies employing samples of white males only. These results, however, were limited to explaining the experiences of work-based relationships among the dominant power group in organizations (Ragins, 1997). In recognition of the fact that it is unlikely that the mentoring models developed from this research will also apply to all other groups in organizations, researchers have addressed the role of gender and diversity in mentoring relationships (O'Neill, 2002).

Diversified mentoring relationships are composed of mentors and mentees who differ in group membership associated with power differences in organizations (for example gender, race, ethnicity, class, disability, sexual orientation). According to Ragins' theory regarding diversified mentoring relationships, (1997; 2002), gender makes a difference in mentoring relationships as individuals are members of groups that have different degrees of power or influence in organizations. Ragins (2002: 24) states that 'these group memberships impact on employee's access to power and resources in organisations, define their roles in the organisation and elicit stereotypes and attributions about their competence and abilities.' The extent to which these groups influence organizations depends on their control over power resources, which involves control over persons, information, and other organizational resources (Ragins, 1997).

Furthermore, Ragins' (1997; 2002) theory asserts that these group memberships are inextricably linked to the mentoring relationship. Members bring their external position and influences with them to the mentoring relationship. Consequently, mentoring relationships involving minority members, including women, differ from their majority counterparts in the development processes and outcomes associated with the relationship. Here, in the following sub-sections, we address the role of gender in these development processes and the outcomes associated with the mentoring relationship in more detail.

The availability of male and female mentors

Numerous researchers have suggested that acquiring a mentoring relationship is particularly problematic for women (Burke and Nelson, 2002; Kram, 1985; Powell and Graves, 2003; Ragins, 1989, 2002; Ragins and Cotton, 1991; Scandura and Ragins, 1993; Scandura and Williams, 2001). It has been suggested that one of the main reasons for this is that aspiring women may prefer to be mentored by other successful women yet the disproportionate amount of women compared to men occupying senior level positions in organizations results in a shortage of potential female mentors (Davidson and Burke, 2004; Powell and Graves, 2003; Wilson, 2003; Ragins and Scandura, 1994). Ragins (2002) argues that even when potential female mentors do exist in organizations, it may be difficult to attract them as mentors, as they are already likely to be inundated with requests.

This has important implications for women as studies of women's career development suggest that one of the major barriers to their participation in a fully developed career, as well as negatively influenced opportunities for career advancement, is the scarcity of role models (Powell and Graves, 2003; Wilson, 2003). Female mentors may share gender-based experiences that aspiring women can relate to. Furthermore, senior female mentors provide other women with visible proof that they can reach the top positions, and their visibility encourages other women to feel that they can achieve the same goals.

Research has suggested that women who are in a position to act as a mentor may be prevented from doing so, further restricting the pool of successful, experienced women for aspiring women to choose from. For example, Ragins and Cotton (1993) controlled for organizational rank and found that women anticipated greater drawbacks or obstacles to becoming a mentor than men did, but expressed similar positive intentions to serve as a mentor. These drawbacks may include increased workload and the need to out-perform male counterparts (Davidson, 1997) which leaves little time to engage in a mentoring relationship either as a mentor or indeed, as a mentee.

In a survey conducted by Ragins and Scandura (1994) that consisted of a matched sample of male and female executives, however, the researchers found no differences between men and women in expected costs, benefits or intention to mentor. Ragins and Scandura's (1994) research suggests that the lack of female mentors in organizations is the result of the relative absence of women at high ranks, rather than of gender differences in intention to mentor. Similarly, in Allen et al.'s (1997) research of first-level supervisors, where the numbers of men and women were roughly equal, women had similar intentions to mentor others and there were no differences between men and women with regards to perceived barriers to becoming a mentor. This research suggests that women are just as likely to become mentors as men, yet more men exist at senior levels to fulfil a mentoring role. While men have an abundance of potential mentors of the same gender from which to choose, women who wish to benefit from a mentoring relationship are invariably faced with approaching mentors of the opposite sex. This has been found to be viewed as problematic by some women (Allen et al., 1997).

Cross-gender mentoring relationships

It is important to note that aspiring women can learn a great deal from male mentors, and as mentoring is a reciprocal relationship, male mentors, can in turn, learn much from their female mentees (Woolnough et al., 2005). Male mentors may provide female mentees with alternative perspectives they may not have considered and female mentees can highlight issues and conflicts that male mentors (as senior members of the organization) may have been previously unaware of. Also, male mentors often occupy more powerful positions than female mentors and may therefore be more likely to have access to important knowledge and information about the organization (Hurley and Fagenson-Eland, 1996). Whilst the life choices and style of male mentors may differ from their female mentees, studies have indicated that gender alone does not determine the success of a mentoring relationship (Ragins and Scandura, 1999). Rather, mentor and mentee competence and level of commitment to the mentoring relationship (among other factors) influence the effectiveness of mentoring relationships (Lane, 2004; Kram, 1985).

Researchers have argued, however, that cross-gender mentoring relationships may be more difficult to initiate than same-gender relationships (Clawson and Kram, 1984; Kram, 1985). Women may be discouraged from initiating a relationship with a man for fear that their approach may be regarded by the mentor or others in the organization as sexual in nature (Bowen, 1985; Fitt and Newton, 1981; Hurley and Fagenson-Eland, 1996). In their study of 30 cross-gender mentoring relationships, Fitt and Newton (1981) found that a close relationship with a member of the opposite sex often created suspicion and jealousy among spouses and colleagues. Therefore, the mere perception of others may act as a barrier for women to approaching male mentors.

Secondly, according to traditional gender role expectations, women invariably take a passive role in initiating relationships (Noe, 1988). This is problematic for women when initiating cross-gender relationships, as they may be concerned that a potential male mentor would regard their proactive approach as inappropriate. Women in Ragins and Cotton's (1991) study, did not, however, express anxiety with regards to being proactive in initiating mentoring relationships, challenging the traditional gender role stereotypes.

The studies highlighted here are relatively dated. The extent to which women are concerned about mentoring relationships creating suspicion and jealousy among spouses and colleagues may differ if addressed in more contemporary research. Similarly, the level of proactivity women show in initiating mentoring relationships may be different and future research may address the relevance of these claims today.

Mentor selection of mentee

Most of the research regarding gender preferences has been conducted from the perspective of the mentee (Ragins, 1999). There has been little empirical research examining mentor gender preferences regarding mentees. In light of the impact mentors have been shown to have on the career and personal development of their mentee, propensity to mentor others, and the choices mentors make when selecting mentees, is an important area of study. Organizational structures, however, tend to resemble a pyramid shape and it is therefore unlikely that every junior employee will have access to a senior employee with whom to form a mentoring relationship. The issue of those with a propensity to engage in a mentoring relationship and the preferences mentors have with regards to their mentee, has important implications in determining who progresses in their career and who aids the career progression of employees (Allen, 2003; Allen et al., 2000; Neilson and Eisenbach, 2003) yet literature examining an individual's motivation to mentor others is scarce (Allen, 2003; Allen et al., 1997).

Research investigating the selection of mentees by mentors has employed social exchange theory (Olian et al., 1993). According to Allen et al. (2000: 272), 'exchange theory presents a model of human behaviour that views an interaction between two people as an exchange where the cost of participation in the relationship is compared to the perceived benefits.' The model proposes that individuals are more inclined to develop relationships with individuals that they perceive to provide greater rewards than costs. Within the context of mentoring, social exchange theory asserts that mentors will be more likely to select mentees they believe can bring certain desirable attributes and/or competencies to the relationship, in order to develop a relationship that benefits both parties.

Mentoring research appears to provide support for this theory. In Kram's definitive study (1985), mentors claimed that they preferred to mentor high performing mentees. Literature has also proposed that individuals select mentees based on the mentee's need for help, as well as the mentee's potential and ability. Allen et al. (2000), however, in their qualitative study found that the mentors interviewed were more interested in high performing mentees than mentees in need of help.

Research also suggests that there are other characteristics valued by mentors when selecting protégés. Kram (1985: 44) stated that senior managers focus 'on those who want to learn and grow.' Allen et al.'s qualitative research (1997) and Allen's (2004) quantitative research reported that high motivation and learning orientation were important variables in selecting mentees. This suggests that individuals are reluctant to mentor high performing mentees who lack a desire to develop.

These results may prevent women from accessing mentors in the same way that men do. Results from studies have consistently shown that women are often not presented with the same opportunities as men to develop a mentoring relationship (Powell and Graves, 2003). Women are not privy to many of the informal networks that involve potential male mentors such as certain clubs and various sports and other recreational activities (Davidson and Burke, 2004). Moreover, some authors have shown that women also have fewer formal opportunities for mentorship. Research has shown that one of the reasons mentors choose a particular mentee is due to their mentee's involvement in key, visible projects (Hunt and Michael, 1983). Undoubtedly, male mentees who are visible as a result of their involvement in key work projects, are more likely to be in a position where they will be aware of potential mentors and the skills, characteristics and knowledge they possess. As women tend to occupy lower-level positions in organizations, they may be less likely than men to become involved in projects that can potentially lead to mentoring relationships. It is therefore likely that mentors seeking to mentor a high performing mentee will be more aware of potential male mentees than potential female mentees.

Another influential factor in the selection of mentees by mentors is the level of interpersonal similarity (Allen et al., 1997). Mentors are likely to be attracted to those they perceive as similar to themselves and often view mentees as younger versions of themselves. Burke, McKeen and McKenna (1993) for example, found that mentors reported providing more mentoring to mentees they regarded as similar to themselves in terms of intelligence, approach to procedures, personality, background, ambition, education and activities outside work.

The tendency to like, communicate with, promote and develop similar individuals is referred to as homophily, and is also known as social similarity (Neilson and Eisenbach, 2003). The tendency of homophily to exist within mentoring relationships as highlighted in Burke et al.'s (1993) research is an important issue as mentors, as senior members of an organization, are likely to be white, males (Davidson and Burke, 2004; Powell and Graves, 2003; Wilson, 2003). By employing this mechanism to select mentees, mentors are in effect perpetuating the status quo by giving support to other white males, at the expense of other employees including women and ethnic minorities.

Whilst the studies described in this sub-section lead to an increased understanding of the initiation of mentoring relationships, there are limitations to the research documented. For example, most studies on mentoring (Chao, 1997; Kram, 1985; Noe, 1988; Scandura, 1992) focus on informal mentoring relationships and it is likely that the initiation of informal mentoring relationships will differ to the initiation of formal mentoring relationships. Willingness to mentor or be a mentee and the selection processes in formal and informal mentoring relationships are also likely to differ. As companies are increasingly recognizing the benefits of mentoring and employing formal programmes in an attempt to replicate the success of informal relationships documented in academic and business literature, this has important implications for the future development of mentoring. It is therefore important to address the role of gender in informal and formal mentoring relationships.

The role of gender in formal and informal mentoring relationships
Murray (1991: 5) defines formalized mentoring as

> a structure and series of processes designed to create effective mentoring relationships, guide the desired behaviour change of those involved, and evaluate the results for the protégés, the mentors and the organisation with the primary purpose of systematically developing the skills and leadership abilities of the less-experienced members of an organisation. (Scandura 1998:451).

The characteristics of formal and informal mentoring relationships differ and this can significantly affect the outcome of the relationship. Formal mentoring relationships, however, minimize the risk of mentors identifying and selecting high performing individuals as mentees, at the expense of others who may benefit more from a mentoring relationship (Feldman, 1999).

According to O'Neill (2002), very little is known about gender or race in formal mentoring relationships as most of the research to date has simply addressed informal mentoring. Two studies have addressed this gap in the literature. Ragins and Cotton (1999) found that mentees in cross-gender relationships that were assigned by the organization and structured more formally reported that their mentors provided fewer challenging assignments than those in informal mentoring relationships. In contrast, mentees in same-gender relationships reported that their mentors provided more challenging assignments when in a formal relationship.

In Ragins et al.'s (2000) study, women with formal mentors were less satisfied with their formal mentoring programmes than their male counterparts, and these women reported less career commitment than formally mentored men and non-mentored men and women. Furthermore, female mentees with male mentors reported less satisfaction with the formal mentoring programme, than male mentees who were paired with either male or female mentors. This suggests that formal programmes may be less effective for women than men. The selection of effective mentors is important for all programmes, but it may be critical for programmes aimed at women (Ragins et al., 2000). This has led Stroh et al. (1992) to conclude that formal mentoring programmes may serve as a springboard to informal mentoring relationships but women should continue to seek out an informal mentor, even when they are assigned a formal mentor by the company.

It is important to recognize however, that women invariably face barriers when attempting to find an informal mentoring relationship. In this respect, women may benefit more from informal mentoring relationships, but may be reluctant to approach potential mentors. In contrast, formal mentoring programmes provide women with a 'licence' to benefit from the skills and expertise of a key, visible, knowledgeable and experienced member of the organization, something they may have previously been prevented from doing. For this reason, formal mentoring programmes have been shown to be particularly useful when addressing diversity issues.

The benefits of formal mentoring programmes for diversity in organizations have been isolated by Clutterbuck and Ragins (2002: 46) who state that formal mentoring programmes provide women and minorities with access to mentors; increase the future pool of diverse mentors; legitimize cross-gender mentoring relationships and help negate sexual innuendoes and destructive rumours about cross-gender mentoring relationships. Furthermore, formal mentoring relationships encourage diversity as opposed to informal mentoring relationships, which can foster similarity in organizations.

In addition, formal mentoring programmes can have many benefits if programmes are researched, administered and evaluated appropriately (Clutterbuck and Ragins, 2002). Findings with regards to formal mentoring programmes may reflect the quality and content of the programme itself, rather than the mentoring relationship per se.

The influence of gender on the type and amount of mentoring received
Studies have produced mixed results with regards to gender differences in the amount and type of mentoring functions received. Ragins (1989) for example, proposed that women may look for socio-emotional support in a mentor whereas men look for instrumental help. Burke et al. (1993) suggested that mentors give psychosocial help to junior women and instrumental help to junior men (Burke and McKeen, 1990; Burke et al., 1993). Similarly, Koberg et al.'s (1994) study found that men reported receiving more career development functions than women, regardless of rank. This suggests that type of mentoring received may perpetuate the culture of career advancement for men. In contrast however, Ragins and McFarlin (1990) found that women and men reported help of the same nature from their mentors.

On the other hand, Young and Perrewe (2000) reported an association between gender and mentee expectations of a mentor. Although gender was not included as a control variable, female mentees in their sample had higher social support expectations as well as higher career-related support expectations for mentors, than did male mentees for their mentors. This suggests that expectations may influence the type and amount of mentoring received.

Ragins and Cotton's (1999) study revealed increased career outcomes provided by male mentors. Specifically, they concluded that mentees with a history of male mentors reported more compensation and more promotions than mentees with a history of female mentors, even after controlling for career interruptions, length of relationship, type of mentor, position tenure and occupation. Furthermore, Allen and Eby (2004) found that consistent with theoretical perspectives such as social role theory, male mentors reported providing more career-related mentoring, whereas female mentors reported providing more psychosocial mentoring to their mentees. The authors concluded that it may therefore be helpful for individuals to cultivate multiple mentoring relationships of different genders, in order to reap the full benefits of mentoring.

Interestingly, Struthers (1995) found that the higher the rank of the mentor, the more likely that women in the study were to report having received instrumental help from that person and the less likely they were to report having received psychosocial support. O'Neill (2002) comments that these results may reflect stereotypical gender differences; adopting this view alone may be misleading when the mentors' gender is confounded with other factors such as rank. O'Neill states that if men tend to occupy senior ranks, and those in senior ranks are more likely to provide instrumental help, it could appear that male mentors are more likely than female mentors to provide instrumental help. Those who do not consider this may then be inaccurate in their conclusion that gender differences apparent.

The role of race and ethnicity in mentoring relationships

It is also likely that race and ethnicity influences mentoring relationships although less work has addressed these issues (Davidson, 1997; Ragins, 1997; Thomas, 1990, 1999). Research has shown that black and ethnic minority men and women are less likely to be involved in mentoring relationships. Davidson (1997) in her study of black and ethnic minority female managers, for example, reported that these managers were less likely to be in mentoring relationships compared to their white female counterparts. Those who did engage in mentoring said they had positive experiences but they believed that they would have benefited from having a 'black' female mentor.

Research has shown that black and ethnic minorities who do engage in mentoring relationships are more likely to form mentoring relationships with white people. Two main reasons for this have been cited in the literature. Firstly, as people from black and ethnic minorities progress to higher managerial ranks, they are less likely to find a mentor of the same ethnic origin. This may be due to extra demands at work, which leaves them little time to act as a mentor (O'Neill, 2002). Secondly, as the dominant group with the most power in organizations is white, people from black and ethnic minorities are at a disadvantage unless they form a mentoring relationship with the dominant group, that is a white senior person (Ragins, 1997).

The mentor's gender has also been found to influence outcomes of mentoring. Dreher and Cox (1996)'s survey of 742 men and 276 women MBAs for example, found that MBAs who had a mentor earned substantially higher salaries than other MBAs, but only if their mentor was a white male. Those with female mentors and mentors of colour did not benefit in terms of salary. Furthermore, Dreher and Chargois's (1998) study of graduates of a historically black college replicated the findings reported by Dreher and Cox (1996).

From the limited relevant literature, a few studies have indicated how race influences the functions received within mentoring relationships. For example, Thomas (1990), in his study of cross-race versus same-race mentoring relationships found that more psychosocial support was reported in same-race relationships than in cross-race relationships. Thomas states that cross-race mentoring pairs experience some discomfort when interacting with each other, which in turn detrimentally affects the development of psychosocial functions within the relationship.

In contrast, Turban, Dougherty and Lee (2002) found that racial similarity did not impact on the levels of support received by mentees in their similar study. They did find, however, that individuals were more likely to be in mentoring relationships with others of similar gender and race, supporting previous research that both parties in a mentoring relationship tend to gravitate to individuals they perceive as similar to themselves. Different reasons have been offered as to why people may or may not initiate cross-race relationships and experience discomfort when interacting with people of a different ethnic origin, including racial taboos and a tendency to form relationships with others from the same identity group (Thomas, 1990, 1999).

The two studies outlined previously (Thomas, 1990; Turban et al., 2002) only considered the mentee's perspective. In Ensher and Murphy's (1997) study, the researchers addressed both mentee and mentor perspectives using a sample of black and ethnic minority mentees. Ensher and Murphy (1997) found that mentees reported receiving more career support from same-race mentors, yet mentors reported providing more psychosocial support to same-race mentees, highlighting contradictions between the reports of mentees and mentors. Interestingly, the researchers also found that racial composition did not influence satisfaction with mentors. Overall, their findings reported that the more similar mentees perceived themselves to their mentors in terms of outlook, values or perspective, the more likely they were to report being satisfied with their mentor. These results suggest that if mentees find themselves to be similar to their mentors on some dimension other than race, then they may be just as satisfied with mentors of a different race as with mentors of the same race.

Furthermore, Turban et al. (2002) found that the duration of the mentoring relationship in their study influenced the level of mentoring received in diversified mentoring relationships. In general, duration of the relationship did not affect the mentoring received by mentees with same-gender mentors but those in cross-gender relationships reported receiving more mentoring in longer duration relationships. This suggests that gender dissimilarity may have negative implications early on in mentoring relationships but that this diversity is beneficial as relationships continue. This may be because mentees and mentors in cross-gender relationships learn to adapt to one another and because over time, a wider array of information exchange takes place, which produces more beneficial outcomes. This may also be evident in cross-race relationships and highlights the need to examine diversified relationships over time to fully investigate their benefits and limitations.

It is worth noting that, as with the vast majority of research on mentoring, most of the literature on black and ethnic minority mentoring relationships focuses on informal relationships. It may be the case that the complex and challenging issues faced by black and ethnic minorities may be somewhat diminished in formal mentoring relationships due to the legitimization of these relationships by the host organization. The negative effects of mentoring may however be more prevalent in cross-race mentoring relationships, and future research is required to address the role of race in mentoring relationships further. According to O'Neill (2002), senior men in organizations provide more instrumental help, which suggests that 'if senior white men in corporations are involved in formal mentoring programmes in which they are expected to provide instrumental help to women and people of colour, but are not expected to develop instant friendships and close emotional ties, some progress toward gender and race equity might be made' (O'Neill, 2002: 10).

The benefits of mentoring for the mentor

Although early work on mentoring raised the potential benefits of mentoring for the mentor (Kram, 1985), the vast majority of mentoring research has focused on the benefits of the relationship for the mentee. There is a scarcity of empirical investigations focusing on the benefits of mentoring for the mentor and indeed, the mentor's experience in general (Allen et al., 1997; Allen and Poteet, 1999; Bozionelos, 2004; Burke et al., 1994; Lane, 2004; Ragins and Scandura, 1999). According to Feldman (1999: 259), the mentor is the 'missing person' in mentoring research. This has important implications for women in business and management who may be inclined to act as mentors, as the benefits of acting as a mentor on the career and personal development of mentors has, until recently, been an under-researched area.

Available literature proposes that mentors can potentially experience an array of both personal and professional benefits from a mentoring relationship. These include personal fulfilment, assistance on projects, increased self-confidence, revitalized interest in work, intellectual challenge, valuable insights regarding their own or external organizations, financial rewards, increased prestige and reputation and recognition from others for developing talent in the organization (Bozionelos, 2004; Burke et al., 1994; Clutterbuck, 2001; Kram, 1985; Lane, 2004; Mullen, 1994). These are important findings for women in business in management, as senior women acting as mentors become visible role models for future generations of senior women and the relationship is also likely to impact on the mentor's visibility and professional advancement.

From their survey of managers in a 10000 strong global engineering company in the UK Tabbron et al. (1997) found that the benefits for the mentor are that it widens the mentor's network of contacts and gives them insight into the issues faced by their staff and colleagues. Further empirical work attempting to tackle the gap in the mentoring literature with regards to the mentor's perspective has produced similar results (Feldman, 1999; Lane, 2004).

Allen et al. (1997) conducted in-depth interviews with 27 mentors from five different organizations in the US, to investigate their experiences of mentoring. They revealed that mentors reported benefits including the building of support networks, job-related rewards that focused on others, job-related rewards that focused on self and self-satisfaction. Allen et al. (1997) found that factors related to the desire to help others and factors related to an increase personal learning were the main reasons mentors gave for mentoring others.

Allen et al. (1997) also reported that the majority of mentors had been involved in a previous mentoring relationship as a mentee. This was also confirmed by Ragins and Scandura (1999) who discovered that previous experience in a mentoring relationship, either as a mentor or mentee, was significantly related to outcomes associated with being a mentor. Individuals who had no prior mentoring experience expected more costs and fewer benefits, than individuals who had previously been involved in mentoring relationships. This is an important finding in relation to the decision to become a mentor, as it appears that individuals with previous positive mentoring experiences are more likely to mentor others. This suggests that the effective dissemination and publication of positive experiences and the benefits that can be accrued from engaging in a mentoring relationship (particularly among female mentors), may entice others to become mentors and in turn encourage the transfer of knowledge in organizations.

Available literature on mentoring paints a one-sided picture of the outcomes for mentors. Yet, there are very real potential costs associated with being a mentor, that to date, have received less attention in the literature (Feldman, 1999; Ragins and Scandura, 1999). Acting as a mentor requires investment in time and energy that usually goes beyond the mentor's formal role. Whilst this can be immensely rewarding, several authors have commented on the detrimental affect that unsuccessful mentoring relationships can have on the mentor. Fitt and Newton (1981) comment that mentoring relationships invariably raise the mentor's profile. First impressions would suggest that this is a positive aspect of being a mentor. Yet, this is only likely to be of benefit to the mentor if the mentee responds to the mentoring relationship and develops in some way. For example, it may be the case that during the course of a mentoring relationship, the mentee's performance deteriorates rather than improves, and this can mean that the mentor's professional reputation is adversely affected as a result. Furthermore, this may have a knock-on effect on the professional reputation of the mentor's peers and superiors.

The potential costs of an underachieving mentee in terms of how this may reflect negatively on the mentor, however, may be higher for female mentors than they are for male mentors (Ragins and Scandura, 1994). The relative absence of women at high ranks within organizations means that fewer women are in a position to become mentors, and those that are, consequently become more visible (Davidson and Burke, 2004; Powell and Graves, 2003; Ragins and Scandura, 1994). This is also likely to be the case for black and ethnic minority mentors who are also under-represented in senior positions (Davidson, 1997). This highlights the need for further awareness of the benefits and risks of becoming a mentor and providing support for those acting as mentors, particularly those who may experience difficulties with their mentoring relationships (Woolnough et al., 2005).

Based on the authors' review of the relevant literature throughout this chapter, Figure 7.1 is a model summarizing the impact of mentoring relationships for white women and female black and ethnic minorities in business and management. We believe it shows how the availability, type and formation of mentoring relationships for women in the workplace and

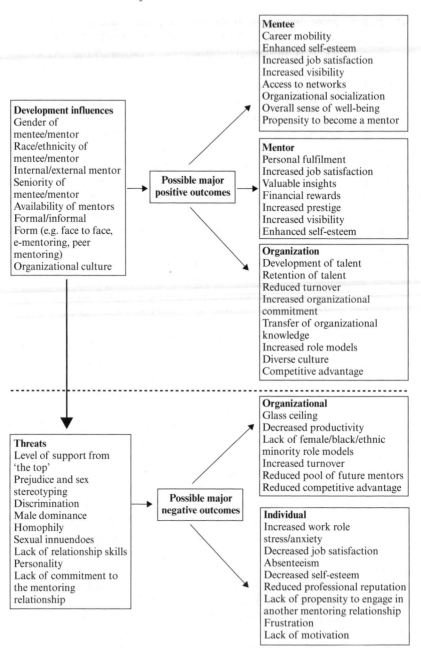

*Figure 7.1   A model of the impact of mentoring relationships for women in
business and management*

the organizational culture in which they exist, can influence the outcomes of a mentoring relationship for the mentee, mentor and the organization in a positive way. It is important that organizations recognize the importance of investing in quality mentoring relationships for women in the workplace, as the individual and organizational benefits can be immense.

There are, however, numerous threats to the availability, type and formation of mentoring relationships for women in the workplace, which can detrimentally affect the extent to which diversified mentoring relationships are supported within the organization, the individuals involved in the mentoring relationship and the organizational business advantage as a whole. If these threats become a reality then the outcomes of mentoring relationships are likely to be negative. Indeed, the very absence of supported mentoring relationships in organizations to foster the future talent of all individuals and provide an effective mechanism for information exchange, can detrimentally affect the overall business success of companies. The effects of devaluing the impact of diversified mentoring relationships can be costly for organizations and this may ultimately influence their ability to secure a competitive advantage.

New alternative forms of mentoring

Virtually all empirical research has focused on the benefits of mentoring in one dyad (one mentee and one mentor) which involves face-to-face interaction (Russell and Adams, 1997). More recently, however, the benefits of alternative forms of mentoring have been addressed. A single mentor can play a key role in women's professional advancement but one mentor does not necessarily guarantee career success. It may not be possible for example, to remain in a mentoring relationship for a number of years in organizations where the workforce is particularly transient. Furthermore, individuals are more likely to experience more than one career during their working life and encounter a variety of roles within different organizations. This may mean that individuals seek different things from different mentors, as they adapt their careers and as their particular development needs change. It may be more appropriate to cultivate a network of mentors who can help with career and professional development in a variety of ways. This can be achieved in numerous ways, by peer and group mentoring for example, as well as e-mentoring.

Peer mentoring
The value of peer mentoring is gaining popularity. The strong bonds that are often developed between co-workers, serve to provide both career and psychosocial support. Peers typically have opportunities to interact and

view each other's performance. They may also be well placed to provide career feedback to each other. Additionally, peers are likely to have similar experiences and they are ideal sources of psychosocial support, particularly for women (Russell and Adams, 1997).

Group mentoring
Group mentoring can take many different forms. Kaye and Jacobson (1995), for example, refer to a formal type of group mentoring which consists of one senior colleague and several junior mentees. Other compositions of group mentoring may differ in terms of hierarchical power and influence, but may provide individuals who do not have access to traditional mentoring relationships with an opportunity to benefit from mentoring (Russell and Adams, 1997). For example, group participation may serve as a substitute for traditional, individual mentors by allowing mentees to capitalize on the benefits of networking, psychosocial support, role modelling and feelings of belonging resulting from the group interaction (Dansky, 1996). Also, group mentoring would allow mentees to benefit from the knowledge and expertise of a mentor, as well as exchange ideas and receive feedback as a group (Russell and Adams, 1997).

The use and application of alternative forms of mentoring such as group and peer mentoring is an important issue. Kram (1985) originally proposed that individuals rarely rely on one individual for developmental support. Rather they call upon multiple individuals. Kram termed this phenomenon, 'relationship constellations'. In this sense, Kram recognized that individuals receive mentoring assistance from many people at any given time. Mentoring assistance can be provided by a range of people from senior colleagues, to peers, family and community members. Higgins and Kram (2001) state that a reconceptualization of mentoring is needed to take into account the potential for this network of mentoring support.

E-mentoring
The fast paced environment in many organizations often means that meeting someone face to face can be problematic and time consuming. It may also be that individuals would prefer to mentor or be mentored by someone external to the organization. E-mentoring is an effective way to facilitate mentoring relationships, particularly when time is scarce and the proximity of mentor and mentee is problematic. Although face-to-face mentoring is the most common form of mentoring, e-mentoring, otherwise known as computer mediated communication (CMC) or virtual mentoring, is receiving greater prominence in the literature (Ensher et al., 2003). Bierema and Merriam (2002:214) define e-mentoring as 'a computer mediated, mutually beneficial relationship between a mentor and a protégé which provides learning, advising, encouraging, promoting and modelling, that is often

boundaryless, egalitarian and qualitatively different than traditional face-to-face mentoring.' While the use of e-mentoring is flourishing, little systematic research has addressed the success and challenges of this method.

The limited available literature highlights the benefits of e-mentoring. E-mentoring can allow for greater flexibility in creating and sustaining relationships. Conversing electronically may also help relationships to develop across barriers of gender, race, geography, age and hierarchy (Bierema and Merriam, 2002; Fagenson-Eland and Yan Lu, 2004). In addition, time constraints often experienced in face-to-face mentoring are alleviated in e-mentoring as pairs are free to communicate at all hours.

Conclusion

As organizations strive to improve, develop and retain talented employees, barriers that exclude women and other minority groups from positions of power will need to be eradicated (O'Neill, 2002). Mentoring has been shown to be an effective mechanism to encourage the professional development of women and black and ethnic minorities in business and management and to encourage the transfer of knowledge, experience, information and values. Research has shown that many women who have mentors experience greater career success and advancement, experience enhanced self-esteem and confidence, are more prepared for leadership roles and are more able to access senior members of staff through their mentor (Kram, 1985; Vance and Olsen, 2002). Furthermore, cross-gender relationships may challenge stereotypical beliefs that women lack the motivation, attitudes, commitment and skills to be good managers (Fagenson, 1993; Ibarra, 1994; Omar and Davidson, 2001; Powell and Graves, 2003). Women face more challenges than men when involved as a mentee or mentor, but embracing this developmental relationship can have a profound positive effect on the careers of women.

There is still a paucity of research relating to the role of women and black and ethnic minorities in mentoring relationships. In particular, the impact of formal mentoring relationships, specifically those designed to increase diversity within organizations deserves more attention in the academic literature. In addition, more longitudinal research is required to examine the impact of diversified mentoring relationships over time. Factors such as gender and race for example have been shown to influence the formation of mentoring relationships. Whilst individuals tend to gravitate towards those they perceive as similar to themselves in terms of demographic characteristics, the benefits of underlying similarity including values and attitudes that are often not at first apparent, may influence the continuation of the relationship and contribute to its overall success over time. This has important implications for the future development of mentoring relationships and requires further attention. It is clear that whilst mentoring has attracted much research over the past thirty years or so, knowledge is still lacking in certain areas, particularly in relation to the roles of women and black and ethnic minorities in mentoring relationships.

References

Allen, T.D. (2003), 'Mentoring others: a dispositional and motivational approach', *Journal of Vocational Behavior*, **62**: 134–54.
Allen, T.D. (2004), 'Protégé selection by mentors: contributing individual and organisational factors', *Journal of Vocational Behaviour* **65**, 469–83.
Allen, T.D. and L.T. Eby (2004), 'Factors related to mentor reports of mentoring functions provided: gender and relational characteristics', *Sex Roles*, **50**(1/2), 129–39.
Allen, T.D. and M.L. Poteet (1999), 'Developing effective mentoring relationships: Strategies from the mentor's viewpoint', *The Career Development Quarterly*, **48**, 59–73.
Allen, T.D., M.L. Poteet and S.M. Burroughs (1997), 'The mentor's perspective: a qualitative inquiry and future research agenda', *Journal of Vocational Behavior*, **51**, 70–89.
Allen, T.D., M.L. Poteet and J.E.A. Russell (2000), 'Protégé selection by mentors: what makes the difference?', *Journal of Organisational Behavior*, **21**, 271–82.
Benabou, C. and R. Benabou (2000), 'Establishing a formal mentoring program for organisational success', *National Productivity Review*, **18**(2), 1–5.
Bierema, L.L. and S.B. Merriam (2002), 'E-mentoring: using computer mediated communication to enhance the mentoring process', *Innovative Higher Education*, **26**(3), 211–27.
Bowen, D.D. (1985), 'Were men meant to mentor women?', *Training and Development Journal*, **39**(2), 30–34.
Bozionelos, N. (2004), 'Mentoring provided: relation to mentor's career success, personality, and mentoring received', *Journal of Vocational Behavior*, **64**, 24–46.
Burke, R.J. and C.A. McKeen (1990), 'Mentoring in organisations: implications for women', *Journal of Business Ethics*, **9**, 317–32.
Burke, R.J. and C.A. McKeen (1997), 'Benefits of mentoring relationships among managerial and professional women: A cautionary tale', *Journal of Vocational Behavior*, **51**, 43–57.
Burke, R.J and D.L. Nelson (2002), *Advancing Women's Careers: Research and Practice*, Oxford, Blackwell.
Burke, R.J., C.A. McKeen and C. McKenna (1993), 'Correlates of mentoring in organizations: the mentor's perspective', *Psychological Reports*, **68**, 883–96.
Burke, R.J., C.A. McKeen and C. McKenna (1994), 'Benefits of mentoring in organisations: the mentor's perspective', *Journal of Managerial Psychology*, **9**(3), 23–32.
Chao, G.T. (1997), 'Mentoring phases and outcomes', *Journal of Vocational Behavior*, **51**, 15–28.
Clawson, J.G. and K.R. Kram (1984), 'Managing cross-gender mentoring', *Buiness Horizons*, **27**(3), 22–32.
Clutterbuck, D. (2001), *Everyone Needs a Mentor: Fostering Talent at Work* (3rd edn), London: Chartered Institute of Personnel and Development.
Clutterbuck, D. and B.R. Ragins (2002), *Mentoring and Diversity: An International Perspective*, Oxford: Butterworth and Heinemann.
Clutterbuck, D. and G. Lane (2004), *The Situational Mentor: An International Review of Competences and Capabilities in Mentoring*, Aldershot: Gower.
Dansky, K.H. (1996), 'The effect of group mentoring on career outcomes', *Group and Organisation Management*, **21**, 5–21.
Davidson, M.J. (1997), *The Black and Ethnic Minority Women Manager: Cracking the Concrete Ceiling*, London: Paul Chapman.

Davidson, M.J. and R.J. Burke (2004), *Women in Management Worldwide: Facts, Figures and Analysis*, Aldershot: Ashgate.

Davidson, M.J. and C.L. Cooper (1992), *Shattering the Glass Ceiling: The Woman Manager*, London: Chapman.

Dreher, G.F. and R.A. Ash (1990), 'A comparative study among men and women in managerial, professional and technical positions', *Journal of Applied Psychology*, **75**(5), 1–8.

Dreher, G.F. and J.A. Chargois (1998), 'Gender, mentoring experiences and salary attainment among graduates of an historically black university', *Journal of Vocational Behaviour*, **53**, 401–16.

Dreher, G.F. and T.H. Cox (1996), 'Race, gender and opportunity: a study of compensation attainment and the establishment of mentoring relationships', *Journal of Applied Psychology*, **8**, 297–308.

Ensher, E.A. and S.E. Murphy (1997), 'Effects of race, gender, perceived similarity and contact on mentor relationships', *Journal of Vocational Behaviour*, **50**, 460–81.

Ensher, E.A., C. Heun and A. Blanchard (2003), 'Online mentoring and computer-mediated communication: new directions in research', *Journal of Vocational Behaviour*, **63**, 264–88.

Fagenson, E.A. (1989), 'The mentor advantage: perceived career/job experiences of protégés versus non-protégés', *Journal of Organisational Behaviour*, **10**, 309–20.

Fagenson, E.A. (1993), *Women in Management: Trends, Issues and Challenges in Managerial Diversity, Women and Work*, Volume 4, Newbury Park, CA: Sage.

Fagenson-Eland, E.A. and R. Yan Lu (2004), 'Virtual mentoring', in D. Clutterback and G. Lane (eds), *The Situational Mentor: An International Review of Competences and Capabilities in Mentoring*, Aldershot: Gower.

Feldman, D.C. (1999), 'Toxic mentors or toxic protégés? A critical re-examination of dysfunctional mentoring', *Human Resource Management Review*, **9**(3), 247–78.

Fitt, L.W. and D.A. Newton (1981), 'When the mentor is a man and the protégé is a woman', *Harvard Business Review*, March–April, 56–8.

Higgins, M.C. and K.E. Kram (2001), 'Reconceptualising mentoring at work: a developmental network perspective', *Academy of Management Review*, **26**(2), 264–88.

Hunt, D.M. and C. Michael (1983), 'Mentorship: a career training and development tool', *Academy of Management Review*, **8**(3), 475–85.

Hurley, A.E. and E.A. Fagenson-Eland (1996), 'Challenges in cross-gender mentoring relationships: psychological intimacy, myths, rumours, innuendoes and sexual harassment', *Leadership and Organization Development Journal*, **17**(3), 42–9.

Ibarra, H. (1994), 'Personal networks of women and minorities in management: a conceptual framework', *Academy of Management Review*, **18**(1), 56–88.

Kaye, B. and B. Jacobson (1995), 'Mentoring: a group guide', *Training and Development*, **49**(4), 22–7.

Keane, D. and R. Napper (2001), *Mentoring Matters*, Oxford: Oxfordshire County Council.

Koberg, C.S., R.W. Boss, D. Chappell and R.C. Ringer (1994), 'Correlates and consequences of protégé mentoring in a large hospital', *Group and Organisation Management*, **19**(2): 219–39.

Kram, K.E. (1985), *Mentoring at Work: Developmental Relationships in Organisational Life*, Glenview, IL: Scott, Foresman.

Kram, K.E. (2004), 'The making of a mentor', in D. Clutterbuck and G. Lane (eds), *The Situational Mentor: An International Review of Competences and Capabilities in Mentoring*, Aldershot: Gower.

Kram, K.E. and L.A. Isabella (1985), 'Mentoring alternatives: The role of peer relationships in career development', *Academy of Management Journal*, **26**(1), 110–32.

Lane, G. (2004), 'A quantititative view of mentor competence', in D. Clutterbuck and G. Lane (eds), *The Situational Mentor: An International Review of Competences and Capabilities in Mentoring*, Aldershot: Gower.

Mullen, E.J. (1994), 'Framing the mentoring relationship as information exchange', *Human Resource Management Review*, **4**(3), 257–81.

Murray, M. (1991), *Beyond the Myths and Magic of Mentoring*, San Francisco, CA: Jossey-Bass.

Neilson, T.R. and R.J. Eisenbach (2003), 'Not all relationships are created equal: Critical factors of high-quality mentoring relationships', *The International Journal of Mentoring and Coaching*, **1**(1), 1–18.

Noe, R.A. (1988), 'Women and mentoring: a review and research agenda', *Academy of Management Review*, **13**(1), 65–78.

Olian, J.D., S.J. Carroll and C.M. Giannantonio (1993), 'Mentor reactions to protégés: an experiment with managers', *Journal of Vocational Behaviour*, **43**, 266–78.

Omar, A. and M.J. Davidson (2001), 'Women in management: a comparative cross-cultural overview', *Cross Cultural Management: An International Journal, Women in Management: Cross Cultural Research*, **8**(3/4), 35–67.

O'Neill, R.M. (2002), 'Gender and race in mentoring relationships: a review of the literature' in D. Clutterbuck and B.R. Ragins (eds), *Mentoring and Diversity: an International Perspective*, Oxford: Butterworth and Heinemann.

Powell, G.N. (1993), *Women and Men in Management* (2nd edn), Newbury Park, CA: Sage.

Powell, G.N. and L.M. Graves (2003), *Women and Men in Management* (3rd edn), Newbury Park, CA: Sage.

Ragins, B.R. (1989), 'Barriers to mentoring: the female manager's dilemma', *Human Relations*, **42**(1), 1–22.

Ragins, B.R. (1997), 'Diversified mentoring relationships in organisations: a power perspective', *Academy of Management Review*, **22**(2), 482–521.

Ragins, B.R. (1999), 'Gender and mentoring relationships: a review and research agenda for the next decade', in G.N. Powell (ed.), *Handbook of Gender in Organizations*, Newbury Park, CA: Sage.

Ragins, B.R. (2002), 'Understanding diversified mentoring relationships: definitions, challenges and strategies', in D. Clutterbuck and B.R. Ragins (eds), *Mentoring and Diversity: An International Perspective*, Oxford: Butterworth and Heinemann.

Ragins, B.R. and J.L. Cotton (1991), 'Easier said than done: gender differences in perceived barriers to gaining a mentor', *Academy of Management Journal*, **34**, (4), 939–51.

Ragins, B.R. and J.L. Cotton (1993), 'Gender and willingness to mentor in organisations', *Journal of Management*, **19**(1), 97–111.

Ragins, B.R. and J.L. Cotton (1999), 'Mentor functions and outcomes: a comparison of men and women in formal and informal mentoring relationships', *Journal of Applied Psychology*, **84**(4), 529–50.

Ragins, B.R. and D.B. McFarlin (1990), 'Perceptions of mentor roles in cross-gender mentoring relationships', *Journal of Vocational Behaviour*, **37**, 321–39.

Ragins, B.R. and T.A. Scandura (1994), 'Gender differences in expected outcomes of mentoring relationships', *Academy of Management Journal*, **37** (4), 957–72.

Ragins, B.R. and T.A. Scandura (1999), 'Burden or blessing? Expected costs and benefits of being a mentor', *Journal of Organizational Behavior*, **20**, 493–509.

Ragins, B.R., J.L. Cotton and J.S. Miller (2000), 'Marginal mentoring: the effects of type of mentor, quality of relationship, and program design on work and career attitudes', *Academy of Management Journal*, **43**(6) 1177–94.

Ragins, B.R., B. Townsend and M. Mattis (1998), 'Gender gap in the executive suite: CEOs and female executives report on breaking the glass ceiling', *Academy of Management Executive*, **12**(1), 28–42.

Roberts, A. (2000), 'Mentoring revisited: a phenomenological reading of the literature', *Mentoring and Tutoring*, **8**(2), 145–70.

Russell, J.E.A. and D.M. Adams (1997), 'The changing nature of mentoring in organisations: an introduction to the special issue on mentoring in organizations', *Journal of Vocational Behavior*, **51**, 1–14.

Scandura, T.A. (1992), 'Mentorship and career mobility: an empirical investigation', *Journal of Organisational Behavior*, **13**, 169–74.

Scandura, T.A. (1998), 'Dysfunctional mentoring relationships and outcomes', *Journal of Management*, **24**(3), 449–67.

Scandura, T.A. and B.R. Ragins (1993), 'The effects of sex and gender role orientation on mentorship in male dominated occupations', *Journal of Vocational Behavior*, **43**, 251–65.

Scandura, T.A. and E.A. Williams (2001), 'An investigation of the moderating effects of gender on the relationships between mentorship initiation and protégé perceptions of mentoring functions', *Journal of Vocational Behavior*, **59**, 342–63.

Singh, V., D. Bains and S. Vinnicombe (2002), 'Informal mentoring as an organisational resource', *Long Range Planning*, **35**, 389–405.

Stroh, L.K., J.M. Brett and A.N. Reilly (1992), 'All the right stuff: a comparison of female and male managers' career progression', *Journal of Applied Psychology*, **77**, 251–60.

Struthers, N.J. (1995), 'Differences in mentoring: a function of gender or organisational rank?', *Journal of Social Behaviour and Personality*, **10**, 265–72.

Tabbron, A., S. Macaulay and S. Cook (1997), 'Making mentoring work', *Training for Quality*, **5**(1), 6–9.

Thomas, D.A. (1990), 'The impact of race on managers' experiences of developmental relationships mentoring and sponsorship: an intra-organisational study', *Journal of Organizational Behavior*, **11**, 479–91.

Thomas, D.A. (1999), 'Beyond the simple demography–power hypothesis: how blacks in power influence white-mentor-black-protégé developmental relationships', in A. Murrell, R. Cosby and R. Ely (eds), *Mentoring Dilemmas: Developmental Relationships within Multicultural Organizations*, Mahwah, NJ: Lawrence Erlbaum Associates.

Turban, D.B., T.W. Dougherty and F.K. Lee (2002), 'Gender, race and perceived similarity effects in developmental relationships: the moderating role of relationship duration', *Journal of Vocational Behavior*, **61**, 240–62.

Vance, C. and R.K. Olsen (2002), *The Mentor Connection in Nursing*, New York: Springer.

Vinnicombe, S. and V. Singh (2003), 'Locks and keys to the boardroom', *Women in Management Review*, **18**(6): 325–33.

Whitley, W., T.W. Dougherty and G.F. Dreher (1991), 'Relationship of career mentoring and socio-economic origin to managers' and professionals' early career progress', *Academy of Management Journal*, **34**(2), 331–51.

Whitmore, J. (2003). *Coaching for Performance: Growing People, Performance and Purpose* (3rd edn), London: Nicholas Brealey.

Wilson, F. (2003), *Organisational Behaviour and Gender*, Aldershot: Ashgate.

Woolnough, H., M. Davidson and S. Fielden (2005), *Challenging Perceptions – Leadership, Career Development and Mentoring Pilot Programme for Female Mental Health Nurses in NHS Trusts, A Report Summary*, The NHS Leadership Centre.

Young, A.M. and P.L. Perrewe (2000), 'What did you expect? An examination of career-related support and social support among mentors and protégés', *Journal of Management Issues*, **26**(1), 611–32.

8 Integration of career and life

Mireia Las Heras and Douglas T. (Tim) Hall

Introduction

In the battle of Lepanto, 1571, the European troops called on Holy Mary asking her 'to stop the sun' so there would be more daylight hours to complete the battle. Apparently she did, and the Europeans defeated the invading troops. Whether this story is true or not, in today's work world people's days only have 24 hours, although professional work and other personal undertakings seem to require much more than that. The complexity of roles and demands lead to difficulties in coping in both family and work domains.

This chapter advocates the concept of integration as a key concept for understanding work–life issues. Human life is a complex system, and as such, over the last decades, researchers have begun to realize that the various domains of an individual's life interact with each other and must be studied in an integrated manner and within a common framework (Carlson and Kacmar, 2000). Senge (1990) points out that although decomposition seems a reasonable way of dealing with complex problems, it has significant limitations in a world of tight couplings and non-linear feedbacks. He claims that the defining characteristic of a system is that it cannot be understood as a function of its isolated components; it must be viewed as a whole to be fully comprehended. Scott (2003) similarly argues that, 'no complex system can be understood by an analysis that attempts to decompose the system into its individual parts as to examine each part and relationship in turn' (p. 93). Consistent with these views, this chapter is concerned with harmonization of roles, diverse domain demands, and the dimensions that make up people's lives. We advocate the need for integration and examine the ramifications of such integration, where *integration is the person's sense that his or her identity is a coherent whole, made up of various sub-identities related to specific life and career roles* (Hall, 2002: 71–2). This chapter examines the difficulties of integrating career in life, especially in the first years of career development and takes a holistic view and a developmental approach of the individual; it views well-being and satisfaction of the individual as the main career outcomes.

In this chapter we first review the literature on work–family: where it originated, how it has developed, and the underlying assumptions behind the main streams of work–life research. Second, we argue the need for an integrative model of study, where work is a dimension of someone's life, and life refers to the whole span of their person's career. Third, we examine how careers develop in the first years for most Americans to whom work is most likely to be full-time and a salient element of personal identity. However, we argue, careers are no longer one single cycle but a series of mini-cycles, and these new career panoramas have several implications for someone pursuing a career. In our approach we take into account the adult's developmental levels, familial situations and personal dispositions that might facilitate or hinder career development; we focus on the first years of career development. We suggest that integration is an outcome of adult development, and suggest how an individual's growing self-awareness about extrinsic and intrinsic career goals can lead to such development and thus to integration. Fourth, we describe what we know about the developmental process of people who are highly integrated and the relationship between career–life integration. Our perspective requires looking at work and non-work domains as parts of a whole. The chapter concludes by revisiting our definition of the integration and the consequences of such redefinition for researchers, individuals, career counselors, and managers.

Forty years of work–family research

Although research in work–family issues started in the mid-1960s (Rapoport and Rapoport, 1965; 1969), the field took off in the late 1970s and the early 1980s. In 1980, Bartolome and Evans (1980) warned the community of practitioners and researchers of the actual cost of success that business executives face. They described the personal cost of 'career success' and challenged the assumption that to achieve such success, people needed to give up personal life and family satisfaction. Bartolome and Evans (1980) had only males in their sample; however, their findings warned of the dangers that careers in business could pose to achieve success and fulfillment in dimensions other than work. Korman, Witting-Berman and Lang (1981) described the effects of career success in a large sample of managers. They stressed that both for managers and professionals, career success was often linked to personal failure, leading to alienation.

From the early 1980s, research in work and family relationships has mostly focused on conflict and spillover, and managerial practice has focused on policies to ameliorate the negative effects in the workplace of such conflict and spillover. Work–family *conflict* appears when pressures from the roles of work and family are mutually incompatible, such that participation in one role makes it more difficult to participate in the other (Greenhaus and Beutell, 1985). The Greenhaus and Beutell literature review shows three major forms of work–family conflict: *time-based conflict, strain-based conflict*, and *behavior-based conflict*. Recent researchers study conflict as emanating from either work or family separately, and emphasize the family-to-work conflict (Kossek and Ozeki, 1998). Although this may be an attempt to legitimize 'family-friendly' policies, it may neglect the fact that who ultimately suffers the conflict is the individual, albeit the consequences have an effect on performance and other outcome measures. *Time-based* conflict appears when involvement in one role is impeded by time pressures in the other; 'there is a good deal of evidence to suggest that the number of hours people work is related to the amount of work–family conflict they are likely to experience' (Milliken and Dunn-Jensen, 2005) (p. 44). *Strain-based* conflict is conceptualized as a transactional process reflecting an imbalance between demands and the resources available to cope with those demands (Scharlach, 2001). Scharlach suggests that 'when demands exceed resources, one result can be role strain, defined as the felt difficulty in fulfilling role obligations (p. 217).' *Behavior-based conflict* appears when fulfilling the requirements of one role is made more difficult by the behavior required in another.

Spillover theory suggests that there is a reciprocal relationship between affective responses in one's work life and in one's family life (Linehan and Walsh, 2000). These two types of spillover, however, may have different effects, and have been studied separately. Spillover theory is based on the assumption that the effects of role expansion depend on the individual's global satisfaction with her current life situation (Campbell and Campbell, 1994). This assumption entails that women who are committed to and effective in their work roles carry on such commitment and enthusiasm to other roles, and vice versa.

Although more scarce in number, there are also studies showing that *positive spillover* in the non-work to work direction is also possible (Kirchmeyer, 1992). Kirchmeyer studies the nature and predictors of such positive spillover from non-work to work domains. The research of positive spillover from non-work to work-to-work domains is based on observation that some people get energy from roles other than work and carry it to work domains, thus increasing their performance. Positive spillover is based on the role accumulation theory. Sieber (1974) suggests that there are four major positive outcomes of role-accumulation: role privilege, status security, status enhancement, and enrichment of the personality.

These two different venues of research (negative and positive effects of multiple work and family roles) are summarized in what Rothbard (2001) calls the depletion and the enriching arguments. The depletion argument focuses on the idea that engagement in a role can lead to a negative emotional response to that role (inter-role conflict and stress) or to other roles (spillover); it looks at the negative emotional responses that people have to role engagement. The enrichment argument bases its claims in role accumulation theory, suggesting that role engagement may bring resources and pleasurable experiences, rather than pain, to the person. This view suggests that the benefits of role involvement may lead to gratification, greater self-esteem, and a positive emotional response to the role. Enrichment theory suggests that the benefits from one role may be carried over to another, so that positive responses from one role increase people's engagement in another. Rothbard's (2001) research provides strong evidence of potential enrichment by role accumulation, which leads her to suggest that 'rather than trying to limit family commitments and participation in other roles, organizations may do well to encourage such activities, as people may gain energy and sustenance from them' (p. 681).

Assumptions of the research and practice on work–family

Much of the research on work and family has focused on measuring static relationships between antecedents and outcomes. The main antecedents are number of roles, time demand, family demands, and spouse's job situation. The main outcomes are spillover, conflict, turnover, burnout and performance measures. One focus of work–life research has been the attempt to understand the mechanisms that affect work–family interactions. There are some research lines that seek to discover such mechanisms. Carlson and Kacmar (2000) studied the role of the values of the individual as a moderator between the antecedents (for example, work role ambiguity, work time demands, and family time demands) and consequences (job satisfaction, family satisfaction and life satisfaction) of experienced work–family conflict. Hansen (2001) advocates the need for harmonizing work and other facets of life and delineates an 'Integrative Life Planning' methodology. Poelmans (2005) studies the decision process that precedes and follows the work–family dilemma which may lead to the discovery of the underlying mechanisms of work–family interaction.

In the area of practice, concern about the interaction between work and family roles has pushed managers to apply policies that help employees to fulfill the demands of both work and family roles. However, these organizational policies do not necessarily reduce individual work–family conflict, for several reasons (Kossek and Ozeki, 1998). First, promotion and career planning often do not accommodate personal situations, thus putting more pressure on people at moments when they personally have demanding commitments outside work domains. Second, daily decision making is driven by deadlines and clients (Milliken and Dunn-Jensen, 2005), which gives work activities advantage over non-work activities when allocating time and resources. Third, some policies make it easy for individuals to neglect their non-work roles (for example, sick child care, concierges) instead of integrating work in life. Fourth, demands on time, effort and availability in work domains have increased at a faster rate than solutions. Fifth, changes in policies have not always been coupled with changes in organizational culture; policies have become 'espoused theories' instead of 'theories in use' (Argyris, 1991).

The first and second abovementioned reasons at least partially depend on the individual. Promotion and career planning often do not accommodate personal situations; nowadays the panorama in which careers develop allows individuals to design their own career paths out of the organizational constraints. In the current employment landscape, individuals do not necessarily pursue 'organizational careers', during which the company is responsible for planning and developing their career progression. Individuals may create their own paths; this new career pattern is what Hall and Mirvis (1996) coin the 'protean career' and Arthur and Rousseau (1996) call 'the boundaryless career'. Whereas in the old days the organization used to decide the possible and optimal pathways for the individual, now the individual might travel as a pilgrim who decides not only the final destination but also the ways to get there. One of the main features of the new ways careers develop is that, more than ever before, careers may be defined by personal choices (Mirvis and Hall, 1996).

Another micro variable that hinders integration of work with the other dimensions of life is the fact that the individual's daily decision making is bound to be driven by deadlines and clients. Milliken and Dunn-Jensen (2005), based on March and Simon (1958), suggest that when people have to prioritize tasks they are likely to do so on the basis of urgency rather than importance. When tasks are urgent, and negative outcomes are derived from neglecting them, people allocate more time than they do to tasks that do not have deadlines or immediate consequences. Similarly, if the tasks have direct clients who are paying for the service, they get more attention than otherwise. As a result, when work and non-work domains compete for time, work-related tasks are more likely to get it. It depends on the individual overcoming the resource allocation bias, and values (Carlson and Kacmar, 2000) and personal identity play an important role in doing so. The more salient the professional identity is in the individual's overall identity, the more the allocation will be likely to benefit work domains. The more the individual values family life, the more the allocation will be likely to benefit non-work domains.

The need for a new lens: career–life integration

The assumptions behind most of the research and practice in the work–life arena regard work and life as opposite or irreconcilable realities. The human being has innate psychological needs that are essential for ongoing psychological growth, integrity and well-being (Deci and Ryan, 2000). These basic innate needs are: the need for competence, relatedness and autonomy. To meet those basic needs is fundamental to developing a trajectory toward vitality, integration and health (Deci and Ryan, 2000). Work is one dimension of human life that might help to fulfill those needs. Likewise, family, community and spiritual life are also domains that might help to fulfill the need for competence, relatedness and autonomy. Thus, people do not necessarily need to *balance* work and life, but rather to *integrate* work with all aspects of life. 'An adult is not only a worker, or a spouse, or a parent. An adult may be all these things' (Kegan, 1994: 6).

Thus, although essential, work is neither the only nor the most important element over the whole course of the lifetime. Family, community, and spiritual life are also crucial for a person to have a balanced identity and achieve well-being. Professor Polo (1997) describes work as a task that requires effort and is specifically human. He remarks that work contributes to the common good and perfects the person who develops it. Thus, through work the person contributes to perfect the world. The person also perfects herself as a human being since work is a means to enact values, to grow personally, to express creativity, and to achieve mastery.

Through family people experience intimacy, love and affiliation. It is in a family where they are valued for being and where they can transmit life. It is also through family that they contribute to society, fulfill the desire of legacy and perpetuation, and give back what they received in childhood. People receive services and goods from the community and as a member of it also fulfill their desires of legacy, contributes to the common good, and develop relationships and affiliation. People's identity also includes their spiritual life, whether or not through joining a religion or subscribing to a doctrine. Such spiritual life shapes people's values, beliefs and aims, and contributes to the sense of affiliation and perpetuation.

Thus, work-related activities can play a key role in someone's development (Dalton and Thompson, 1986). However, if work takes over other dimensions it may hinder the meeting of developmental needs associated with dimensions other than work. Similarly, if one's career does not provide proper developmental opportunities, the career may be experienced as frustrating and unrewarding (Dalton and Thompson, 1986). Cultural subgroups, such as families, clubs and work groups, provide tools, practices and values that can allow people to satisfy basic needs, to feel volition and choice as well as cohesion and relatedness. Insofar as this occurs, we find human health and well-being. However, if the values and goals are not well integrated, for example because the cultural or sub-cultural context is chaotic and pressuring rather than optimally challenging and supportive, we would expect to find not only constituents who evidence less well-being, but cultures themselves that are less stable and more fragmented (Deci and Ryan, 2000).

Developmental models of careers

The word 'career' has a connotation of progression or development along some course (Dalton and Thompson, 1986). Nicholson and Andrews (2005) point out that the 'etymological root of the word, career, denotes a pathway, conveying the image of a traveler in a landscape.' Developmental models of careers have evolved over time, reflecting changes in the panorama where careers develop. Life-span models (Super, 1957) (Miller and Form 1951) describe long cycles in which the individual gets introduced to the work place, adapts and masters different tasks. Organizational-based models (Dalton and Thompson, 1986; Schein, 1984) also describe lifelong cycles where the individual gets initiated and masters tasks; although contrary to the life-span models, those stages are not age-related.

In contrast to life-span models, Hall (1994) has proposed that contemporary careers may be viewed more accurately as a series of short cycles of initiation, learning and mastery. Hall (1994, 2002) claims that because the life cycle of technologies and products is so shortened, so too are personal career mastery cycles. As a result, people's careers become increasingly a succession of cycles of exploration–trial–establishment–mastery–exit, as they move in and out of various product areas, technologies, functions, organizations and the like. This should facilitate the integration of career with other dimensions of life, since people might be slower in one mini-cycle or may even go out of the job market during one cycle and still be able to come back and be employable. Moreover, as we will argue later in the chapter, when coming back to the job market, people may have fulfilled other developmental tasks, so they are likely to be a better and more mature employee, more suited for managerial tasks and leadership roles. However, it seems that people have not changed the old assumption that career is only one long cycle; if they 'break' it at some point, they might be compromising it forever.

Denise might be a good example of the functioning of mini-cycles. Although Denise is only 27, she has already undergone a whole career mini-cycle and has spent some time out of the job market to take care of her family. Denise graduated with a degree in political science at the age of 22, having worked in Washington for two years. After her graduation she worked in Washington for another year and then studied for a Master's degree in political science. Afterwards, she decided to pursue a Ph.D. in the same field. Before doing so, she went to Europe and studied for a Master's degree in art management for one year. After her European experience Denise had to take care of her sick parents, and during that time she temped for one year, which for her felt like being out of the job market, since she had very restricted options due to her parents' residence in the countryside and to her time availability. Once the family situation improved, Denise started her Ph.D. After two years, in which she objectively did very well, she realized that she did not like it and quit the program. It was then that she looked for a job in business and after six months in this, she got into an MBA.

Denise's story is paradigmatic of the shorter career cycles that the technologies, products and fast knowledge creation have created. Denise initiated a mini-career-cycle in political science, mastered it, took some time off, and started a new career cycle.

Career integration in life during the first years of professional life

One necessary step toward integration of career in life is the integration of the different life dimensions in an individual's identity. However, over the professional life of a person, a number of socially held assumptions and forces may jeopardize proper decision-making. The first years of professional life are crucial to determine the panorama in which career and family life develop. However, these years are full of competing needs that make the individual prone to overemphasize time and energy allocation in career undertakings.

There are four main reasons why young professionals focus so heavily on professional goals when they start their careers, overlooking dimensions other than work. First, they invest a great deal, in money and in time, energy and ego, on training and development for their career before entering the job market and during the first years of professional activity. Second, the life developmental stage they are in when they start their professional life is one of forming an initial life structure, of which work is a major part (Levinson, 1978, 1996.) Third, career is salient for the role models of young professionals. Last, organizational decision makers monitor young professionals to decide whether or not they are high potential, fast-track employees.

First, young professional adults in the US make a big investment in their careers. When still adolescents, approximately at the age of 16, they start a thorough college search. At the age of 17–18 they move out of their family's home after an exhausting search–application–decision process. During the college years they strive to at least keep the same pace as their peers. They learn to compete and to compare. They have rewards for being at the top – whether receiving compliments, awards or scholarships. Accelerating their studies is judged as successful, whereas slowing them is stigmatized. During college years, students feel the financial burden of tuition and room and board, which leads them to work, make some money, ask for a loan, or at least to witness the sacrifice their parents make to pay for everything. Over the summers they either take classes to speed up their pace, or get a job to explore the professional world while earning some money.

When graduation comes, students desire to get the return of such an investment. Moreover, a high percentage of young graduates go back to school after a few years of professional experience, or even without such experience. This aggravates the financial burden and the need of a return.

Third, people adapt to new roles by observing role models that enable them to establish potential identities (Ibarra, 1999). During college years, students have two main sources of establishing potential identities: their peers and the media. Their peers, however, are still a 'work in progress'; people with whom to compete, compare and share, but not to identify with. The other source is the media. On TV shows, as well as in films, novels and magazines, professionals are often portrayed as well-respected and happy when they make a lot of money and get to positions where they exert influence. Thus, young people starting their professional lives identify with such models and aspire to be happy having power and money.

Finally, organizational settings are designed for people to advance at a fast pace during their first years of professional work. Whether with policies of up-or-out or fast-track paths, companies convey the need to advance quickly during the first years of one's career. These policies are coupled with the generalized belief that long hours at work, availability during weekends and vacations, and willingness to transfer or to travel mean high commitment. Such common beliefs put pressure on the young person who is starting their career to allocate time and energies according to what is expected from them. Moreover, in most companies there are stories and experiences of people who have been sidelined after turning down promotions or refusing overseas assignments.

As a consequence of the investment, the developmental stage in which young people start their careers and the role models available at the time, young professionals set high career goals for the first years of work. Commitments that make them slow the pace toward the accomplishment of such goals are regarded as hurdles to overcome. However, it is in these years that the young professional may establish a family, have children, and desire to share and enjoy time with them.

Some people commit to new roles thinking that the freedom to choose also implies that they are going to be able to manage new role demands. People do not like the verb 'compromise'. We implicitly compromise all the time; however, we are not equipped to accept that we do so. As a young mother reported in a weekly magazine's article about the difficulties of simultaneously working and parenting, 'We grew up believing that we had fantastic, unlimited freedom of choice' (Warner, 2005). As a result, there is a sense of control over life events in which assuming new roles does not necessitate cutting back old ones. Compromise is equated to lack of freedom – or to lack of ability. Our society is not prepared to accept either one or the other. However, one cannot, or should not, talk about work and family as if they were two independent, unrelated realities. A person's life is like one complete puzzle with several pieces. Both work and family are crucial pieces of the puzzle that makes up life. As Cleveland (2005) suggests, 'our current criteria for success are deficient because we ignore the facets and structures of work that affect non-work areas of our lives' (p. 340).

Let us present a vignette. It is Monday at noon. You go with your peers to a fabulous salad buffet. You are a salad lover, and there it is: all kind of ingredients available for you. It is your first time in this place, so you observe to see how it works. Got it. You need to pay, then you take your tray, and you can start choosing ingredients. You can take as many as you want. There is only one little constraint: you need to eat all you put on your plate. Perfect. You follow your friends, who you think might know the place well. You see delicious ingredients and you take them. You even take some cucumbers. You don't like them, but you have heard how healthy they are. You do not even finish seeing everything, because your plate is already full. You sit and start. The waiter passes by and offers some meat and bread. You had not counted on that. Anyway, you say, 'Thank you. Leave it here.'

Let us translate. An individual is guided by what others do. She does not even finish exploring the possibilities. She even takes assignments she does not like, because they are portrayed as 'healthy', career wise. After following her friends, she takes what seems 'satisfying', so she is happy with that. Her decision is based on what her friends do and in what is portrayed by the media as good. This reflects that she has had a restricted number of potential identities. Besides, the developmental needs of the life stage of the young person lead her to focus on specific goals that are more salient in this stage. Both the potential identities available for her and her own developmental stage, lead her to put a lot on her plate, in terms of career commitments. In the vignette the person takes enough when wandering around, and because she is hungry, she probably takes even more than she needs. During the first years of professional life the person establishes a family. In this vignette she had not envisioned that the waiter was going to pass. So, she had committed enough, and now she is adding even more. However, she is not able to cut back in previous commitments, either because psychologically she cannot or because of external pressures.

The bottom line is that integration needs to exist first in the individual's mind. It is not a matter of compromising, but of being aware of how the different pieces fit together. If the pieces are harmoniously integrated, the picture is nice and clear. If one of the pieces takes over, the rest of the picture may end up being grotesque. At different life stages and in different familial and personal circumstances each piece may have a different shape and importance. The young person who is starting his career without any major responsibility other than work may have very different pieces from the father of three children in their middle school years or from the daughter of an Alzheimer's sufferer. Life is dynamic and so are the requirements of each life domain. However, not giving proper room to a piece in a life stage may compromise the whole picture in following stages.

These ideas are clearly illustrated in the story of Javi, an MBA graduate from a leading Spanish Business School. In his story, it is clear that he has the big, integrated picture as his goal in life. He realizes that there are forces that might bias his decision-making, and he tries to overcome them. Moreover, Javi realizes that his life is composed of several domains and that overemphasizing one of them would mean to diminish others. Moreover, he takes into account not only his life goals, but also his wife's:

> The last semester of the MBA we decided to get married [to Edurne, another MBA student at the time]. Career and personal wise you need to be very clear: what you want to do and why. There are a lot of external pressures, but you are the one who knows your expectations, your circumstances, your situation, your preferences and your dreams. You need to not let others decide … because that would make no sense … From the very beginning [when we got married] children were part of the picture. My plan is for my life, and my career is only one part of my life.

Looking in more depth at integrating as a way of framing the work–life relationship

Let us recap what we have been saying here. In contrast to traditional ways of viewing the work–life interface, which see work roles and family or personal roles as two separate kinds of entities that have to be juggled, balanced, or somehow played off against each other, the concept of integrating suggests that work and personal activities are simply two parts of a whole identity. In much of our thinking about this topic, we seem to be making the assumption that the person is living a divided life, one in which he or she is pulled in different directions, with two quite different identities. If, on the other hand, we see them as two parts of a whole, then we can focus more on the whole and on the ways that the parts mesh together to create a strong and unified whole. It is this holistic model of role behavior that we propose as a more useful model for having a satisfying and fulfilling life – a 'life worth living', as Herb Shepard called it.

Executives, managers and other agents of organizations often seem also to make the assumption that family, personal and work roles are different entities that need to compete for resources. Rosabeth Kanter (1977), in an early classic report on work and family life, used the term 'the myth of separate worlds' to describe a phenomenon in which the organization acted as if the employee's home simply did not exist, as if all that mattered was their life at work. Despite Kanter's call for a remedy, we still see organizations making time and work demands on employees that suggest a clear lack of awareness of the existence of their private lives. Let us now look in a deeper way at what this concept of work–life integration is all about.

Joyce Fletcher (1998) has made the distinction between the employee's public life and her private life. As Fletcher points out, when there is a clash between the public work role and the private sphere (home and personal activities), the private side 'disappears'. That is, the public side always seems to have greater visibility and credibility.[1]

However, if we take a more holistic perspective, we view the 'public' and the 'private' as simply two parts of the same whole. The public side is the externally visible part, the one that most people observe in an individual's work activities. The private side, when the individual is at work, is often less visible in the work setting. However, if people choose to make them both visible at work and to openly discuss home and family experiences and make them part of their public self at work, then the public–private dichotomy vanishes. In fact, both are part of people's overall life and identity and to keep one part of one's self concealed can be a stressful and energy-consuming (and energy-wasting) activity. Or, on the other hand, if people are not consciously concealing the private side but rather neglecting it, then this would represent a 'lopsided identity' in which their private life is being under-represented.

Integration as an outcome of adult development

How does the process of becoming more integrated or congruent at work take place? Several bodies of relevant literature can assist us in this inquiry. First, in the area of adult development, we know from Kegan's (1982) research that identity integration is, in fact, a major part of what adult development is all about. As people move through the various levels of growth, the self becomes more differentiated. That is, people's lives become richer, with more varied activities in more varied roles. Their emotional world becomes bigger and more complex. And the self must grow and create new components that serve to connect people to this richer set of engagements with the world.

However, as the self becomes more differentiated and complex, it is also necessary for it to be able to integrate all of these new facets, so that the individual feels whole. That is, even though one sees oneself engaging with the world in very different and complicated ways, one also needs to have a sense of oneself as one person with one self, not multiple selves or multiple personalities. The psychologically healthy person is able to hold all of these different parts of the self, or 'subidentities', in one single clear identity. This attainment of an integrated identity is a highly demanding activity, as one is literally growing a new self as one moves through various levels of development.

Perhaps the level in the Kegan (1982) model that is most relevant to our discussion here is the fourth or *institutional* level. Here the individual has moved from the interpersonal level, where the self is embedded in his different roles, to a new level where he can see a separation between his sense of self and his role activities – in this case his work activities. In level three, the *interpersonal* level, the individual can not see a distinction between the self and his work – he *is* his work. And if he is successful at work, he is successful as a person, in his total sense of self, or vice versa. However, in level four, the self has created a distance from the work role, so that he has more perspective on the work. In this new view, he *has* a work role, whereas for the individual at level three, he *is* his work role. Thus, if the individual at level four encounters a setback at work, he does not feel like a failure as a person; he is simply aware that he is having a difficulty in one part of his life.

We realize that this is a very subtle distinction that we are making. In this holistic view of identity, work and home still can represent two different types of activities. Integration does not mean that the person is simultaneously engaged in both at the same time, although this is sometimes possible. Rather, the person at level four is able to engage in work activities and still hold his identity as a father, son, husband, and so on, and have that as a public part of his self at work.

The evolution from level three, interpersonal, to level four, institutional, is relevant for professionals in leadership positions. Kegan (1994) claims that managerial work requires: to own and to invent one's work, to be self-initiating, self-correcting, and self-evaluating rather than dependent on others to frame problems and initiate adjustments, to be guided by one's visions, to take responsibility for what happens at work, rather than attributing all internal and external circumstances to someone else, to master the work roles, and to see the relation of the parts to the whole. Only someone who is at least at level four of development is able to master these requirements. For people at the third level, 'the fundamental and most trustworthy source of knowledge is outside of oneself' (p. 164), thus, those at the third level want outside control to make decisions and to take responsibilities. Someone at the third level experiences irreconcilable expectations, inherent in leadership roles, has difficulty in holding himself together and is directly and 'immediately' affected by each thing that happens to him; someone at the fourth level is only 'mediately' affected by the loyalties, values and expectations that are important to her (Kegan, 1994). The individual at the fourth level is guided by her own vision and by her own internal way of authorizing.

By 'integration', we mean *the person's sense that his or her identity is a coherent whole, made up of various sub-identities related to specific life and career roles* (Hall, 2002: 71–2.) Integrating the career as a part of an individual's life can help them to evolve from lower to higher levels of consciousness, which enables them to take on the mental demands of managerial jobs. Some employers want nothing from their employees but well-socialized, responsible, loyal workers who can perform assigned duties. For such employers, individuals in the third level of conscientiousness will be the perfect fit. However, leadership roles demand the employee to own her work, to make decisions, to self-initiate, self-evaluate and self-correct herself. To commit to family and community roles facilitates an individual's evolving to the fourth level which enables her to perform such leadership requirements, because people grow best when they experience support and challenge.

The work environment might provide challenge, in the form of variety and difficulty, but it usually lacks support. It could promote 'defensiveness and constriction' (p. 42). The experience of challenge without support is painful, and 'it can generate feelings of anger, helplessness and futility' (p. 43). However, when young adults commit to family and community roles those roles might provide the adequate blend of challenge and support. They experience new demands coupled with support. In the family, as parents, the individuals are expected, for instance, to institute a vision of leadership, maintain boundaries, and set limits (Kegan, 1994). These expectations are challenges that they face in the presence of support – from their partner, friends and extended family among others. As spouses, adults are expected to develop a 'separate identity' distinct from the one of the spouse, to overcome romanticized love, to love *despite* personal differences, and to set limits to preserve the couple as a distinct subgroup of the family (Kegan, 1994). In developing the capabilities to fulfill these expectations the adults are evolving to higher levels of conscientiousness. In developing such capabilities the individual is valued for who she is and is supported despite her mistakes and shortcomings. This kind of supportive context containing psychological safety for experimentation and personal growth is what Kegan calls a 'holding environment'. This safe setting facilitates her willingness to try again following errors and personal faults. Such a holding environment may lead to vital engagement and growth, which is positive for the individual as a whole, and as a consequence is positive for her professional undertakings and personal commitments. Kegan claims that the willingness and capacity of someone to self-initiate, self-evaluate and self-correct herself requires 'a theory or a philosophy of what makes something valuable, a meta-leap beyond the third order' (p. 169), and effective commitment to family, community, and spiritual life might facilitate acquiring such an underlying philosophy.

How to foster development as a way to facilitate integration

As we have just seen, integration is a consequence of adult development. However, how do people grow? Kegan (1982) suggests that individuals grow through challenge and support. Additionally, goal theorists show that human action always 'pursues goals, although individuals vary in the degree to which they are explicitly aware of those goals in daily life' (Sheldon and Elliot, 1999: 482). Furthermore, 'goals define the pursuits of individuals, regardless of awareness or volition' (Austin and Vancouver, 1996: 340). Taking into account both adult development theory and goal-setting theory one can conclude that human development requires challenge, and that such challenge can be provided by personal goals, which drive human activity. Goal attainment facilitates personal growth and adult development if those goals are *self-concordant* (Sheldon and Elliot, 1999). Self-concordant goals are those that seek to meet personal needs of autonomy, competence, and relatedness of the individual. According to development theories (Kegan, 1982; Levinson, 1978), the salience of those needs varies through the life span of the individual. The concretization of the goals should adapt to suit the different weight of the needs through the life span of the individual.

In short, human activity is driven by goals. The attainment of those goals triggers growth if the goals are self-concordant. To be self-concordant the goals need to adapt to different developmental levels and needs. The fact that goals are self-concordant 'is manifested in the fact that goals pursued tend to have an internal perceived locus of causality; that is, they are felt to emanate directly from self-choices' (Sheldon and Elliot, 1999: 483).

In the career domain goals might target extrinsic or intrinsic rewards. Extrinsic rewards are those that others give to the individual for doing the job, such as financial income, promotion, and recognition. Intrinsic rewards are those that the person gets while engaging in the work, such as developing creativity and other abilities, and intellectual stimulation;

thus, intrinsic rewards are not granted by others (Betz et al., 1989). Both extrinsic and intrinsic rewards might enable the individual to meet the needs of autonomy, competence and relatedness. At different moments a preponderance of either extrinsic or intrinsic will be better suited to fulfill those needs of autonomy, competence and relatedness. Human beings are active and are naturally inclined toward growth and development. Sheldon and Elliot (1999), along with other authors, suggest that individuals have innate developmental trends and propensities that may be given voice as their lives go forward. 'This voice might be difficult to hear, but current research suggests that the ability to hear it is of crucial importance for the pursuit of happiness' (Sheldon and Elliot, 1999: 495).

As mentioned earlier, for someone to feel satisfaction and well-being, the attainment of goals should be concordant with their personal needs and dispositions. 'Different goal contents have different relations to the quality of behavior and mental health, specifically because different goal contents are associated with differing degrees of need satisfaction' (Deci and Ryan, 2000: 227). Thus, the attainment of goals that lead to needs satisfaction, trigger well-being and fulfillment. The attainment of goals that do not satisfy the needs for autonomy, competence and relatedness, might be experienced as frustrating or unsatisfactory. As a result, if the needs of the individual in each of the quadrants of the model in Figure 8.1 are aligned with those goals, the attainment of them will trigger growth and fulfillment. Otherwise, if goals and needs are not aligned, the attainment might be felt as unrewarding.

In Figure 8.1 we can see combinations of extrinsic and intrinsic goals for rewards that might facilitate growth and development, thus, they might facilitate growth and, in the end, career–life integration.

It is interesting to note that in the Faster–Higher–Stronger category (quadrant 1 in Figure 8.1) the individual might, for 'a period of time', fulfill her needs for autonomy, competence and relatedness. However, extrinsic rewards are, by definition, granted by others. Thus, extrinsic rewards cannot lead to high degrees of autonomy satisfaction. The case of the Making-A-Living category (quadrant 4 in Figure 8.1) is even more critical. There the person does not seek to fulfill any of her or his needs in the work domain. However, such a person might make a little psychological investment in their work, and spend those energies in fulfilling their needs in domains other than work.

Having the proper goals in each stage of life might facilitate adult development and integration. However, there is a pervasive danger: to get stuck in the FHS category (quadrant 1), that is, in the high goal-setting for extrinsic rewards and low for intrinsic. Previously we have explained why young professionals are likely to enter their professional life in this category.

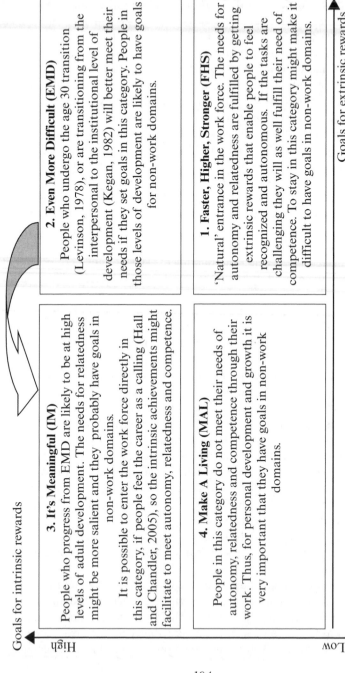

Goals for intrinsic rewards

High ↑

3. It's Meaningful (IM)

People who progress from EMD are likely to be at high levels of adult development. The needs for relatedness might be more salient and they probably have goals in non-work domains.

It is possible to enter the work force directly in this category, if people feel the career as a calling (Hall and Chandler, 2005), so the intrinsic achievements might facilitate to meet autonomy, relatedness and competence.

2. Even More Difficult (EMD)

People who undergo the age 30 transition (Levinson, 1978), or are transitioning from the interpersonal to the institutional level of development (Kegan, 1982) will better meet their needs if they set goals in this category. People in those levels of development are likely to have goals for non-work domains.

4. Make A Living (MAL)

People in this category do not meet their needs of autonomy, relatedness and competence through their work. Thus, for personal development and growth it is very important that they have goals in non-work domains.

1. Faster, Higher, Stronger (FHS)

'Natural' entrance in the work force. The needs for autonomy and relatedness are fulfilled by getting extrinsic rewards that enable people to feel recognized and autonomous. If the tasks are challenging they will as well fulfill their need of competence. To stay in this category might make it difficult to have goals in non-work domains.

Low

Low   Goals for extrinsic rewards   High ↑

Figure 8.1   Self-concordant goals for work rewards that facilitate development and growth at different life stages and growth levels

The problem is not in starting professional life there, but in remaining in it over the years, since this makes some of their needs remain unmet, and leads them to develop compensatory motives.

> One ramification of the development of strong compensatory motives such as extrinsic aspirations is that they not only result from lack of basic need satisfaction but they also tend to perpetuate the lack of need satisfaction because they are likely to keep people focused on the need substitutes or extrinsic goals, thus strengthening the 'wrong' goals and exacerbating the negative, ill-being consequences (Deci and Ryan, 2000)

This effect is likely to have cognitive roots. Bazerman and Watkins (2004) suggest that 'researchers have shown that human judgment and decision-making deviates from rationality.' In their book, Bazerman and Watkins mention four common errors or biases that might account for the effect of over-committing to the wrong goals even when they do not yield the expected satisfaction. First, people have the tendency to think that the problem is not 'severe enough' to merit action or change in one's behavior. Second, individuals tend to allocate blame to others; thus, the cause of the lack of well-being is identified as external rather than internal (to have the wrong goals). Third, people tend to overly discount the future, so thinking that future bad effects will in fact not be that bad. Fourth, and extremely important, individuals tend to maintain the status quo, especially if the change is experienced as a recognition of having made a wrong decision.

Let us consider an example. The case of over-committing to 'the wrong goals' would be the case of someone who enters the work force after graduating from college at the age of 22. She gets a job in a very demanding industry where she needs to be very available in terms of time and geographical mobility. She aims to be promoted, to get exposed to different projects and people, and to make a lot of money. She perceives that all these things will make her be respected, and thus will fulfill her need of relatedness. Moreover, these work rewards will also make her financially autonomous, since she will feel 'as a grown up'. Moreover, she aims to feel competent in showing that she can do a good job. Thus, in a first career stage her aims are aligned with her developmental needs.

However, over the years, she might enter new networks and commit to new roles, as for instance, she might get married, be a mother and participate in a fellowship. If she does not change her goals, and keeps the same commitment and drive toward money, promotion and learning, such 'old' commitment might interfere with her efforts toward her 'newly' acquired intrinsic goals. Thus, getting stuck in the same career goals might jeopardize her development in the new roles. She most likely will experience marriage, motherhood and fellowship as unrewarding, because she is not investing enough to take something out of them. As a result she may re-emphasize her investment in her old roles, which are the only ones that are yielding satisfaction. Besides, she may think that the problem is not that severe, since she still has 'her old rewards'. Second, she might blame her husband, her company or even the governmental laws for not making it easier for young people to care for their families (all these reasons might be partially true, but she would not be admitting her stake in the problem). Third, she may think that in the future she will find everything more compatible, and also she might think that her decisions now will not have repercussions for future actions. Thus, she will postpone taking action. Lastly, the tendency to maintain the status quo may make it easier for her to keep doing what she is good at, and so avoid change. Thus, the reinforcement of investment in her 'old' goals might seriously hinder her capacity to grow and develop through the new challenges and support. Even more serious, she might, in the future, be less willing to try new roles, since the experience had been felt as stressful.

One prominent example of a person moving from the Faster, Higher, Stronger cell to the Even More Difficult perspective would be Bill Gates. He achieved perhaps the most extreme form of success measured by extrinsic goals by becoming the world's richest person. Then, after he married and became a father, and presumably went through some other kinds of personal development, he became interested in philanthropy. He and his wife founded the Bill and Melinda Gates Foundation and took on the mission of making a difference in world health. He obviously still strives for financial success, as his company, Microsoft, is as competitive as ever, but he is also motivated by the intrinsic goals of sharing his resources, helping others, and making a better world.

Integration and social identity

Another set of literature that can be helpful here is that dealing with various kinds of difference in organizations. For example, Bell and Nkomo's (2001) study of black professional women discusses the issues of having a bicultural identity. They report many examples of their respondents' constant awareness that they live in two different worlds – a black world at home and a predominantly white or more mixed-race world at work. They have to be able to constantly hold those two sometimes-competing parts of their selves – being authentic and true to themselves at the same time that they are engaging in a competent and satisfying way with their family, friends and colleagues. Here is how one woman, Dawn Stanley, described the task. She sees the black and white communities in which she lives as two separate drawers, two separate faces, and two separate uniforms. I get up Monday through Friday and I think about acting, behaving, and interacting with one group of people where I am more formal and maintain an emotional distance. Then on Friday evenings, I close the door to my office. The weekend is back to me, back to family, back to being in safe territory. It's not that I don't do things with white folks from time to time, but my worlds are not very integrated, they are separate and distinct...It's just two closets: they both work and I know what to expect in both of them. (Bell and Nkomo, 2001: 231)

However, Bell and Nkomo report that not all of the women in their sample reported having this sense of a bicultural identity:

Rather, they speak of themselves as centered in one universe, one they describe as richly diverse. They are not interested in being 'incog-Negro', a black person who attempts to disguise, hide, or deny their racial identity. Their willingness to reveal their sense of identity keeps them strongly connected to black womanhood. These women see African-Americans as an important part of the national fabric, and because of that, carry inside them a sense of self-worth that many black women in a white world have to fight to discover. (p. 233)

Bell and Nkomo quote Julia Smith, who described the basis of her integrated identity:

I don't know if you would call it being in a limbo world or if you would call it having access to things that have been traditionally opened only to whites... I guess the notion of functioning in a white world becomes uncomfortable when you view yourself as having sort of given up and you have cut away a piece of yourself in order to deal with white people. Now I am not saying that I open my life like a book to white folks, but I am clear on who I am. I think I'm accepted on my own terms to a certain extent as a black woman. I position myself not as a threat, but as a person of strength. That's important to me. (p. 233)

Other relevant difference situations would involve people's invisible parts of the self, such as sexual orientation or chronic illnesses, at work. How do individuals make choices about where to disclose information about their illness or lifestyle? And if they disclose, how and when do they do it?

Beatty (2003) examined these issues for people with two invisible illnesses, epilepsy and MS. Disclosure can be a difficult issue, as there are real consequences, many of them negative, of revealing a chronic illness. Job and career discrimination, distancing from colleagues, and well intended but not always helpful actions of co-workers are but a few of the possibilities. And on the positive side, it can be tremendously liberating to see that one can be one's true self at work, being open about one's illness, and be a fully functioning and accepted part of the work group. Clair et al. (2005) discuss the issue of invisible social identities, such as those related to sexuality, illness and racial diversity. They created a general model of how individuals manage invisible identities, focusing on the choice to 'pass' (that is, to conceal the identity) or to reveal. We would assume that the decision to reveal would suggest that the person had integrated this personal characteristic into the larger personal identity. Their model proposes that people are more likely to reveal as a function of certain individual differences (propensity toward risk taking, self-monitoring, developmental stage and motives). One of the motives they cite is the desire to 'maintain a coherent sense of self' (p. 88): 'Declaring one's difference allows one to be a complete and integrated person and obviates the difficult task of constantly being engaged in information management to conceal aspects of oneself' (Clair et al., 2005: 88). The authors also propose that factors in the interpersonal and environmental context, such as diversity climate, norms, legal protections and qualities of the other person, can affect the pass/reveal choice, as well.

Briscoe (1998) examined these issues of when an individual is able to express herself at work and when she chooses to withhold information about herself. Some values are restricted on a 'routine' basis, while others are expressed or suppressed on a 'restricted' basis. He found that some of the most difficult parts of the self to reveal at work do, in fact, involve personal or private life, such as religious beliefs. Some of the intrapersonal factors that drive the decision to express or suppress values include: identity, affect, standards, pragmatism and role-fulfillment. There are also external factors that affect this process, which include: authority, external values or culture, personal support, advocacy, familiarity and dialogue structures. Briscoe also found that, although these factors do exert a strong influence, some people were found to have a higher need than others to express their values in their behavior.

Another informative study is Ibarra's (2003) examination of how people make important life and career changes. She found that in many cases people did not tend to make big, momentous decisions to change. Rather, they often would simply try out some new activities in an experimental way. And then, if they enjoyed them and liked the results, they might move more and more in that direction. In time, this might result in a significant change in career. Ibarra also found that these new activities required the person to change their identity in a way that was congruent with the new activities. Like the activity changes, the identity changes often occurred in an incremental and evolving way. This process illustrates the evolving self that Kegan discusses, as the person self becomes more complex with the addition of the new activities, and then the person has to make sense of the changes by creating a new identity that holds a coherent view of and perspective on the life and career changes.

The importance of boundaries

When we talk about integrating work and family activities it does not mean that there is no separation or boundary between them. Any living system needs to have separated and differentiated functions, and work activities and family activities call for, most of the time, quite different sorts of behavior. These different behaviors are bounded in various ways, usually in time or in space (location). These boundaries are necessary to help maintain the person's focus in each area. What lessons do these streams of research hold regarding identity integration in the work–life arena? One observation that we can make on this other research is that it *is* possible to integrate career in life. Some people are able to find ways to bring their whole selves to work, or at least the important parts that they want to bring to work. Our words 'want to' suggest another point: part of the integration process consists of our finding the level of disclosure at work about home and personal life that feels comfortable to us. For example, someone may talk about a chronic illness at work but choose not to give out details about specific symptoms or yesterday's visit to the doctor. In the same way many people find ways to make their family part of their work world and vice versa, but they also have a sense of boundaries. These boundaries are constantly being renegotiated as one deals with the various developmental tasks of life. Moreover, the words 'want to' stress the fact that one needs to take into account the desire of integration when making decisions about and weighing alternatives for career moves. As we have reviewed, it does mean to be able to give room to different domains at different points in time. Giving room to family, community and spiritual life domains may promote psychological evolution that is needed to master the order and complexity demanded in managerial and leadership work roles.

A richly textured description of this process of work–life integration was provided by Crary (1996). In an essay entitled, 'Holding it all together', she provided the details of a day in the life of a professional woman, married, with a young daughter. Her theme of holding the parts together is what we mean here by integration. Here is how she described one part of the experience:

> The challenge of 'integrating' seems to me to be one of being able to hold adequately within my life space, in some harmonious whole, the different kinds of investments and commitments (to relationships, to work) that deeply engage and stimulate me, and make a contribution to the world in some fashion. However, the act of holding them all together within my life structure seems to require continuous calibration, questioning of time, energy, and payback across these different contexts. (Crary, 1996: 213)

She goes on to say that this integration is not a solitary process. It must be done 'in sync' with her immediate family members (husband and daughter). As she says, 'The more flexible Tim [her husband] can be with his commitments, the easier it is for me to maintain my outside-of-the-home work commitments, relationships, and activities (and I'm sure the reverse is true as well)' (p. 213).[2] Thus, as Crary shows us, work–life integration is indeed a *process* more than an outcome. It is not something one achieves at a certain moment in life. Rather, like any developmental process, it is a work in progress.

For example, she describes some of the 'psychological tyrannies that I can fall prey to while navigating through my days' that affect her sense of internal balance:

1. There are many moments when I doubt my own professional competence...
2. I can become absorbed in worrying about how others are perceiving me...
3. At times, I doubt how good a job I am doing as a parent...
4. I worry about my mental competence... (p. 214.)

What seems important to us in reading Crary's personal integrative journey is, first the need for self-awareness as she addresses these tasks and interdependencies and how adaptable she can be in changing herself in appropriate ways as she moves through the challenges. Second, not only does the journey benefit the person, but it is highly beneficial to develop effective leaders.

Conclusion

What, then, can we say about work–life integration? First, *it is a process that involves psychological development*. It is not a state of being. One must undergo personal change to be effective in this process. This is what makes it so difficult.

More specifically, the identity integration process requires *the ability to see simultaneously the complexity and the wholeness of the different facets of one's life*. It means being comfortable with the different parts and with the role senders' knowledge of these different facets. In sum, integration is a developmental process, whereby as one faces new life tasks and challenges, one is constantly coming to terms with and learning to accept an evolving sense of self, while seeing how all of the pieces together form a coherent whole.

Careers no longer develop in lifelong cycles but in a series of shorter learning cycles over the span of a individual's work life span. Such a panorama requires them to develop a protean career, that

> involves horizontal growth, expanding one's range of competencies and ways of connecting to work and other people, as opposed to the more traditional vertical model of success (upward mobility). In the protean form of growth, the goal is learning, psychological success, and expansion of the identity. In the more traditional vertical form, the goal was advancement, success and esteem in the eyes of others, and power. Thus the protean form can embrace both mastery and relational growth. (Hall and Mirvis, 1996: 35)

Career–life integration may both facilitate the enactment of a protean career and at the same time be facilitated by the nature of the protean career. First, it might facilitate the development of a protean career because, as argued in the chapter, the individuals might develop psychological capacity to cope with the demands of the work arena in their family, community and spiritual life. On the other hand, the nature of the protean career might facilitate to integrate career in life, because the shorter cycles of career development do not necessitate continuity in time, which means that to slow the career pace one does not jeopardize future career development.

These short cycles can be a way that an individual moves through the various career goal orientations shown in Figure 8.1. Although we are not arguing that there is any particular direction of change that all people go through, we would argue that one frequent progression is from an early-career focus on extrinsic goals (the 'Faster, Higher, Stronger' mindset) to an incorporation of more intrinsic rewards to accompany this extrinsic striving ('Even More Difficult' orientation). This model can also be used to understand other kinds of shifts, such as a person who starts with a sense of calling in her work ('It's Meaningful') and then becomes concerned with pursuing this calling and also becoming rich and famous (EMD).

To make these short cycles of career development work effectively requires two 'metacompetencies' (Hall, 2002): self-awareness and adaptability. Self-awareness is required so that the individual can know what her goals are and how well her current life is aligned with those goals. And then adaptability is needed so that she is able to make the necessary changes if her current life structure is not aligned with her goals. These qualities help her to develop an internal compass, to help her identify and to follow what Shepard called 'the path with a heart.'

Another potent influence on an individual's developing personal integration and a clearer understanding of what career success means for herself is her key relationships. In particular, this means reference groups and developmental networks. As people change, for example by moving from the FHS quadrant to the EMD quadrant in Figure 8.1, they would probably have to shift their attention from the reference group associated with their early career stage (for example, co-workers for whom striving and vertical success are paramount) to a new reference group that highly values intrinsic rewards. In fact, this may mean cutting ties with the old reference group. As Ibarra (2003) points out, the people who have a stake in where you are right now are probably not those who will help you get to somewhere else.

Unfortunately, it is more difficult to identify a reference group that values intrinsic rewards than one favoring extrinsic goals. The latter can be observed through their ambitious work behavior, their choice of possessions such as homes, cars and other external rewards, and other observations of the visible indicators of extrinsic rewards. But finding a new group of referent others who valued intrinsic goals would be aided through consciously attempting to create a new developmental network of people with the EMD orientation. Ibarra (2003) discusses how personal and career changes are greatly facilitated through these sorts of new connections. The good news here is that this change process can start with small steps, such as new projects, new volunteer activities, taking a course, joining a new club, exploration of new career opportunities, and the like.

All of this suggests to us that researchers should consciously use the lens of integration as they study work–life issues. They should not only take into account the detrimental effects of spillover and conflict, but should also seek the mechanisms that might prevent them, mechanisms that help people see the different spheres of their lives as part of one unified whole. Such mechanisms might ameliorate spillover and conflict; thus, being beneficial for the employees as well as for the organizations.

We argue that, in managerial careers, such mechanisms lie in long-term career planning and management processes that build an individual's self-awareness and adaptability. The more she sees and accepts the various parts of the self that are related to various activities and roles in her life, the more whole she will feel, and the less stress she will feel. And the more she is able to be proactive and make changes in her life when her activities feel out of alignment with her values, again, the more likely she is to experience identity integration.

To support this integration perspective, future research must develop instruments to measure career–life integration that will help uncover the conditions that facilitate or hinder career integration in life. Reliable measurement would also enable the exploration of outcomes and other implications of integration that would benefit both individuals and the organization.

Notes

1. In a later paper, Fletcher and Ragins (forthcoming) go on to show how relational theory from the Wellesley Stone Center and more recent ideas from positive organizational scholarship can be applied to produce beneficial developmental relationships in the form of relational mentoring.
2. In the spirit of full disclosure, we should say that the husband in question here is the second author of this chapter.

References

Argyris, C. (1991), 'Teaching smart people how to learn', *Harvard Business Review*, 5–15 (HBS Reprint # 4304).

Arthur, M.B. and D.M. Rousseau (1996), *The Boundaryless Career. A New Employment Principle for a New Organizational Era*, New York: Oxford University Press.

Austin, J.T. and J.B. Vancouver (1996), 'Goal constructs in psychology: structure, process, and content', *Psychological Bulletin*, **120**(3), 338.

Bartolome, F. and L.P. Evans (1980), 'Must success cost so much?', *Harvard Business Review*, **58**, 137–48.

Bazerman, M.H., and M.D. Watkins (2004), *Predictable Surprises: the Disasters you Should Have Seen Coming, and How to Prevent Them*, Boston, MA: Harvard Business School Press.

Beatty, J.E. (2003), 'Chronic illness disclosure in the workplace', unpublished doctoral dissertation, Boston College, Boston, MA.

Bell, E.L.J.E. and S.M. Nkomo (2001), *Our Separate Ways: Black and White Women and the Struggle for Professional Identity*, Boston, MA: Harvard Business School Press.

Betz, N.E., L.F. Fitzgerald and R.E. Hill (1989), 'Trait factor theories: traditional cornerstone of career theory', in M.B. Arthur, D. Hall and B.S. Lawrence (eds), *Handbook of Career Theory*, New York: Cambridge University Press, pp. 26–41.

Briscoe, J.P. (1998), 'The expression and suppression of personal values in the workplace', unpublished doctoral dissertation, Boston University, Boston, MA.

Campbell, D.J. and K.M. Campbell (1994), 'The effects of family responsibilities on the work commitment and job performance of non-professional women', *Journal of Occupational & Organizational Psychology*, **67**, p. 283.

Carlson, D.S. and K.M. Kacmar (2000), ,Work–family conflict in the organization: do life role values make a difference?', *Journal of Management*, **26**, pp. 1031–54.

Charmaz, K. (2000), 'Experiencing chronic illness', in G.L. Albrecht, R. Fitzpatrick and S.C. Scrimshaw (eds), *Handbook of Social Studies in Health and Medicine*, Thousand Oaks, CA: Sage, pp. 277–92.

Clair, J.A., J.E. Beatty and T.L. Maclean (2005), 'Out of sight but not out of mind: managing invisible social identities in the workplace', *Academy of Management Review*, **30**(1), 78–95.

Cleveland, J.N. (2005), 'What is success? Who defines it? Perspectives on the criterion problem as it relates to work and family', in E.E. Kossek and S.J. Lambert (eds), *Work and Life Integration*, New Jersey: Lawrence Erlbaum Associates, pp. 319–46.

Crary, M. (1996), 'Holding it all together', in P. Frost and S. Taylor (eds), *Rhythms of Academic Life: Personal Accounts of Careers in Academia*, Thousand Oaks, CA: Sage, pp. 207, 218.

Dalton, G. and P.H. Thompson (1986), *Novations. Strategies or Career Management*, Glenview, IL: Scott, Foresman and Company.

Deci, E.L. and R.M. Ryan (2000), 'The "what" and "why" of goal pursuits: human needs and the self-determination of behavior', *Psychological Inquiry*, **11**(4), 227–68.

Fletcher, J. (1998), *Disapperaring Acts*, Cambridge, MA: MIT Press.

Fletcher, J.K. and B.R. Ragins (forthcoming), 'Stone Center Relational–Cultural Theory: a window on relational mentoring cheer', in K. Kram and B.R. Ragins (eds), *The Handbook of Mentoring at Work: Research, Theory and Practice*, Thousand Oaks, CA: Sage.

Friskopp, A. and S. Silverstein (1995), *Straight Jobs, Gay Lives*, New York: Touchstone.

Greenhaus, J.H. and N.J. Beutell (1985), 'Sources of conflict between work and family roles', *Academy of Management Review*, **10**, p. 76.

Hall, D. (1986), 'Breaking the career routines: midcareer choice and identity development', in D.T. Hall (ed.), *Career Development in Organizations*, San Francisco, CA: Jossey-Bass, pp. 120–59.

Hall, D. (1994), 'The new "career contract": wrong on both counts?', unpublished technical report, Executive Development Roundtable, Boston University, Boston, MA.

Hall, D.T. (2002), *Careers In and Out of Organizations*, Thousand Oaks, CA: Sage.

Hall, D.T. and D.E. Chandler (2005), 'Psychological success: when the career is a calling', *Journal of Organizational Behavior*, **26**, pp. 155–78.

Hall, D. and P. Mirvis (1996), 'The new protean career', in D.T. Hall (ed.) *The Career is Dead: Long Live the Career*, San Francisco, CA: Jossey-Bass, pp. 15–46.

Hansen, L.S. (2001), 'Integrating work, family, and community through holistic life planning', *Career Development Quarterly*, **49**, pp. 261–74.

Ibarra, H. (1999), 'Provisional selves: experimenting with image and identity in professional adaptation', *Administrative Science Quarterly*, **764**(44), 764–91.

Ibarra, H. (2003), *Working Identity: Unconventional Strategies for Reinventing Your Career*, Cambridge, MA: Harvard Business School Press.

Kanter, R.M. (1977), *Work and Family in the United States: A Critical Review and Policy Agenda*, New York: Russel Sage.

Kegan, R. (ed.) (1982), *The Evolving Self: Problem and Process in Human Development*, Cambridge, MA: Harvard University Press.

Kegan, R. (ed.) (1994), *In Over Our Heads: The Mental Demands of Modern Life*, Cambridge, MA: Harvard University Press.

Kirchmeyer, C. (1992), 'Perceptions of nonwork-to-work spillover: challenging the common view of conflict-ridden domain relationships', *Basic & Applied Social Psychology*, **13**, p. 231.

Korman, A.K., U. Wittig-Berman and D. Long (1981), 'Career success and personal failure: alienation in professional managers', *Academy of Management Journal*, **24**, 342.

Kossek, E.E. and C. Ozeki (1998), 'Work–family conflict, policies, and the job-life satisfaction relationship: a review and directions for organizational behavior-human resources research', *Journal of Applied Psychology*, **83**, pp. 139–49.

Kossek, E.E., B. Lautsch and S. Eaton (2005), 'Flexibility enactment theory: implications of flexibility type, control, and boundary management for work-family effectiveness', in E.E. Kossek and S.J. Lambert (eds), *Work and Life Integration*, New Jersey: Lawrence Erlbaum Associates, pp. 243–62.

Levinson, D. (1978), *The Seasons of a Man's Life*, New York: Alfred A. Knopf.

Levinson, D. (1996), *The Seasons of a Woman's Life*, New York: Alfred A. Knopf.

Linehan, M and J.S. Walsh (2000), 'Work–family conflict and the senior female international manager', *British Journal of Management*, 11, p. S49.

March, J. and H.A. Simon (1958), *Organizations*, New York: Wiley.

Miller, D. (1994), 'What happens after success: the perils of excellence', *The Journal of Management Studies*, **31**(3), 325.

Miller, D.T. and W.H. Form (1951), *Industrial Sociology*, New York: Harper.

Milliken, F.J. and L.M. Dunn-Jensen (2005), 'The changing time demands of managerial and professional work: implications for managing the work–life boundary', in E.E. Kossek and S.J. Lambert (eds), *Work and Life Integration*, New Jersey: Lawrence Erlbaum Associates.

Mirvis, P. and D. Hall (1996), 'Psychological success and the boundaryless career', in M.B. Arthur and D.M. Rousseau (eds), *The Boundaryless Career. A New Employment Principle for a New Organizational Era*, New York: Oxford University Press, pp. 237–55.

Nicholson, N. and W. Andrews (2005), 'Playing to win: biological imperatives, self-regulation and trade-offs in the game of career success', *Journal of Organizational Behavior*, **26**.

Poelmans, S. (2005), 'The decision process theory of work and family', in E.E. Kossek and S.J. Lambert (eds), *Work and Life Integration*, Mahwah, NJ: Lawrence Erlbaum Associates, pp. 263–87.

Polo, L. (1997), 'Ética. Hacia una versión moderna de los temas clásicos', (in Spanish), Union editorial, 2nd edn, Madrid: Aedos.

Rapoport, R. and R. Rapoport (1965), 'Work and family in contemporary society', *American Sociological Review*, **30**(3), 381–94.

Rapoport, R. and R.N. Rapoport (1969), 'The dual career family: a variant pattern and social change, *Human Relations* **22**(1), 3–30.

Rothbard, N.P. (2001), 'Enriching or depleting? The dynamics of engagement in work and family roles', *Administrative Science Quarterly*, **46**, p. 655.

Scott, R.W. (2003), *Organizations: Rational, Natural, and Open Systems*, 5th edn, Upper Saddle River, NJ: Pearson Education.

Scharlach, A.E. (2001), 'Role strain among working parents: implications for workplace and community', *Community, Work & Family*, **4**, pp. 215–30.

Schein, E.H. (1984), 'Culture as an environmental context for careers', *Journal of Occupational Behavior*, **5**, p. 71.

Senge, P.M. (1990), *The Fifth Discipline: The Art and Practice of the Learning Organization*, New York: Doubleday.

Sheldon, K.M. and A.J. Elliot (1999), 'Goal striving, need satisfaction, and longitudinal well-being: the self-concordance model', *Journal of Personality and Social Psychology*, **76**(3), 482–97.

Sieber, S.D. (1974), 'Toward a theory of role accumulation', *American Sociological Review*, **39**, 567–78.

Super, D. (1957), *The Psychology of Careers*, New York: Harper & Row.

Warner, J. (2005), 'Mommy madness', *Newsweek*, 21 February, pp. 42–51.

9 Balance, integration and harmonization: selected metaphors for managing the parts and the whole of living

Sandy Kristin Piderit

The study of work–life issues is several decades old, and has evolved significantly. In this chapter, I comment on two dominant metaphors which have been used to frame such scholarship. While a plethora of other conceptual labels are sometimes invoked in the field, including conflict, enhancement, interaction, juggling, reconciliation and spillover, two metaphorical terms have been dominant. Lambert and Kossek (2005) point out that scholars 'have tended to adopt the most commonly used terms' (p. 518) which they identify as work–family *balance* and work–life *integration*. These are the first two metaphors I consider in this chapter. Next, I draw out the potential merits of a third metaphor recently advanced by Rapoport, Lewis and Gambles (2005).

When I first began to explore the work–life literature, I was puzzled by the coexistence of the two conceptual labels, balance and integration. At first, I tried to make sense of the two labels, which seemed inconsistent with one another, by testing the assumption that 'balance' was a label used in writing for practitioners, and 'integration' was reserved for more theoretically grounded writing for scholars. However, I soon found that there are valuable and informative practitioner articles using the 'integration' label (for example, Shellenbarger, 1999) and carefully crafted scholarly articles using the 'balance' label (for example, Caproni, 2004; Kofodimos, 2004). I realized that my starting assumption could not withstand testing. I began to try to track down the transition from the balance to the integration metaphor, and to seek out and size up other possibilities as well.

Balance

The balance metaphor suggests a performer walking along a tightrope high above a circus ring, carrying two packages. In the left hand she carries her work responsibilities, and in the right hand she carries her family responsibilities. If either package gets too heavy, she will not be able to continue her forward motion in a controlled way, but will fall to the net or the floor, risking her poise or her very life. If she succeeds in traversing the tightrope from one end to the other, her reward is the opportunity to turn around and do it again for the next group of circus spectators who buy tickets.

This description suggests that a balancing act is something that women perform while men watch (perhaps in anger, perhaps in anxiety, perhaps in amusement). Similarly, the first scholarship on work–family issues portrayed role conflict and balance as an issue for married women (MacDermid, 2005), with the presumption being that only women who marry and do not resign from the paid workforce have to manage work and family. Early studies of role conflict, dating from the 1950s, focused on husbands' and wives' views of the women's role, and on the costs to women of deviating from their stereotypical role by pursuing employment after marriage and childbirth (MacDermid, 2005). For women to remain in the workforce while raising children and maintaining their commitments to their husbands was seen as something eccentric – a circus act.

More recently, writers have criticized the work–family balance metaphor, and proposed alternatives. Prominent critics of the balance metaphor include Halpern and Murphy (2002), who point out that balance shares with juggling the tendency to provoke anxiety among those engaged in managing the boundaries between work and non-work parts of life. They argue that the metaphor should be changed, because 'work and family are not a zero-sum game.' (p. 3) As an alternative, they propose work–family interaction, because in statistical terms an interaction effect suggests the possibility that work and family might have independent effects on productivity and satisfaction, but together they might create synergistic effects (positive interactions).

Another forceful call to get unstuck from this balance metaphor was made by Rapoport et al. (2002). Rapoport and her colleagues argued that the phrase 'work–life balance' 'implies that work is not part of life and that everyone's time should be split equally between the two' (p. 16). As an alternative, they suggested 'work–life integration', which suggests that individuals 'should be able to function and find satisfaction in *both* work and personal life, independent of the amount of time they actually spend in each domain at different stages of their lives' (p. 17). At the individual level, work–life integration is meaningful for all individuals, not just for women or for people with children. At the organizational level, Rapoport and her colleagues call for a focus on gender equity. Throughout the book, they provide evidence that workplace practices that make it difficult to attain work–life integration in an equitable way, for both men and women, also undermine employee productivity.

Will this move away from balance and toward integration be sufficient to reorient our scholarly efforts so that the study of work–life issues is no longer seen as marginal and relevant only for women who wish to combine employment and motherhood? As I considered this question, some of the the differences between the balance and integration metaphors became apparent.

Comparing balance and integration

The integration metaphor suggests a woodworker assembling pieces into a pleasing whole, whether a functional piece of furniture or a beautiful decorative sculpture. The pieces of wood, representing work, family, hobbies, religion, self-care and other activities, may fit together easily to form a whole, or they may not. The pieces which do not fit together neatly with the developing construction can be sanded down, or trimmed with a knife, a chisel, or a saw. Gaps between pieces can be filled in with shims or caulk so that the finished work will stand square, plumb and level.

The merits of this metaphor are obvious. Both men and women may work towards integration, and the different ways in which individuals construct their lives are not constrained to a 50–50 formula. It does not suggest that life can be divided into work and family, with no pieces left over. It makes room for other pieces of personal life, besides family responsibilities and enjoyment of time with family, that are significant parts of individuals' identity and contributors to their life satisfaction. Furthermore, integration as a metaphor makes room for individual differences, personal taste, and time horizons appropriate for individuals at different stages of life.

However, a common drawback of the balance and integration metaphors is their underlying assumption, a powerful one in US society – the assumption that the balancing or integrating is an individual task. This assumption is not unique to American society, but is shared with other countries such as the United Kingdom, Canada and Australia. Den Dulk (2005) reviews the literature on liberal welfare state regimes, in which governmental provisions for work–family arrangements are rare and the assumption is that market forces will encourage companies to adopt work–family policies and practices when it is in their best interests. Her study contrasts these regimes with social-democratic states like Sweden, and conservative regimes like Italy and the Netherlands, and thus illustrates how societal values differ and are put into action in defining the roles of the government, employers, and employees in addressing work–life issues. Similarly, Poster (2005) makes the point that 'responsibility for work-life policies in the United States has been placed largely in the hands of the private sector…. [and] these firms are retreating from their accountability to U.S. working families' (p. 379).

Both the balance and the integration metaphors, drawing attention to a solo high-wire walker or woodworker, reinforce this assumption that each individual adult must manage work–life issues on his or her own. Although this may not be the intent of the scholars who make use of the terms, the danger of this potential for misinterpretation cannot be overlooked. Certainly, it is possible to imagine more than one woodworker collaborating in the design and assembly of a sculpture. Nevertheless, the echoes of older writing about work–family conflict and work–family balance leave the impression that these dilemmas can be managed individually.

The drawback of the integration metaphor is that it does not address the societal values which send us signals about what pieces must be included in our life sculptures in order for our lives to be considered significant. Those societal values, in the United States, still privilege paid work over unpaid work (Schor, 1991; Wohl, 2002). If we aren't doing enough paid work to be able to pay someone else to do our laundry or cook our dinners, our society tells us that we should 'pull ourselves up by our bootstraps', work harder or more hours, and hire a housekeeper. Although some scholars (including Rapoport et al., 2002) who discuss work–life integration do not wish the term to evoke an individual process, they still use integration as an individual-level term, and then talk about equity as the organizational and societal aim towards which we should strive collectively.

Rapoport, Lewis, Bailyn and Gambles (2005) acknowledge that the working terminology of work–personal life integration 'remains problematic' (p. 468), and have begun to experiment with a third alternative label. Exploring and extending the notion of a third way for conceptualizing the management of work–life issues is my aim in the remainder of this chapter.

Seeking a third way

An alternative to expecting individuals to manage the boundaries between their personal lives and their paid work is to expect that individuals will share that task with one another, in families, in work groups, and in communities. This alternative is represented by the third metaphor I will discuss in this chapter. I first heard this metaphor in a keynote session at the first international conference on Community, Work, and Family, which was held in Manchester (UK). The session, 'Richenda Gambles and Rhona Rapoport, in conversation…', which took place on Thursday, 17 March, 2005, was summarized on the conference website as follows:

- Why is it so difficult to get over the important ideas in harmonising paid work with the rest of life? Getting people to think [about] how work practices (rather than just policies) need to change [is an enduring challenge.]

- How can we address issues about harmonising work and the rest of life at different points in a life's course? [We are still learning what harmony sounds and feels like in] the later stages of life when earlier forms of work are over, [but] there is still the energy and need to do work.

Bringing paid work into harmony with the rest of life is a striking notion. After all, musicians understand that melody can be created by a single voice, but harmony can only be created by the juxtaposition of different voices which sound simultaneously. Work–life harmonization could never be an exclusively individual task. While Lewis and Rapoport (2005) have begun to use the label of harmonization interchangeably with the label of integration, they have not yet explored the specific implications of the new label in their published work. In the remainder of this chapter, I work with the metaphor quite deliberately, in order to explore its distinctive possibilities for informing research.

The harmonization metaphor suggests a group of people singing a series of songs. Sometimes the group sings songs they have rehearsed together. In those cases, the backbone of the group is the piano player, who uses the left hand to play chords and the right hand to play melodies, synchronized on the same tempo and in the same key. Each singer joins in to sing one part of the melody (soprano, alto, tenor or bass) or to provide background notes which underscore the piano's chords. At other times, the group improvises, a cappella, and no one person conducts or leads the singing. Instead, the group relies on familiar lyrics and tempos to begin their singing, and then innovates spontaneously, playing with tempo, melodic variations, atypical harmonizations, and unexpected combinations of voices.

What is notable about this metaphor, in contrast with the balance and integration metaphors, is that it does not suggest that work and other parts of living must be managed by a single individual. Certainly, it is possible for a soloist singing a cappella to create a beautiful melody. It is equally possible for an unmarried person with no dependents to create a rich life, which might include employment or retirement; church, synagogue, or walks in the outdoors; pets, gardening and crafts; and time spent with neighbors, brothers or sisters, cousins, nieces or nephews. Still, that melody by itself may or may not be in harmony with the other melodies played around the soloist. His or her life might be rich, but it might also create discord if it is always lived without regard for what is going on in the lives of others. We cannot assess the harmony of a single person's song.

Harmony can only be assessed in the context of a group of voices, whether the group is defined in terms of a neighborhood, a work team or a family. Another song might be performed by a husband (tenor), a wife (alto), and a daughter (soprano), each of which alternates between a lead role and backup roles in telling the story about their family's work and learning, with choruses supported by teachers, a nanny, grandparents, friends, home repair workers, and the neighborhood mail delivery person. This is also a song with the possibility of discordant notes, but also with the possibility of true harmonization – a collective achievement.

Equally important is that the image of a group of singers improvising, rather than simply rehearsing for a performance as directed by the pianist or conductor, underscores the idea that not all of life can be planned. This notion that plans are needed in managing work–life issues is a limited one, since even the best-laid plans sometimes cannot be implemented. Unexpected occurrences create the need for adjustments and revisions to previous plans, and crises can create the need for immediate actions without time for preplanning.

Future research directions

We live our lives within changing sets of relationships, both with others in our families, workplaces, neighborhoods and countries, and with our planet and the non-human life it sustains. When those relationships support our desire to live in harmony with our shared values, they can empower us; when they make our desires undiscussable, or frame our values as eccentric, they can trap us within the status quo. The notion that we work in order to allow company stockholders to earn a profit on their investments, which ignores the impact of company actions on people and the planet, has led us to accept a variety of practices that are not consistent with harmonious life. Critics of global capitalism (Korten, 1995) and advocates of the triple bottom line (Elkington, 1997) are already moving beyond such outdated notions as stockholders' profit orientations driving all company activities. By adopting the metaphor of living in harmony, scholars of work–life issues can build on this momentum to understand and accelerate the practices which allow harmonious living.

Less of this work–life scholarship will involve studies of existing government policies that may facilitate or hamper the harmonization of citizens' personal lives and paid work. Political scientists, economists and sociologists will continue to debate which policies are desirable and effective, and which are feasible to implement in different societal contexts. However, scholars in those disciplines will increasingly keep in mind that policies which are not in harmony with citizens' values are not likely to have the desired impact on citizens' behavior, and that behavioral change is what is needed.

More of this work–life scholarship will involve critiques of existing corporate policies, and case studies of workplaces which are setting new trends and experimenting with new ways of supporting individuals' diverse desires for harmonizing work and personal life. In organizational studies and anthropology, there is still a need for studies examining why some employers implement flexible work policies and others do not; why some employees take advantage of such policies, and others do not; and how a variety of workplaces are adapting practices to their own particular contexts. These studies represent contributions to scholarship, and the case studies will create new opportunities for generating rich and nuanced dialogue in the classroom. Writers in those arenas should keep in mind that just as workplaces vary in optimal organizational structures, so too will they vary in the ways in which they foster harmonious lives.

Perhaps most importantly, more of this work–life scholarship in the future will involve inquiry into practices at the margins, where people are innovating to discover the practices which create harmony in their lives. For the majority, it may be more comfortable to rely on time-tested practices which define family roles and work options, but for others, the old rules may be too constraining, and the new practices those minorities invent may become valuable guides for future generations. In organizational behavior, social psychology and family studies, research into the ways that roles are enacted, discord is expressed, and change is advocated should continue. Studies of evolving patterns of family life should document how people are responding to global pressures in their work and non-work lives, and reflect on inequities in how those pressures affect different individuals and social groups. Scholars in those disciplines should keep in mind that individuals seek ways to live in harmony with one another, and also with their self-defined values, and may find more than one workable set of new societal norms depending on the communities within which they make their homes.

Across this broad array of scholarly endeavors into work–life issues, scholars working in different disciplines must continue to seek connections and opportunities for mutual reinforcement. Without sacrificing the rigor of intellectual debate and without silencing reasoned disagreement, we must reach across our disciplinary boundaries in search of common language and a common vision of a desirable future. It is important that the study of work–life issues using the metaphor of harmonious living not remain marginal in the disciplines where scholars make their homes.

Implications

As Lambert and Kossek (2005) note, 'The terms scholars adopt paint an image of the relationship between work and personal life, thus opening or closing possibilities for intervention.' (p. 518). In this chapter, I have commented on three terms that scholars might adopt for examining the relationships between work and personal lives, drawing out the potential limitations of the terms 'balance' and 'integration', which are currently dominant in US scholarship on work–life issues, and advancing some of the potential benefits of a new term, 'harmonization'. This term, which Rapoport and her colleagues Gambles and Lewis have coined in their examination of how work–life issues are managed in different countries around the globe, encourages readers to focus on how lives are lived in practice, rather than on what policies might be invoked to facilitate work–life harmonization (whether the policies are ever put into practice or not). Most importantly, working toward harmonization encourages us to manage work–life issues not as individual issues or even issues for individual families, but collectively, through experiments that challenge old societal norms which may not support the values we wish to advance in the next century.

References

Caproni, Paula J. (2004), 'Work/life balance: you can't get there from here', *Journal of Applied Behavioral Science*, **40**, 208–18.

Den Dulk, Laura (2005), 'Workplace work–family arrangements: a study and explanatory framework of differences between organizational provisions in different welfare states', in Steven A.Y. Poelmans (ed.), *Work and Family: An International Research Perspective*, Mahwah, NJ: Lawrence Erlbaum Associates, pp. 211–38.

Elkington, John (1997), *Cannibals with Forks: The Triple Bottom Line of 21st Century Business*, Oxford: Capstone Publishing Ltd.

Halpern, Diane F. and Susan Elaine Murphy (2002), 'From balance to interaction: why the metaphor is important', in D.F. Halpern and S.E. Murphy (eds), *From Work–Family Balance to Work–Family Interaction: Changing the Metaphor*, Mahwah, NJ: Lawrence Erlbaum Associates, pp. 3–9.

Kofodimos, Joan (2004), 'Interpreting lessons learned: a comment on Paula Caproni's journey into balance', *Journal of Applied Behavioral Science*, **40**, 219–25.

Korten, David C. (1995), *When Corporations Rule the World*, San Francisco, CA: Berrett-Koehler Publishers.

Kossek, Ellen E. and Susan J. Lambert (eds) (2005), *Work and Life Integration: Organizational, Cultural, and Individual Perspectives*, Mahwah, NJ: Lawrence Erlbaum Associates.

Lambert, Susan J. and Ellen E. Kossek (2005), 'Future frontiers: enduring challenges and established assumptions in the work–life field', in E.E. Kossek and S.J. Lambert (eds), *Work and Life Integration: Organizational, Cultural, and Individual Perspectives*, Mahwah, NJ: Lawrence Erlbaum Associates, pp. 513–32.

Lewis, Suzan and Rhona Rapoport (2005), 'Looking backwards to go forwards: the integration of paid work and personal life', in Bram Peper, A. van Doorne-Huiskes and L. den Dulk (eds), *Flexible Working and Organisational Change: The Integration of Work and Personal Life*, Cheltenham, UK and Northampton, MA, USA: Edward Elgar, pp. 297–311.

MacDermid, Shelley M. (2005), '(Re)Considering conflict between work and family', in E.E. Kossek and S.J. Lambert (eds), *Work and Life Integration: Organizational, Cultural, and Individual Perspectives*, Mahwah, NJ: Lawrence Erlbaum Associates, pp. 19–40.

Poelmans, Steven A.Y. (ed.) (2005), *Work and Family: An International Research Perspective*, Mahwah, NJ: Lawrence Erlbaum Associates.

Poster, Winifred R. (2005), 'Three reasons for a transnational approach to work–life policy', in E.E. Kossek and S.J. Lambert (eds), *Work and Life Integration: Organizational, Cultural, and Individual Perspectives*, Mahwah, NJ: Lawrence Erlbaum Associates, pp. 375–400.

Rapoport, Rhona, Suzan Lewis and Richenda Gambles (2005), 'Work–personal life harmonisation: visions and pragmatic strategies for change', pp. 129–58 in S. Lewis and C.L. Cooper (eds), *Work–Life Integration: Case Studies of Organisational Change*, Chichester, UK: Wiley.

Rapoport, Rhona, Lotte Bailyn, Joyce K. Fletcher and Bettye H. Pruitt (2002), *Beyond Work–Family Balance: Advancing Gender Equity and Workplace Performance*, San Francisco, CA: Jossey-Bass.

Rapoport, Rhona, Suzan Lewis, Lotte Bailyn and Richenda Gambles (2005), 'Globalization and the integration of work with personal life', in Steven A.Y. Poelmans (ed.) *Work and Family: An International Research Perspective*, Mahwah, NJ: Lawrence Erlbaum Associates.

Schor, Juliet B. (1991), *The Overworked American*, New York: Basic Books.

Shellenbarger, Sue (1999), 'Forget juggling and forget walls; now, it's integration', in S. Shellenbarger, *Work and Family: Essays from the Work & Family Column of the Wall Street Journal*, New York: Ballantine Books, pp. 119–21, Originally published in the *Wall Street Journal*, 18 February 1998, p. B1.

Wohl, Faith A. (2002), 'Imagining the future: a dialogue on the societal value of care', in D.F. Halpern and S.E. Murphy (eds), *From Work–Family Balance to Work–Family Interaction: Changing the Metaphor*, Mahwah, NJ: Lawrence Erlbaum Associates, pp. 237–50.

PART 3

ORGANIZATIONAL PROCESSES AFFECTING WOMEN IN BUSINESS AND MANAGEMENT

10 Sex, sex similarity and sex diversity effects in teams: the importance of situational factors[1]

Laura M. Graves and Gary N. Powell

Today's organizations are increasingly using work teams as tools to achieve their strategic objectives (Cohen and Bailey, 1997; Lawler et al., 1995; Marquardt and Horvarth, 2001; Snow et al., 1996; Stewart et al., 1999). Teams produce goods and provide services, design new products, solve organizational problems, and even lead entire organizations. Teams are common across industries as diverse as health care, automobile manufacturing, financial services and electronics. Moreover, the proliferation of teams is a worldwide phenomenon. Global organizations such as IBM, Heineken, BP and Glaxo-Wellcome use teams to achieve global efficiencies, respond to regional markets, and transfer knowledge throughout their organizations.

As a result of women's increased participation in the global labor force (Powell and Graves, 2003), teams are more likely to include both women and men than ever before. Diversity in teams on the basis of member sex may affect the experiences of individual team members and overall team effectiveness. At the individual level, two types of effects may occur: sex effects and sex similarity effects. *Sex effects* arise when men's and women's experiences as team members differ (for example, Eagly and Karau, 1991). *Sex similarity effects* occur when team members' experiences differ as a function of the extent to which they are similar to their team mates on the basis of sex (for example, Chatman and O'Reilly, 2004; Konrad et al., 1992; Tsui et al., 1992). At the team level, *sex diversity effects* arise when team cohesion and performance vary as a function of the extent to which the team is heterogeneous with respect to sex (for example, Jehn et al., 1999; Pelled et al., 1999; Polzer et al., 2002).

In this chapter, we briefly review theories and research evidence regarding the effects of sex, sex similarity and sex diversity in mixed-sex teams. We then consider how key aspects of the situations in which mixed-sex teams function may determine whether these effects are manifested. In so doing, we address two general questions:

1. What do the effects of sex, sex similarity, and sex diversity in mixed-sex teams look like when they occur?
2. How do situational factors influence the nature of these effects?

Compared to recent reviews of the literature on diverse work teams (for example, Jackson et al., 2003; Williams and O'Reilly, 1998), this review is unique in focusing on sex as opposed to a broad set of demographic factors. By focusing on sex, we are able to consider dynamics that are associated exclusively with sex (for example, gender roles). A second unique aspect of the review is its simultaneous focus on sex, sex similarity and sex diversity effects. Despite the fact that all three types of effects simultaneously influence the dynamics that occur in teams, the literature on sex effects (for example, Eagly and Karau, 1991; Carli and Eagly, 1999) is distinct from the literature on sex similarity and sex diversity effects (for example, Riordan, 2000; Tolbert et al., 1999; Williams and O'Reilly, 1998).

Sex effects

Both status characteristics theory and social role theory suggest that team members have different expectations regarding the roles of women and men in teams (Carli and Eagly, 1999). Status characteristics theory (Berger et al., 1998; Ridgeway, 1991; Ridgeway and Smith-Lovin, 1999; Wagner and Berger, 1997) suggests that differences in women's and men's social status will lead to differences in their experiences in mixed-sex teams. According to the theory, individuals are assigned status based on their demographic characteristics. High-status individuals view themselves and are viewed by others as more competent than low-status individuals (Berger et al., 1998; Wagner and Berger, 1997). As a result, high-status individuals are expected to perform at higher levels than low-status individuals. Since women are generally assigned lower status or worthiness in Western societies than men, women are likely to be viewed as less competent with lower performance expectations (Ridgeway, 1991; Ridgeway and Smith-Lovin, 1999). These expectations are reflected in team interactions such that high-status men make more task contributions, act more confidently and assertively, receive more positive feedback for their contributions, and are more influential (Carli and Bukatko, 2000; Carli and Eagly, 1999). When low-status women violate performance expectations by making task contributions or acting confidently and assertively, their contributions are likely to be rejected (Rudman, 1998).

Social role theory (Eagly, 1987; Eagly et al., 2000) suggests that differences in the behavior of women and men and how they are evaluated in mixed-sex teams are due to differences in their social roles. Women and men are typically employed in different types of jobs (Blau et al., 2002; Jacobs,

1999). Consistent with gender stereotypes (Deaux and Kite, 1993; Deaux and LaFrance, 1998), women's jobs require more expressive and subordinate behaviors (for example, nurturing, caretaking), and men's jobs require more instrumental and dominant behaviors (for example, leading, directing). As a result, women and men develop different skills and modify their behaviors to be consistent with gender roles. Moreover, people expect, or even demand, that women and men behave differently. Consequently, women in teams are expected to engage in more expressive and subordinate behavior than men, whereas men are expected to engage in more instrumental and dominant behavior.

Research evidence on differences in women's and men's behavior in teams and in evaluations of women's and men's performance, influence and leadership in teams generally supports these theories (cf. Carli, 2001; Carli and Bukatko, 2000; Carli and Eagly, 1999; Powell and Graves, 2003). Men display more self-assertion and dominance and less deference and warmth in their interactions with other team members than women. In addition, men exhibit more task-oriented behavior that contributes directly to accomplishment of the team's task and less social-oriented behavior that helps to maintain team morale and positive interpersonal relations among team members. Further, men's task contributions are evaluated more positively than those of women. Men exert more influence than women in teams and are more likely to emerge as informal leaders when the team has no assigned leader.

There is some question, however, about the robustness of the sex effects described above. Much of the research evidence for these effects comes from laboratory studies in which team members interact briefly and have little information about each other – the very conditions that are most likely to invoke gender-based expectations (Carli and Bukatko, 2000; Carli and Eagly, 1999; Eagly and Karau, 1991; Powell and Graves, 2003). Moreover, there is some evidence that these effects disappear when team members have information about each other's competence (Dovidio et al., 1988; Wood and Karten, 1986) or interact extensively over time (Eagly and Karau, 1991; Goktepe and Schneier, 1989; Webber, 1987). When team members know each other better and have worked together for a longer period of time, status judgments and gender roles could play less of a role in dictating behavior.

Sex similarity effects

Theories of social identification (Ashforth and Mael, 1989; Tajfel and Turner, 1986) and similarity-attraction dynamics (Byrne, 1971; Byrne and Neuman, 1992) suggest that individuals who are similar to their team mates with respect to sex have more positive experiences than those who are dissimilar (Tsui et al., 1992). According to social identity theory (Ashforth and Mael, 1989; Tajfel and Turner, 1986), team members are likely to categorize one another based on their demographic characteristics (for example, sex, race, age). After categorization occurs, individuals typically identify with and favor those who share their characteristics. Since sex is a highly visible and, thus, frequently used basis for categorization (Deaux and Major, 1987; Frable, 1997), team members are likely to identify with and favor same-sex others. Similarly, the similarity-attraction paradigm (Byrne, 1971; Byrne and Neuman, 1992) suggests that sex similarity between an individual and his/her team mates will enhance the perceived similarity between that individual and the team. This increase in perceived similarity, in turn, strengthens interpersonal attraction, thereby facilitating positive interpersonal interactions. As a result of these dynamics, individuals who are similar to their team mates with respect to sex are likely to have more positive team experiences (for example, opportunities to contribute, inclusion in social activities) than individuals who are different from their team mates with respect to sex.

Kanter's (1977) work on tokenism reinforces the notion that negative experiences are associated with being dissimilar with respect to sex. According to Kanter, when a team is comprised of a distinct numerical minority or a token member of one sex, members of the majority perceive members of the minority as dissimilar, have few interactions with them, and display prejudice and discrimination toward them (Fiske, 1998). In contrast, when a group is made up of a more equal representation of both sexes, the majority finds it difficult to avoid interacting with the minority. Members of the majority are more likely to view members of the minority as individuals rather than simply as representatives of their sex, resulting in a reduction of prejudice and discrimination directed toward the minority.

Scholars have recently suggested that the effects of sex similarity are more complex than those described above. In particular, they argue that the impact of being different is likely to vary across the sexes (Chattopadhyay, 1999; Konrad et al., 1992; Tsui et al., 1992). Regardless of sex, most individuals seek to maintain a positive social identity, which may be accomplished by identifying and associating with individuals with high social status (Ashforth and Mael, 1989; Tajfel and Turner, 1986). This drive for a positive identity has different implications for low- and high-status individuals. Individuals who belong to a low-status group (for example, women) are likely to distance themselves from their own group and identify with the high-status group (for example, men). In contrast, individuals who belong to a high-status group (for example, men) maintain a positive identity by identifying with their own group and distancing themselves from the other group (for example, women).

As a result, men are more likely to be welcomed as members of predominantly female teams than women are to be welcomed as members of predominantly male teams, which could make the effects of being different with respect to sex *less* detrimental for men than for women. However, it is also possible that the effects of being different may be *more* detrimental for men than for women because association with low-status females may threaten their status and self-esteem (Chattopadhyay, 1999; Tsui et al., 1992).

Research evidence regarding the existence of sex similarity effects (for example, Chatman & O'Reilly, 2004; Chattopadhyay, 1999; Graves and Elsass, 2005; Konrad et al., 1992; Riordan and Shore, 1997; Tsui et al., 1992) is mixed and does not offer a clear indication of whether these effects are similar or different for men and women (cf. Powell and Graves, 2003). Early field studies found that the effects of being in the minority for women in male-intensive settings such as the military, law enforcement and medicine were more negative than those for men in female-intensive settings such as nursing, teaching and social work; having minority status in a team worked to the advantage of men and the disadvantage of women. However, more recent field studies have yielded highly variable results, with women being more disadvantaged from being in the minority in some instances and men in others.

To make sense of the seemingly erratic effects of sex similarity in teams, the role of situational factors in creating these effects needs to be examined. For example, sex similarity effects may be less likely to occur when organizations stress the value of teamwork (Chatman et al., 1998) or have a high level of integration or equality on the basis of sex (Brewer and Miller, 1984; Graves and Elsass, 2005; Riordan and Shore, 1997). In contrast, when situational factors stress the importance of acting independently of other team members or emphasize status differences between the sexes, sex similarity effects may be more likely to occur.

Sex diversity effects

There are two opposing views of the effect of diversity on team effectiveness. One suggests that diversity reduces team effectiveness (Tsui et al., 1992; Pfeffer, 1985; Williams and O'Reilly, 1998). According to this view, similarity-attraction and social identification processes cause team members to reject those who are different from themselves. In diverse teams, this leads to the creation of factions, conflict and communication problems. Ultimately, the performance of the group is impaired and members' satisfaction with and commitment to the group is reduced.

The second view suggests that diversity enhances team effectiveness (Cox, 1993; Jehn et al., 1999; Pelled et al., 1999; Williams and O'Reilly, 1998).

In diverse teams, members have different experiences, values, attitudes, and cognitive approaches. They bring varied knowledge and perspectives to the team's task, which will enhance the team's creativity and problem solving ability. The positive impact of diversity is especially likely to occur on complex tasks such as new product design and innovation, which require multiple perspectives and varied knowledge. The benefits of diversity may also extend to member attraction to the team. Greater diversity increases the amount of interaction between the two sexes over time and decreases sex-based prejudice and discrimination, thereby improving relations among team members and enhancing attachment to the team.

Which of these two views better describes what occurs in ongoing mixed-sex teams? The research evidence regarding sex diversity effects is mixed (cf. Jackson et al., 2003; Powell and Graves, 2003). Some studies have found that sex diversity has a positive effect on team performance (Jackson and Joshi, 2004; Rentsch and Klimoski, 2001); other studies have found a negative effect (Jehn and Bezrukova, 2004); and still other studies have found a non-significant effect (Ely, 2004; Richard, 2000; Sacco and Schmitt, 2005; Watson et al., 1998). There is no discernible pattern in these results.

Given the mixed nature of the research evidence, the moderating effect of situational factors on the relationship between sex diversity and team performance warrants close attention. For example, the relationship between sex diversity and team effectiveness may be moderated by factors such as diversity education (Ely, 2004), interpersonal congruence among team members (Polzer et al., 2002), outcome interdependence (Schippers et al., 2003), and team longevity (Chatman and Flynn, 2001; Harrison et al., 1998; Pelled et al., 1999; Schippers et al., 2003), all of which would be likely to contribute to a more positive relationship.

The importance of situational factors

According to our review, prior research on the effects of sex, sex similarity and sex diversity in teams has yielded generally inconsistent results. Some research findings have suggested that these effects are dependent on situational factors. Yet most studies of these effects fail to consider situational effects in their designs, and researchers typically provide little, if any, information about the context in which studies were conducted (Jackson et al., 2003).

It would seem that the effects of sex, sex similarity, and sex diversity in teams are likely to vary according to whether the context emphasizes or de-emphasizes sex (Brewer and Miller, 1984; Deaux and Major, 1987). When the conditions under which mixed-sex teams operate de-emphasize the importance of sex as a component of members' identities or create equality between the sexes, negative outcomes may be averted. However, when these conditions emphasize the importance of sex or do not discourage sex-based categorization, at least some team members, if not the entire team, may experience negative outcomes. Several situational factors appear to be important, including characteristics of the team, the nature of the task, the demographic composition of the organization and its senior officials, the organizational culture, and the societal culture.

The team's overall demographic composition is likely to affect the occurrence of sex-related effects in teams. Scholars (Brewer, 2000; Lau and Murnighan, 1998) have suggested that the number and nature of the demographic subgroups (for example, young black males, young white males, young Asian females, middle-aged white females, middle-aged white males) within a mixed-sex team may be especially important. When there are many possible subgroups and these subgroups are demographically heterogeneous, sex-related effects are unlikely to occur (Brewer, 2000; Lau and Murnighan, 1998). For example, a team comprised of a 40-year-old white male engineer, a 65-year-old black female engineer, a 45-year-old Asian male sales representative, and a 20-year-old white female sales representative could form coalitions based on age, race, occupation or sex. Because forming a coalition based on any one category would lead to differences within the coalition on other categories, coalition formation is unlikely, and sex-related effects should not occur. However, in a team composed of two middle-aged white male engineers and two young black female sales representatives, sex is highly related to age, race and occupation. There are only two possible subgroups in this team, one composed of men and one composed of women. This presumably increases the emphasis on sex as a demographic characteristic; coalitions are likely to be formed on the basis of sex, and sex-related effects are likely to occur (Powell and Graves, 2003). The results of a recent study (Lau and Murnighan, 2005) are consistent with the idea that the number and nature of demographic subgroups within a team influences the occurrence of sex-related effects.

The team's longevity is another critical factor (Chatman and Flynn, 2001; Pelled, 1996; Schippers et al., 2003). As team members interact over extended periods of time, they are likely to gain additional information about each another, which, in turn, should reduce gender-based categorization and stereotyping. Relationships between members should then be formed based on factors such as abilities, attitudes, values and beliefs, not sex (Graves and Elsass, 2005; Harrison et al., 1998). Consistent with this logic, research on sex effects in teams indicates that these effects diminish as teams spend more time interacting (Eagly and Karau, 1991). Findings regarding the influence of time on the occurrence of sex similarity and sex diversity effects are less clear. Some evidence suggests that the effects of sex similarity (Sacco and Schmitt, 2005) and sex diversity (Chatman and Flynn, 2001; Harrison et al., 1998) decline as the tenure of the team member or longevity of the team increases. Other evidence (for example, Mohammed and Angell, 2004; Schippers et al., 2003), however, suggests that the passage of time does not affect the likelihood of sex diversity effects.

The gender orientation of the task (that is, whether it is associated primarily with members of one sex or is regarded as sex-neutral) may also influence whether sex-related effects occur (Hall et al., 1998; Karakowsky and Siegel, 1999). Tasks that are typically performed by members of one sex or the other (for example, nursing, police work) or create coalitions based on sex (for example, developing affirmative action plans) increase the likelihood of sex-based categorization that may detract from individual and team outcomes. In contrast, tasks that are less associated with either sex reduce the occurrence of sex-related effects.

Research evidence on the moderating effect of the gender orientation of the task is inconclusive. Although a meta-analysis of early research on sex effects in teams suggested that males were more likely to emerge as team leaders when the task was masculine rather than feminine, most of the studies included in the meta-analysis used gender-neutral tasks (Eagly and Karau, 1991). Moreover, recent research on the moderating effect of the gender orientation of the task yielded mixed results concerning its influence on both sex (Hall et al., 1998; Karakowsky and Siegel, 1999) and sex similarity (Karakowsky and Siegel, 1999; Yoder, 1994) effects. The influence of the gender orientation of the task on the occurrence of sex diversity effects is relatively untested.

The structure of the team's task is also likely to influence whether sex-related effects occur. When tasks and outcomes are interdependent and team members must work jointly to achieve collective goals, they are presumably motivated to form accurate rather than stereotypical impressions of one another and to view themselves as a team, thereby minimizing sex-related effects (Brewer and Miller, 1984; Chatman et al., 1998; Elsass and Graves, 1997; Fiske, 2000). Demography researchers have recently begun to study the moderating effects of factors such as task interdependence and collective goals, with mixed results. Some findings suggest that a sense of team inter-dependence or collective goals reduces the occurrence of sex similarity or sex diversity effects (for example, Chatman et al., 1998; Schippers et al., 2003), whereas other findings provide no evidence of a moderating effect (Jehn and Bezrukova, 2004; Jehn et al., 1999).

The gender composition of the larger organization affects the emphasis on sex in relationships between men and women in teams (Milliken and Martins, 1996; Powell and Graves, 2003). Sex differences may be less important in organizations where there is a great deal of sex diversity than in organizations where there is little. In organizations with a balanced gender composition, team members should be accustomed to differences in sex and should not use sex as the basis for categorization. Further, negative outcomes may be less likely to occur in female-intensive than male-intensive organizations (Williams and O'Reilly, 1998). In female-intensive organizations, increasing sex diversity means that males are added to female-dominated teams. In male-intensive organizations, the reverse is true. According to status characteristics theory (Berger et al., 1998; Wagner and Berger, 1997), females are more likely to welcome the addition of males to their teams than vice versa. Thus, increasing sex diversity may cause fewer problems in female-intensive organizations than in male-intensive organizations. Unfortunately, the effect of organizational gender composition on the occurrence of sex-related effects in teams remains largely untested because researchers typically study teams in a handful of organizations.

The gender composition of the organization's senior management may affect team members' interactions by influencing the relative status of women and men (Burke and McKeen, 1996; Elvira & Cohen, 2001; Ely, 1995). When women work in organizations with few women in key roles, they are more likely to invoke gender stereotypes, devalue their own abilities, avoid organizational activities, and compete with their female peers. In such organizations, female team members are likely to behave as inferiors, and male team members are likely to behave as superiors. In contrast, when women and men share power at the top of the organization, status differences between women and men in the team should be eliminated or reduced. Although being in the minority still might have a negative effect on women or men, such effects should be lessened by the relative equality of the two sexes. Researchers (Burke and McKeen, 1996; Elvira and Cohen, 2001; Ely, 1995; Mellor, 1995) have confirmed the importance of the gender composition of top officials on the construction of gender in organizations as well as women's peer relationships, participation, and intentions to remain with their organizations. Research on the effect of the gender composition of top management on interactions in mixed-sex teams, however, is lacking.

The organization's culture, especially its values regarding cooperation and diversity, may have a strong influence on the emphasis placed on sex in teams (Powell and Graves, 2003). Organizations with positive diversity cultures reduce the likelihood of negative consequences in mixed-sex teams (Ely and Thomas, 2001; Kossek and Zonia, 1993). In a positive diversity culture, organizational members value efforts to increase the representation of women, people of color, and individuals with disabilities, and view members of these groups as qualified. Equality is stressed, and differences in status based on sex, race and disability are reduced. Further, in a positive diversity culture, employees acknowledge differences among women and among men as well as between women and men. Recognition that individual differences are present within each sex allows team members to view each other as distinct persons, not just as representatives of the two sexes. Moreover, organizations that regard the insights, skills and experiences of individuals from different backgrounds as valuable business resources create a particularly productive environment for diverse teams. In such settings, the input of each individual is valued and respected because of, rather than in spite of, his or her background.

Diversity researchers have begun to explore the effects of diversity climate on the occurrence of sex-related effects in teams, with mixed results. One study (Hobman et al., 2004) found that the negative effects of visible diversity (sex, ethnicity and age) were reduced when the diversity climate was positive. However, other research (Ely, 2004; Jehn and Bezrukova, 2004) suggests that the presence of human resources practices designed to create a supportive diversity environment does not moderate the effects of sex diversity. Of course, such practices may not necessarily create a positive diversity climate.

Finally, the societal culture may influence the emphasis on sex in teams. Sex-related effects may be most likely to occur in teams operating in countries where traditional gender roles are emphasized and women's workplace participation is constrained (for example, Spain, Japan) (Yamauchi, 1995; Johnson, 2005). Although researchers have recently begun to study the effects of national culture diversity on teams (Earley and Mosakowski, 2000), there is little research on the effects of national culture on the occurrence of sex-related effects in teams. A study of symphony orchestras in Germany (Allmendinger and Hackman, 1995), however, is suggestive of such effects. Women, who have historically comprised a very small proportion of symphony musicians in Germany, are now being integrated into orchestras. This process has been more positive in the former East Germany than the former West Germany. Members of symphonies located in the former East Germany believe that male and female orchestra members support one another and work together to achieve common goals. In contrast, in the former West Germany, there is substantial tension over the integration of women into orchestras, and the musicians believe that male and female musicians are treated differently. Prior to the unification of Germany, East German women had higher rates of workforce participation than West German women. It is possible that differences in societal norms concerning women's participation in the workforce led to a disparity in the acceptance of female musicians in the two areas of Germany.

In summary, numerous situational factors may affect the occurrence of sex-related effects in mixed-sex teams. These factors include the characteristics of the team, task, organization and society. Existing evidence on the role that these characteristics play in moderating the effects of sex, sex similarity and sex diversity in teams is fairly limited and does not allow us to reach definitive conclusions. Several areas warrant attention from researchers. In particular, further examination of the extent to which the characteristics of the team (overall demographic composition, team member tenure, team longevity) and the nature of the task (for example, gender orientation, task interdependence) moderate the occurrence of all three types of sex-related effects would be desirable. Researchers also need to extend their focus to the moderating effects of organizational factors, including the diversity climate and the gender composition of the organization and its top management. Research on the effects of national culture on the occurrence of sex-related effects in teams is also needed.

Moreover, researchers should explore the combined effects of the situational factors outlined above. Researchers must recognize that situational factors are likely to act together to determine whether sex-related effects occur in teams. For instance, the moderating effects of the team's demographic composition and longevity may depend on whether it operates in an organization where gender diversity is valued and women comprise a substantial portion of the organization and top management. Similarly, the moderating effects of the organization's diversity climate or gender composition may depend on the larger societal context in which the organization operates.

Conclusions

In conclusion, we recommend future research on sex-related effects in teams that specifically focuses on the role of situational factors. With respect to sex effects, additional field research is needed in ongoing teams to shed light on the conditions under which women are marginalized as team members. With respect to sex similarity effects, more research is needed to specify the situational factors that determine these effects and whether being different is more detrimental to female or male members of teams. With respect to sex diversity effects, further research is needed to determine the conditions under which these effects are positive, negative or non-existent. Interactions between these effects and analogous effects stemming from the influence of other dimensions of diversity (for example, race, ethnicity, age, socioeconomic class) also warrant research attention (Ferdman, 1999; Frable, 1997). It would be desirable for researchers to test all three types of sex-related effects simultaneously to determine the unique contributions of each type of effect and their influence on each other; multilevel models that account for both individual-level and team-level effects are recommended.

Moreover, a comprehensive research program that simultaneously examines the influence of a wide array of situational factors is recommended. Such research should increase our understanding of how to create situations that enhance the likelihood that *all* team members will have positive experiences and that their teams will be highly effective.

Note

1. An earlier version of this chapter was presented at the 2005 British Academy of Management Meeting, Oxford, UK.

References

Allmendinger, J. and J.R. Hackman (1995), 'Study of the inclusion of women in symphony orchestras', *Social Forces*, **74**, 423–60.

Ashforth, B.E. and F. Mael (1989), 'Social identity theory and the organization', *Academy of Management Review*, **14**, 20–39.

Berger, J., M.H. Fisek and R.Z. Norman (1998), 'The evolution of status expectations: a theoretical extension', in J. Berger and M. Zelditch, Jr. (eds), *Status, Power and Legitimacy: Strategies and Theories*, New Brunswick, NJ: Transaction, pp. 175–205.

Blau, F.D., M.A. Ferber and A.E. Winkler (2002), *The Economics of Women, Men, and Work*, 4th edn, Upper Saddle River, NJ: Prentice-Hall.

Brewer, M.B. (2000), 'Reducing prejudice through cross-categorization: Effects of multiple social identities', in S. Oskamp (ed.), *Reducing Prejudice and Discrimination*, Mahwah, NJ: Lawrence Erlbaum, pp. 165–83.

Brewer, M.B. and N. Miller (1984), 'Beyond the contact hypothesis: theoretical perspectives on desegregation', in N. Miller and M.B. Brewer (ed.), *Groups in Contact: The Psychology of Desegregation*, Orlando, FL: Academic Press, pp. 281–302.

Burke, R.J. and C.A. McKeen (1996), 'Do women at the top make a difference? Gender proportions and the experiences of managerial and professional women', *Human Relations*, **49**, 1093–104.

Byrne, D. (1971), *The Attraction Paradigm*, New York: Academic Press.

Byrne, D. and J.H. Neuman (1992), 'The implications of attraction research for organizational issues', in K. Kelley (ed.), *Issues, Theory, and Research in Industrial/Organizational Psychology*, Amsterdam: Elsevier Science, pp. 29–70.

Carli, L.L. (2001), 'Gender and social influence', *Journal of Social Issues*, **74**, 725–41.

Carli, L.L. and D. Bukatko (2000), 'Gender, communication, and social influence: a developmental perspective', in T. Eckes and H.M. Trautner (eds), *The Developmental Social Psychology of Gender*, Mahwah, NJ: Lawrence Erlbaum Associates, pp. 295–331.

Carli, L.L. and A.H. Eagly (1999), 'Gender effects on social influence and emergent leadership', in G.N. Powell (ed.), *Handbook of Gender and Work*, Thousand Oaks, CA: Sage, pp. 203–22.

Chatman, J.A. and F.J. Flynn (2001), 'The influence of demographic heterogeneity on the emergence and consequences of cooperative norms in work teams', *Academy of Management Journal*, **44**, 956–74.

Chatman, J.A. and C.A. O'Reilly (2004), 'Asymmetric reactions to work group sex diversity among men and women', *Academy of Management Journal*, **47**, 193–208.

Chatman, J.A., J.T. Polzer, S.G. Barsade and M.A. Neale (1998), 'Being different yet feeling similar: the influence of demographic composition and organizational culture on work processes and outcomes', *Administrative Sciences Quarterly*, **43**, 749–80.

Chattopadhyay, P. (1999), 'Beyond direct and symmetrical effects: the influence of demographic dissimilarity on organizational citizenship behavior', *Academy of Management Journal*, **42**, 273–87.

Cohen, S.G. and D.E. Bailey (1997), 'What makes teams work: group effectiveness research from the shop floor to the executive suite', *Journal of Management*, **23**, 239–90.

Cox, T.H. (1993), *Cultural Diversity in Organizations: Theory, Research, and Practice*, San Francisco, CA: Berrett-Koehler.

Deaux, K. and M. Kite (1993), 'Gender stereotypes', in F.L. Denmark and M.A. Paludi (eds), *Psychology of Women: A Handbook of Issues and Theories*, Westport, CT: Greenwood, pp. 107–39.

Deaux, K. and M. LaFrance (1998), 'Gender', in D.T. Gilbert, S.T. Fiske and G. Lindzey (eds), *The Handbook of Social Psychology*, 4th edn, Volume 1, Boston, MA: McGraw-Hill, pp. 788–827.

Deaux, K. and B. Major (1987), 'Putting gender into context: an interactive model of gender-related behavior', *Psychological Review*, **94**, 369–89.

Dovidio, J.F., S.L. Ellyson, C.F. Keating, K. Heltman and C.E. Brown (1988), 'The relationship of social power to visual displays of dominance between men and women', *Journal of Personality and Social Psychology*, **54**, 233–42.

Eagly, A.H. (1987), *Sex Differences in Social Behavior: A Social-Role Interpretation*, Hillsdale, NJ: Lawrence Erlbaum Associates.

Eagly, A.H. and S.J. Karau (1991), 'Gender and emergence of leaders: a meta-analysis', *Journal of Personality and Social Psychology*, **60**, 685–710.

Eagly, A.H., W. Wood and A.B. Diekman (2000), 'Social role theory of sex differences and similarities: a current appraisal', in T. Eckes and H.M. Trautner (eds), *The Developmental Social Psychology of Gender*, Mahwah, NJ: Lawrence Erlbaum Associates, pp. 123–74.

Earley, P.C. and E. Mosakowski (2000), 'Creating hybrid team cultures: an empirical test of transnational team functioning', *Academy of Management Journal*, **43**, 26–49.

Elsass, P.M. and L.M. Graves (1997), 'Demographic diversity in decision-making groups: the experiences of women and people of color', *Academy of Management Review*, **22**, 946–73.

Elvira, M.M. and L.E. Cohen (2001), 'Location matters: a cross-level analysis of the effects of organizational sex composition on turnover', *Academy of Management Journal*, **44**, 591–605.

Ely, R.J. (1995), 'The power in demography: women's social constructions of gender identity at work', *Academy of Management Journal*, **38**, 589–634.

Ely, R.J. (2004), 'A field study of group diversity, participation in diversity education programs, and performance', *Journal of Organizational Behavior*, **25**, 755–80.

Ely, R.J. and D.A. Thomas (2001), 'Cultural diversity at work: the effects of diversity perspectives on work group processes and outcomes', *Administrative Science Quarterly*, **46**, 229–73.

Ferdman, B.M. (1999), 'The color and culture of gender in organizations: attending to race and ethnicity', in G.N. Powell (ed.), *Handbook of Gender and Work*, Thousand Oaks, CA: Sage, pp. 17–34.

Fiske, S.T. (1998), 'Stereotyping, prejudice, and discrimination', in D.T. Gilbert, S.T. Fiske and G. Lindzey (eds), *The Handbook of Social Psychology*, 4th edn, Volume 2, Boston, MA: McGraw-Hill, pp. 357–411.

Fiske, S.T. (2000), 'Interdependence and the reduction of prejudice', in S. Oskamp (ed.), *Reducing Prejudice and Discrimination*, Mahwah, NJ: Lawrence Erlbaum Associates, pp. 115–35.

Frable, D.E.S. (1997), 'Gender, racial, ethnic, sexual, and class identities', *Annual Review of Psychology*, **48**, 139–62.

Goktepe, J.R. and C.E. Schneier (1989), 'Role of sex, gender roles, and attraction in predicting emergent leaders', *Journal of Applied Psychology*, **74**, 165–7.

Graves, L.M. and P.M. Elsass (2005), 'Sex and sex dissimilarity effects in ongoing teams: some surprising findings', *Human Relations*, **58**, 191–221.

Hall, R.J., J.W. Workman and C.A. Marchioro (1998), 'Sex, task, and behavioral flexibility effects on leadership perceptions', *Organizational Behavior and Human Decision Processes*, **74**, 1–32.

Harrison, D.A., K.H. Price and M.P. Bell (1998), 'Beyond relational demography: time and the effects of surface- and deep-level diversity on work group cohesion', *Academy of Management Journal*, **41**, 96–107.

Hobman, E.V., P. Bordia and C. Gallois (2004), 'Perceived dissimilarity and work group involvement: the moderating effects of group openness to diversity', *Group and Organization Management*, **29**, 560–87.

Jackson, S.E. and A. Joshi (2004), 'A multi-attribute, multilevel analysis of team diversity and sales performance', *Journal of Organizational Behavior*, **25**, 675–702.

Jackson, S.J., A. Joshi and N.L. Erhardt (2003), 'Recent research on team and organizational diversity: SWOT analysis and implications', *Journal of Management*, **29**, 801–30.

Jacobs, J.A. (1999), 'The sex segregation of occupations: prospects for the 21st century', in G.N. Powell (ed.), *Handbook of Gender and Work*, Thousand Oaks, CA: Sage, pp. 125–41.

Jehn, K.A. and K. Bezrukova (2004), 'A field study of group diversity, workgroup context, and performance', *Journal of Organizational Behavior*, **25**, 703–29.

Jehn, K.A., G.B. Northcraft and M.A. Neale (1999), 'Why differences make a difference: a field study of diversity, conflict, and performance in work groups', *Administrative Science Quarterly*, **44**, 741–63.

Johnson, K. (2005), 'Spain tries to get macho men to lift a finger on washday', *Wall Street Journal*, 1 October, p. A1.

Kanter, R.M. (1977), *Men and Women of the Corporation*, New York: Basic Books.

Karakowsky, L. and J.P. Siegel (1999), 'The effects of proportional representation and gender orientation of the task on emergent leadership behavior in mixed-sex groups', *Journal of Applied Psychology*, **84**, 620–31.

Konrad, A., S. Winter and B.A. Gutek (1992), 'Diversity in work group sex composition: Implications for majority and minority members', in P. Tolbert and S.B. Bacharach (eds), *Research in the Sociology of Organizations*, Volume 10, Greenwich, CT: JAI Press, pp. 115–40.

Kossek, E.E. and S.C. Zonia (1993), 'Assessing diversity climate: a field study of reactions to employer efforts to promote diversity', *Journal of Organizational Behavior*, **14**, 61–81.

Lau, D.C. and J.K. Murnighan (1998), 'Demographic diversity and faultlines: the compositional dynamics of organizational groups', *Academy of Management Review*, **23**, 325–40.

Lau, D.C. and J.K. Murnighan (2005), 'Interactions within groups and subgroups: the effects of demographic faultlines', *Academy of Management Journal*, **48**, 645–59.

Lawler, E.E., III, S.A. Mohrman and G.E. Ledford, Jr (1995), *Creating High Performance Organizations: Practices and Results of Employee Involvement and Total Quality Management in Fortune 1000 Companies*, San Francisco, CA: Jossey-Bass.

Marquardt, M.J. and L. Horvarth (2001), *Global Teams: How Top Multinationals Span Boundaries and Cultures with High-Speed Teamwork*, Palo Alto, CA: Davies-Black.

Mellor, S. (1995), 'Gender composition and gender representation in local unions: relationships between women's participation in local office and women's participation in local activities', *Journal of Applied Psychology*, **80**, 706–20.

Milliken, F.J. and L.L. Martins (1996), 'Searching for common threads: understanding the multiple effects of diversity on occupational groups', *Academy of Management Review*, **21**, 402–33.

Mohammed, S. and L.C. Angell (2004), 'Surface- and deep-level diversity in workgroups: Examining the moderating effects of team orientation and team process on relationship conflict', *Journal of Organizational Behavior*, **25**, 1015–39.

Pelled, L.H. (1996), 'Demographic diversity, conflict, and work group outcomes: an intervening process theory', *Organizational Science*, **7**, 615–31.

Pelled, L.H., K.M. Eisenhardt and K.R. Xin (1999), 'Exploring the black box: an analysis of work group diversity, conflict, and performance', *Administrative Science Quarterly*, **44**, 1–28.

Pfeffer, J. (1985), 'Organizational demography: implications for management', *California Management Review*, **18**(1), 67–81.

Polzer, J.T., L.P. Milton and W.B. Swann, Jr (2002), 'Capitalizing on diversity: congruence in small work groups', *Administrative Science Quarterly*, **47**, 296–324.

Powell, G.N. and L.M. Graves (2003), *Women and Men in Management*, 3rd edn, Thousand Oaks, CA: Sage.

Rentsch, J.R. and R.J. Klimoski (2001), 'Why do "great minds" think alike? Antecedents of team member schema agreement', *Journal of Organizational Behavior*, **22**, 107–22.

Richard, O.C. (2000), 'Racial diversity, business strategy, and firm performance: a resource-based view', *Academy of Management Journal*, **43**, 164–77.

Ridgeway, C.L. (1991), 'The social construction of status value: gender and other nominal characteristics', *Social Forces*, **70**, 367–86.

Ridgeway, C.L. and L. Smith-Lovin (1999), 'Gender and interaction', in J.S. Chafetz (ed.), *Handbook of the Sociology of Gender*, New York: Kluwer Academic/Plenum, pp. 247–74.

Riordan, C.M. (2000), 'Relational demography within groups: past developments, contradictions, and new directions', in G. Ferris (ed.), *Research in Personnel and Human Resource Management*, Volume 19, New York: Elsevier, pp. 131–73.

Riordan, C.M. and L.M. Shore (1997), 'Demographic diversity and employee attitudes: an empirical examination of relational demography within work units', *Journal of Applied Psychology*, **82**, 342–58.

Rudman, L.A. (1998), 'Self-promotion as a risk factor for women: the costs and benefits of counterstereotypical impression management', *Journal of Personality and Social Psychology*, **74**, 629–45.

Sacco, J.M. and N. Schmitt (2005), 'A dynamic multilevel model of demographic diversity and misfit effects', *Journal of Applied Psychology*, **90**, 203–31.

Schippers, M.C., D.N. Den Hartog, P.L. Koopman and J.A. Wienk (2003), 'Diversity and team outcomes: the moderating effects of outcome interdependence and group longevity and the mediating effect of reflexivity', *Journal of Organizational Behavior*, **24**, 779–802.

Snow, C.C., S.A. Snell, S.C. Davison and D.C. Hambrick (1996), 'Use transnational teams to globalize your company', *Organizational Dynamics*, **24**(1), 50–66.

Stewart, G.L., C.C. Manz and H.P. Sims (1999), *Teamwork and Group Dynamics*, New York: Wiley.

Tajfel, H. and J.C. Turner (1986), 'The social identity theory of intergroup behavior', in S. Worchel and W.G. Austin (eds), *Psychology of Intergroup Relations*, 2nd edn, Chicago, IL: Nelson-Hall, pp. 7–24.

Tolbert, P.S., M.E. Graham and A.O. Andrews (1999), 'Group gender composition and work group relations: theories, evidence, and issues', in G.N. Powell (ed.), *Handbook of Gender and Work*, Thousand Oaks, CA: Sage, pp. 179–202.

Tsui, A.S., T.D. Egan, and C.A. O'Reilly, III (1992), 'Being different: relational demography and organizational attachment', *Administrative Science Quarterly*, **37**, 549–79.

Wagner, D.G. and J. Berger (1997), 'Gender and interpersonal task behaviors: status expectation accounts', *Sociological Perspectives*, **40**, 1–32.

Watson, W.E., L. Johnson and D. Merritt (1998), 'Team orientation, self-orientation, and diversity in task groups: Their connection to team performance over time', *Group and Organization Management*, **23**, 161–89.

Webber, R.A. (1987), 'Changes in perception and behavior in mixed-gender teams', *Human Resource Management*, **26**, 455–67.

Williams, K.Y. and C.A. O'Reilly III (1998), 'Demography and diversity in organizations: a review of 40 years of research', in B.M. Staw and L.L. Cummings (eds), *Research in Organizational Behavior*, Volume 20, Stamford, CT: JAI, pp. 77–140.

Wood, W. and S.J. Karten (1986), 'Sex differences in interaction style as a product of perceived sex differences in competence', *Journal of Personality and Social Psychology*, **50**, 341–7.

Yamauchi, H. (1995), 'Factor structure of preferences for job attributes among Japanese workers', *Psychological Reports*, **77**, 787–91.

Yoder, J.D. (1994), 'Looking beyond numbers: the effects of gender status, job prestige, occupational gender-typing on tokenism processes', *Social Psychology Quarterly*, **57**, 150–59.

11 Influence and inclusion: a framework for researching women's advancement in organizations

Diana Bilimoria, Lindsey Godwin and Deborah Dahlen Zelechowski

Steadily the importance of women is gaining not only in the routine tasks of industry, but in executive responsibility... Women constitute a part of our industrial achievement. (Herbert Hoover, US President 1928)

Women's workplace responsibilities have arguably advanced considerably in the past several decades. Certain indicators would suggest that gender equality has been reached in the workplace, as statistics show that women today comprise 46 per cent of all US workers (US Bureau of Labor Statistics, 2004) and hold 50 per cent of all professional positions. While these statistics are promising for women's advancement, other numbers suggest that the glass ceiling has not yet been totally shattered. Particularly disconcerting is the fact that although the number of women qualified for management positions continues to rise – with 51 per cent of bachelor's degrees and 45 per cent of all advanced degrees being granted to women (US Bureau of the Census, 2000) – an examination of the end of the managerial pipeline shows that very few women are actually moving up to top-level management positions (Ragins et al., 1998). Today, almost 80 years after President Hoover declared women to be a vital part of 'our industrial achievement', among *Fortune* 500 companies, only 7.9 per cent of the top earners, 15.7 per cent of the corporate officers, and less than 2 per cent of the CEOs are women (Catalyst, 2005).

The trend of unequal gender representation in the upper echelon of organizations leads us and many other researchers to ask questions such as: why are there so few women in top corporate tiers? What are the continuing barriers to women's advancement in organizations (for example Fagenson, 1990; Heilman, 2001; Catalyst 2005)? The answer to these questions is not a simple one, including a variety of contributive explanatory variables such as the lack of mentoring (Ragins and Sundstrom, 1989, Higgins and Kram, 2001), networking challenges (Oakley, 2000; Brass, 1985), gender stereotypes (Oakley, 2000), and work-life balance issues (Rapoport et al., 2002). In this chapter, we provide a review of these factors, both individual and organizational, under the rubrics of two dimensions: personal *influence* and social *inclusion*. In particular, we argue that research on women's career progression must include a simultaneous examination of the individual characteristics that enable them to be successful as well as the nature of the organizational contexts they face that facilitate or constrain their career development. Through this integrative framework, we derive a number of questions that are likely to provide more fine-grained analyses than have been undertaken by most research to date to understand the unique barriers to women's career advancement in organizations.

Before we can understand what individual and organizational factors are necessary for women to succeed in organizations, we first examine the contextual dynamics facing women in organizations, and how these create the unique set of circumstances that women (not men) encounter in their career advancement within business and management.

The unique circumstances faced by women in organizations

The discourse about the different realities that men and women face on the path toward the executive suite is filled with many voices, opinions and theories. O'Neil and Bilimoria (2005a; 2005b) identify three key gender-related factors that suggest that women in organizations face situations and realities that are considerably different from men's experiences. These factors uniquely shape and constrain women's career progress, as follows:

1. The continued under-representation of women within the top tiers of organizations, resulting in their persistent token status and stereotyping, poses unique barriers to women's advancement.
2. The inability of organizations to adjust work structures and success criteria to accommodate women's life and family responsibilities as primary care-givers uniquely impacts their prospects for advancement.
3. A relational approach to career development frequently shapes women's career choices and progression.

Building on O'Neil and Bilimoria's (2005a, 2005b) framework, we will elaborate on each of these factors to detail how the career advancement dynamics women face are markedly different than men's experiences.

Under-representation, token dynamics and stereotyping
While today there are more women in management positions than compared to years past, the proportion of women in top management positions still

leaves them facing token dynamics behind the doors of the executive suite. In her seminal work in this area, Kanter (1977) proposed three perceptual phenomena that result in negative implications for minority groups: (1) heightened visibility, which exacerbates performance pressures for them; (2) polarization, which leads to a sense of isolation from informal and social and professional networks; and (3) assimilation, where they are encouraged to act in a gender-defined manner. Research has suggested that tokenism dynamics will remain for women in top management until there is at least a 7–12-fold increase in the numbers of females in top positions (Oakley, 2000). As long as women remain tokens in number, especially within upper management, they have the unique disadvantage of being stereotyped and thus treated differently than their male counterparts.

The in-group favoritism among the male majority, as suggested by social identity theory, may serve as the mechanism perpetuating the 'old boys' network', the informal male social system in place both within and across organizations that serves to preserve males' status at the top (Oakley, 2000). Social identity theory also helps explain the process of gender-based stereotyping, which women continue to face as a minority group within upper management. A majority of the stereotypic beliefs about the sexes pertain to communal and agentic attributes, with women viewed as being more communal and socially oriented and men seen as more task-oriented and aggressive (Eagly, 1987, Eagly et al., 2000).

The impact of such stereotyping can be detrimental for women, resulting in unique gender-related barriers for women's career advancement including a perceived lack of fit with the organization (Simpson, 2000; Heilman, 1983), and lower job satisfaction (Burke and McKeen, 1996). Building upon Schein's work (1973; 2001), Powell et al. (2002) found that a good manager is still perceived as predominantly masculine. The norm in management is so strongly male, women are even looked upon as deviant based upon their innate characteristics such as their higher tone of voice and more feminine physical appearance (Larwood, 1991; Heilman and Stopeck, 1985). These findings suggest that society has sex-typed the executive suite, perpetuating the 'think manager, think male' mental model, making it particularly difficult for women to progress to the top of organizations.

Life responsibilities clash with organizational structure
Women have gone to work, but they have not relinquished their duties at home, as 70 per cent of women in dual-earner couples report that they have to take a greater responsibility for child care than their male partners, and 72 per cent of family members who provide care to the elderly are women (Families and Work Institute, 2005). Documenting the stressful dynamics that these women face as work awaits them around the clock,

Hochschild (1989) discussed this issue of women's dual role in society today as both career-woman and care-giver, dubbing the phenomenon 'the second-shift'.

Despite their broader familial responsibilities, however, women continue to face career trajectories that are based on the traditional male model of continuous employment and advancement (Mavin, 2001; Pringle and Dixon, 2003). The archetype of the 'ideal worker' as someone who can devote all the hours in the day necessary to work, including reorganizing their private life to meet work needs, seems still to pervade organizational definitions of career success (Williams, 2000). For example, Simpson's (1998) study illustrated how today's organizations are environments where face-time, or as she calls it, *presenteeism*, has become a new competitive element across the genders. Even if one is able to get their work done at home or in off-hours, being seen in the office early and late are equated to being committed and dependable. Because women remain responsible for a larger portion of domestic responsibilities, however, they have a harder time putting in the same hours as men, and thus are at a disadvantage (cf, Simpson, 1988). Yet the ideal worker can only exist if he or she has a domestic worker at home meeting all the other needs of a family and household (Williams, 2000).

While there have been a range of different organizational responses (for example day care, after-school programs, to information services and alternative work scheduling policies) attempting to help women (and men) balance their familial obligations (Auerbach, 1990), many argue that these do not solve the core issue of women continuing to carry most of the burden of care-giving duties in society. Other research has suggested that even when these policies are in place, workers report that using flexible schedules and taking time off for family reasons when these options are available hinders their job advancement (Families and Work Institute, 2005). The idea that women who try to balance work and home are put on a 'mommy track' has been the focus of research for nearly two decades now (Schwartz, 1989). Recent research, however, has suggested that the introduction of these choices for today's women has given women a sense of illusionary freedom of choice and control over their lives, when in reality they are now held even more responsible for how they combine child care with professional responsibilities (Elvin-Nowak, 1999). As a result, guilt is a common consequence of women trying to juggle both career and family pressures (Holcomb, 1998). The tension between home and work responsibilities, and the failure of organizational reward and promotion systems to adequately adjust to women's societally-mandated life responsibilities, thus create unique challenges to women's career progression in organizations.

Relational orientation as career driver

Studies have suggested that 'for women, the primary experience of self is relational, that is, the self is organized and developed in the context of important relationships' (Surrey, 1991: 52). Most women view themselves in terms of their relationships either as mother, friend, wife, co-worker, with connection to others key to their identity (Gilligan, 1982). Based on such findings, O'Neil and Bilimoria (2005b: 8) argue that, 'because of their general preference for relationality, women's careers may develop different patterns, paths, concerns, and responsibilities than men's careers.'

For example, Bardwick (1980) challenged Levinson's et al. (1978) male-based model of adult development. Discussing the 'seasons of a woman's life', she suggested that women's lives tend to focus both on relationships and career advancement, which impacts how their lives and careers unfold. Gallos (1989) argued that male-based standards for defining career success are not necessarily applicable to women. Building on Gilligan's work (1982), Gallos suggested that women may have fundamentally different outlooks on their desired career trajectory, perceived options, and priorities which are informed by their role in the family, societal expectations and socialization and career opportunities. Powell and Mainiero (1992) proposed a conceptualization of women's career development as 'cross currents in a river of time' which takes into account the impact of personal, organizational and societal factors on women's career choices. They suggested that, 'women may focus more on measures of satisfaction that represent how they are feeling about their careers, rather than what their careers actually look like' and they 'attempt to strike a balance between their relationships with others and their personal achievements at work', seeking subjective satisfaction in both realms (p. 2). More recently, Mainiero and Sullivan (2005) suggest a 'kaleidoscope model' to explain the changing relational nature of women's careers. They suggest that, 'like a kaleidoscope that produces changing patterns when the tube is rotated, women shift the pattern of their careers by rotating different aspects in their lives to arrange their roles and relationships in new ways' (p. 106).

Based on relational preferences, a woman's career may ebb and flow in ways altogether different from that of the traditional male model, primarily focused on linear career progression. Because a woman's life cycle may involve intense relational experiences such as childbirth and child care, her developmental stages may be different from a man's as she travels in and out of the organizational work sphere. Research has suggested that women may take longer to reach the same organizational status as their male counterparts because of the focus that family and relational life takes throughout their careers (Bailyn, 1989). However, research has also suggested that during middle adulthood, women discover a renewed sense of purpose and increased energy for work (Bardwick, 1980; Borysenko, 1996). Gordon and Whelan (1998) suggest that many women undergo a significant change during their mid-life, which organizations need to understand better in order to support and integrate women effectively into the organization. According to her life stage concerns, therefore, a woman's career advancement and family responsibilities may shift from foreground and background throughout her life differently than they do for men (O'Neil and Bilimoria, 2005a).

Taken together, these three factors – token status, life responsibilities and relational orientation – paint a social and organizational landscape which is unique to women. From a societal perspective, women remain primary care-givers and continue to value relational identity patterns as drivers of their life choices. From an organizational perspective, 'institutionalized patriarchy and hegemonic masculinity continue to affect women's abilities to advance and to succeed, particularly at the highest organizational levels, thus resulting in a general pattern of few or no women in top corporate positions.' (O'Neil and Bilimoria, 2005a: 170). As such, we argue that women's career advancement, especially to the highest levels of organizational leadership, continues to deserve specific attention. We now turn our attention to the factors impacting women's career progression in light of the contextual features discussed above.

Dimensions for women's effectiveness at the top: influence and inclusion

There are many pieces to examine when trying to understand the puzzle of women's career advancement. Ragins and Sundstrom (1989) suggested that a variety of factors be examined when explaining women's promotion to powerful positions, including organizational features and interpersonal influences. A scan of the literature reveals that the research to date, however, has typically fallen into one of two categories (Oakley, 2000; Fagenson, 1990; Ragins and Sundstrom, 1989). One category of work focuses on personal characteristics and behaviors of women leaders, including their physical traits, attitudes and behaviors to explain the lack of women in top management. This body of work has been referred to as the 'gender-centered' or 'person-centered' perspective (Fagenson, 1990). The second category of research, referred to as the 'organization structure' perspective, focuses not on women themselves, but rather on the structural features of organizations that constrain women's rise to the executive echelons (Fagenson, 1990). Some studies have examined both personal and situational factors (for example Gattiker and Larwood, 1988; Tharenou et al., 1994). However, most research is 'bound by the theoretical perspective embraced by the researcher' and thus has been grounded in either the gender-centered perspective or the organization structure perspective, minimizing our explanations to an either-or situation (Fagenson, 1990: 267).

While each of these approaches adds insight to our understanding of the obstacles women face on the way to the top, most theory and research of women's managerial progression has rarely simultaneously 'examined a range of personal and situational determinants' (Kirchmeyer, 1998: 673). Because of the myopic tendency for researchers to focus on either a woman's personal characteristics or on the organization's structural features, the dynamic interaction of these factors has often been neglected. Building upon prior research that has demonstrated the importance of these factors individually, we reason that for a woman to be successful at the top of an organization, she needs to possess and employ certain personal charac-teristics and skills which we term her *influence* characteristics, while at the same time being in a supportive organizational environment that allows her to use these skills, which we term her *inclusion* characteristics. We argue that in order to explore women's career progression fully in organizations, researchers need to concurrently examine *both* of these factors – what a woman does in a particular organizational context, as well as the nature of the context itself.

Recent headlines highlight the argument that focusing on either influence or inclusion in isolation is not sufficient and results in a limited understanding of women's experience as they advance in organizations. Take, for instance, the case of Laura Zubulake, a top-ranked executive with UBS, one of Europe's largest banks, who was recently awarded $29 million in damages from a sexual discrimination suit she filed against the bank (The *Guardian*, 2005). Given her professional success, Zubulake's personal level of influence was arguably quite high, she was educated, experienced and qualified. However, she found herself in an environment that not only did not include her, but as her lawsuit revealed, it actively *ex*cluded her. Being told that she was old, ugly, should smile more and be 'softer', in addition to being excluded from trips (which were often to golf courses, baseball stadiums and sometimes strip clubs) with clients, were only some of the many charges brought against UBS (The *Guardian*, 2005). Unfortunately, Ms Zubulake's story is not unique among businesses, where many recent lawsuits have reflected the problems that arise when influential women find themselves in an environment that is not inclusive, and is even hostile, toward them (for example, Anderson, 2006; Majumdar, 2004).

Women, however, can also find themselves in an environment that is (or is potentially) inclusive of them, but they do not have the personal skill set, or influence, needed to advance. The media storm that evolved in the aftermath of Harriet Miers' nomination to the US Supreme Court illustrates this dynamic. A large criticism of Miers' nomination – from both Democrats and Republicans alike – was the perception that she lacked the qualifications to serve on the highest court in the country. After female justices O'Connor and Ginsburg broke the supreme court's gender barrier, one can argue that the court is inclusive of women; as such, gender did not appear to be the fodder for criticism of Miers' nomination (in fact some thought that her gender was an advantage toward her confirmation since it would maintain the current proportion of women on the bench). Instead, her lack of judicial experience (and courtroom experience in general) seemed to seal the fate of her nomination to the bench; as reflected in Senator Trent Lott's (R-Mississippi) comment, he did not think that she had 'enough experience in the constitutional area to be on the Supreme Court' (CNN, 2005). Thus, Miers' credentials, or lack thereof, resulted in low levels of the personal influence that she needed to advance to the highest court.

As both these examples illustrate, organizational advancement can be fraught with various obstacles for women, both personal and situational. To systematically understand the nature of the complex barriers to women's advancement, especially to the executive suite, we must simultaneously examine their individual characteristics (which determine their influence) as well as their organizational contexts (which determine their inclusion). Below we discuss each of these factors and the integrative framework in more detail, proposing integrative research questions for future studies to examine women's ascent and success in organizations more comprehensively.

Influence: the personal factors in women's advancement and success

Influence pertains to the ways women contribute to the organization through the extension of personal authority and effectiveness in their roles (Zelechowski and Bilimoria, 2003). Within the general rubric of 'influence' we include all factors that compose a woman's human capital and individual social capital characteristics that pertain to her performance and effectiveness and that contribute to her career advancement. A woman's human capital characteristics may include her education, training, skills, knowledge and prior work experience (Becker, 1993). Where human capital encompasses individuals' unique skills and abilities, social capital is more a reflection of one's opportunities within their context (Burt, 1998). It is defined as any aspect of social structure that creates value and facilitates the actions of the individuals within the social structure; it is created when relations among people change in ways that facilitate instrumental action (Coleman, 1990), and may include social networks and mentoring relationships (Portes, 1998). Individual social capital characteristics that result in the accumulation of influence refer to how a person takes advantage of these opportunities (for example, connecting to valuable resources through networks and mentors) to achieve desired outcomes.

Social capital skills thus pertain to how a person creates and sustains their personal effectiveness through building connections and relationships that yield valuable resources and opportunities.

Paying heed to these human and social capital characteristics, research has documented the myriad ways by which women can augment their career success in organizations. For example, managerial advancement and other positive career outcomes such as increased salary are related to a variety of human capital characteristics including: higher levels of educational attainment (Tharenou et al., 1994; Becker, 1993); longer organizational tenure (Judge and Bretz, 1994), and participation in training and development (Tharenou et al., 1994; Ragins and Sundstrom, 1989). Individuals with longer job and organization tenure, educational attainment and training develop expertise both within their specific positions and their general field of knowledge (Wayne et al., 1999). Such knowledge becomes a source of power and influence, relative to the need that others have for the specific skill and expertise the individual possesses (French and Raven, 1960). Women with higher levels of education, tenure and training are able to wield a wider circle of influence within their organization because they are credited with possessing enhanced knowledge and understanding around certain topics that others within the organization need. Ragins et al. (1998) found that many successful women executives have become influential and successful by developing a unique skill set which makes them indispensable to the organization. As one woman in this study commented, 'I think you have to have a specialty and you have to do it better than anybody else can conceivably know how to do it' (Ragins et al., 1998: 30).

Individual social capital skills may contribute to a woman's level of influence as well. For instance, there are many reasons to believe that increased social connections and networks will also lead to positive outcomes in one's career mobility. Research has found that the social resources embedded within networks provide benefits such as greater and more timely access to information, greater access to financial or material resources, and greater visibility, legitimacy and sponsorship within the social system (Seibert and Kramer, 2001). Additionally, Mintzberg (1983) suggests that a person who is influential needs not only a source of personal power, but must also have political skill. Perrewe (2000) defines political skill as, 'knowing what to do in a particular work situation with how to execute the behaviors in a convincing manner' suggesting that executives high in 'political skill are better able to cope with the chronic workplace stressors they encounter.' Referring to women specifically, Mainiero (1994) stated, 'political skill is a necessary, even vital, aspect of women's career advancement – that breaking the glass ceiling without shattering hopes for a promising executive career requires delicate political skill.'

These various skills and characteristics taken together help determine a woman's personal influence within an organization. This factor, embedding both human and individual social capital elements, helps explain a woman's advancement in the organization. Influence is a non-static individual characteristic that can increase or decrease over time in comparison to others, as a woman's skill level, experience and connections change over time.

Inclusion: the contextual factors in women's advancement and success
As reflected in the statement by Ellen Hancock, Chairman and CEO of Exodus Communications, 'Your employees get you promoted; your peers allow you to be promoted', organizational inclusion is a critical factor in women's career success (Pestrak, 2000: 1). Inclusion pertains to the organizational characteristics that appear to determine how women are integrated into their corporate setting (Zelechowski and Bilimoria, 2003). Women who are in more inclusive environments are able to use their skills and talents to their fullest capacity. In contrast, a woman who is in an *ex*clusive environment, where she is not invited into or perhaps actively excluded from various networks, may have a stunted career trajectory in that environment, regardless of her personal abilities.

Inclusive environments are characterized by cultural norms that support positive relations between men and women, freedom from stereotyping about women's and men's roles and occupations, conditions (work schedules, job titles, physical environment) that are inclusive of both men and women, a strong 'critical mass' of women; opportunities for advancement based on talent rather than gender, and work policies that help support work–life balance (McLean, 2003). While no company may be perfect, there are several firms emerging as models of inclusive working environments for women. For example, Xerox is routinely ranked among the best places for women to work – not necessarily because it is one of the few *Fortune* 500 companies with a female CEO, but because gender inclusion does not stop at the door of the executive suite (McGinn, 2005). At Xerox, management is comprised of over 30 per cent women, managers are held accountable for meeting diversity goals, and the corporate culture is reported to be one where 'no one hesitates to reschedule a meeting to take a child to the pediatrician' (McGinn, 2005: 151).

We know, however, that not all organizational cultures are as inclusive to women. Researchers have documented a variety of organizational-level barriers that can impede a woman's career advancement, regardless of her personal credentials, including corporate policies and practices in training, career development, promotion and compensation (Oakley, 2000). For instance, a study by Simpson (1995: 7) showed that an MBA does not seem to be as successful for women in terms of subsequent career advancement and salary levels as it is for men, illustrating that 'an organizational culture which excludes or devalues women can make any qualification effectively redundant.' In a study of European female executives, Linehan and Scullion (2001) found support for organizational bias against females in the selection process for international assignments, a severe shortage of pre-departure training and very little organizational attention given to female career development. Similarly, Oakley (2000: 323) observes that women often find themselves 'excluded from the upper ranks of management due to improper tracking earlier in their career,' because they are 'often not offered experience in areas like operations and manufacturing, which are deemed an essential prerequisite for the CEO position and other senior management positions'.

Women are often left out of the 'old boys' network', as well as from mentoring relationships and other informal social networks that may exist within the organization, giving the men who are tapped into these resources an advantage (Vincent and Seymour, 1994; Reinhold, 2005). Research has suggested that women may actually gain from mentoring relationships more than men because they have more obstacles to overcome in order to advance (Ragins, 1989; Tharenou, 1999; Wallace, 2001). Mentoring helps provide women with access to networks (Burt, 1998), as well as challenging assignments, increased visibility and credibility (Tharenou, 1999).

Whether it is a context where stereotypes quietly persist, where working conditions and compensation favor men, where mentoring is absent for women, or women managers remain token in number, subtle sex discrimination is occurring and women are excluded from participating fully. Subtle sex discrimination is defined as 'the unequal and harmful treatment of women that is visible but often not noticed because [women] have internalized sexist behavior as acceptable or customary' (Benokraitis and Feagin, 1994: 30). While the different system-level obstacles that continue to inhibit women's full inclusion into the organization may be more subtle and covert than the discriminatory practices of yesterday, they are just as dangerous – if not more so – because they are actually harder to identify and confront than overt discrimination (Ragins et al., 1998; Meyerson and Fletcher, 2000; Benokraitis and Feagin, 1994). Such barriers impact women and corporations alike, as Reinhold (2005: 43) states, 'organizational, and leadership issues still limit women's representation at the top levels of US corporations, and the resulting brain drain does not bode well for companies competing for a shrinking pool of talented potential leaders'.

Inclusion is an important variable in understanding women's advancement, since a woman's personal skills and influence will not translate into career advancement if she is in an organization that does not support her participation and development. While a woman can try to influence the culture of the organization within which she works, ultimately it is the characteristics and practices of the organization that determine her level of inclusion. Inclusion is a non-static organizational characteristic that can increase or decrease over time in comparison to others, as an organizational environment changes its treatment of women over time.

An integrated framework: opportunities for future research

In this chapter we have argued that researchers must simultaneously study both influence and inclusion factors as explanations of women's successful rise to top management positions. Furthermore, we suggest that influence and inclusion are not uni-dimensional variables, but rather multi-dimensional, where either factor can be high or low. A graphical representation of the possible interaction between influence and inclusion results in a framework ripe for further research, as illustrated in Figure 11.1. While derived from the literature, this framework was also informed by interviews conducted in a pilot study with six women inside (executive) directors in *Fortune* 1000 corporations (Zelechowski and Bilimoria, 2003). These women were high-ranking executives, who in addition to their executive role have been elevated to a seat on the board of directors – a rare role for women.

As depicted in Figure 11.1, a woman can reflect higher or lower levels of influence as determined by her personal (human and social capital) characteristics. For example, a woman with an advanced educational degree, greater expertise and experience, and a range of workplace and social connections, could possess higher influence within her organization than a woman lacking these qualities. Separate from her influence, however, a woman can also experience various levels of inclusion by her organization as determined by the degree of support and integration offered specifically to her. Low inclusion environments are marked by unsupportive or uncooperative behaviors, including exclusion from work-related social functions, exclusion from business information and resources, unavailability of challenging and high profile assignments, and a generally unsupportive environment with little mentoring or feedback, discounting of contributions, and marginalization of ideas.

The emergent typology in Figure 11.1 helps frame the dynamic interaction between influence and inclusion that women may encounter on the way to the executive suite. Using this framework as a springboard for future research, we propose four possible profiles of women: *strivers*, *silent servants*, *accommodators* and *socialized achievers*. We argue that a woman's career advancement is connected to her profile within the framework. Based on the dynamic interaction between influence and inclusion factors, each profile of women has different experiences surrounding career progression and

| | INCLUSION | |
	Lower	Higher
Higher	Strivers	Socialized achievers
INFLUENCE		
Lower	Silent servants	Accommodators

Figure 11.1   Influence and inclusion: an integrated framework for studying women's advancement in organizations

satisfaction. Describing each profile below, we also frame possible questions for future research.

Silent servants: neither included nor influential
Women who are low on the factor of personal influence as well as inclusion, we label *silent servants*. They are not highly skilled, connected, or educated and thus lack high levels of influence within an organization. Additionally, the exclusive culture of their organization compounds the situation by excluding them from the social networks within the organization, severely limiting their access to support and development resources. Silent servants could be positioned in the organization – even within upper-management positions – literally as tokens, selected to fill an artificial quota for the sake of appearance, rather than with the expectation that they will contribute to the organization. As Oakley notes, 'the highly noticeable under-representation of women creates pressures from stakeholders for more visible participation from women in corporate boards and upper management positions' (2000, p. 322). Yet research has shown that women who are selected for a leadership role on the basis of preference rather than merit rate their performance more negatively, take less credit for their successful outcomes, view themselves as more deficient in leadership skills, and are less motivated to pursue leadership roles (Heilman et al., 1987).

While we might hope this is not happening today, there is evidence that women who are low on both inclusion and influence continue to be used as 'window dressing' at the top of corporations. A recent study with executive women at a major US banking company (Godwin and Brenner, 2005) found that given the striking imbalance of female representation in the upper echelons of this organization, some of the women at these levels have sensed that they were appointed mostly as tokens at the top. As one senior woman from this study reported, 'They put women up front so that their face is seen [in certain meetings]... Oh, that's the best part! [I was at one of these meetings and] I have in my drawer a piece of paper with the word "token" written on it that the guys gave me. The only thing that kept me from punching out people was that I knew that they were joking.'

Based on such findings, we expect that initially silent servants may be grateful for the opportunity they are given, especially when they land senior positions. Ultimately, however, it is unlikely that they will be satisfied with their token roles as they realize that they do not wield real influence within the organization and as they reach a more visible glass ceiling. If a silent servant's influence increases, either through improved skills, connection, knowledge or expertise, she may become a frustrated striver unless the organization also changes to become more welcoming of her contributions.

The personal and organizational dynamics that foster silent servants raise interesting research questions such as: are silent servants the least likely to experience career advancement into top management positions? What organizational dynamics result in a silent server being promoted into upper management positions? How satisfied are silent servants with their career opportunities? What factors lead to a silent servant becoming a striver, accommodator or socialized achiever? How does top management treat silent servers?

Strivers: influential, but not included

We use the term *strivers* to describe the women who possess a high degree of influence within their organization either from higher levels of education, training, organizational tenure, a range of connections, or personal ability. Due to organizational structures and peer behaviors that stymie their contribution to the organization, however, they remain low on inclusion, and thus have tremendous potential, which often remains untapped. Strivers are those talented women who find themselves hitting their head on the glass ceiling, striving to break through and reach top-level positions. On paper, these women are qualified for organizational success and advancement, but their contributions are discounted and/or they are not given access to the social networks and mentoring necessary to help them advance (Metz and Tharenou, 2001; Becker, 1993).

We hypothesize that these women find themselves in a catch-22 situation: they possess the skills and talents required of successful executives; however, they can not enact them because the organization is not supportive of women's participation in the male-dominated executive suite. Women in these environments may find themselves in a lose–lose situation where acting in a feminine manner is equated with incompetence, but acting in a competent way (that is, masculine, authoritative) is seen as being unfeminine and thus not encouraged (Oakley, 2000). Jamieson (1995) refers to this as the 'femininity/competency' bind that many women face within organizations.

Ms Zubulake's story at UBS, referred to above, illustrates the difficulties a striver can face in an exclusive environment that has double standards for men and women. In her testimony, she described how she was 'accused of insubordination while male colleagues were allowed to yell back' at her boss, while her peer evaluations also said that she should 'smile more' and be 'softer' (The *Guardian*, 2005). Despite her skills and qualifications for a higher position, her organizational context thwarted her ability to achieve to her fullest potential. Strivers like Ms Zubulake who have influential skills and talents, yet find themselves in an unsupportive, exclusionary environment are faced with a variety of career decisions. Among other options, they can choose to remain in an organization that does not allow them to utilize their skills and talents fully and are likely to come up against a glass ceiling; they can bear the high costs of filing a complaint or lawsuit against their company, leave and join an organization that will include them more fully, or begin their own businesses. While there are growing headlines about high-profile discrimination lawsuits like those recently seen among Wall Street banks (The *Guardian*, 2005), increasingly, it seems that many skilled women are choosing to leave the corporate world altogether because of the continued obstacles they must face because of their gender (Hefferman, 2002; Einhart, 2001).

The experiences, career trajectories and exit patterns of strivers offer many interesting research questions awaiting further exploration, including: what are the most typical exclusionary behaviors strivers face? What kinds of tactics do strivers use to advance in an exclusionary environment? What career opportunities do strivers perceive they have within their organizations? What exit patterns are observable for strivers: what makes them stay within an exclusionary environment and what triggers them to leave? Where do they go if they leave? What causes a striver to file a complaint against her organization? What are the personal stress implications for strivers?

Accommodators: included, but not influential

Accommodators are women with low personal influence who are situated within an organization that is (or would be) inclusive to her. Unlike silent servants, accommodators' inclusionary environment makes support systems such as social networks, mentoring and training available to them. While accommodators are likely to need additional experience and training before they are able to move into top management positions (Oakley, 2000), we expect that training and developmental opportunities are more likely to be given to them than to women in an exclusionary organization.

Developing critical skills and experiences is often a strategy accommodators pursue to move into higher positions. Ragins, Townsend, and Mattis's (1998: 29) survey of the highest ranked women in *Fortune* 1000 companies found that in addition to hard work, 'developing specialized expertise is another effective means for women to become known as high performers' as specialized skills helped them become indispensable to the organization. Once accommodators gain greater visibility and experience within the organization, they may move toward becoming socialized achievers. Further research is needed to understand the experience and career movement of accommodators, including: do accommodators who receive training, mentoring or challenge assignments have a greater likelihood of achieving top-management positions? How do accommodators compare to strivers and silent servants in their experience and attainment of executive roles? How does an accommodator recognize and leverage her inclusive environment and gain the skills/connections she needs to move into upper-level jobs? What factors foster an inclusive organizational culture for women?

Socialized achievers: influential and included

Socialized achievers are women who are high on both the influence and inclusion dimensions. These women are educated, skilled, connected and experienced within their work domain, and as a result they repeatedly excel at the tasks they undertake. They have gained influence within the organization by continually proving their credibility in each new work situation (Ragins et al., 1998). At the same time, they work in an organizational setting that embraces and supports them, allowing them to use their skills and talents to their full potential. Their contributions are valued and even sought after, they are included in the social networks of the organization, with access to both informal and formal networks, and have equal opportunities for advancement as do their male counterparts.

Socialized achievers may not only be primed for personal advancement within the organization; they are likely also to be a valuable link for other women. By virtue of their success and inclusion in the social structure of the organization, they may be more likely and able to serve as positive mentors to junior women (and men). Their success may also function to help perpetuate an inclusive culture. As prior research has shown, the presence alone of high level women is associated with improvements in the representation and treatment of other women in the organization (Bilimoria, 2006; Ely, 1995); it appears that traditional female stereotypes may be overcome by the presence of positive female role models (Noe, 1988). Studies (Eagly and Steffen, 1984; Geis et al., 1985) have found that 'the experience of working with female authority models or having information regarding competent women results in a more positive evaluation of women' (Noe,

1988: 70). Thus, we reason that socialized achievers, particularly in senior organizational positions, help beget more successful women by reinforcing an inclusive culture for women within the organization.

Take the story of Andrea Jung, the first female CEO of Avon as an example of socialized achievement. A closer look at Jung's profile reveals that having both influence and inclusion helped her reach the coveted corner office. Personal influence derived from her Ivy League education at Princeton, as well as her experience with high-end cosmetics gained from serving as an executive vice president at Neiman Marcus, helped lay the groundwork for her to succeed in her first stint with the company as an external consultant (Setoodeh, 2005). Fortunately for Jung, her influence was able to blossom fully in an inclusive environment at Avon. Thus, after demonstrating her savvy market prowess to the then-CEO, her successes were rewarded with additional responsibilities and promotions, until she was finally tapped as CEO in 1999 (Setoodeh, 2005). While the majority of the company's employees are women (the chief operating officer is also a woman), having a woman at the top has resulted in additional changes that may help other women advance within the company as well, as 'colleagues say she's introduced a culture at Avon that lets parents take time off, guilt-free, to attend crucial school activities' (Setoodeh, 2005). The success of her tenure is seen not only in the organizational culture, but also in the bottom line. Since her ascent to the top spot in 1999, she has worked on a major overhaul of the company's products and marketing which have resulted in a 45 per cent increase in sales, from $5.3 billion to $7.7 billion, with stock prices up 164 per cent (Setoodeh, 2005). As Avon continues to successfully knock on doors, there are rumors that even bigger corporations may be knocking on Jung's door offering her other CEO positions (Setoodeh, 2005). Jung exemplifies the successes that can be achieved when influence and inclusion are found in combination.

Future research questions for exploration of the circumstances and successes of socialized achievers include: in comparison with other types, do socialized achievers experience the highest levels of objective and subjective career success? What are the organizational consequences (both culturally and financially) of having a socialized achiever as a CEO? How do socialized achievers in senior positions influence the career trajectory of other women within the organization? How do the early career decisions of socialized achievers prepare them for top-level positions later on?

Discussion

Not every situation and obstacle that women in organizations face is equal. Thus, researchers must study the varied barriers to career advancement and success more systematically: the factors that comprise the paths to personal influence and social inclusion. We argue here that future research must hold both sets of obstacles (personal and contextual) in simultaneous tension. In doing so, we become more aware of the subtle differences in the problems that various women face, and may gain a more comprehensive picture of women's patterns of career progression within organizations. The practical implications of such a framework include creating multi-faceted and tailored solutions to individual cases – strengthening a woman's human capital when that is needed, or gaining awareness of and focusing on improving the environment's inclusion when that is a hindrance.

Gaining a better understanding of women's career advancement may be beneficial to organizations as well as individual women. As Oakley (2000: 324) reports, 'Almost all of the top ranked companies have an upper management that actively demonstrates support for the promotion of women, almost all of these companies target women to participate in executive education programs, and almost all of these companies take steps to facilitate the movement of women into line positions.' By gaining a finer-grained understanding of the paths to advancement, organizations may be better able to remove the impediments constraining women's progression to the executive suite.

The research questions raised in this chapter are just some of the directions we call on future studies to undertake. Other research should explore the nature of a woman's movement from one quadrant to another. While we argue that both inclusion and influence are necessary for career advancement especially to the highest corporate levels, future studies may examine the circumstances under which one dimension may be the more dominant. Finally, it may be interesting to determine how each dimension drives or hinders the development of the other.

References

Anderson, J. (2006), 'Six women at Dresdner file bias suit', *New York Times*, 10 January, Business/Financial Desk, Late Edition; Section C, Page 1, Column 6.

Auerbach, J. (1990), 'Employer-supported child care as a women-responsive policy', *Journal of Family Issues*, **11** (4), 384–400.

Bailyn, L. (1989), 'Understanding individual experience at work: comments on the theory and practice of careers', in M.B. Arthur, D.T. Hall and B.S. Lawrence (eds), *Handbook of Career Theory*, Cambridge: Cambridge University Press, pp. 477–89.

Bardwick, J.M. (1980), 'The seasons of a woman's life', in D. McGuigan (ed.), *Women's Lives: New Theory, Research and Policy*, Ann Arbor, MI: University of Michigan, Center for Continuing Education of Women, pp. 35–55.

Becker, G.S. (1993), *Human Capital*, Chicago, IL: University of Chicago Press.

Benokraitis, N. and J. Feagin (1994), *Modern Sexism: Blatant, Subtle, and Covert*, New York: Prentice Hall.

Bilimoria, D. (2006), 'The relationship between women corporate directors and women corporate officers', *Journal of Managerial Issues*, **18**(1), 47–61.

Borysenko, J. (1996), *A Woman's Book of Life*, New York: Riverhead Books.

Brass, D.J. (1985), 'Men's and women's networks: a study of interaction patterns and influence in an organization', *Academy of Management Journal*, **28**(2), 327–43.

Burke, R.J. and C.A. McKeen (1996), 'Do women at the top make a difference? Gender proportions and the experiences of managerial and professional women', *Human Relations*, **49**(8), 1093–104.

Burt, R. (1998), 'The gender of social capital' *Rationality and Society*, **10**(1), 5–46

Catalyst (2005), 'Women "take care". Men "take charge": Stereotyping of US business leaders exposed', www.catalystwomen.org/.

CNN (2005), 'Miers withdraws Supreme Court nomination', 28 October, www.cnn.com/2005/POLITICS/10/27/miers.nominations/.

Coleman, J. (1990), *Foundations of Social Theory*, Cambridge, MA: Harvard University Press.

Eagly, A.H. (1987), *Sex Differences in Social Behavior: A Social-Role Interpretation*, Hillsdale, NJ: Erlbaum.

Eagly, A.H. and S. Karau (2002), 'Role congruity theory of prejudice toward female leaders', *Psychological Review*, **109**(3), 573–98.

Eagly, A.H. and V. Steffen (1984), 'Gender stereotypes stem from the distribution of women and men in social roles', *Journal of Personality and Social Psychology*, **46**(4), 735–54.

Eagly, A.H., W. Wood and A.B. Diekman (2000), 'Social role theory of sex differences and similarities: a current appraisal', in T. Eckes and H.M. Trautner (eds), *The Developmental Social Psychology of Gender*, Mahwah, NJ: Lawrence Erlbaum Associates, pp. 123–74.

Einhart, N. (2001), 'Survival tactic: recognize your female talent', *Fast Company*, www.fastcompany.com/articles/2001/01/act_fineline.html.

Elvin-Nowak, Y. (1999), 'The meaning of guilt: a phenomenological description of employed mothers' experiences of guilt', *Scandinavian Journal of Psychology*, **40**(1), 73–83.

Ely, R.J. (1995), 'The power in demography: women's social constructions of gender identity at work', *Academy of Management Journal*, **38**(3), 589–634.

Fagenson, E. (1990), 'At the heart of women in management research: theoretical and methodological approaches and their biases', *Journal of Business Ethics*, **9**(4/5), 267–74.

Families and Work Institute (2005), www.familiesandwork.org/.

French, J.P.R. Jr and B. Raven (1960), 'The bases of social power', in D. Cartwright and A. Zander (ed.), *Group Dynamics*, New York: Harper and Row, pp. 607–23.

Gallos, J. (1989), 'Exploring women's development: implications for career theory, practice, and research', in M.B. Arthur, D.T. Hall and B.S. Lawrence (eds), *Handbook of Career Theory,* Cambridge: Cambridge University Press, pp. 110–31.

Gattiker, U.E. and L. Larwood (1988), 'Predictors for managers' career mobility, success, and satisfaction', *Human Relations*, **41**(8), 569–91.

Geis, F.L., M.B. Boston and N. Hottman (1985), 'Sex of authority role models and achievement by men and women: leadership performance and recognition', *Journal of Personality and Social Psychology*, **49**(3), 636–56.

Gilligan, C. (1982), *In a Different Voice: Psychological Theory and Women's Development*, Cambridge, MA: Harvard University Press.

Godwin, L. and N. Brenner (2005), 'Seeing only shadows: a theory of gender-blindness among executive women', presented at the Academy of Management Annual Conference, Honolulu, HI.

Gordon, J.R. and K.S. Whelan (1998), 'Successful professional women in midlife: how organizations can more effectively understand and respond to the challenges', *The Academy of Management Executive*, **12**(1), 8–27.

Guardian, The (2005), '$29M payout for woman belittled and excluded by Wall Street boss', 7 April, www.guardian.co.uk/usa/story/0,12271,1454895,00.html.

Hefferman, M. (2002), 'Exhibit A: the female CEO', *Fast Company*, **61** (August), 58–66.

Heilman, M. (1983), 'Sex bias in work settings: the lack of fit model', in L.L. Cummings and B.M. Staw (eds), *Research in Organizational Behavior*, Volume 5, Greenwich. CT: JAI, pp. 269–98.

Heilman, M. (2001), 'Description and prescription: how gender stereotypes prevent women's ascent up the organizational ladder', *Journal of Social Issues*, **57**(4), 657–74.

Heilman, M. and M. Stopeck (1985), 'Attractiveness and corporate success: different causal attributions for males and females', *Journal of Applied Psychology*, **70**(2), 379–88.

Heilman, M., M.C. Simon, D.P. Repper (1987), 'Internationally favored, unintentionally harmed? Impact of sex-based preferential selection on self-perceptions and self-evaluations', *Journal of Applied Psychology*, **72**(1), 62–8.

Higgins, C. and K.E. Kram (2001), 'Reconceptualizing mentoring at work: a developmental network perspective', *Academy of Management Review*, **26**(2), 264–98.

Hochschild, A. (1989), *The Second Shift*, New York: Avon.

Holcomb, B. (1998), *Not Guilty: The Good News About Working Mothers*, New York: Scribner.

Jamieson, K.H. (1995), *Beyond the Double Bind: Women in Leadership*, New York: Oxford University Press.

Judge, T.A. and R.D. Bretz, Jr (1994), 'Political influence behavior and career success', *Journal of Management*, **20**(1), 43–65.

Kanter, R.M. (1977), *Men and Women of the Corporation*, New York: Basic Books.

Kirchmeyer, C. (1998), 'Determinants of managerial success', *Journal of Management*, **24**(6), 673–92.

Larwood, L. (1991), 'Start with a rational group of people...Gender effects of impression management in organizations', in R.A. Giacalone and P. Rosenfeld (eds), *Applied Impression Management: How Image-making Affects Managerial Decisions*, Newbury Park, CA: Sage, pp. 177–94.

Levinson, D., D. Darrow, M. Levinson and B. McKee (1978), *Seasons of a Man's Life*, New York: Knopf.

Linehan, M. and H. Scullion (2001), 'Challenges for female international managers: evidence from Europe', *Journal of Managerial Psychology*, **16**(3), 215–28.

Mainiero, L.A. (1994), 'On breaking the glass ceiling: the political seasoning of powerful women executives', *Organizational Dynamics*, **22**(4), 4–20.

Mainiero, L.A. and S.E. Sullivan (2005), 'Kaleidoscope careers: an alternate explanation for the opt-out revolution', *The Academy of Management Executive*, **19**(1), 106–23.

Majumdar, S. (2004), 'From glass ceiling to pay gap', 16 July, in.rediff.com/money/2004/jul/16spec.htm.

Mavin, S. (2001), 'Women's careers in theory & practice: time for change?' *Women in Management Review*, **16**(4), 183–192.

McDonald, P., K. Brown and L. Bradley (2005), 'Have traditional career paths given way to protean ones?', *Career Development International*, **10**(2), 109–29.

McGinn, D. (2005), 'In good company', *Newsweek*, 24 October, www.msnbc.msn.com/id/9709961/site/newsweek/.

McLean, D. (2003), *Workplaces that Work: Creating A Workplace Culture that Attracts, Retains and Promotes Women*, report for The Centre of Excellence for Women's Advancement, The Conference Board of Canada, Ontario.

Metz, I. and P. Tharenou (2001), 'Women's career advancement: the relative contribution of human and social capital', *Group & Organizational Management*, **26**(3), 312–42.

Meyerson, D.E. and J.K. Fletcher (2000), 'A modest manifesto for shattering the glass ceiling', *Harvard Business Review*, **78**(1), 126–37.

Mintzberg, H. (1983), *Power In and Around Organizations*, Englewood Cliffs, NJ: Prentice-Hall.

Noe, R. (1988), 'Women and mentoring: a review and research agenda', *Academy of Management Review*, **13**(1), 65–78.

Oakley, J. (2000), 'Gender-based barriers to senior management positions: understanding the scarcity of female CEOs,' *Journal of Business Ethics*, **27**(4), 321–34.

O'Neil, D.A. and D. Bilimoria (2005a), 'Women's career development phases: idealism, endurance, and reinvention', *Career Development International*, **10**(3), 168–93.

O'Neil, D.A. and D. Bilimoria (2005b), 'Women and careers: a critical perspective on the theory and practice of women in organizations', Working Paper Series (WP-06–05), Department of Organizational Behavior, Case Western Reserve University, Cleveland, Ohio.

Perrewe, P. (2000), 'Political skill: an antidote for workplace stressors,' *Academy of Management Executive*, **14**(3), 115–23.

Pestrak, D. (2000), 'The glass ceiling: what you don't know, won't hurt you', www.debrapestrak. com/success_view_200012.htm.

Portes, Alejandro (1998), 'Social capital: its origins and applications in contemporary sociology', *Annual Review of Sociology*, **24**(1), 1–24

Powell, G.N. and L.A. Mainiero (1992), 'Cross-currents in the river of time: Conceptualizing the complexities of women's careers', *Journal of Management*, **18**(2), 215–37.

Powell, G.N., D.A. Butterfield and J. D. Parent (2002), 'Gender and managerial stereotypes: have the times changed?', *Journal of Management*, **28**(2), 177–93.

Pringle, J.K. and K.M. Dixon (2003), 'Re-incarnating life in the careers of women', *Career Development International*, **8**(6), 291–300.

Ragins, B.R. (1996), 'Jumping the hurdles: barriers to mentoring for women in organizations', *Leadership & Organization Development Journal*, **17**(3), 37–41.

Ragins, B.R. (1989), 'Barriers to mentoring: the female manager's dilemma', *Human Relations*, **42**(1), 1–22

Ragins, B.R. and E. Sundstrom (1989), 'Gender and power in organizations', *Psychological Bulletin*, **105**(1), 51–88.

Ragins, B.R., B. Townsend and M. Mattis (1998), 'Gender gap in the executive suite: CEOs and female executives report on breaking the glass ceiling', *The Academy of Management Executive*, **12**(1), 28–42.

Rapoport, R., L. Bailyn, J. Fletcher and B. Pruitt (2002), *Beyond Work Life Balance*, San Fransisco: Jossey-Bass.

Reinhold, B. (2005), 'Smashing glass ceilings: why women still find it tough to advance to the executive suite', *Journal of Organizational Excellence*, **24**(3), 43–55.

Schein, V. (1973), 'The relationship between sex role stereotypes and requisite management characteristics', *Journal of Applied Psychology*, **57**(2), 95–100.

Schein, V. (2001), A global look at psychological barriers to women's progress in management', *Journal of Social Issues*, **57**(4), 675–88.

Schwartz, E.N. (1989), 'Management women and the new facts of life', *Harvard Business Review*, **67**(1), 65–76.

Seibert, S.E. and M.L. Kraimer (2001), 'A social capital theory of career success', *Academy of Management Journal*, **44**(2), 219–37.

Setoodeh, R. (2005), 'Calling Avon's lady', *Newsweek*, 27 December/3 January, www.msnbc. msn.com/id/6733211/site/newsweek/.

Simpson, R. (1995), 'Is management education the right track for women?', *Women in Management Review*, **10**(6), 3–8.

Simpson R. (1998), 'Presenteeism, power and organizational change: long hours as a career barrier and the impact on working lives of women managers', *British Journal of Management*, **9**(3), 37–52.

Simpson, R. (2000), 'Gender mix and organizational fit: how gender imbalance at different levels of the organization impacts on women managers', *Women in Management Review*, **15**(1), 5–19.

South, S.J., W.T. Markham, C.M. Bonjean and J. Corder (1987), 'Sex differences in support for organizational advancement', *Work and Occupations*, **14**(2), 261–85.

Stewart, L.P. and W.B. Gudykunst (1982), 'Differential factors influencing the hierarchical level and number of promotions of males and females within an organization', *Academy of Management Journal*, **25**(3), 586–97.

Stroh, L.K., J.M. Brett and A.H. Reilly (1992), 'All the right stuff: a comparison of male and female managers', *Journal of Applied Psychology*, **77**(3), 251–60.

Surrey, J.L. (1991), 'The "self-in-relation": a theory of women's development', in J.V. Jordan, A.G. Kaplan, J.B. Miller, I.P. Stiver and J.L. Surrey (eds), *Women's Growth in Connection: Writings from the Stone Center*, New York: The Guilford Press, pp. 51–66.

Tharenou, P. (1999), 'Gender differences in advancing to the top', *International Journal of Management Reviews*, **2**(1), 1–22.

Tharenou, P. (2001), 'Going up? Do traits and informational social processes predict advancing in management', *Academy of Management Journal*, **44**(5), 1005–18.

Tharenou, P., S. Latimer and D. Conroy (1994), 'How do you make it to the top? An examination of influences on women's and men's managerial advancement', *Academy of Management Journal*, **37**(4), 899–931.

US Bureau of the Census (2000), www.census.gov/.

US Bureau of Labor Statistics (2004), www.dol.gov/wb/stats/main.htm.

Vincent A. and J. Seymour (1994), 'Mentoring among female executives', *Women in Management Review*, **9**(7), 15–20.

Wallace, J.E. (2001), 'The benefit of mentoring for female lawyers', *Journal of Vocational Behavior*, **58**, 366–91.

Wayne, S.J., R.C. Liden, M.L. Kraimer and I.K. Graf (1999), 'The role of human capital, motivation and supervisor sponsorship in predicting career success', *Journal of Organizational Behavior*, **20**(5), 577–95.

Williams, Joan (2000), *Unbending Gender: Why Family and Work Conflict And What to Do About It*, Oxford: Oxford University Press.

Zelechowski, D.D. and D. Bilimoria (2003), 'The experience of women corporate inside directors on the boards of *Fortune* 1000 firms', *Women In Management Review*, **18**(7), 376–81.

12 The effectiveness of human resource management practices for promoting women's careers

Alison M. Konrad

Since the late 1980s and early 1990s, management researchers have shown increasing interest in organizational Human Resource Management (HRM) practices, their antecedents and their effects. Evidence that HRM practices can contribute to firm financial performance (for example Huselid et al., 1997; Welbourne and Cyr, 1999) spawned the management subfield of Strategic Human Resource Management, which resulted in a burgeoning and influential stream of literature (Colbert, 2004; Wright and Snell, 1998).

At about the same time, the field of workplace diversity emerged. The primary impetus of the development of the workplace diversity field was the Hudson Institute's publication of *Workforce 2000: Work and Workers in the 21st Century* (Johnston and Packer, 1987). *Workforce 2000* made the case that in order to remain competitive, organizations would have to change their HRM practices to attract, motivate and retain the new, more demographically diverse workforce entering the US labor market in the year 2000. Subsequent authors elaborated these arguments to develop the business case for diversity (for example, Cox and Blake, 1991; Robinson and Dechant, 1997). The business case for diversity has three major components:

- Diverse groups can outperform homogeneous groups in tasks requiring problem-solving or creativity
- Market intelligence provided by a diverse employee group can provide organizations with better methods for reaching a diverse customer base
- Firms that manage diversity well will attract, motivate, develop and retain the best talent from all demographic groups, thereby outperforming firms that cannot manage diversity effectively.

The business case for diversity implies that one of the ways HRM practices can provide strategic value to the firm is by bringing a more diverse cohort into the workplace and finding ways to develop, motivate and retain that cohort. But how effective are HRM practices for accomplishing these goals? The purpose of this chapter is to review and synthesize the literature on HRM practices and women's career outcomes to summarize the state of the field and identify questions for further research. We begin by examining the wide variety of diversity-related practices implemented in organizations and their effects on women's careers. We then examine the conditions under which organizations are likely to adopt diversity-related HRM practices aimed at promoting the careers of the new, more diverse cohort of workers, including women. We examine the performance question raised by the field of strategic HRM by summarizing research linking diversity-related HRM practices to organizational performance. We close by identifying unanswered questions and areas where future research is needed.

What HRM practices have been developed to enhance women's careers?

Diversity-related HRM practices involve systems for recruitment, selection, training and development, career progression and retention (Fine, 1995; Heneman et al., 1996). Explicitly paying attention to diversity in the staffing process is important for reducing the effects of individual gender and race biases resulting from stereotypes learned in early childhood (Poehlman et al., 2004) and the natural human tendency to prefer similar others (Byrne, 1971). Attention to diversity can also help decision-makers to identify talented people who aren't connected to the usual networks (Ibarra, 1993; Brown and Konrad, 2001a, 2001b) and feeder pools where the organization has traditionally found its job candidates, including internal talent stuck in dead-end jobs without a career ladder (DiPrete and Soule, 1986, 1988).

In recruiting, organizations can undertake a variety of actions to identify and tap feeder pools likely to generate a demographically diverse set of qualified job candidates, such as placing ads in publications targeting women or specific ethnic groups, participating in job fairs dedicated to developing a diverse pool of job candidates, or working with employment agencies and search firms specializing in finding highly qualified women and/or specific ethnic groups (Equal Opportunities Commission, 2004; Fine, 1995; Konrad and Linnehan, 1995a). Using a diverse team of recruiters and ensuring that brochures, websites and other materials communicate a welcoming environment for diversity can help to attract a diverse set of candidates to the organization (Perkins et al., 2000).

If feeder pools are not very diverse, employers can help to diversify them by supporting training programs in the local schools and/or creating a set of internships for high school and university students (Fine, 1995; Konrad and Linnehan, 1995a). An example of such an initiative can be found on the website for Canadian Women in Communications (CWC), a professional association dedicated to promoting the advancement and involvement of women in the communications field. CWC offers mentoring, professional development courses and speakers at local and national levels to enlarge and strengthen the pool of women candidates for the field of communications in general as well as for senior executive and Corporate Board positions (see the website at cwc-afc.com/about.html).

In selection, organizations can examine selection ratios by demographic group to determine whether certain groups are more likely to be hired than others. If differences are found, organizations can investigate reasons and develop strategies for enhancing diversity (Equal Opportunities Commission, 2004; Fine, 1995; Konrad and Linnehan, 1995a). Organizations can try to use a diverse team to interview all job candidates in order to ensure that someone on the interviewing team can tap into candidates' qualifications despite differences in communication style or culture. A diverse interviewing team also allows the organization to get a sense of how well candidates will function in a diverse workplace. Another important technique in selecting for diversity is to use a structured interview process, which ensures that all candidates are asked the same set of questions and therefore have the same opportunities to demonstrate their abilities and qualifications. A meta-analysis of 31 US studies showed that although whites received higher interview ratings than Black and Hispanic candidates on average, high-structure interviews resulted in lower group differences than low-structure interviews (Huffcutt and Roth, 1998).

Providing internal leadership development programs is useful in the area of training and development for a diverse workforce, because members of historically excluded groups often have less access to traditional sources of knowledge and skill-building. Organizations can also institute high potential programs, which involve identifying people with the ability to rise substantially in the organization and connecting them with training, mentoring and development opportunities. Ensuring that each cohort of leadership development candidates and high potential employees is diverse builds a strong feeder pool for creating a diverse top management team in the future (Fine, 1995; Konrad and Linnehan, 1995a). Vinnicombe and Singh (2003) argue that in addition, women-only leadership training can help women better develop their leadership strengths in order to access leadership positions.

To ensure career progression for a diverse workforce, organizations can try to ensure that a diverse set of candidates is interviewed for each hire, each promotion, and each management opening (Fine, 1995; Konrad and Linnehan, 1995a). In addition, organizations can institute career planning for all employees, where managers meet with each employee individually on an annual basis and discuss their career options (Perlmutter et al., in press). In these meetings, employees participate in developing their own individually-tailored career plans and develop an understanding of the skills and achievements they will need in order to attain their goals.

Two factors that may be the most important to employee retention are growth opportunities and fairness (Konrad and Deckop, 2001). As such, ensuring that a diverse set of employees receives training and chances for promotion should lead to enhanced retention of all groups. The organizational justice literature demonstrates that fairness means ensuring that organizational decisions are made through a rational and transparent process so that ability and achievement is rewarded. Additionally, fairness means that employees are treated with dignity and respect and are provided with reasonable explanations for the tough decisions that are made (Colquitt, 2001). To get a better insight into employee retention, employers can examine turnover rates by demographic group to see if certain groups are more likely than others to leave the organization. Exit interviews can provide invaluable information regarding why employees are leaving the organization and strategies for improving retention in the future (Fine, 1995; Heneman et al., 1996; Konrad and Linnehan, 1995a).

What do we know about the impact of HRM practices on women's careers?

Researchers have linked four types of HRM practices with career outcomes for women and for a diverse workforce in general: 1) practices associated with employment equity (Australia, Canada) or equal opportunity (the UK, the US); 2) practices providing development opportunities; 3) practices that formalize the HRM system; and 4) work–life flexibility benefits. In this section, we describe each of these types of HRM practices and the impact on women's careers.

Employment equity, equal employment opportunity, and affirmative action
Considerable research has examined whether government programs intended to improve equity in employment opportunities have enhanced women's career outcomes (for example, French, 2001; Leck 2002; Leck and Saunders, 1992; Leck et al., 1995; Leonard, 1984, 1985, 1986). A key finding in this area showed that government programs resulted in the development of more diversity-related HRM practices among the employers most directly targeted by government enforcement (Konrad and Linnehan, 1995a; Holzer and Neumark, 2000). Research has fairly consistently shown these practices to be positively associated with women's employment outcomes as well as the outcomes of other groups designated by legislation.

In a study of 294 Canadian employers subject to the Employment Equity Act from 1989 to 1993, Leck and Saunders (1992) found that organizations with more extensive employment equity programs (which Leck and Saunders labeled EEP effectiveness in their Tables) were more likely to hire representative numbers of women, including women who were visible minorities, aboriginal, disabled, and white without disabilities. Using the same sample of organizations, Leck et al. (1995) found that growth in pay was positively associated with the extensiveness of the employer's employment equity programs for white women, women who were disabled, and women who were visible minorities, as well as white men and aboriginal men. In a more recent study of 286 Canadian firms, Ng and his colleagues (Ng et al., 2005a) found that employers subject to the Employment Equity Act were more likely than others to have diversity policies, to recruit for diversity, to have diversity training, and to hold their managers accountable for diversity effectiveness.

In the US, Leonard (1984; 1985; 1986) concluded that federal law outlawing employment discrimination and federal regulation requiring contractors to the federal government to develop and undertake affirmative action in employment improved the employment opportunities of women and minorities significantly. Sass and Troyer (1999) found that affirmative action litigation increased the hiring of new female recruits in police departments. Konrad and Linnehan (1995a) found in a study of 138 Philadelphia-area organizations that employers subject to affirmative action regulations or equal employment lawsuits developed more identity-conscious HRM structures to combat discrimination. Comparing the effects of identity-blind and identity-conscious HRM practices, they also found that employers who adopted more identity-conscious practices had women in higher-ranking management positions and had more visible minorities in management. Identity-blind structures that aimed at creating fairness for all but that did not take a particular focus on gender or racial identity, were unrelated to employment statistics. Holzer and Neumark (2000) found in a study of 2092 firms that affirmative action regulations resulted in employers using more recruitment, screening, performance evaluation and training practices. Affirmative action resulted in employers attracting more female and minority applicants and hiring more female and minority employees.

In a study of 1976 Australian organizations, French (2001) found that employers taking an affirmative action stance toward gender equity by developing gender-specific strategies to overcome bias against women and by developing gender-specific structures including mentoring and networking (which French labeled Cluster 3 in her Tables) had more women in management and more women at higher levels of management than employers taking little action toward gender equity (which French labeled

Cluster 1 in her Tables). Affirmative action employers also had more women in management than employers who took what French called a gender diversity approach, which involved consultation with the union, inclusion of employment equity issues in enterprise bargaining and the provision of work–life flexibility benefits (which French labeled Cluster 4 in her Tables). This finding is consistent with the international picture of trade unions as showing a significant level of under-representation of women and visible minorities in decision-making (Greene and Kirton, 2005).

In sum, the research in multiple countries fairly consistently supports the positive effect on women's employment opportunities of HRM practices related to employment equity or equal employment programs. In particular, HRM practices that are identity conscious in that they focus attention on decisions regarding members of historically under-represented groups seem to increase the diversity of organizational employment statistics.

But is paying attention to demographic identity when making staffing decisions fair? Researchers have questioned whether employment equity, equal employment, and affirmative action raise fairness concerns among employees. A study of 133 students in a Canadian university showed that 91 per cent believed that a focus on employment equity inevitably results in reverse discrimination against white men (Leck, 2002). Similarly, a study of 349 university students in the US documented negative views of affirmative action (Kravitz and Platania, 1993). Bell et al. (2000) found that many of their respondents believed that affirmative action programs cause employers to hire less qualified applicants and reject more qualified applicants. Consistent with this belief, Heilman et al. (1997) found that managers rated the performance of hypothetical female employees associated with affirmative action more negatively than they rated males or females not associated with affirmative action.

Interestingly, both the Kravitz and Platania (1993) and Leck (2002) studies also showed that the participants had a very poor understanding of what employment equity programs in Canada and affirmative action programs in the US entail. Both studies showed participants thought employment equity or affirmative action involved hiring quotas. In fact, quotas are only imposed upon US public sector organizations when a judge determines that a public sector employer has intentionally engaged in systematic and widespread discrimination. Private-sector firms are strictly forbidden from using hiring quotas in the US (Konrad and Linnehan, 2003).

People respond much more positively to the actual HRM practices associated with staffing for a diverse workforce. Konrad and Linnehan's (1995b) study showed that line managers rated most identity-conscious staffing processes positively, including aggressive recruiting of women and minorities for management, targeting women and minorities to receive management training, and tracking the percentage of women and minorities in jobs that lead to management. Parker, Baltes and Christiansen (1997) found that all employees, including white men in a US organization with a strong Affirmative Action program considered their organization to be fair.

One reason people respond positively to diversity-focused staffing processes is the fact that prior to equal employment, employment equity, and affirmative action initiatives, many employers made personnel decisions in very unsystematic and arbitrary ways. Legal mandates that employers demonstrate fairness to a diverse labor force required employers to rationalize their processes and make them more transparent (Dobbin et al., 1993). Requiring employers to identify the qualifications needed for job performance and to select job candidates on the basis of 'bona fide occupational qualifications' created improved opportunities for everyone wishing to rise in the organization through merit.

Because people who have a poor understanding of diversity staffing programs also have negative attitudes toward them, providing transparency by explaining the organization's staffing process to employees may improve perceptions of fairness. In addition Leck (2002) recommends employee involvement in developing diversity staffing programs. She also argues that organizational leaders should process all employee-raised concerns thoroughly in order to identify any unintended negative results of diversity staffing programs.

Development opportunities

Beyond employment equity and equal employment programs, researchers have examined whether the provision of internal training and development opportunities enhances women's career outcomes. Research is fairly consistent in showing positive results. For example, Lyness and Thompson (2000) found that developmental job assignments were important positive predictors of career success for both women and men in a large multinational financial services corporation. Lyness and Judiesch (1999) found that women in this firm were more likely to be promoted than hired into management positions, emphasizing the importance of developing women for internal promotion opportunities. Also emphasizing the importance of development opportunities, Blum et al. (1994) found that employers emphasizing promotion and development had more women in management positions in a sample of 201 firms in Georgia (US). Goodman, Fields and Blum (2003) replicated those findings using subsequent data collected from the same sample. Fields, Goodman and Blum (2005) found that an emphasis on promotion and development was positively associated with the percentage of black managers in the same set of firms at a later point in time.

Replicating the importance of training and development opportunities in Australia, Tharenou, Latimer and Conroy (1994) found that training and development experiences were positive predictors of managerial advancement for both women and men. Metz and Tharenou (2001) similarly found that training and development were positive predictors of advancement for a large sample of women working in the Australian finance and banking sector.

Mentoring has been identified as a critically important resource for professional and managerial development (Fagenson, 1989; Scandura, 1992). Findings from Australia and the US have indicated a larger positive effect of mentoring on career success for women (Lyness and Thompson, 2000; Tharenou, 2005), although others have found that men accrue greater benefits than women (Kirchmeyer, 1998). Unfortunately, Ragins and Cotton (1991) found that women perceived more barriers to obtaining a mentor than men did. In order to provide access to mentoring, a number of organizations have instituted formal mentoring programs. Ragins and Cotton (1999) found that formally-assigned mentors were less effective than mentorships that developed informally for career development. They also found that female protégés in formal mentoring relationships received less coaching, role-modeling, friendship and social interaction from their mentors than their counterparts in informal mentoring relationships, while male protégés received equal amounts of these mentoring functions from formal and informal mentors.

Another important source of knowledge and information essential to career development is access to professional networks (Brown and Konrad, 2001a; 2001b; Ibarra, 1993), although Kirchmeyer (1998) and Forret and Dougherty (2004) found that network support had a stronger positive impact on men's career outcomes than on women's. Burke et al. (1995) compared the internal and external networks of women and men in management in three large organizations and found that these networks were typically gender-segregated such that women had fewer links to senior managers in the organization, who were predominantly male. Similarly, Linehan (2001) found that European women managers perceived a lack of networking opportunities with senior men. Ibarra (1995) found that relative to whites, minority managers in the US had fewer intimate connections in their networks and viewed their networks as less useful for gaining access to career benefits. Combs (2003) summarizes the research on black women's access to informal networks and concludes that this group may be forced into out-group status in managerial social networks. Proudford and Smith (2003)'s study of interpersonal conflict resolution confirms that conflicts are likely to be resolved in ways that preserve the social bond between members of the same gender and racioethnic groups. Their research and theorizing supporting Combs' assertion that black women managers suffer social ostracism from dual distinction of gender and race.

To help women and racioethnic minorities gain access to informal social networks, organizations have sponsored employee memberships in professional associations developed around gender and racioethnic identities and/or have chartered employee affinity. Linehan (2001) found that managerial women perceived female organizational networks to be useful for developing women's knowledge and skills and for promoting women's careers, although a lack of integration into men's networks could limit the effectiveness of this strategy. Pini, Brown and Ryan (2004) studied the Australian Local Government Women's Association and found that members cited many benefits in terms of social support and knowledge building, although there were critics of the Association's women-only policy and questions of how influential the Association could be. Research by Friedman and his colleagues in the US has linked participation in affinity groups for minorities with reduced turnover (Friedman and Holtom, 2002), greater opportunities to receive mentoring and improved career optimism (Friedman et al., 1998). In sum, professional associations and employee affinity groups targeting women and racioethnic minorities seem to be valuable resources for both social support and knowledge building among their members, resulting in positive outcomes for employers.

Formalization
As Huffcutt and Roth's (1998) meta-analysis showed, formalizing the selection process by requiring structured interviewing can reduce race differentials in interview ratings substantially. Other research has shown that formalizing the personnel decision-making processes in organizations is beneficial for women's career outcomes as well. For example, Reskin and McBrier (2000) found that organizations using more formalized recruiting methods, specifically, job posting, advertising or using employment agencies to recruit applicants, had more women in management positions. Elvira and Graham (2002) found that the degree of formalization in the compensation process was positively associated with equal pay for women. Yang, Konrad and Cannings (2005) found that a more informal compensation process combined with greater pay dispersion in a medical specialty resulted in lower earnings for female doctors in Sweden. In sum, the research implies that formalization of the HRM decision-making process appears to be effective for improving career outcomes for women and racioethnic minority groups.

Work–life flexibility benefits

Because women take responsibility for two-thirds or more of caretaking and household labor around the world (Bianchi et al., 2000; Davis and Greenstein, 2004; Fuwa, 2004; Geist, 2005; Halleröd, 2005; Lee and Waite, 2005; Li, 2005), work–life flexibility benefits can be important for women's career development. The responsibilities associated with family formation affect women's career development, although the impact differs in different societies. For instance, in the United States, marriage is no longer associated with a reduction in women's labor force participation, but the arrival of children continues to impact women's hours of paid work (Cohen and Bianchi, 1999). In Taiwan, almost a third of women drop out of the labor force upon marriage, and an additional 10 per cent drop out upon the arrival of children. By comparison, in mainland China, marriage and children have little impact on women's participation in the paid labor force (Yi and Chien, 2002).

Complicating the picture further, the structure of families is changing, and people's definitions of family are becoming broader and more flexible (Lobel et al., 1999). For instance, the percentage of babies born to single mothers has risen dramatically. In 2002, only 63.4 per cent of live births in Canada were to married women, and fully 27.5 per cent were to mothers who had never been married (Statistics Canada, 2004). In the US, 34 per cent of births in 2002 were to unmarried women (US Census Bureau, 2004). Single mothers face the challenge of combining work and family effectively to both care for their children and provide income for the family. In addition, welfare reform efforts are moving poor women with children into the workforce, which is challenging employers to find ways of employing and retaining former welfare clients, many of whom must juggle paid work with considerable family obligations (Kossek et al., 1997). Elder care responsibilities also result in increased work–family conflict, especially for women (Singleton, 2000).

In sum, the double burden of full-time employment and demanding caretaking and household labor responsibilities causes women to seek options that reduce the pressures of work–family conflict. Dropping out of the labor force or engaging in entrepreneurship (Arai, 2000) are possible options, and to retain female workers, employers are finding that they need to provide work–life flexibility benefits. In addition, younger cohorts of workers desire organizations to provide flexibility to allow better balance between work and other aspects of life (Smola and Sutton, 2002). As the number of dual-career families increases, men are experiencing more work–family conflict (Higgins and Duxbury, 1992), and some evidence suggests that men in dual-career families experience reduced career outcomes compared to men who do not have to share responsibility for caretaking and household tasks (Schneer and Reitman, 1993; Stroh and Brett, 1996; Tharenou, 1999).

Research shows that work–life flexibility benefits have positive effects on employees. Kossek and Nichol's (1992) study showed that providing an on-site child care center was associated with reduced work–family conflict and more positive attitudes toward the organization's benefits package. Holtzman and Glass's (1999) study of 324 new mothers showed that longer parental leaves were positively related to job satisfaction. Lyness et al. (1999) interviewed 86 pregnant women and found that those whose organizations offered guaranteed jobs after childbirth and who perceived a supportive work–life culture in the organization planned to return to work more quickly after childbirth. Grover and Crooker's (1995) study of 745 randomly selected workers found that employees who had access to work–life flexibility benefits showed significantly greater organizational commitment and significantly lower intentions to quit their jobs. Thompson et al.'s (1999) study of 276 managers and professionals found that people were more likely to use work–life flexibility benefits if they perceived a supportive work–family culture in the organization. In addition, perceptions of a supportive culture and the presence of work–life flexibility benefits were positively related to organizational commitment and negatively related to work–family conflict and intentions to turnover.

Flexibility in the time and place of work also appears to be beneficial. Holtzman and Glass's (1999) study of 324 new mothers mentioned above also found that flexible work schedules and the ability to work at home were positively related to job satisfaction. A meta-analysis of 41 studies of flextime work schedules showed positive effects on productivity, job satisfaction, and satisfaction with work scheduling, as well as reduced absenteeism, and a meta-analysis of 25 studies of compressed workweeks showed positive effects on supervisory performance ratings, job satisfaction, and satisfaction with the work schedule (Baltes et al., 1999). A study of 104 telecommuting employees compared to 121 regular employees showed that the telecommuters were more committed to the organization and happier with their supervisors (Igbaria and Guimaraes, 1999).

In summary, work–life flexibility benefits are associated with more positive employee attitudes and may benefit employers by reducing turnover. There is some evidence that work–life flexibility benefits are associated with positive outcomes for women's careers, although more work needs to be done in this area. Dreher (2003) found that the number of work–life flexibility benefits provided in 1994 was positively associated with the representation of women in senior management positions in 1999 in his study of 72 *Fortune* 500 firms in the US.

Who adopts diversity-related HRM practices?

Organizational adoption of diversity-related HRM practices is variable. For instance, Konrad and Linnehan (1995a) found that on average, the 138 employers in their sample had adopted only 58 per cent of the identity-blind and 37 per cent of the identity-conscious HRM practices listed in their survey. Balser (1999) reported that while 80 per cent of the 118 employers in her study reported reviewing advertisements of job openings to eliminate discriminatory language, only 43 per cent reported training on how to provide accommodation to employees with disabilities. Regarding work–life flexibility benefits, Konrad and Mangel (2000) found that on average, the 849 large organizations in their sample had adopted only 3 out of 19 possible benefits listed in their survey instrument. Similarly, Pitt-Catsouphes et al. (2004) found that fewer than 40 per cent of the 1057 employers responding to a 1998 survey examining work–life practices in organizations provided a child care resource and referral service, and even fewer provided resource and referral services for elder care. People working for smaller employers are even less likely to receive extensive work–life flexibility benefits. The US Bureau of Labor Statistics estimates that only 14 per cent of US workers received assistance for child care from their employers, and only 3 per cent received financial support for child care from their employers in 2004. In that same year, on-site child care was available to 2 per cent of US workers, and employer-sponsored off-site child care was available to 1 per cent. Also in 2004, only 4 per cent of US workers had access to flexible workplace benefits, and only 9 per cent received adoption assistance (US Department of Labor, 2004).

Given the positive impact of diversity-related HRM practices on women's careers and the variability in employer adoption, it is useful to identify the factors linked with higher adoption levels. Like any organizational initiative, leadership is important to the adoption of diversity-related HRM practices, and more practices are adopted by organizations whose leaders consider diversity to be important (Konrad and Linnehan, 1995a; Milliken al., 1998; Moore et al., 2001; Ng et al., 2005b; Rynes and Rosen, 1995). Consistent with the classic size-formalization hypothesis, organization size appears to be important, with large organizations adopting more diversity-related practices (Goodstein, 1994; 1995; Ingram and Simons, 1995; Konrad and Linnehan, 1995a; Konrad and Mangel, 2000; Moore et al., 2004; Pitt-Catsouphes et al., 2004; Rynes and Rosen, 1995). Organizations in industries and regions where there is a high level of adoption among competitors are more likely to adopt diversity-related practices (Goodstein, 1994; 1995; Ingram and Simons, 1995), indicating the importance of mimetic isomorphism. Organizations with an HRM department or a diversity officer are more likely to adopt practices (Osterman, 1995; Rynes and Rosen, 1995), indicating the influence of professional expertise. Studies have also shown that employers adopt more practices if they are required to by law and if they experience lawsuits based on government anti-discrimination statutes (Balser, 1999; Konrad and Linnehan, 1995a; Moore et al., 2001). Balser's (1999) study also indicated the importance of a law orientation and having legal representation on retainer to the adoption of practices related to accommodating disability in the workplace, further indicating the value of government policies.

Organizations can also adopt diversity-related HRM practices for strategic reasons, and organizations perceiving such practices to be useful are more likely to adopt them. For instance, organizations employing more women are more likely to offer work–life flexibility benefits (Goodstein, 1994, 1995; Ingram and Simons, 1995; Konrad and Mangel, 2000; Osterman, 1995), although some studies have reported null findings regarding this association (Milliken et al., 1998; Pitt-Catsouphes et al., 2004). Organizations receiving more requests for accommodation have more accommodation activity and develop more extensive practices to develop an inclusive organizational culture for workers with disabilities (Balser, 1999). One study indicated that organizations utilizing high commitment work practices were more likely to provide work–life flexibility benefits (Osterman, 1995). Osterman's finding indicates the importance of a strategic view to the adoption of diversity-related practices, although more work needs to be done in this area.

Finally, the diversity of decision-makers in an organization can also make a difference, although this area requires additional research. Pitt-Catsouphes et al., (2004) found that organizations with more women in executive positions were more likely to develop work–life initiatives. This finding suggests that women leaders may be more cognizant of employees' needs for work–life initiatives.

How do diversity-related HRM practices affect performance?

Although the potential benefits outlined in the business case for diversity are clear, research findings on the relationship between diversity and organizational performance are mixed. A number of studies show that workplace diversity is positively related to effectiveness. For example, in two studies examining 291 and 410 US firms, respectively, Frink et al. (2003) demonstrated that organizations with about equal numbers of women and men showed better financial performance than organizations with either a predominantly male or a predominantly female workforce. Richard (2000) found that racial diversity was positively associated with the financial performance of 63 US banks pursuing a growth strategy. Similarly, in a study of 177 US banks, Richard et al., (2003) found that racial diversity was positively related to financial performance for banks pursuing an innovation strategy.

Not all studies have shown positive effects of diversity, however. Richard et al., (2004) found that the association between racial diversity in top-management teams and firm performance was curvilinear and complex. Kochan et al. (2003) conducted research at four major US firms that were leaders in supporting workforce diversity. Comparing performance, group process and financial results for comparable business units, the authors concluded that workforce diversity was unrelated to organizational performance. Combining the results of 24 studies of intact work groups, Weber and Donahue (2001) concluded that neither job-related human capital diversity nor surface-level demographic diversity was related to group cohesion or group performance. Finally, Williams and O'Reilly (1998) concluded from their review of the research literature that demographic diversity in work groups might be associated with *less* cohesion and *lower* performance.

Clearly, workplace diversity does not automatically result in positive performance, and it is likely that effective management is needed to overcome the initial barriers of surface-level stereotyping and longer term issues associated with deep-level differences in values, beliefs and styles. For this reason, a few researchers have examined the link between diversity-related HRM practices and firm financial performance. Wright et al., (1995) found that the stock price of 34 firms rose after the announcement that they had been awarded an Exemplary Voluntary Effort (EVE) award for affirmative action from the US federal government. Hannon and Milkovich (1996) found that stock prices rose for the 74 firms listed in *Working Mother* magazine as 'best for working mothers'. In the same study, however, no gains were shown for the firms listed in *Black Enterprise* magazine as 'best for blacks', the firms listed in the *New York Times* as the '100 best companies to work for in America', the firms listed in *USA Today* as the 'best companies for women', or the firms listed in the *National Society of Black Engineers* magazine as 'best for black engineers'. In a study of 195 for-profit US firms, Konrad and Mangel (2000) found that work–life benefits were associated with higher productivity for firms employing a higher percentage of women. In a study of 527 US firms, Perry-Smith and Blum (2000) found that firms with more extensive work–life benefits were more likely to be perceived by their peers as high performers. In sum, human resource practices aimed at effective diversity management may be associated with better firm financial performance, although more research is needed on this issue.

Unanswered questions and directions for future research

In this chapter, I have identified a variety of HRM practices implemented in organizations to enhance the diversity of the workplace. Research has generally shown that these practices are associated with positive career outcomes for historically excluded groups. While such practices can raise questions of fairness, research indicates that implementation of reasonable practices aimed at eliminating discriminatory barriers and accommodating diversity can result in positive justice perceptions among all organizational members, including historically dominant groups. Organizations vary in the extent to which they implement diversity-related HRM practices, and the presence of these practices is associated with leadership support of diversity as well as organization size, the use of such practices by competitors, the presence of an HRM department, legal requirements, and perceptions that such practices can contribute to achieving business goals. The following sections outline specific directions for future research in this area.

The strategic impact of HRM and diversity

Preliminary evidence indicates that organizations with more diversity-related HRM practices outperform their counterparts financially, although identifying the causal direction of this association requires further research. Research has not addressed the extent to which organizations have linked diversity-related HRM practices to their business strategy. To what extent have organizations developed an understanding of the relationship between workplace diversity and firm financial performance? The link between effective diversity management and firm financial performance is distal rather than proximal, and decision-makers need to develop an understanding of the entire value chain to identify the specific practices needed for success. In order to articulate this logic so that it has an impact on the direction of the firm, HRM needs to be included in strategic decision-making. Strategic HRM planning ensures that the organization has the right talent in the right positions at the right time for effective execution of the business strategy, and research is needed to investigate the impact of incorporating diversity at this level of strategic planning.

Effectiveness of diversity training

Many organizations respond to workplace diversity by instituting training (Rynes and Rosen, 1995), but little is known about what makes a diversity-related training program effective (Roberson et al., 2003). For example, although sexual harassment training is mandatory for managers in many US organizations, research on training effectiveness seems to be at the stage of examining employee perceptions (for example, Reese and Lindenberg,

2004). Given the impact of sexual harassment on women's job attitudes and intentions to quit (Laband and Lentz, 1998), developing sexual harassment training programs that are effective in reducing the incidence of harassment is an important goal for research and practice.

Diversity among women

Research on the effects of diversity-related HRM practices also needs to become more cognizant of diversity among women. Leck (Leck and Saunders, 1992; Leck et al., 1995), who conducted separate analyses on white women, women of color, aboriginal women, and women with disabilities to examine the impact of Canadian employment equity programs is the exception in literature that primarily focuses on white professional and managerial women. It is likely that different types of practices are needed to improve the employment outcomes of different groups of women (Proudford, 1999).

Diversity-related practices that advance the careers of white women are generally not sufficient for removing barriers to career advancement faced by women of color (Bell and Nkomo, 2001). Histories of social injustice resulting in unequal power relations between identity groups create dynamics in workplaces that make women of color outsiders, even when they hold positions inside the organization (Collins, 1999). The status of being an *outsider within* an organization can result in disparate interpersonal treatment (Bell and Nkomo, 1999; 2001), reduced satisfaction with mentoring (Blake-Beard, 1999), and escalation of conflict (Proudford, 1999). In addition, considerable diversity exists within the category of 'women of color', as Collins (1999) notes, 'African American women, Asian Indian women, Japanese American women, and White American women may all be considered "outsiders within" in a given corporation, but quite different group histories got them there' (p. 86). As a result of these differing histories, different groups of women perceive different organizational needs. For instance, Proudford (1999) reports that while both white and black women considered transportation support to be important, white women focused on the availability of parking spaces while black women desired subsidies for public transport. To make research relevant to the diversity of women in organizations, researchers need to focus on a wider variety of diversity-related HRM practices to serve the differing needs of these populations.

Age differences among women influence their needs for diversity-related HRM practices. Negative stereotypes of older workers affect both women and men (Perry and Parlamis, 2006). Evidence suggesting that views of older women are more negative than views of older men (McClellan and McKelvie, 1993; McKelvie, 1993) implies that the impact of ageing on career outcomes may be gendered. Goldberg et al. (2004) found that older women in young-typed industries received fewer promotions than younger women did, while age did not affect men's promotions in these industries. This finding indicated that matching the age profile of the industry was more important for women than for men. Interestingly, the same authors found that older men in old-typed industries received fewer promotions than younger men, indicating that mismatches between age and industry age-type did not hurt career prospects for men. Considerably more research is needed to examine whether ageing has a different impact on career outcomes for women and men as well as on the effectiveness for women of HRM practices designed to protect workers against age discrimination.

Class differences between women affect the extent of diversity-related HRM practices they are offered by employers. Work-at-home options or flexible work times are more difficult to implement for women in manufacturing jobs or women in front-line customer service positions. Poor women of color involuntarily find themselves in low-paying jobs requiring non-standard hours such as shift work or night work (Catanzarite, 2002; Presser, 2003), even though non-standard schedules can be more difficult to integrate with caretaking responsibilities than regular 9-to-5 work. An important issue for future research is identifying the actions employers can take to increase the access of poor women to jobs providing a living wage, a good quality of worklife and flexibility for caretaking responsibilities (Kossek et al., 1997). As one step in this research program, Perlmutter et al. (in press) found women transitioning from welfare in Philadelphia were more likely to retain their jobs if their employers paid higher wages with financial benefits and provided career counseling.

US research has shown that although gay men experience earnings penalties compared to straight men, straight women earn 17 to 34 per cent less than their lesbian counterparts (Black et al., 2003; Blandford, 2003). The reasons for these earnings differences need to be examined, as well as the effectiveness of HRM practices intended to make the workplace more welcoming for lesbian, gay, bisexual and transgendered employees (Thomas, 2004).

Finally, the experience of workers with disabilities may vary by gender. For instance, a study of sexual harassment victims in Canada based on 17 interviews and 12 focus groups found that women with disabilities were particularly vulnerable and that their disabilities were often exploited and used to humiliate them sexually (Carr et al., 2003). More research is needed to examine the effectiveness of HRM practices intended to accommodate workers with disabilities, and the experiences of women with disabilities require particular attention.

References

Arai, A.B. (2000), 'Self-employment as a response to the double day for women and men in Canada', *Canadian Review of Sociology and Anthropology*, **37**, 125–42.

Balser, D.B. (1999), 'Implementing New Employment Law: A Contested Terrain', dissertation, Cornell University, available from Dissertation Abstracts International.

Baltes, B.B., T.E. Briggs, J.W. Huff, J.A. Wright and G.A. Neuman (1999), 'Flexible and compressed workweek schedules: A meta-analysis of their effects on work-related criteria', *Journal of Applied Psychology*, **84**, 496–513.

Bell, E.E. and S.M. Nkomo (1999), 'Postcards from the borderlands: building a career from the outside/within', *Journal of Career Development*, **26**, 69–84.

Bell, E.E. and S.M. Nkomo (2001), *Our Separate Ways: Black and White Women and the Struggle for Professional Identity*, Boston, MA: Harvard Business School Press.

Bell, M.P., D.A. Harrison and M.E. McLaughlin (2000), 'Forming, changing, and acting on attitude toward affirmative action programs in employment: a theory-driven approach', *Journal of Applied Psychology*, **85**, 784–98.

Bianchi, S.M., M.A. Milkie, L.C. Sayer and J.P. Robinson (2000), 'Is anyone doing the housework? Trends in the gender division of household labor', *Social Forces*, **79**, 191–228.

Black, D.A., H.R. Makar, S.G. Sanders and L.J. Taylor (2003), 'The earnings effects of sexual orientation', *Industrial and Labor Relations Review*, **56**, 449–69.

Blake-Beard, S.D. (1999), 'The costs of living as an outsider within: an analysis of the mentoring relationships and career success of Black and White women in the corporate sector', *Journal of Career Development*, **26**, 21–36.

Blandford, J.M. (2003), 'The nexus of sexual orientation and gender in the determination of earnings', *Industrial and Labor Relations Review*, **56**, 622–42.

Blum, T.C., D.L. Fields and J.S. Goodman (1994), 'Organization-level determinants of women in management', *Academy of Management Journal*, **37**, 241–68.

Brown, D.W. and A.M. Konrad (2001a), 'Granovetter was right! Using networks to find a job', *Group and Organization Management*, **26**, 434–62.

Brown, D.W. and A.M. Konrad (2001b), 'Job seeking in a turbulent economy: social networks and the importance of cross-industry ties to an industry change', *Human Relations*, **54**, 1015–44.

Burke, R.J., M.G. Rothstein and J.M. Bristor (1995), 'Interpersonal networks of managerial and professional women and men: Descriptive characteristics', *Women in Management Review*, **10**, 21–7.

Byrne, D.E. (1971), *The Attraction Paradigm*, New York: Academic Press.

Carr, J., A. Huntley, B. MacQuarrie and S. Welsh (2003), *Workplace Harassment and Violence*, Report to Status of Women Canada.

Catanzarite, L. (2002), 'Dynamics of segregation and earnings in brown-collar occupations', *Work and Occupations*, **29**, 300–45.

Cohen, P.N. and S.M. Bianchi (1999), 'Marriage, children, and women's employment: what do we know?', *Monthly Labor Review*, **122**(12), 22–31.

Colbert, B.A. (2004), 'The complex resource-based view: implications for theory and practice in strategic human resource management', *Academy of Management Review*, **29**, 341–58.

Collins, P.H. (1999), 'Reflections on the outsider within', *Journal of Career Development*, **26**, 85–8.

Colquitt, J.A. (2001), 'On the dimensionality of organizational justice: a construct validation of a measure', *Journal of Applied Psychology*, **86**, 386–400.

Combs, G.M. (2003), 'The duality of race and gender for managerial African American women: implications of informal social networks on career advancement', *Human Resource Development Review*, **2**, 385–405.

Cox, J., Jr and S. Blake (1991), 'Managing cultural diversity: implications for organizational competitiveness', *Academy of Management Executive*, **5**(3), 45–56.

Davis, S.N. and T.N. Greenstein (2004), 'Cross-national variations in the division of household labor', *Journal of Marriage and the Family*, **66**, 1260–71.

DiPrete, T.A. and W.T. Soule (1986), 'The organization of career, lines: equal employment opportunity and status achievement in a Federal bureaucracy', *American Sociological Review*, **53**, 295–309.

DiPrete, T.A. and W.T. Soule (1988), 'Gender and promotion in segmented job ladder systems', *American Sociological Review*, **53**, 26–40.

Dobbin, F., J.R. Sutton, J.W. Meyer and W.R. Scott (1993), 'Equal employment opportunity law and the construction of internal labor markets', *American Journal of Sociology*, **99**, 396–427.

Dreher, G.F. (2003), 'Breaking the glass ceiling: the effects of sex ratios and work–life programs on female leadership at the top', *Human Relations*, **56**, 541–62.

Elvira, M.M. and M.E. Graham (2002), 'Not just a formality: pay system formalization and sex-related earnings effects', *Organization Science*, **13**, 601–17.

Equal Opportunities Commission (2004), 'Recruiting staff: guidance for managers and supervisors', available on the Equal Opportunities Commission (UK) website: www.eoc. org.uk/EOCeng/dynpages/EqualityChecklist.asp.

Fagenson, E.A. (1989), 'The mentor advantage: perceived career/job experiences of protégés vs. non-protégés', *Journal of Organizational Behavior*, **10**, 309–20.

Fields, D.L., J.S. Goodman and T.C. Blum (2005), 'Human resource dependence and organizational demography: a study of minority employment in private sector companies', *Journal of Management*, **31**, 167–85.

Fine, M.G. (1995), *Building Successful Multicultural Organizations: Challenges and Opportunities*, Westport, CT: Greenwood.

Forret, M.L. and T.W. Dougherty (2004), 'Networking behaviors and career outcomes: Differences for men and women?', *Journal of Organizational Behavior*, **25**, 419–37.

French, E. (2001), 'Approaches to equity management and their relationship to women in management', *British Journal of Management*, **12**, 267–85.

Friedman, R.A. and B. Holtom (2002), 'The effects of network groups on minority employee turnover intentions', *Human Resource Management*, **41**, 405–21.

Friedman, R.A., M. Kane and D.B. Cornfield (1998), 'Social support and career optimism: examining the effectiveness of network groups among Black managers', *Human Relations*, **51**, 1155–77.

Frink, D.D., R.K. Robinson, B. Reithel, M.M. Arthur, A.P. Ammeter, G.R. Ferris et al. (2003), 'Gender demography and organization performance: a two-study investigation with convergence', *Group and Organization Management*, **28**, 127–47.

Fuwa, M. (2004), 'Macro-level gender inequality and the division of household labor in 22 countries', *American Sociological Review*, **69**, 751–67.

Geist, C. (2005), 'The welfare state and the home: regime differences in the domestic division of labour', *European Sociological Review*, **21**, 23–41.

Goldberg, C.B., L.M. Finkelstein, E.L. Perry and A.M. Konrad (2004), 'Job and industry fit: the effects of age and gender matches on career progress outcomes', *Journal of Organizational Behavior*, **25**, 807–29.

Goodman, J.S., D.L. Fields and T.C. Blum (2003), 'Cracks in the glass ceiling: in what kinds of organizations do women make it to the top?', *Group & Organizaion Management*, **28**, 475–501.

Goodstein, J.D. (1994), 'Institutional pressures and strategic responsiveness: employer involvement in work–family issues', *Academy of Management Journal*, **37**, 350–82.

Goodstein, J.D. (1995), 'Employer involvement in eldercare: an organizational adaptation perspective', *Academy of Management Journal*, **38**, 1657–71.

Greene, A. and G. Kirton (2005), 'Trade unions and equality and diversity', in A.M. Konrad, P. Prasad and J.K. Pringle (eds), *Handbook of Workplace Diversity*, London, UK and Thousand Oaks, CA: Sage, pp. 489–510.

Grover, S.L. and K.J. Crooker (1995), 'Who appreciates family-responsive human resource policies: the impact of family-friendly policies on the organizational attachment of parents and non-parents', *Personnel Psychology*, **48**, 271–88.

Halleröd, B. (2005), 'Sharing of housework and money among Swedish couples: do they behave rationally?', *European Sociological Review*, **21**, 273–88.

Hannon, J.M. and G.T. Milkovich (1996), 'The effect of human resource reputation signals on share price: an event study', *Human Resource Management*, **33**, 405–24.

Heilman, M.E., C.J. Block and P. Stathatos (1997), 'The affirmative action stigma of incompetence: Effects of performance information ambiguity', *Academy of Management Journal*, **40**, 603–25.

Heneman, R.L., N.E. Waldeck and M. Cushnie (1996), 'Diversity considerations in staffing decision-making', in E.E. Kossek and S.A. Lobel (eds), *Managing Diversity: Human Resource Strategies for Transfoming the Workplace*, New York: Blackwell, pp. 74–102.

Higgins, C.A. and L.E. Duxbury (1992), 'Work–family conflict: a comparison of dual-career and traditional-career men', *Journal of Organizational Behavior*, **13**, 389–411.

Holzer, H.J. and D. Neumark (2000), 'What does affirmative action do?', *Industrial and Labor Relations Review*, **53**, 240–71.

Holtzman, J. and J. Glass (1999), 'Explaining changes in mothers' job satisfaction following childbirth', *Work and Occupations*, **26**, 365–404.

Huffcutt, A.I. and P.L. Roth (1998), 'Racial group differences in employment interview evaluations', *Journal of Applied Psychology*, **83**, 179–89.

Huselid, M.A., S.E. Jackson and R.S. Schuler (1997), 'Technical and strategic human resource management effectiveness as determinants of firm performance', *Academy of Management Journal*, **40**, 171–88.

Ibarra, H. (1993), 'Network centrality, power and innovation involvement: determinants of technical and administrative roles', *Academy of Management Journal*, **36**, 471–501.

Ibarra, H. (1995), 'Race, opportunity and diversity of social circles in managerial networks', *Academy of Management Journal*, **38**, 673–703.

Igbaria, M. and T. Guimaraes (1999), 'Exploring differences in employee turnover intentions and its determinants among telecommuters and non-telecommuters', *Journal of Management Information Systems*, **16**, 147–64.

Ingram, P. and T. Simons (1995), 'Institutional and resource dependence determinants of responsiveness to work–family issues', *Academy of Management Journal*, **38**, 1466–82.

Johnston, W.B. and A.H. Packer (1987), *Workforce 2000: Work and Workers in the 21st Century*, Indianapolis: Hudson Institute.

Kirchmeyer, C. (1998), 'Determinants of managerial career success: evidence and explanation of male/female differences', *Journal of Management*, **24**, 673–92.

Kochan, T., K. Bezrukova, R. Ely, S.E. Jackson, A. Joshi, K.E. Jehn et al. (2003), 'The effects of diversity on business performance: report of a feasibility study of the diversity research network', *Human Resource Management*, **42**, 3–21.

Konrad, A.M. and J. Deckop (2001), 'Human resource trends in the United States: challenges in the midst of prosperity', *International Journal of Manpower*, **22**, 269–78.

Konrad, A.M. and F. Linnehan (1995a), 'Formalized HRM structures: coordinating equal employment opportunity or concealing organizational practices?', *Academy of Management Journal*, **38**, 787–820.

Konrad, A.M. and F. Linnehan (1995b), 'Race and sex differences in line managers' reactions to equal employment opportunity and affirmative action interventions', *Group and Organization Management*, **20**, 409–39.

Konrad, A.M. and F. Linnehan (2003), 'Affirmative action as a means of increasing workforce diversity', in M.J. Davidson and S.L. Fielden (eds), *Individual Diversity and Psychology in Organizations*, New York: Wiley, pp. 96–111.

Konrad, A.M. and R. Mangel (2000), 'The impact of work–life programs on firm productivity', *Strategic Management Journal*, **21**, 1225–37.

Kossek, E.E. and V. Nichol (1992), 'The effects of on-site child care on employee attitudes and performance', *Personnel Psychology*, **45**, 485–509.

Kossek, E.E., M. Huber-Yoder, D. Castellino and J. Lerner (1997), 'The working poor: locked out of careers and the organizational mainstream?', *Academy of Management Executive*, **11**(1), 76–92.

Kravitz, D.A. and J. Platania (1993), 'Attitudes and beliefs about affirmative action: Effects of target and of respondent sex and ethnicity', *Journal of Applied Psychology*, **78**, 928–38.

Laband, D.N. and B.F. Lentz (1998), 'The effects of sexual harassment on job satisfaction, earnings and turnover among female lawyers', *Industrial and Labor Relations Review*, **51**, 594–607.

Leck, J.D. (2002), 'Making employment equity programs work for women', *Canadian Public Policy*, 28, S85–S100.

Leck, J.D. and D.M. Saunders (1992), 'Hiring women: the effects of Canada's Employment Equity Act', *Canadian Public Policy*, **18**, 203–20.

Leck, J.D., S. St. Onge and I. Lalancette (1995), 'Wage gap changes among organizations subject to the Employment Equity Act', *Canadian Public Policy*, **21**, 387–400.

Lee, Y. and L.J. Waite (2005), 'Husbands' and wives' time spent on housework: a comparison of measures', *Journal of Marriage and the Family*, **67**, 328–36.

Leonard, J.S. (1984), 'Antidiscrimination or reverse discrimination: the impact of changing demographics, Title VII, and affirmative action on productivity', *Journal of Human Resources*, **19**, 145–74.

Leonard, J.S. (1985), 'What promises are worth: the impact of affirmative action goals', *Journal of Human Resources*, **20**, 3–20.

Leonard, J.S. (1986), 'The effectiveness of equal employment law and affirmative action regulation', in R.G. Ehrenberg (ed.), *Research in Labor Economics*, Volume 8, Part B, Greenwich, CT: JAI Press, pp. 319–50.

Li, J. (2005), 'Women's status in a rural Chinese setting', *Rural Sociology*, **70**, 229–52.

Linehan, M. (2001), 'Networking for female managers' career development: empirical evidence', *Journal of Management Development*, **20**, 823–29.

Lobel, S.A., B.K. Googins and E. Bankert (1999), 'The future of work and family: critical trends for policy, practice and research', *Human Resource Management*, **38**, 243–54.

Lyness, K.S. and M.K. Judiesch (1999), 'Are women more likely to be hired or promoted into management positions?', *Journal of Vocational Behavior*, **54**, 158–73.

Lyness, K.S. and D.E. Thompson (2000), 'Climbing the corporate ladder: do female and male executives follow the same route?', *Journal of Applied Psychology*, **85**, 86–101.

Lyness, K.S., C.A. Thompson, A.M. Francesco and M.K. Judiesch (1999), 'Work and pregnancy: individual and organizational factors influencing organizational commitment, timing of maternity leave, and return to work', *Sex Roles*, **41**, 485–508.

McKelvie, S. (1993), 'Stereotyping in perception of attractiveness, age, and gender in schematic faces', *Social Behavior and Personality*, **21**, 121–28.

McLellan, B. and S. McKelvie (1993), 'Effects of age and gender on perceived facial attractiveness', *Canadian Journal of Behavioural Science*, **25**, 135–42.

Metz, I. and P. Tharenou (2001), 'Women's career advancement: the relative contribution of human and social capital', *Group and Organization Management*, **26**, 312–42.

Milliken, F.J., L.L. Martins and H. Morgan (1998), 'Explaining organizational responsiveness to work–family issues: the role of human resources executives as issue interpreters', *Academy of Management Journal*, **41**, 580–92.

Moore, M.E., B.L. Parkhouse and A.M. Konrad (2001), 'Women in sport management: Advancing the representation through HRM structures', *Women in Management Review*, **16**, 51–61.

Moore, M.E., B.L. Parkhouse and A.M. Konrad (2004), 'Diversity programs: influencing female students to sport management?', *Women in Management Review*, **19**, 304–16.

Ng, E.S.W., R.J. Burke and H.C. Jain (2005a), 'Legislation, contract compliance and diversity practices: do these matter?', paper presented at the annual meeting of the Administrative Sciences Association of Canada, Toronto, May.

Ng., E.S.W., R.J. Wiesner and H.C. Jain (2005b), 'CEO commitment, perceptions of CEO commitment, and actual diversity outcomes', paper presented at the annual meeting of the Academy of Management, Honolulu, August.

Osterman, P. (1995), 'Work/family programs and the employment relationship', *Administrative Science Quarterly*, **40**, 681–700.

Parker, C.P., B.B. Baltes and N.D. Christiansen (1997), 'Support for affirmative action, justice perceptions, and work attitudes: a study of gender and racial-ethnic group differences', *Journal of Applied Psychology*, **82**, 376–89.

Perkins, L.A., K.M. Thomas and G.A.Taylor (2000), 'Advertising and recruitment: marketing to minorities', *Psychology and Marketing*, **17**, 235–55.

Perlmutter, F.D., J. Deckop, A.M. Konrad and J. Freely (in press), 'Nonprofits and the job retention of former welfare clients', *Nonprofit and Voluntary Leadership Quarterly*.

Perry, E.L. and J.D. Parlamis (2006), 'Age and ageism in organizations: A review and consideration of national culture', in A.M. Konrad, P. Prasad, and J.K. Pringle (eds), *Handbook of Workplace Diversity*, London, UK and Thousand Oaks, CA: Sage, pp. 345–70.

Perry-Smith, J.E. and T.C. Blum (2000), 'Work–family human resource bundles and perceived organizational performance', *Academy of Management Journal*, **43**, 1107–17.

Pini, B., K. Brown and C. Ryan (2004), 'Women-only networks as a strategy for change? A case study from local government', *Women in Management Review*, **19**, 286–92.

Pitt-Catsouphes, M., J.E. Swanberg, J.T. Bond and E. Galinsky (2004), 'Work–life policies and programs: comparing the responsiveness of nonprofit and for-profit organizations', *Nonprofit Management and Leadership*, **14**, 291–312.

Poehlman, T.A., E. Uhlmann, A.G. Greenwald, and M.R. Banaji (2004), 'Understanding and using the implicit association test: meta-analysis of predictive validity', unpublished paper, Harvard University, Cambridge, MA.

Presser, H.B. (2003), 'Race-ethnic and gender differences in nonstandard work shifts', *Work and Occupations*, **30**, 412–39.

Proudford, K.L. (1999), 'The dynamics of stigmatizing difference', *Journal of Career Development*, **26**, 7–20.

Proudford, K.L. and K.K. Smith (2003), 'Group membership salience and the movement of conflict: reconceptualizing the interaction among races, gender and hierarchy', *Group & Organization Management*, **28**, 18–44.

Ragins, B.R. and J.L. Cotton (1991), 'Easier said than done: gender differences in perceived barriers to gaining a mentor', *Academy of Management Journal*, **34**, 939–51.

Ragins, B.R. and J.L. Cotton (1999), 'Mentor functions and outcomes: a comparison of men and women in formal and informal mentoring relationships', *Journal of Applied Psychology*, **84**, 529–50.

Reese, L.A. and K.E. Lindenberg (2004), 'Employee satisfaction with sexual harassment policies: the training connection', *Public Personnel Management*, **33**(1), 99–119.

Reskin, B.F. and D.B. McBrier (2000), 'Why not ascription? Organizations' employment of male and female managers', *American Sociological Review*, **65**, 210–33.

Richard, O.C. (2000), 'Racial diversity, business strategy, and firm performance: a resource-based view', *Academy of Management Journal*, **43**, 164–77.

Richard, O.C., T. Barnett, S. Dwyer and K. Chadwick (2004), 'Cultural diversity in management, firm performance, and the moderating role of entrepreneurial orientation dimensions', *Academy of Management Journal*, **47**, 255–66.

Richard, O.C., A. McMillan, K. Chadwick and S. Dwyer (2003), 'Employing an innovation strategy in racially diverse workforces: effects on firm performance', *Group and Organization Management*, **28**, 107–26.

Roberson, L., C.T. Kulik and M.B. Pepper (2003), 'Using needs assessment to resolve controversies in diversity training design', *Group and Organization Management*, **28**, 148–74.

Robinson, G. and K. Dechant (1997), 'Building a business case for diversity', *Academy of Management Executive*, **11**(3), 21–31.

Rynes, S. and B. Rosen (1995), 'A field survey of factors affecting the adoption and perceived success of diversity training', *Personnel Psychology*, **48**, 247–70.

Sass, T.R. and J.L. Troyer (1999), 'Affirmative action, political representation, unions, and female police employment', *Journal of Labor Research*, **20**, 571–87.

Scandura, T. (1992), 'Mentorship and career mobility: an empirical investigation', *Journal of Organizational Behavior*, **13**, 169–74.

Schneer, J.A. and F. Reitman (1993), 'Effects of alternate family structures on managerial career paths', *Academy of Management Journal*, **36**, 830–43.

Singleton, J. (2000), 'Women caring for elderly family members: shaping non-traditional work and family initiatives', *Journal of Comparative Family Studies*, **31**, 367–75.

Smola, K.W. and C.D. Sutton (2002), 'Generational differences: revisiting generational work values for the new millennium', *Journal of Organizational Behavior*, **23**, 363–82.

Statistics Canada (2004), 'Births, 2002', CANSIM Data Tables, www.statcan.ca/english/freepub/84F0210XIE/2002000/tables.htm (last accessed 24 April, 2005).

Stroh, L.K. and J.M. Brett (1996), 'The dual-earner dad penalty in salary progression', *Human Resource Management*, **35**, 181–201.

Tharenou, P. (1999), 'Is there a link between family structures and women's and men's managerial career advancement?', *Journal of Organizational Behavior*, **20**, 837–63.

Tharenou, P. (2005), 'Does mentor support increase women's career advancement more than men's? The differential effects of career and psychosocial support', *Australian Journal of Management*, **30**, 77–109.

Tharenou, P., S. Latimer and D. Conroy (1994), 'How do you make it to the top? An examination of influences on women's and men's managerial advancement', *Academy of Management Journal*, **37**, 899–931.

Thomas, D.A. (2004), 'Diversity as strategy', *Harvard Business Review*, **82**(9), 98–107.

Thompson, C.A., L.L. Beauvais and K.S. Lyness (1999), 'When work–family benefits are not enough: the influence of work–family culture on benefit utilization, organizational attachment, and work–family conflict', *Journal of Vocational Behavior*, **54**, 392–415.

US Census Bureau (2004), 'Statistical Abstract of the United States', www.census.gov/prod/www/statistical-abstract-04.html (last accessed 24 April, 2005).

US Department of Labor (2004), 'National Compensation Survey – Benefits', www.bls.gov/ncs/ebs/home.htm#data (accessed 15 April, 2005).

Vinnicombe, S. and V. Singh (2003), 'Women-only management training: an essential part of women's leadership development', *Journal of Change Management*, **3**, 294–306.

Weber, S.S. and L.M. Donahue (2001), 'Impact of highly and less job-related diversity on work group cohesion and performance: a meta-analysis', *Journal of Management*, **27**, 141–62.

Welbourne, T.M. and L.A. Cyr (1999), 'The human resources executive effect initial public offering firms', *Academy of Management Journal*, **42**, 616–31.

Williams, K.Y. and C.A. O'Reilly, III. (1998), 'Demography and diversity in organizations: a review of 40 years of research', in B.M. Staw and L.L. Cummings (eds), *Research in Organizational Behavior*, Volume 20, Greenwich, CT: JAI, pp. 77–140.

Wright, P.M. and S.A. Snell (1998), 'Toward a unifying framework for exploring fit and flexibility in strategic human resource management', *Academy of Management Review*, **23**, 756–72.

Wright, P., S.P. Ferris, J.S. Hiller and M. Kroll (1995), 'Competitiveness through management of diversity: effects on stock price valuation', *Academy of Management Journal*, **38**, 272–87.

Yang, Y., A.M. Konrad and K. Cannings (2005), 'Pay dispersion and earnings for women and men: a study of Swedish doctors', paper presented at the annual meeting of the Academy of Management, Honolulu, August.

Yi, C.-C. and W.-Y. Chien (2002), 'The linkage between work and family: female's employment patterns in three Chinese societies', *Journal of Comparative Family Studies*, **33**, 451–74.

PART 4

WOMEN AS LEADERS IN BUSINESS AND MANAGEMENT

13   Leadership style matters: the small, but important, style differences between male and female leaders

Alice H. Eagly and Mary C. Johannesen-Schmidt

Condoleezza Rice, Ruth Bader Ginsburg and Meg Whitman have become familiar names – women in prominent leadership positions whose photographs appear regularly in newspapers and magazines. They are but three examples of women who hold powerful positions in government or business. Although these women are well known, there exist a large number of less famous women who hold important leadership positions. In fact, in 2004 women occupied 23.3 per cent of all chief executive positions (US Bureau of Labor Statistics, 2005, Table 11). The percentage of women among all managers is much higher. The occupational category that has defined management in federal record-keeping, 'executive, administrative, and managerial occupations', is the category for which women's share of employment has shown the greatest increase in recent decades (Wootton, 1997), rising from only 17.6 per cent in 1972 to 45.9 per cent in 2002 (US Bureau of Labor Statistics, 1982, Table 1; 2002, January, Table A-19). An apparent small decline in this percentage after 2002 reflects the redefinition of the manager occupational category to include agricultural managers, a relatively male-dominated group (see Bowler et al., 2003).

Women's ascent into managerial positions has been accompanied by much attention to the ways in which women lead and possible differences between the leadership styles of women and men. We address these issues in this chapter by reviewing the debate about difference versus similarity in leadership styles and summarizing research evidence relevant to this issue.

In both popular writing and psychological research, leadership style has received considerable scrutiny. Styles are viewed as relatively consistent patterns of interaction that typify leaders as individuals. Leaders of course vary their behaviors within the confines of their style, depending on the situation and audience. For example, a leader with a typically democratic style might display the collaborative behaviors of consulting, discussing or negotiating, depending on the circumstance. Moreover, leaders may abandon their characteristic styles under certain situations. In a crisis situation, for example, a leader whose typical mode is democratic might become highly directive because the situation demands quick, decisive action.

Claims regarding the leadership styles of men and women have important ramifications for women's advancement into positions of leadership because leadership styles show varying degrees of effectiveness. One indication of the importance accorded leadership style is that the failure of individual leaders is often attributed to their leadership style. The 2003 downfall of Howell Raines, *New York Times* editor, precipitated by the journalistic fraud of one of his writers, was followed by the revelation of 'long-simmering complaints' regarding his 'top-down management style' (Steinberg, 2003, p. A1). Lawrence Summers, the former president of Harvard University, has also received much criticism for his 'hierarchical management style' (Steinberg, 2003, p. A1). Consistent with this informal emphasis on leadership style, systematic research confirms that some leadership styles are more effective than others (for example, Judge and Piccolo, 2004; Judge et al., 2004).

If men and women differ systematically in their leadership style, leaders of one sex may be generally more effective, at least in some situations. Even beliefs regarding sex differences in style (for example, Heilman et al., 1989), regardless of their veracity, could sway popular belief regarding the types of leadership positions that men and women should hold.

Following the social psychological principle that individuals focus greater attention on unusual, or non-prototypical, members of groups (Miller et al., 1991), popular writing tends to focus on the leadership styles of women more than those of men. Because women remain somewhat unusual in high-level positions, they receive more attention than their male counterparts. As but one example, merely compare the familiarity of the former CEO of Hewlett-Packard, Carly Fiorina, and the current CEO, Mark Head. This increased attention to women leaders and their leadership style can be unwelcome. They sometimes get the impression that 'issues of style with respect to women can unfortunately often be more important than issues of substance', as stated by Elaine La Roche, executive at Morgan Stanley (Thrall, 1996, 2 July, p. C4).

Because men have been the prototypical occupants of leadership roles, their styles have come to be associated with these roles. As research by Schein (2001) has shown, when people think about the characteristics of managers, those that come to mind are similar to those ordinarily associated with men. Because of the substantial overlap between people's associations about men and leaders, male leaders seem usual or 'natural' in most leadership roles. Therefore, men do not need to concern themselves with tailoring their leadership style to be accepted as legitimate. Nor do men ordinarily need to worry about coming across as too masculine or too feminine. In short, men typically enjoy relative freedom from the scrutiny of their leadership style, except if they lose the support of their subordinates. Then it is common that leadership style is blamed for their failure.

The leadership style debate

The degree to which women and men exhibit distinct leadership styles has been the subject of much debate, and experts have come to sharply divergent conclusions. The intensity of this debate resembles others focusing on whether men and women are best characterized as similar or dissimilar (see Kimball, 1995).

The similarity position

Leadership researchers traditionally claimed that men and women do not differ in leadership style. These researchers generally bolstered this claim by citing a few relevant studies that had not produced a statistically significant difference between male and female leaders on some measure of leadership style. Although the individual studies discussed by these reviewers may have been excellent, these generalizations were subject to error due to the informal methods by which they reached their conclusions. Without attempts to include more than a few studies comparing men's and women's leadership, reviewers were not adequately grounded in the available empirical research. Reviewers understandably favored those studies whose conclusions matched their own pre-existing views on the matter.

A typical conclusion of the 1980s, as stated by Bass, a well-known leadership scholar, is the following: 'The preponderance of available evidence is that no consistently clear pattern of differences can be discerned in the supervisory style of female as compared to male leaders' (Bass, 1981: 499). Similarly, Rosabeth Moss Kanter, in the influential book *Men and Women of the Corporation*, stated, 'There is as yet no research evidence that makes a case for sex differences in either leadership aptitude or style' (Kanter, 1977: 199).

In an early attempt to quantify the results of the relevant research, a 1986 meta-analysis of the leadership styles of men and women claimed an absence of sex differences. However, this review accessed only a small portion of the available studies and mistakenly included experiments that had deliberately insured the exact equality of male and female behavior by experimental manipulation (Dobbins and Platz, 1986). Therefore, this meta-analysis did not provide valid conclusions regarding the leadership behavior of women and men (see Eagly and Carli, 2003a, 2003b). Additional skepticism about sex differences in leadership style appeared in a widely read article in *Academy of Management Executive* (Powell, 1990). Despite these myriad claims for similarity, the opinions of authors and researchers on the leadership styles of women and men were far from unanimous, and a sizable camp of writers claimed that men and women lead with distinctively different styles.

The difference position

Unlike the researchers arguing for similarity, the early advocates for difference consisted mainly of authors with substantial experience in organizations who wrote for management audiences and the general public. Perhaps the best known of these advocates is Judy Rosener, a Professor of Management at University of California, Irvine. Her claims concerning men's and women's distinct ways of leading were first articulated in her 1990 article entitled 'Ways women lead', which appeared in *Harvard Business Review*. She labeled the female style as *interactive* and noted that female leaders emphasized 'encouraging others to have a say in almost every aspect of work, from setting performance goals to determining strategy. To facilitate inclusion, they create mechanisms that get people to participate and they use a conversational style that sends signals inviting people to get involved' (Rosener, 1990: 120).

Rosener based these claims on her qualitative summary of the results of a questionnaire study of women who were members of the International Women's Forum, an organization dedicated to promoting women's success in business, government and other fields. The male comparison group consisted of a sample of respondents formed by asking each female respondent to identify a man whose position was similar to her own.

Sally Helgesen made similar claims regarding women's leadership style in her 1990 book, *The Female Advantage: Women's Ways of Leadership*. Her conclusions derived from a qualitative study of four prominent women executives. Helgesen described the female style as a 'web of inclusion' characterized by the leveling of workplace hierarchies, collaboration with employees, and a personal connection with clients or customers. Earlier advocates of difference included Alice Sargent (1981), who contended that the behavior of male and female managers was in line with their respective gender stereotypes. And subsequent to Sargent, Marilyn Loden (1985) characterized feminine leadership style as emphasizing cooperation, collaboration, lack of hierarchy, and problem-solving based on intuition and empathy. In contrast, she characterized masculine leadership style as emphasizing competition, hierarchy, leader-held control and problem-solving free of emotion.

Given the provocative quality of these authors' conclusions favoring differences and the stark contrast of their claims with social scientists' claims of similarity of men and women, it is not surprising that a debate ensued. A key event in this debate was an exchange in the *Harvard Business*

Review following the publication of Rosener's article in which experts on leadership and gender faced off in agreement or disagreement with its methods and conclusions (Epstein et al., 1991). It is appropriate that neither side prevailed in this debate because neither set of proponents had derived their conclusions by methods that would be considered at all rigorous by the standards of contemporary science.

One of the keys to producing conclusions that can withstand critical scrutiny is to use more sophisticated methods of integrating research findings. Better methods would allow the discussion to move beyond the simple dichotomy of similarity versus difference by considering the size of any sex differences and their variability across settings. Careful attention to these issues in the context of the complete body of research can bring this debate forward to a satisfactory conclusion.

Rationale for expectations of similarity versus difference in men's and women's leadership styles

Arguments for similarity

Close examination of the situations of male and female leaders offers rationales for both similarity and difference. In favor of similarity, an obvious argument is that leadership roles influence the behavior of those who occupy them. Like other organizational roles, leadership roles are accompanied by norms that guide the performance of tasks, and these norms apply to all who hold the same role. Managers are obligated to perform certain duties, such as monitoring others' performance and disseminating information. Consequently, the behavior of men and women in similar roles should be similar because they all encounter similar norms for behavior. The socialization that men and women receive in an organization guides their performance of their duties. Women may learn to enact a leader role in a seemingly masculine way if they realize that such behaviors are necessary to its satisfactory enactment of their role.

Another argument for similarity is that male and female managers are ordinarily selected for their roles by fulfilling generally similar criteria. For example, management positions in some organizations require an MBA degree and a certain amount and type of work experience. Because such requirements apply to men and women alike, the resulting similarity of the experience and training of female and male leaders would encourage similar enactment of their roles.

An additional reason to expect similarity in leadership styles comes from research on stereotype threat. This research indicates that individuals who are subject to negative stereotypes based on their group membership face a psychological burden from knowing that their confirmation of these stereotypes may serve to reinforce assumptions commonly held about their group (Steele and Aronson, 1995). To the extent that people hold the belief that women are poor leaders, women in leader roles can face stereotype threat.

One consequence of stereotype threat can be *identity bifurcation* by which individuals so threatened may respond by disidentifying, not with all characteristics associated with their group, but selectively with those stereotypical qualities that seem disabling in a particular domain of performance. In research on this phenomenon, women strongly identified with success in mathematics, when confronted with threat, distanced themselves from female stereotypical characteristics relevant to beliefs about women's lesser mathematics ability (Pronin et al., 2004). If this principle applies to leadership, women strongly identified with success as leaders may similarly distance themselves from female stereotypical characteristics relevant to beliefs about women's lesser leadership ability. The following statement by a female executive in the financial industry is suggestive of this identity bifurcation:

> I don't know exactly when it happened, but I learned that you had to be slightly less warm, slightly less good-natured, slightly less laughing, carefree, and happy. You have to put on a more serious demeanor, to establish credibility more quickly. I don't advocate trying to be nasty, but you stop trying to be warm, wonderful, and nice. It works better. (McBroom, 1986: 72)

To the extent that female leaders dissociate themselves from some feminine qualities and abandon behaviors that are stereotypically feminine, men and women would lead in a more similar manner.

In summary, there are several processes that are likely to contribute to similarity in the behavior of male and female leaders: shared norms governing particular roles, organizational socialization concerning appropriate ways to carry out these roles, similar criteria for leader selection, and possibly, female leaders' dissociation from some feminine qualities. Researchers who focus on processes that enhance similarity have claimed that any differences in the styles of male and female leaders are illusory because they are artifacts of the placement of women and men into different leadership roles (for example, Bartol and Martin, 1986; Kanter, 1977; Nieva and Gutek, 1981; van Engen et al., 2001). This view acknowledges sex differences in leadership style only to the extent that men and women occupy different types of leadership roles – for example, men concentrated in line management and women in human resources management. Different roles favor different styles.

Arguments for difference

Despite the straightforward logic that men and women in similar roles are constrained by their roles to fulfill their duties with very similar behavioral styles, such an argument proves to be too simple. In addition to leader roles, leaders respond to the constraints of their gender roles, which are shared beliefs that apply to individuals based on their status as either male or female. These beliefs convey the agentic focus of the male gender role and the communal focus of the female gender role.

Consistent with the idea that gender roles exert influence even in the presence of organizational roles, we demonstrate in this chapter that only some gender-stereotypical differences in behavior erode under the influence of organizational roles. In short, the influence of gender roles is present in the workplace and continues to affect behavior with the consequence that even men and women in similar roles usually enact these roles somewhat differently (Gutek and Morasch, 1982; Gutek, 2001). The influence of gender roles emerges because other people hold these expectations and because people themselves have internalized these expectations to some extent as aspects of their own identities.

Others' gender-role expectations

Because of the agentic focus of the male gender role, people expect that male leaders will speak assertively, compete for attention, influence others, stick fairly narrowly to the assigned task, and make problem-focused suggestions. In contrast, because of the communal focus of the female gender role, people expect that female leaders will speak more tentatively, draw attention to others rather than themselves, be receptive to the suggestions from others, concentrate on supporting others, and focus on relational and interpersonal harmony. As a woman participating in a study of female executives' leadership styles observed, 'There's a basic expectation that a woman is going to be the comfortable, team-building, soft, forgiving type' (Manuel et al., 1999: 8).

Internalized gender-role expectations

The influence of gender roles on leaders' behavior occurs at least in part because they internalize their gender role to some extent so that they think of themselves in gender-specific ways. Much work in social psychology emphasizes the ways in which self-concepts differ between men and women (for example, Cross and Madson, 1997; Deaux and Major, 1987; Gabriel and Gardner, 1999; Wood et al., 1997). The identity bifurcation process that we have discussed may press female leaders to relinquish some female-stereotypical aspects of their workplace identities, but the extent to which the self-concepts of male and female leaders become similar is unknown.

Organizational scholars have argued that male and female managers tend to hold different expectations for their workplace behavior, at least in part because of their differing social identities (for example, Ely, 1995).

Women's expectations for themselves in the workplace are exemplified by the answers that Boston female executives provided when describing their leadership style (Manuel et al., 1999). In this group of executive women, 98 per cent included the characteristics of collaborative, flexible, inclusive and participative in describing their own style. It is doubtful that almost all male executives would have chosen such communal qualities. Yet, female executives do not view themselves as exclusively communal, as nearly as many women also described their style as assertive, decisive, team-oriented and strong.

In a study of the ways in which managers influence their superiors, differences between male and female middle managers emerged with female managers more likely to report that they acted more out of organizational interest than self interest, considered others' viewpoints, and focused on the interpersonal aspects of their influence attempts in addition to the task aspects (Lauterbach and Weiner, 1996). These self descriptions suggest an integration of the managerial role with the female gender role.

Research on sex differences in workplace behavior

Research on workplace behavior has produced findings consistent with the concurrent influence of dual gender and employment roles, regardless of whether these effects on behavior emerge from others' expectations or from employees' own identities. One example is Moskowitz et al.'s (1994) study of Canadian employees' behavior. The researchers sampled employees' experiences by having them report on their agentic and communal interpersonal behavior in the workplace for a period of 20 days.

Analysis of the data gathered in this field study indicated, in general, that agentic behavior, such as an assertive, confident interaction style, intensified the higher an employee's workplace status. Employees behaved most agentically when interacting with a subordinate and least agentically when interacting with a superior. In contrast, communal behavior, such as a friendly, unselfish and expressive interaction style, varied depending upon the sex of the employee. Regardless of their workplace status as superior or subordinate, women behaved more communally than men. This tendency was especially pronounced when women interacted with other women.

Parallel findings come from research on physicians' interactions with their patients. A quantitative review of these studies indicated that female physicians, more than their male counterparts, displayed communal behaviors, including more positive, friendly talk, greater questioning about medical and psychosocial matters, more psychosocial counseling, and more nodding and smiling (Roter et al., 2002; Roter and Hall, 2004). Although these studies of employees and physicians focused on general workplace behavior and not specifically on leadership style, their findings indicate that men and women in the same or similar roles show gender stereotypical behavior while on the job, at least with respect to communal behaviors.

These findings suggest that people have some freedom to vary the way in which they carry out their duties in workplaces. Employees may exceed the minimum requirements of their roles by being innovative, giving extra effort, or otherwise engaging in behaviors not obligated by their role. Thus, managers who are fulfilling their role may nonetheless be friendly or more remote, exhibit much or little excitement about future goals, consult few or many colleagues in making decisions, provide extensive or limited mentoring of subordinates, and so forth. Behaviors such as these, which are usually not narrowly prescribed by the norms associated with their leader role, are most susceptible to the influence of gender norms.

The effects of role incongruity
One feature of women's situation that is not shared by men is that their gender role and leadership roles are usually not consistent in the qualities that they emphasize. Because of this incongruity between the primarily communal qualities that people associate with women and the primarily agentic qualities that people associate with successful leaders (and with men), women face cross-pressures. If they conform to their gender roles, they can seem too feminine to be a good leader. If they conform to their leader role, they can seem too masculine to be a good exemplar of womanhood.

This incongruity between the female gender role and the traditional leader role may result in less favorable evaluation of women's potential for leadership because women are thought to be somewhat deficient in agentic qualities. In addition, women who hold leadership positions may encounter negative reactions when they behave in a clearly agentic manner because they appear somewhat deficient in communal qualities (Eagly and Karau, 2002; Heilman, 2001). The norms associated with male and female gender roles allow people to tolerate harsh, controlling, and competitive behaviors from men more than from women. Indeed, people may to some extent expect such behaviors in men but sanction women for similar behaviors.

Because of the incongruity between the female gender role and most leader roles, finding a leadership style that is well-received, appropriate and effective is a delicate task for women. Catalyst's 1996 study of *Fortune* 1000 female executives thus found that 96 per cent rated as *critical* or *fairly important* 'developing a style with which male managers are comfortable' (Catalyst, 2001; see also Ragins et al., 1998). Endorsements of the importance of style were similarly high among Canadian executives (90 per cent) and

UK executives (94 per cent). However, finding that style that facilitates interaction with male colleagues can be challenging.

In sum, despite the factors encouraging similar leadership styles when men and women hold the same workplace roles, gender roles nevertheless spill over to the workplace and exert pressure toward gender stereotypical behavior. Leaders' gendered views of themselves as well as the expectations of others reflect gender roles and can constrain women's and men's behavior in a gender-stereotypical direction.

Classic research on the leadership styles of women and men

To inform the debate that has surrounded these questions, researchers have turned to empirical research to assess leadership styles. These methods follow a long-standing tradition of psychological research on leadership style. Psychologists have made significant contributions to the understanding of leader behavior and the consequences of these behaviors. In this tradition, thousands of studies representing diverse theories and methods have addressed leadership style.

Task-oriented and interpersonally oriented styles

The majority of leadership style research conducted before 1990 focused on the distinction between *task-oriented style*, or behavior related to the accomplishment of assigned tasks, and *interpersonally oriented style*, or behavior related to the maintenance of interpersonal relationships. These distinctions match well with analyses of gender because of their resemblance to the agency and communion dimensions of gender stereotypes. If gender stereotypes are applied, male leaders should favor a task-oriented style, and female leaders should favor an interpersonally oriented style. Yet, because all leaders must attend to both task and interpersonal issues at least to some extent, any sex differences found would be expected to be relatively small. In addition, as we have already stated in this chapter, each leader role is defined within an organization by norms that exert additional pressures on male and female leaders to behave similarly.

This distinction between task and interpersonal orientations first emerged in research on small group interaction by social psychologist R. Freed Bales (1950). Additional researchers developed this distinction, the most notable being a group of industrial/organizational psychologists working at Ohio State University in the 1950s (Halpin, 1957; Halpin and Winer, 1957; Hemphill and Coons, 1957; Stogdill, 1950). In this line of research, task orientation, labeled *initiation of structure*, entails behaviors such as getting subordinates to follow rules and procedures, maintaining high standards for performance, and making leader and subordinate roles explicit. These researchers labeled interpersonal orientation as *consideration*, which encompasses behavior such as helping and doing favors for subordinates, looking out for their welfare, explaining procedures, and being friendly and available. These leadership styles were assessed in various ways, most commonly by questionnaire items describing the behaviors typical of each style. In these questionnaires, observers would judge the frequency with which leaders engaged in these behaviors. Observers most often were leaders' followers or subordinates, but peer leaders, organizational leaders, and the leaders themselves served as observers in some studies.

Despite becoming a less popular approach to understanding leadership style after critiques emerged, a very large body of research was produced assessing the task and interpersonal behaviors of leaders. After a period of waning interest, this research has taken on renewed importance due to the relations demonstrated between these style variables and leader outcomes. Specifically, a quantitative integration of the results of 130 studies found that both task-oriented and interpersonally oriented behaviors contribute to leaders' effectiveness (Judge et al., 2004). Interpersonally oriented leadership was especially strongly related to followers' satisfaction with their leader.

Comparison of women and men on task-oriented and interpersonally oriented leadership styles

Given the many studies of these leadership styles, sex differences were examined meta-analytically. Carrying out this task, Eagly and Johnson (1990) integrated 139 comparisons of women and men on various measures of their task-oriented and interpersonally oriented styles. In this review of the available research, no overall sex difference in task orientation appeared, but there was a very small tendency for women to manifest more of the interpersonally oriented behaviors than men.

The tendency for women to display interpersonally oriented behaviors slightly more than men appeared in laboratory studies with student participants and studies of general (non-managerial) employees or business school students. However, among people in positions as organizational managers, women and men did not differ in their display of the interpersonally oriented style. Thus, these findings suggest that managerial roles can constrain behavior and reduce this sex difference. However, even among managers, women tended to be more interpersonally oriented than men to the extent that their roles were less male dominated. In managerial roles that were more integrated by sex, women did have a somewhat more interpersonally oriented style than men.

One reason why women managing in very masculine or male-dominated settings do not differ from men in their interpersonally oriented behavior may be that they lose credibility or authority if they display stereotypically feminine behavior. Where very few women are present, the typical behaviors of male leaders may come to be seen as the only legitimate styles.

Task-oriented behaviors also showed interesting variability across settings. When leading in a role congruent with their gender role, both male and female leaders were more likely to focus on task accomplishment. This finding stems from ratings of how traditionally masculine or feminine leaders' roles were. For example, these ratings suggested that military officer and athletic director were especially masculine roles and elementary school principal and social service agency director were especially feminine roles. Leaders occupying a role less congruent with their own gender (for example, the female military officer or male elementary school principal) tended to be less task-oriented (or were perceived to be less task-oriented). In this sense, leaders facing incongruity between their gender role and their leader role may be at a disadvantage, given the importance of attention to task accomplishment to the success of a leader. This finding underscores the risks of role incongruity that we discussed earlier in this chapter.

Democratic and autocratic styles
Another tradition of leadership style research distinguishes between *democratic* and *autocratic* styles. Some researchers have made a similar distinction between *participative* and *directive* leadership. Regardless of label, a democratic or participative leader is one who considers others' opinions and knowledge when making decisions, whereas an autocratic or directive leader does not. This focus of leadership style is more specific than interpersonal and task orientation because it relates mainly to decision making.

Attention to these aspects of style first emerged in the 1930s in studies conducted by Kurt Lewin, a founding father of social psychology (Lewin and Lippitt, 1938; Lewin et al., 1939). Since that time, a host of researchers have investigated these aspects of leadership style by studying leaders in organizations and small groups (for example, Vroom and Yetton, 1973).

The relative merits of democratic and autocratic styles are not as simply put as for other styles. Under some circumstances, a democratic approach is particularly effective, and under other circumstances, the autocratic approach is more effective (Ayman, 2004; Yukl, 2002). Although autocratic leadership can lead to effective decision making, it may come at the cost of subordinates' morale. Especially when their group membership is voluntary, subordinates are more likely to exit groups with autocratic leaders than democratic leaders (Van Vugt et al., 2004). Thus, there is a small tendency in research studies for group members to be less satisfied with autocratic than democratic leaders. However, satisfaction with leaders does not necessarily predict greater effectiveness in terms of productivity and other outcomes.

Comparisons of women and men on democratic and autocratic leadership styles

In thinking about possible sex differences in this aspect of style, researchers need to keep in mind the negative or ambivalent reactions that women often receive when they are judged as acting in too masculine a manner. When women lead in an autocratic or take-charge manner, they may be successful in achieving goals, but this success may come at interpersonal cost. Although autocratic men are not necessarily well liked, they are accepted to a greater degree than autocratic women (Eagly et al., 1992; Jago and Vroom, 1982). Women may therefore seek ways to soften their leadership styles by including others in the decision making process.

Although a democratic, collaborative style may be better received than an autocratic style, democratic collaboration is not necessarily the default style of women. Rather, it may be that a leader's style changes after autocratic behaviors are met with resistance or are otherwise not well received. As one woman leader described the evolution of her style toward greater collaboration:

> I can be abrasive at times, and I have had to be over the years, and there have been stages in our development when I've been very tough – but basically, my style is collaborative and to try to pull people in, and I have grown even more sophisticated at it over the years because I'm more sensitive to what's causing the problem. I certainly in the early years didn't understand as much about human nature as I do now, so when I meet impediments now I am more able to work it in a calmer and supportive style to help people come around to something that I need to do. (Astin and Leland, 1991: 115)

Given that unfavorable reactions to autocratic behavior are directed more to female leaders than male leaders, it follows that women would exhibit autocratic style less frequently than men.

In line with this expectation, Eagly and Johnson's (1990) meta-analysis found that women adopted a more democratic or participative style and a less autocratic or directive style than men. This integration, which was based on 23 studies and various measures of democratic and autocratic leadership styles, produced a relatively small overall effect, yet 92 per cent of the available comparisons were in the direction of women's greater democratic or participative style. In a related meta-analysis that included studies conducted in the 1990s, van Engen and Willemsen (2004) found a similar pattern of differences.

Other evidence that women lead through facilitating others' participation comes from a study of social interaction in state legislative committees (Kathlene, 1994). In their roles as committee chairs, women legislators, more than their male peers, acted as facilitators rather than as traditional directive or 'take charge' leaders. In another study of political leaders, Barth and Ferguson (2002) compared the inaugural addresses of governors and found that female governors expressed more affiliative, collaborative themes than their male counterparts.

Just as with findings for interpersonally oriented style, women's greater display of democratic behaviors eroded in especially male-dominated roles. When female leaders are not surrounded by a critical mass of female peers, women tend to use a more autocratic style, presumably similar to that of their male colleagues, even though they can be especially disliked when using such a style. In contrast, female-dominated settings may be particularly welcoming to democratic and collaborative behavior. According to many observers, women's organizations tend to have a more egalitarian structure, especially if they are feminist organizations (for example, Reinelt, 1994; Riger, 1994).

In summary, one difference between the leadership styles of men and women is that women appear to be somewhat more democratic and less autocratic than men. In some settings, especially feminist organizations, women's democratic collaboration may be very pronounced. However, in a wider range of settings, the differences between male and female leadership are relatively small, with considerable overlap in the styles of men and women.

To the extent that people react negatively to women who behave autocratically, women's democratic style may be primarily a response to others' expectations. Thoughtful women leaders detect that they are generally better accepted when behaving in a collaborative, democratic manner. Yet, women's self-identities as collaborators may affect their behavior as well. Whatever the sources of women's tendencies toward democracy and participation, there are circumstances that favor an autocratic approach – for example, situations demanding quick, decisive action. Women leaders would be at a disadvantage if they did not take charge in a relatively directive and autocratic manner in such situations, even if such actions came at the cost of being resented by some people within the organization. Emergencies exemplify situations that demand intelligent, directive and decisive leadership – a disaster is generally not a time for democratic negotiations between various stakeholders.

Contemporary research on the leadership styles of women and men

During the 1980s and 1990s, new distinctions about leadership styles became the focus of much research. This research examined leadership that is future oriented rather than present oriented, and that strengthens organizations by inspiring commitment among followers and fostering their creative contributions. Leadership researchers sought to understand the aspects of style that would be especially effective under the contemporary conditions faced by organizations. In the environment of modern organizations, leadership consists, not only of the skilled actions of a few leaders at the top of the hierarchy, but also of the actions of many individuals placed throughout an organization. Some have labeled this focus *postheroic* because it emphasizes, not the charismatic leadership of a single individual, but instead shared processes of social influence (Fletcher, 2004). Although this contemporary approach includes some aspects of earlier research on leadership style, it offers some new themes.

James MacGregor Burns (1978) was an early influence on this line of inquiry with his delineation of a leadership style that he labeled *transformational*. This style was subsequently elaborated by Bernard Bass, who described transformational leaders as those who establish themselves as a role model by gaining the trust and confidence of followers. These leaders clearly state future goals, develop plans for achieving these goals, and are innovative even in the midst of a relatively successful organization. Through their mentoring and empowering of followers, transformational leaders encourage them to reach their full potential and become more effective contributors to the organization (Bass, 1985, 1998).

This transformational style contrasts with *transactional* style, which refers to leaders who appeal to subordinates' self-interest by establishing exchange relationships such that desirable behavior is rewarded and undesirable behavior is punished. This type of leadership involves more traditional aspects of managing by clarifying responsibilities, rewarding subordinates for attaining objectives, and correcting them for failing to meet these objectives. Although conceptually and empirically separable, both transformational and transactional leadership styles can contribute to effective leadership in an organization. Most leaders are not exclusively transformational or transactional but include aspects of each type of leadership. In addition to the distinction between transformational and transactional leadership, researchers in this tradition also noted a third style, *laissez-faire*, which is characterized as an extreme 'hands-off' approach and a general failure to execute the role of manager.

Researchers typically assess these leadership style distinctions with a questionnaire measure known as the Multifactor Leadership Questionnaire (or MLQ; Avolio et al., 1999). As described in Table 13.1, this instrument represents transformational leadership by five subscales representing specific aspects of this type of leadership, transactional leadership by three subscales, and laissez-faire leadership by a single scale (Antonakis et al., 2003).

Table 13.1   Definitions of transformational, transactional and laissez-faire
leadership styles in the Multifactor Leadership Questionnaire
(MLQ) and mean effect sizes comparing men and women

MLQ scale and subscale	Description of leadership style	Effect size
Transformational		–0.10
Idealized influence (attribute)	Demonstrates qualities that motivate respect and pride from association with him or her	–0.09
Idealized influence (behavior)	Communicates values, purpose, and importance of organization's mission	–0.12
Inspirational motivation	Exhibits optimism and excitement about goals and future states	–0.02
Intellectual stimulation	Examines new perspectives for solving problems and completing tasks	–0.05
Individualized consideration	Focuses on development and mentoring of followers and attends to their individual needs	–0.19
Transactional		
Contingent reward	Provides rewards for satisfactory performance by followers	–0.13
Active management-by-exception	Attends to followers' mistakes and failures to meet standards	0.12
Passive management-by-exception	Waits until problems become severe before attending to them and intervening	0.27
Laissez-faire	Exhibits frequent absence and lack of involvement during critical junctures	0.16

Note: Table is from Eagly et al., 2003, Tables 1 and 3. Effect sizes are means of all available studies, with more reliable values weighted more heavily. Positive effect sizes for a given leadership style indicate that men had higher scores than women, and negative effect sizes indicate that women had higher scores than men. No effect size appears for overall transactional leadership because its component subscales did not manifest a consistent direction.

Effectiveness of styles

Comparisons of men's and women's transformational and transactional styles are important because researchers intended the characteristics of a transformational leader to epitomize effective leadership in the modern organization. In addition, there is substantial evidence that transformational leadership and the contingent reward subscale of transactional leadership are especially effective. In a meta-analysis of 87 studies examining the relationships between these forms of leadership and effectiveness outcomes, transformational leadership was found to be positively correlated with effectiveness (Judge and Piccolo, 2004).

This meta-analysis revealed a more complex outcome for transactional leadership. Effectiveness was positively related to the contingent reward subscale, which focuses on the rewarding of subordinates for their appropriate behavior. This aspect of transactional style was nearly as effective as transformational style and was especially related to followers' satisfaction with their leaders. There was a weak positive relation between leaders' effectiveness and their display of active management by exception, which involves drawing attention to the shortcomings of followers. However, leaders' effectiveness was negatively related to passive management by exception, which describes a leader who delays until situations become severe before intervening, and to laissez-faire leadership, which describes a leader who is largely absent as a manager.

Comparison of women and men on transformational, transactional and laissez-faire styles

A sufficient body of research on these styles enabled a meta-analysis comparing the styles of men and women. We carried out this project, together with Marloes van Engen, based on 45 studies comparing male and female managers on measures of transformational, transactional and laissez-faire leadership (Eagly et al., 2003). This review included both large studies assessing thousands of managers and many smaller studies conducted within specific organizations or groups of organizations. The resulting sample included managers from a myriad of organizations, but the majority of managers were from business or educational settings. The measures of leadership style were completed by leaders' superiors, peers, subordinates or the leaders themselves.

In general, as shown in Table 13.1, this review showed that female leaders engaged in more transformational behaviors and contingent reward transactional behaviors than male leaders. On the five subscales of transformational leadership, women especially exceeded men on the individualized consideration subscale that encompasses the supportive, encouraging treatment of subordinates. Men were more likely to display the two other aspects of transactional leadership (active and passive management by exception) as well as laissez-faire leadership. These differences remained even when accounting for several types of potential bias, such as the placement of men and women into disparate roles, or a publication bias among researchers. Another large-scale study consisting primarily of business managers, which was published around the same time as the meta-analysis, produced quite similar results (Antonakis et al., 2003). Also, a study of leadership within state legislatures showed that female chairs were more likely than their male counterparts to display an *integrative style*, which was defined similarly to transformational leadership, and male chairs were more likely to display an *aggregative style* that resembles aspects of transactional leadership (Rosenthal, 1998). Thus, across a host of studies and settings, it seems that women and men do differ in transformational, transactional and laissez-faire leadership styles.

At least part of this trend may reflect the ability of women who adopt a transformational style to resolve some of the incongruity between the disparate demands of their leader role and the female gender role. As Yoder (2001) argued, the transformational style affords women a way to manage effectively and with less cost to interpersonal outcomes by tempering their leadership with behaviors consistent with the female gender role. Some aspects of transformational and contingent reward styles thus overlap with behaviors congruent with the female gender role, such as caring, supportive and considerate behaviors. Especially consistent with the female gender role's communal characteristics are the individualized consideration behaviors, which consist of developing and mentoring followers and attending to their needs as individuals. This subscale of transformational leadership, which produced the largest difference favoring female leaders (see Table 13.1), is highly consistent with the communal theme of nurturing and caring. Although some aspects of transformational leadership are not especially aligned with either gender role, none of the dimensions of transformational leadership connotes a distinctly masculine style.

In addition to the consistency between various aspects of transformational leadership and the female gender role, another reason why women may display more of the effective transformational and transactional behaviors than men is that a double standard may be present in gaining leadership positions in the first place. Women in positions of leadership may have to be relatively more qualified than men to attain these roles, and they may be more quickly deselected if they exhibit failure to lead successfully in these roles (Eagly et al., 2003; Eagly and Carli, 2004). The net result would be that women leaders are, in general, more skilled than their male counterparts because they are held to a higher standard of performance.

The core question: do women and men differ in leadership style?

Meta-analyses of leadership styles revealed that gender-stereotypical sex differences emerged among leaders who were arbitrarily placed into leader roles in laboratory experiments. Under such conditions, women focused more on interpersonal considerations and men focused more on task-relevant considerations, and women adopted a more democratic and participative style than men. Without selection or preparation for a leadership role, leaders apparently use gender roles to guide their behavior.

Occupying a leadership role in an organizational setting is a different matter. Performing as a manager weakens the effect of gender roles because the leader role itself has a strong influence on behavior. Yet, even among managers, some stylistic differences between women and men emerge. Women, more than men, tend to have a democratic, participative, collaborative style. This difference is especially evident in female-dominated or gender-integrated roles and erodes in male-dominated roles and settings.

Female managers, more than male managers, tend to adopt a transformational style, especially in their mentoring of followers and attending to them as individuals. In addition, female managers use rewards to encourage appropriate behavior among subordinates more than male managers do. In contrast, male leaders, more than female leaders, display more of the less effective styles that involve avoiding solving problems until they become acute, and being absent or uninvolved at critical times.

These differences certainly do not describe all male and female managers. Nearly all behavioral and psychological sex differences, including those described here, should be viewed as highly overlapping distributions, with the differences between the sexes existing in averages or central tendencies. It is certainly the case that there exist male managers more democratic and collaborative than the average female manager, and female managers more autocratic than the average male manager. Nevertheless, even when group-level differences are small and variability within each sex is substantial, perceivers are able to accurately detect overall sex differences (Hall and Carter, 1999; Swim, 1994).

Implications for the sex difference debate

The meta-analytic findings on sex differences in leadership styles are no doubt welcomed by both the advocates of differences and the advocates of similarity. However, to regard either the difference or similarity position as vindicated would be a distortion of the findings that we have presented. We found small differences, which were generally gender stereotypical, but variable across settings.

The differences that emerged in these integrations of the available research evidence could be regarded as supporting the assertions of managerial writers who have contended that women lead with an especially collaborative, interactive, participative style and that this style produces female advantage.

With respect to transformational and transactional leadership, the pattern of differences especially favors women, because all of the aspects of these styles on which women exceed men have positive relations to leaders' effectiveness, and all of the aspects on which men exceed women have negative or very weak positive relations to effectiveness.

The small size of the sex differences that emerged in the meta-analyses could be regarded as supporting the assertions of the social scientists who have argued that male and female managers who hold the same role do not differ in leadership style. Meta-analyses are able to detect small differences that emerge when many studies are integrated. Given the constraints of leader roles, it does not come as a surprise that the behaviors of men and women who hold the same or similar leadership positions are small. As discussed earlier, these behaviors reflect the simultaneous influence of gender roles, which encourage differences between men and women, and organizational roles, which encourage similarity.

Whether these small differences in leadership style have real world implications is open to some debate. In general, effects that researchers may label as quite small may have considerable importance in a variety of contexts (Rosenthal, 1990). For example, the relation between taking aspirin and the prevention of heart attacks in a randomized double blind experiment amounted to only a very weak relation, statistically represented by a correlation of 0.034, yet this effect translated to 3.4 per cent fewer people experiencing heart attacks, a drop meaningful enough to induce researchers to end the experiment prematurely. It was considered unethical to deny the benefits of the aspirin treatment to the individuals in the control group (Rosnow and Rosenthal, 1989). Bushman and Anderson (2001) noted a number of other small correlations that have been judged important despite their small size (for example, calcium intake and bone density, self examination and extent of breast cancer, exposure to asbestos and laryngeal cancer).

The small size of the observed differences in style does not show that they lack implications in natural settings. When small differences are repeatedly enacted and observed over a long period, their implications are magnified. In other words, if female managers on the average are slightly more encouraging and rewarding to followers than male managers, or are more collaborative and democratic, people detect this difference, formulate gender stereotypes about it, and react to female and male leaders with divergent expectations. The power of leadership roles to lessen sex differences in behavior thus does not eliminate these differences or render them inconsequential.

Implications for the participation of women as leaders

The body of research on leadership style provides no reason for denying women leadership opportunities because they favor inappropriate or ineffective styles. Rather, the evidence indicates that the opposite conclusion must be drawn. For twenty years, leadership researchers have called for leaders to adopt transformational and collaborative styles to manage the complexities facing contemporary organizations (for example, Lipman-Blumen, 1996). If women are more likely to manifest these very styles, even by a small amount, they should surely enjoy at least an equal opportunity to serve as leaders and managers.

Given evidence of bias against women in attaining leadership roles (Eagly and Carli, 2004), it seems that these small differences in leadership style either do not give an advantage to women seeking leadership positions or are counteracted by prejudicial processes. It may be the case that these styles are viewed as 'natural' for women and thus they do not receive much credit for enacting democratic, participative, transformational and collaborative styles.

Perhaps in addition there is a disconnect between leadership behaviors shown to be effective and the traditional definitions of managerial roles within many organizations. This possibility is corroborated by evidence that managers who are successful in the sense that they rise rapidly in hierarchies are somewhat different from managers who are effective in the sense that they have profitable units and committed, satisfied subordinates. In Luthans' (1988) research, managers who were quickly promoted

> spent relatively more time and effort socializing, politicking, and interacting with outsiders than did their less successful counterparts ... [and] did not give much time or attention to the traditional management activities of planning, decision making, and controlling or to the human resource management activities of motivating/reinforcing, staffing, training/developing, and managing conflict (p. 130).

When it comes to ascending in organizational hierarchies, building social capital may be more important than effective managerial performance. The route to executive leadership may not be paved primarily with effective on-the-job performance.

Clearly, much remains to be understood regarding the styles of male and female leaders. What journalists, business writers and researchers alike must resist is the promotion of inappropriate simplifications or premature conclusions. Understanding of these differences has been delayed by far too many one-dimensional generalizations – contentions that either male and female leaders are quite different or that their styles are indistinguishable. Propagating simplifications impedes richer understanding of the ways in which men and women lead and the responsiveness of both sexes to situational pressures.

References

Antonakis, J., B.J. Avolio and N. Sivasubramaniam (2003), 'Context and leadership: an examination of the nine-factor full-range leadership theory using the Multifactor Leadership Questionnaire', *Leadership Quarterly*, **14**, 261–95.

Astin, H.S. and C. Leland (1991), *Women of Influence, Women of Vision: A Cross-Generational Study of Leaders and Social Change*, San Francisco, CA: Jossey-Bass.

Avolio, B.J., B.M. Bass and D.I. Jung (1999), 'Re-examining the components of transformational and transactional leadership using the Multifactor Leadership Questionnaire', *Journal of Occupational and Organizational Psychology*, **72**, 441–62.

Ayman, R. (2004), 'Situational and contingency approaches to leadership', in J. Antonakis, A.T. Cianciolo and R.J. Sternberg (eds), *The Nature of Leadership*, Thousand Oaks, CA: Sage, pp. 148–70.

Bales, R.F. (1950), *Interaction Process Analysis: A Method for the Study of Small Groups*, Reading, MA: Addison-Wesley.

Barth, J. and M.R. Ferguson (2002), 'Gender and gubernatorial personality', *Women and Politics*, **24**, 63–82.

Bartol, K.M. and D.C. Martin (1986), 'Women and men in task groups', in R.D. Ashmore and F.K. Del Boca (eds), *The Social Psychology of Female-Male Relations*, Orlando, FL: Academic Press, pp. 259–310.

Bass, B.M. (1981), *Stogdill's Handbook of Leadership: A Survey of Theory and Research* (rev. edn), New York: Free Press.

Bass, B.M. (1985), *Leadership and Performance Beyond Expectations*, New York: Free Press.

Bass, B.M. (1998), *Transformational Leadership: Industrial, Military, and Educational Impact*, Mahwah, NJ: Erlbaum.

Bowler, M., R.E. Ilg, S. Miller, E. Robinson and A. Polivka (2003), 'Revisions to the Current Population Survey effective in January 2003', retrieved 4 June, 2005 from www.bls.gov/cps/rvcps03.pdf.

Burns, J.M. (1978), *Leadership*, New York: Harper and Row.

Bushman, B.J. and C.A. Anderson (2001), 'Media violence and the American public: scientific facts versus media misinformation', *American Psychologist*, **56**, 477–89.

Catalyst (2001), 'Women in corporate leadership: comparisons among the US, the UK, and Canada', retrieved 30 November, 2006 from www.catalyst.org/files/fact/US,%20UK,%20Canada%20WICL%20Comparisons.pdf.

Cross, S.E. and L. Madson (1997), 'Models of the self: self-construals and gender', *Psychological Bulletin*, **122**, 5–37.

Deaux, K. and B. Major (1987), 'Putting gender into context: an interactive model of gender-related behavior', *Psychological Review*, **94**, 369–89.

Dobbins, G.H. and S.J. Platz (1986), 'Sex differences in leadership: how real are they?', *Academy of Management Review*, **11**, 118–27.

Eagly, A.H. and L.L. Carli (2003a), 'The female leadership advantage: an evaluation of the evidence', *Leadership Quarterly*, **14**, 807–34.

Eagly, A.H. and L.L. Carli (2003b), 'Finding gender advantage and disadvantage: systematic research integration is the solution', *Leadership Quarterly*, **14**, 851–59.

Eagly, A.H. and L.L. Carli (2004), 'Women and men as leaders', in J. Antonakis, A.T. Cianciolo and R.J. Sternberg (eds), *The Nature of Leadership*, Thousand Oaks, CA: Sage, pp. 279–301.

Eagly, A.H. and B.T. Johnson (1990), 'Gender and leadership style: a meta-analysis', *Psychological Bulletin*, **108**, 233–56.

Eagly, A.H. and S.J. Karau (2002), 'Role congruity theory of prejudice toward female leaders', *Psychological Review*, **109**, 573–98.

Eagly, A.H., M.G. Makhijani and B.G. Klonsky (1992), 'Gender and the evaluation of leaders: a meta-analysis', *Psychological Bulletin*, **111**, 3–22.

Eagly, A.H., M.C. Johannesen-Schmidt and M. van Engen (2003), 'Transformational, transactional, and laissez-faire leadership styles: a meta-analysis comparing women and men', *Psychological Bulletin*, **129**, 569–91.

Ely, R.J. (1995), 'The power in demography: women's social constructions of gender identity at work', *Academy of Management Journal*, **38**, 589–634.

Epstein, F.C., F. Olivares, P. Graham, F.N. Schwartz, M.R. Siegel, J. Mansbridge et al. (1991), 'Ways men and women lead', *Harvard Business Review*, **69**(1), 150–60.

Fletcher, J.K. (2004), 'The paradox of postheroic leadership: an essay on gender, power, and transformational change', *Leadership Quarterly*, **15**, 647–61.

Gabriel, S. and W.L. Gardner (1999), 'Are there "his" and "hers" types of interdependence? The implications of gender differences in collective versus relational interdependence for affect, behavior, and cognition', *Journal of Personality and Social Psychology*, **77**, 642–55.

Gutek, B.A. (2001), 'Women and paid work', *Psychology of Women Quarterly*, **25**, 379–93.

Gutek, B.A. and B. Morasch (1982), 'Sex-ratios, sex-role spillover, and sexual harassment of women at work', *Journal of Social Issues*, **38**(4), 55–74.

Hall, J.A. and J.D. Carter (1999), 'Gender-stereotype accuracy as an individual difference', *Journal of Personality and Social Psychology*, **77**, 350–59.

Halpin, A.W. (1957), *Manual for the Leader Behavior Description Questionnaire*, Columbus: Bureau of Business Research, Ohio State University.

Halpin, A.W. and B.J. Winer (1957), 'A factorial study of the leader behavior descriptions', in R.M. Stodgill and A.E. Coons (eds), *Leader Behavior: Its Description and Measurement*, Columbus: Bureau of Business Research, Ohio State University, pp. 39–51.

Heilman, M.E. (2001), 'Description and prescription: How gender stereotypes prevent women's ascent up the organizational ladder', *Journal of Social Issues*, **57**, 657–74.

Heilman, M.E., C.J. Block, R.E. Martell and M.C. Simon (1989), 'Has anything changed? Current characterizations of males, females and managers', *Journal of Applied Psychology*, **74**, 935–42.

Helgesen, S. (1990), *The Female Advantage: Women's Ways of Leadership*, New York: Currency/Doubleday.

Hemphill, J.K. and A.E. Coons (1957), 'Development of the leader behavior description questionnaire', in R.M. Stogdill and A.E. Coons (eds), *Leader Behavior: Its Description and Measurement*, Columbus, OH: Bureau of Business Research, Ohio State University, pp. 6–38.

Jago, A.G. and V.H. Vroom (1982), 'Sex differences in the incidence and evaluation of participative leader behavior', *Journal of Applied Psychology*, **67**, 766–83.

Judge, T.A. and R.F. Piccolo (2004), 'Transformational and transactional leadership: a meta-analytic test of their relative validity', *Journal of Applied Psychology*, **89**, 901–10.

Judge, T.A., R.F. Piccolo and R. Ilies (2004), 'The forgotten ones? The validity of consideration and initiating structure in leadership research', *Journal of Applied Psychology*, **89**, 36–51.

Kanter, R.M. (1977), *Men and Women of the Corporation*, New York: Basic Books.

Kathlene, L. (1994), 'Power and influence in state legislative policymaking: the interaction of gender and position in committee hearing debates', *American Political Science Review*, **3**, 560–76.

Kimball, M.M. (1995), *Feminist Visions of Gender Similarities and Differences*, Binghampton, NY: Haworth Press.

Lauterbach, K.E. and B.J. Weiner (1996), 'Dynamics of upward influence: how male and female managers get their way', *Leadership Quarterly*, **7**, 87–107.

Lewin, K. and R. Lippitt (1938), 'An experimental approach to the study of autocracy and democracy: a preliminary note', *Sociometry*, **1**, 292–300.

Lewin, K., R. Lippitt and R.K. White (1939), 'Patterns of aggressive behavior in experimentally created "social climates"', *Journal of Social Psychology*, **10**, 271–99.

Lipman-Blumen, J. (1996), *The Connective Edge: Leading in an Interdependent World*, San Francisco, CA: Jossey-Bass.

Lipman-Blumen, J. (2005), *The Allure of Toxic Leaders: Why We Follow Destructive Bosses and Corrupt Politicians – And How We Can Survive Them*, New York: Oxford University Press.

Loden, M. (1985), *Feminine Leadership: Or How To Succeed in Business Without Being One of the Boys*, New York: Times Books.

Luthans, F. (1988), 'Successful vs. effective real managers', *Academy of Management Executive*, **2**(2), 127–32.

Manuel, T., S. Shefte and D.J. Swiss (1999), *Suiting Themselves: Women's Leadership Styles in Today's Workplace*, Cambridge, MA: Radcliffe Public Policy Institute and the Boston Club.

McBroom, P. (1986), *The Third Sex: The New Professional Woman*, New York: W. Morrow.

Miller, D.T., B. Taylor and M.L. Buck (1991), 'Gender gaps: who needs to be explained?', *Journal of Personality and Social Psychology*, **61**, 5–12.

Moskowitz, D.S., E.J. Suh and J. Desaulniers (1994), 'Situational influences on gender differences in agency and communion', *Journal of Personality and Social Psychology*, **66**, 753–61.

Nieva, V.G. and B.A. Gutek (1981), *Women and Work: A Psychological Perspective*, New York: Praeger.

Powell, G.N. (1990), 'One more time: do male and female managers differ?', *Academy of Management Executive*, **4**(3), 68–75.

Pronin, E., C.M. Steele and L. Ross (2004), 'Identity bifurcation in response to stereotype threat: women and mathematics', *Journal of Experimental Social Psychology*, **40**, 152–68.

Ragins, B.R., B. Townsend and M. Mattis (1998), 'Gender gap in the executive suite: CEOs and female executive report on breaking the glass ceiling', *Academy of Management Executive*, **12**, 28–42.

Reinelt, C. (1994), 'Fostering empowerment, building community: the challenge for state-funded feminist organizations', *Human Relations*, **47**, 685–705.

Riger, S. (1994), 'Challenges of success: stages of growth in feminist organizations', *Feminist Studies*, **20**, 275–300.

Rosener, J.B. (1990), 'Ways women lead', *Harvard Business Review*, **68**(6), 119–25.

Rosenthal, C.S. (1998), *When Women Lead: Integrative Leadership in State Legislatures*, New York: Oxford University Press.

Rosenthal, R. (1990), 'How are we doing in soft psychology?' *American Psychologist*, **45**, 775–77.

Rosnow, R.L. and R. Rosenthal (1989), 'Statistical procedures and the justification of knowledge in psychological science', *American Psychologist*, **44**, 1276–84.

Roter, D.L. and J.A. Hall (2004), 'Physician gender and patient-centered communication: a critical review of empirical research', *Annual Review of Public Health*, **25**, 497–519.

Roter, D.L., J.A. Hall and Y. Aoki (2002), 'Physician gender effects in medical communication: a meta-analytic review', *Journal of the American Medical Association*, **288**, 756–64.

Sargent, A.G. (1981), *The Androgynous Manager*, New York: AMACOM.

Schein, V.E. (2001), 'A global look at psychological barriers to women's progress in management', *Journal of Social Issues*, **57**, 675–88.

Steele, C.M. and J. Aronson (1995), 'Stereotype threat and the intellectual test performance of African Americans', *Journal of Personality and Social Psychology*, **69**, 797–811.

Steinberg, J. (2003, June 5), 'Executive Editor of *The Times* and top deputy step down', *New York Times*, retrieved 11 June, 2003 from www.nytimes.com/2003/06/05/national/05CND-RESI.html.

Stogdill, R.M. (1950), 'Leadership, membership and organization', *Psychological Bulletin*, **47**, 1–14.

Swim, J.K. (1994), 'Perceived versus meta-analytic effect sizes: an assessment of the accuracy of gender stereotypes', *Journal of Personality and Social Psychology*, **66**, 21–36.

Thrall, P. (1996), 'Success and sharp elbows: one woman's path to lofty heights on Wall Street', *New York Times*, 2 July p. C4.

US Bureau of Labor Statistics (1982), *Labor Force Statistics Derived from the Current Population Survey: A Databook* (Vol. 1: Bulletin 2096), Washington, DC: US Department of Labor.

US Bureau of Labor Statistics (2002, January), *Employment and Earnings*, Washington, DC: US Department of Labor.

US Bureau of Labor Statistics (2005), 'Women in the labor force: a databook', Report 985, retrieved 4 June, 2005 from www.bls.gov/cps/wlf-databook-2005.pdf.

van Engen, M., R. van der Leeden and T.M. Willemsen (2001), 'Gender, context and leadership styles: a field study', *Journal of Occupational and Organizational Psychology*, **74**, 581–98.

van Engen, M.L. and T.M. Willemsen (2004), 'Sex and leadership styles: a meta-analysis of research published in the 1990s', *Psychological Reports*, **94**, 3–18.

Van Vugt, M., S.F. Jepson, C.M. Hart and D. De Cremer (2004), 'Autocratic leadership in social dilemmas: a threat to group stability', *Journal of Experimental Social Psychology*, **40**, 1–13.

Vroom, V.H. and P.W. Yetton (1973), *Leadership and Decision-Making*, Pittsburgh, PA: University of Pittsburgh Press.

Wood, W., P.N. Christensen, M.R. Hebl and H. Rothgerber (1997), 'Conformity to sex-typed norms, affect, and the self-concept', *Journal of Personality and Social Psychology*, **73**, 523–35.

Wootton, B.H. (1997), 'Gender differences in occupational employment', *Monthly Labor Review*, **120**, 14–24.

Yoder, J.D. (2001), 'Making leadership work more effectively for women', *Journal of Social Issues*, **57**, 815–28.

Yukl, G. (2002), *Leadership in Organizations* (5th edn), Upper Saddle River, NJ: Prentice Hall.

14 Women advancing onto the corporate board

Val Singh, Susan Vinnicombe and Siri Terjesen

Introduction

In the last decade, there has been increasing awareness of the slow pace of advancement of women onto corporate boards, despite over thirty years of equal opportunities policies. The lack of female representation in corporate decision-making is now an important issue for policy-makers, particularly in Scandinavia where political intervention is underway. Gender diversity on corporate boards is an emergent issue for developing economies such as India and China, and some countries in the Middle East (Tunisia, Jordan, Egypt and Morocco) are also starting to recognize the importance of developing their female talent up to board level. Indeed, until recently, the lack of women on top corporate boards appeared to be a global phenomenon, with women constituting less than 15 per cent of members of top company boards in the USA, the UK, Canada, Australia, New Zealand and many European countries. However, by 2005, Norway, Sweden, Slovenia, Estonia, Bulgaria, Romania and Finland had at least 15 per cent female representation on their top 50 corporate boards (European Commission, 2005).

In this chapter, we consider theoretical perspectives that shed light upon the persistence of this phenomenon and how positive change can be achieved. We examine the international statistics on women directors, including those from Scandinavia where quota systems have recently been introduced. We then consider the characteristics of companies that have appointed women directors. This is followed by an examination of the characteristics of women directors on large corporate boards, including their human capital. We then consider the links between women on boards and corporate performance, reviewing extant research on the business case, the relationship between gender diversity on corporate boards and firm financial performance, as well as the link with good corporate governance.

Highlighting the approaches selected by the USA, UK and Scandinavia, we consider next how different countries have addressed the issue of lack of female representation on corporate boards. We report a new mentoring scheme in the UK involving top chairmen and senior women managers in non-competing companies. We conclude with suggestions for further research.

Before we begin, we should clarify the terms for the different types of directors and boards. In the US, the term for a corporate board director with executive responsibility and an employment contract with the firm is 'inside director'. In the UK, such directors are 'executive directors' (ED), but do not include the company secretary, the legal officer who is generally considered an inside director in the USA. Similarly, the American term 'outside director' is equivalent to 'non-executive director' (NED) in the UK, and 'supervisory board director' in other parts of Europe. In the US and UK, single tier boards comprise both inside and outside directors, including both chairman and chief executive, all with legal status as directors. In most European governance systems, there is a two-tier board, with the chief executive running the executive board (whose members do not have legal status) and the chairman running the supervisory board of directors.

Theoretical considerations

Scholars have suggested a number of theories to explain women's slow progress into the boardroom. We begin by considering why women are often overlooked as potential talent for directorships. In the 1970s and 1980s, theories focused on women's lack of personal qualities for leadership that enabled them to follow their male peers up the career ladder (Oakley, 2000). These person-centred explanations include sex differences in individual psychological traits that make males more suitable for management, such as their assertiveness and analytical skills, and motivation for advancement. A contributory factor is the different socialization of males and females in childhood, leading to gender-role stereotyping of behaviours and choices of career. There is little evidence of differences in relevant psychological traits between managerial and professional men and women (Burke and Nelson, 2002). A further person-centred explanation is that women do not invest as much as men in the acquisition of human capital such as education, work experience and other investments in skills development (Tharenou et al., 1994).

Later theorists turned to situation-centred explanations, those barriers resulting from systemic but often invisible bias in corporate practices (Kanter, 1977), due to stereotyping and discrimination by the majority. The informal promotion practices and opportunities for challenge and development that depend upon knowing and being known by those at the top of the hierarchy in male-dominated firms are examples of such barriers. The lack of organizational and societal support structures for women with caring responsibilities presents a major barrier for women seeking to combine career and motherhood, or increasingly, elder care.

A third set of explanations draws on the structural bias theories and the interaction of gendered power relations in which women do not have equal access to opportunities for development, sponsorship and information, for example, in gendered cultures by the social exclusion of women from powerful networks (Ragins and Sundstrom, 1989). Employers who have instigated apparently gender-neutral employment systems fail to recognize the bias inherent in the structures and implementation of those systems and the resistant attitudes of the (mostly male) gatekeepers to offering women organizational rewards such as training, developmental experiences, promotion and pay (Oakley, 2000). The gender schema held by those gatekeepers provides a framework that sets their views of gender-appropriate behaviours, roles and expectations. Thus a combination of individual and organizational factors sustains the continued exclusion of talented women from top management positions (Burke and Nelson, 2002). Other articles in this book deal in depth with many of these issues, particularly the gender–power relations and differences in leadership style, the promotion systems, the diversity management systems and definitions of success.

Few women ever reach the talent pool for directorships, and those that do face more hurdles at the door to the boardroom. A number of theories of social exclusion shed light on those hurdles (Singh and Vinnicombe, 2004a). Social identity theory (Tajfel and Turner, 1986) holds that people define themselves and others on the basis of membership of groups such as race, class, sex and professions. According to social identity theory, people prefer to be with, and hence to recruit and promote, people like themselves. Some identity categories such as sex and race are highly visible, and are associated with 'otherness', particularly in the higher tiers of organizations. Kanter (1977) drew attention to homosocial reproduction, the way in which those in powerful positions replicate the male-dominated power structures in corporations. Those at senior organizational levels tend to be white, male, middle class and from prestigious schools (Norburn, 1989). Within the group, people gain a collective sense of themselves, enhancing their self-esteem, and trusting and privileging the in-group members with higher evaluations of their performance than the out-group individuals. Hence it becomes difficult for women to join the elite groups that constitute the power base for future directorships.

The elite group can be seen as a social network. Social network theory predicts that individuals who have access to resources valuable to the company are likely to have the best chance of entering the elite network. Directors are nodes in a network of organizational linkages, and contribute resources such as information and knowledge to their board, their organization and to other members of the network, sharing power, and acting as a socially cohesive group (Westphal and Zajac, 1995; Windolf, 1998). Directors form a privileged closed group with its own rules and ways of thinking. They facilitate invitations to join other boards, by recommending and sponsoring colleagues like themselves, whom they know are likely to fit the existing mould. As powerful positions are a marker of relevant experience, contacts and endorsement, those who have held CEO positions are particularly attractive to the network.

Resource dependency theory provides more detailed insight, suggesting that organizations seek to minimize risk by ensuring access to unique resources, as survival is dependent upon the ability to acquire and retain resources from other actors in the environment (Pfeffer and Salancik, 1978). Resource dependency theory suggests that, given an increasingly uncertain business environment, boards should be composed of individuals who can provide access to a breadth of resources. These can be secured through actions such as mergers, alliances and board interlocks. Critical resources include access to prestige and legitimacy, financing, key functional or geographic market knowledge and, we would argue, diversity. Based on resource dependency theory, we might expect that individuals who recruit members to the board would be interested in widening the scope of resources available and thus welcome people from different occupations and backgrounds.

The board of directors therefore provides external links to experience and contacts, by accessing their human and social capital as needed, as the environment changes. Human capital refers to the education, skills and experience acquired (Becker, 1964), whilst social capital refers to the value embedded in the personal contacts and wider networks of the individual directors. Each director has a unique set of human and social capital assets, and individuals must obtain extensive stocks of human capital in order to be considered for executive management roles including board directorships (Kesner, 1988). Using resource dependency theory, Hillman et al. (2000) suggest a typology of four types of directors. Inside directors contribute expertise on corporate strategy, and have specific knowledge in functional areas. Business expert directors contribute expertise gained by experience as directors in similar large firms, in similar markets, with experience as decision-makers, and can often provide alternative views gained from internal and external experience and their network ties. Support specialists provide access to specialized sources of information and financial and legal resources. The fourth category consists of the community influentials, those bringing experience and understanding from the public world, politics, academia and local government, and providing linkages to those arenas. The more expertise of the individuals, the greater is the legitimacy contributed to the board. As women are less likely to have access to positions that offer them the opportunity to build their human and social capital to the same degree as men, women are less likely to be seen as valuable business experts.

The symbolic value of gender diversity on the board is important, as women employees are more likely to aspire to senior levels when they can see evidence that women can get there in their organization (Bilimoria and Wheeler, 2000). The symbolic value may also result in affirmation by stakeholders such as investors and future employees (Pfeffer and Salancik, 1978). As some companies gain legitimacy from their female directors, particularly in terms of having diversity at decision-making levels, other forces come into play. Institutional theory, which holds that organizations are strongly influenced by external belief systems that construct the way in which the organization behaves and how it is understood (Powell and DiMaggio, 1991), predicts that when gender diversity on board is a feature of many successful companies, mimetic pressures would lead other companies to follow suit, by appointing at least one woman to the board. Most companies reveal the composition of their corporate board, as this is usually a requirement for proxy statements and annual reports, and similar information is frequently provided on corporate websites. Few companies provide information on the entire executive team, so the mimetic pressure results in their addressing the visible lack of diversity rather than the total lack of diversity in leadership. The former can be remedied by appointing a female non-executive director, rather than addressing the longer-term issue of the underdeveloped talent pool of senior women. Hence the proportion of female non-executive directors far exceeds that of executive women.

The statistics on women directors: some international comparisons

The numbers of female directors are slowly but steadily increasing in terms of non-executive/external directors on corporate boards. But Daily et al. (1999) highlighted that little progress into the executive suites of US companies had been made. Internationally, there is growing interest in monitoring the advance of women into the boardroom, following the example of Catalyst in the USA.

Examining the situation in the largest global companies, a study of the *Fortune* Global 200 companies in 2004 showed that women held 10.4 per cent of all board seats in that index and just over a quarter of the companies had no women directors at all (Corporate Women Directors International, 2004). Almost half of the firms with women directors had only one female, although all of the American firms had women directors, in contrast to the

27 Japanese companies with only three female directors among them. An American retailer, Albertsons, topped the *Fortune* Global 200 list in terms of female representation with a gender-balanced board (50 per cent), whilst the Norwegian company, Statoil, followed close behind with a 44 per cent female board.

Women directors in North America
Catalyst undertakes a biennial survey of women in corporate director positions in *Fortune* 500 and 1000 companies, reporting that in 2003, 13.6 per cent of *Fortune* 500 seats were held by women, up from 9.6 per cent in 1995, and 89 per cent of the companies had at least one female director. Whilst only 11 companies had at least 25 per cent women directors in 1995, by 2003 this figure had risen to 54 companies. All of the top 100 companies had at least one female director on their board. The percentage of women directors in the top 100 companies was 16 per cent, whilst for those from 401–500, the percentage dropped to 11.3 per cent. There were six female CEOs, the most prominent being Carly Fiorina of Hewlett Packard, who has since lost her position. Women of colour held 3 per cent of board seats in 415 of the *Fortune* 500 companies, up from 2.5 per cent in 1999.

However, whilst the proportion of women outside directors has increased almost to the level of 15 per cent regarded as the beginning of the end of tokenism by Kanter (1977), there is no such progress in the executive team. The proportion of women inside (executive) directors in *Fortune* 1000 companies in 1999 was only 4.6 per cent of inside directors, albeit up from 0.9 per cent in 1996 (Catalyst, 1999).

At the last Canadian census (Catalyst, 2004a), less than half of top boards had even one female director. The Catalyst survey indicated that whilst women held 11.2 per cent of board seats in the top 500 Canadian companies, the proportion of boards with no women remained unchanged at 51 per cent. The sectors with more women directors were financial services, retail, entertainment and insurance.

Women directors in Europe
In September 2005, a census was undertaken by this chapter's authors of the proportions of women directors in the *Financial Times* European Top 100 company index. Of the 1663 directors, 140 were female (8.4 per cent), but women constituted only 2 per cent of the executive directors, although the 131 women non-executive directors represented 10.8 per cent of NEDs, closely following the *Fortune* 500 proportions in companies listed in the USA. However, closer inspection of the situation across Europe reveals considerable variance in the proportions of women directors.

The European Commission (2005) commissioned a study of women in decision-making positions across the expanded European Union on the

50 largest (by market capital) listed company boards, and reported results
as shown in Table 14.1. With an average of 10 per cent, the proportion of
female directors in the top 50 listed companies across the expanded EU

*Table 14.1   Percentages of female directors on main boards of the 50
largest (by market capitalization) listed companies in each
European country, 2005*

Country (number of companies included)	% Female directors on main boards
Norway (50)	21
Sweden (49)	20
Estonia (16)	19
Slovenia (40)	18
Bulgaria (38)	18
Romania (39)	15
Finland (50)	15
United Kingdom (50)	14
Latvia (32)	12
Germany (50)	12
Lithuania (28)	11
Hungary (48)	11
Denmark (48)	11
Slovakia (24)	10
Czech Republic (49)	10
Average (%)	10
Greece (50)	9
Poland (49)	8
Cyprus (50)	7
Belgium (50)	7
France (49)	6
The Netherlands (50)	5
Spain (50)	5
Portugal (48)	5
Ireland (47)	5
Iceland (46)	5
Austria (48)	5
Luxembourg (23)	3
Malta (12)	2
Italy (50)	2

Source: European Commission, DG EMPL, Database on women and men in decision-making.

varied from 2 per cent in Malta and Italy to 21 per cent in Norway. There are some patterns, such as the Scandinavian and Baltic countries topping the list, but then why did Danish companies have only 11 per cent female directors? Further investigation is needed into these differences across Europe. There are some improvements since the EC's first such study in 2004, when only four countries had 15 per cent or more female representation on the top 50 boards.

Women directors in the Scandinavian countries

The Norwegian government in 2003 introduced legislation for a 40 per cent quota of female directorships if that target was not met voluntarily by private companies by 2005. Such a target had already been achieved in the public sector. Reviewing the results of the initiative in January 2006, during which time the percentage of women directors rose from 6 per cent in 2002 to 22 per cent in listed companies in 2006, the Norwegian equality minister commented that she didn't want to wait for 20 to 30 years for men with enough intelligence to finally appoint women to their boards. Firms not complying within a further period of two years are threatened with penalties including being shut down, although the minister is reportedly reviewing that draconian proposal following angry responses from industry leaders. Similar quota legislation has been introduced by the Swedish government, although they opted for a 25 per cent quota for women directors.

The first index of the top 500 Scandinavian companies and their women directors in 2004 revealed that 63 per cent of companies had women on the corporate board (Center for Corporate Diversity, 2004). However, the pattern across these countries varied, from Norway (73 per cent), Sweden (69 per cent), Denmark (57 per cent), Finland (54 per cent) to Iceland (50 per cent, but only 14 Icelandic companies were included in the Nordic 500). As in the USA and UK, the largest firms have the highest rates of female representation; 82 per cent of the top 50 companies by turnover had women directors compared to only 58 per cent of the remainder. Average board size was 7.6 directors in 2004. Other than in Denmark, two-tier boards were prevalent, and hence these statistics relate to the supervisory board, the non-executive directors. However, it should be noted that the Nordic 500 includes many companies that are part state-owned, which is not the case in the *Fortune* or Financial Times/Stock Exchange (FTSE) companies.

Across the Nordic 500 companies, women constituted 16.5 per cent of all directors. However, in the 240 companies in the Nordic 500 listed on the national stock exchanges, women directors constituted 18 per cent of all directors, with 25 per cent in Norway, 19 per cent in Sweden, 15 per cent in Finland and Denmark, yet only 5 per cent in Iceland, where 42 per cent of women work part-time. Norwegian and Swedish companies have reached high levels of female representation on some boards, with 16.5 per cent and 10 per cent respectively of Nordic 500 companies reaching 40 per cent female boards. Norsk Tipping had the highest proportion with a 67 per cent female board.

Women directors in the UK

The Cranfield Centre for Developing Women Business Leaders has undertaken an annual census of FTSE 100 companies (now referred to as the Female FTSE Index) and women directors since 1999. The UK has a unitary board governance system, and FTSE 100 companies have an average of eleven members, a non-executive chairman, three or four executive directors (chief executive, chief financial officer, and often a chief operations officer) and six or seven non-executive directors. In 2005, 78 per cent of the UK's top 100 companies had women directors, up from 58 per cent in 2000 (Singh and Vinnicombe, 2005). Thirty per cent of companies had more than one woman on board, compared with only 12 per cent in 2000. So women are making inroads into the all-male boardrooms, particularly into non-executive seats. Indeed, women took 17 per cent of new board appointments in 2004 and 2005, compared to a share of only 11 per cent in 2000, at a time when boards on average were reducing in size.

Whilst overall in 2005, women held 10.5 per cent of FTSE 100 directorships, compared to 5.8 per cent in 2000, the percentage of non-executive directors rose from 9 per cent to 14.5 per cent in that five-year period, during which time the first female chair of a FTSE 100 company was appointed (Baroness Hogg of 3i). There was only one female chief executive in the top 100 firms (an American, Dame Marjorie Scardino of Pearson). Indeed, progress of women into executive directorships has been very slow, rising from 2 per cent in 2000 to 3.4 per cent in 2005. Only 11 per cent of FTSE 100 companies had women executive directors.

Characteristics of companies with women directors

There are some significant differences between companies with and without women directors. Market capitalization tends to be significantly higher in companies with women directors than those with only male directors. This trend continued in 2005 in the UK, and similar findings have been reported by Catalyst regarding *Fortune* 500 companies in the USA. In the UK FTSE 100 companies, board size in 2005 was also slightly higher, averaging 11.9 directors for companies with women directors compared with 10.3 directors for all-male boards, against an overall average of 11.3 members (Singh and Vinnicombe, 2005). A related finding was that the number of non-executive directors was also significantly higher ($p = 0.004$) in companies with women directors than companies with all-male boards. Chief executives of companies with women on the board are significantly more likely to be younger than in all-male board companies, with an average age of 52 compared to 55 (Singh and Vinnicombe, 2004b).

Characteristics of women directors

In order to understand better the nature of the barriers for women to reach the boardroom, it is important to research the characteristics of the women who do get there, and to contrast them with their male peers so that the general as well as the gendered aspects of directors' careers can be revealed. Whilst the older generation of women directors were very much pioneers in a male world, women aspiring to the boardroom now face some of those same hurdles but also new challenges that may or may not be shared by their male peers. It is important therefore to understand the characteristics of the directors who succeed in this changing business context from a career perspective. We also need to know more about the contributions made by women and men when they have reached the boardroom. Given the token position of most women directors, their influence on board performance may derive more from their human and social capital than from old boys' club alliances that favour male directors (Fondas and Sassalos, 2000), so a better understanding is needed of any relevant sex differences in the characteristics of directors.

A number of studies have examined the characteristics of corporate directors (Kesner, 1988; Bilimoria and Piderit, 1994), and a recent study of inside directors in the USA by Zelechowski and Bilimoria (2004) reveals that women inside directors had less influence and stature than their male peers, and would therefore be likely to be treated as tokens in the executive suite. Although the women had similar board and company tenure, they were less likely to hold interlocking seats on external boards, they had less powerful titles, they were more likely to be in staff and support functions and they earned considerably less than their male colleagues.

A consistent finding in past research is that female board members are generally younger than male board members (Ibrahim and Angelidis, 1995). Singh and Vinnicombe (2005) reported that the average age of all female FTSE 100 directors (53.0 years) was significantly lower (p < 0.000) than that of male directors (55.6 years). Women directors had only slightly shorter tenure than their male peers, with an average of 3.2 years compared to 3.7 for men. In a meta-analysis of studies in Australia, USA, Canada, New Zealand, Israel and the UK, Burgess and Tharenou (2002) reported that between 70–98 per cent of female directors were aged over 40, between

68–93 per cent had university degrees, that between 65–71 per cent were married and between 44–74 per cent had children.

International experience is an important asset for directors in a globalizing world. Over a decade ago, a survey of CEOs of large American firms found that international experience was less desirable than other types of experience required of corporate board candidates (Catalyst, 1993). However, more recent research by Daily et al. (2000) suggested that international experience would enhance the likelihood of achieving top executive positions in other companies. A study of 40 FTSE 100 chairmen found that they valued international experience over gender and ethnic diversity (Russell Reynolds & Associates, 2002). Singh and Vinnicombe (2004b) found that around half of both men and women directors in FTSE 100 firms had international executive experience and that 30 per cent of female directors in FTSE 100 firms were from outside the UK.

In a study based on US firms, Mattis (2000) reported a preference for 'branded women' directors. The presence of female directors with titles on UK boards was noted in early studies (Howe and McRae, 1991). The titles were academic, political, hereditary titles, life peerages, knighthoods, military and senior job-related titles, as well as civic honours, with some directors having several such labels of 'presumed acceptability' to shareholders as directors. Singh and Vinnicombe (2004b) reported that 29 per cent of all FTSE 100 female directors had titles in 2004 compared to only 18 per cent of all FTSE 100 male directors. This suggests the possibility that men are appointed on expectations whilst women are appointed on what they have already achieved.

A US study found that 58 per cent of directors said that boards would prefer women with prior board experience (Mattis, 2000). Singh and Vinnicombe (2004b) analysed the experience of newly appointed female directors in the FTSE 100. Twenty-four women were appointed in 2004, and a major surprise was that a third of them already had FTSE 100 board experience, rebuffing the conventional view that women do not possess such experience. A third also had public sector board experience, a fifth had been on the boards of financial institutions and a further fifth had been on voluntary sector boards. Nearly two-thirds served on government advisory bodies and commissions, running arts organizations and directing professional organizations. All but one of the women had experience from more than one sector. This is similar to the findings of Bilimoria and Piderit (1994) that women directors were more likely than men to sit on non-profit, social and cultural boards.

Previous research suggests that women directors do not easily gain access to the powerful board committees, particularly the nominating and executive committees, and that the basis for this discrimination is based on a lack of experience rather than gender-based bias (Kesner, 1988). Extending that work, Bilimoria and Piderit (1994) explored the relationship between membership of six types of committee and a broader range of director characteristics, using a sample of around two thousand directors. Women were found to be more likely to serve on public affairs committees, at the periphery of board work, whilst the core committees were more populated by men. Whilst there was no sex bias relating to membership of the powerful audit committee (a heavily regulated board structure), that was not the case for the powerful compensation (equivalent to the British remuneration) committee which favoured male membership. Female board members appeared to be equally qualified to men on most characteristics, except for board tenure which was lower for women. Women directors with business experience were favoured over males in terms of finance committee membership, and women with interlocking ties to the non-business world were appointed over similar males. The data reported was based on 1983 proxy statements, and Bilimoria and Piderit concluded that more attention needed to be given to the selection process for board committees, given the tendency for bias emanating from propensity to stereotype, and to select people like themselves. Twenty years later, in FTSE 100 firms, female directors were evident on all three main board committees: nomination, remuneration and audit (Singh and Vinnicombe, 2005). On average, females sat on 1.2 committees. Proportionally, women were more likely than men to be members of remuneration committees, in contrast to Bilimoria and Piderit (1994), but there was no significant difference for the nomination and audit committees. Interestingly, women were just as likely to chair the remuneration committee, with 7 per cent headed by a female compared to 9 per cent headed by a male. However, it is clear that women still find it extremely difficult to gain access to the company executive committees, as evidenced by the minuscule proportion (3.4 per cent) of women executive directors in the UK.

Women on boards and corporate performance

The business case for gender diversity on boards
The business case for more women on corporate boards is frequently made by policy-makers and diversity champions, and this is evidenced in the support given in the UK by the Secretary of State for Trade & Industry, Patricia Hewitt, in her foreword to the 2004 Female FTSE Report. She stated that 'Diversity in our boardrooms isn't about political correctness or box-ticking – it's about getting the right people appointed to the right jobs every time.' She continued: 'If we are serious about creating a modern economy, recognising diversity and utilising the skills of everyone, there is

still much to do' (Singh and Vinnicombe, 2004b: 1). The development of women's talent is a key issue. Diverse board appointments of women and those from ethnic minorities make use of the entire talent pool, not just half of it.

Drawing on part of Huse's (2005) model for researching board behaviour, Figure 14.1 maps out the process whereby gender diversity on boards could impact board performance, building in the various elements in the business case. There are two sets of intangible benefits of board diversity, one relating to the boardroom and the other relating to the company. Directors' characteristics of diversity (the visible and invisible ways in which they differ by education, age, sex, race, experience, career paths, thinking style and so on), sometimes organized as human and social capital, impact the nature of the board. The board then acquires a certain degree of diversity, depending on the variety of attributes from its members, and also has their aggregated human and social capital. As board members engage in their roles, they draw on their diversity of skills, knowledge and experience as well as their social ties. The business case for diversity argues that the result of diversity should be more effective boardroom behaviours, a better understanding of the marketplace and the workforce, better decision-making and increased independence. Thus diversity should have a positive effect on board performance, although it is at present an area that needs more exploration by researchers. Corporate performance is not only directly impacted by board performance, through the boardroom interactions of diverse members, but indirectly from the symbolic value added by board diversity. These intangible benefits of diversity are derived from the symbolic value of having women on the board, enhancing the reputation of the company, bringing legitimacy, attracting funds from ethical investors, and inspiring women at lower management tiers in the organization. The latter benefit would have added value that would be picked up in employee satisfaction and social performance surveys. Social performance includes both internal and external aspects. These issues are now developed further from the literature.

Bilimoria (2000) summarizes the business case for gender diversity on corporate boards as overall corporate financial status and reputation; strategic input on women's products/market issues and corporate direction; effective boardroom behaviours, and contributions to corporate women employees. When overall corporate financial status and reputation are examined, certainly there is a relationship between company market capitalization (a proxy for size) and the presence of women directors, and this has been found not only in the USA, but also in Canada and the UK (Catalyst, 2003; Singh and Vinnicombe, 2005).

In the UK and across Europe, the business case is strengthened by concerns about the changing demographic profiles. The number of women in the UK

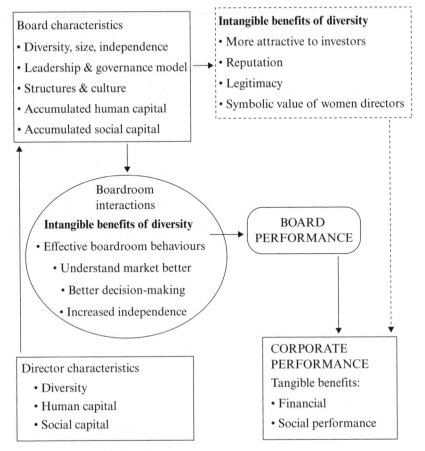

Source: Developed from Huse (2005).

Figure 14.1   Relationships among gender diversity on boards, board performance and corporate performance

workforce is predicted to overtake the number of men in 2018, with overall numbers for both men and women to decline from 2021 (Women & Equality Unit, 2002). So ignoring half the talent pool does not make business sense. In 2005, women owned 48 per cent of the personal wealth of Britain, and this is expected to rise to 60 per cent by 2025. So women will be increasingly important as investors in the future (BBC, 2006).

The increasing voice of corporate investors may encourage firms to work towards gender diversity on boards, because the investors, such as large union pension fund holders, may prefer to invest in companies with good diversity management evidenced by women on the board (Bilimoria, 2000).

Another reason may be that the investors see outcomes of good diversity management (such as women on the board) as an indicator of forward planning and future value in a globalizing world where sensitivity to different cultures and diversity is essential for longer term survival. Companies with all-male boards and that employ many women, or sell products targeted at women are particularly likely to be challenged by stakeholders. Women are increasingly the decision makers when it comes to making major purchases such as houses, cars and holidays. Women directors may suggest new ways of bringing products to market, based on knowledge of females as customers. Daily et al. (1999) state that where companies use market segmentation approaches, women's involvement in firm strategies is critical because of the potential to develop and tailor products to women.

Better corporate governance may be achieved through the sharing of a broader and different range of experiences and opinions (Fondas and Sassalos, 2000). Women have different experiences of the workplace, the market place, public services and the community, and therefore women directors bring a different voice to the debates and decision-making of their boards. Women are likely to take the role seriously, preparing conscientiously for meetings, and asking questions (Izraeli, 2000). This means that decisions would be less likely to be nodded through because of the old boys' club membership, and hence the presence of women may positively influence the independence of the board. Women's presence in the boardroom is also said to lead to a more civilized behaviour and sensitivity to other perspectives (Fondas and Sassalos, 2000; Bilimoria, 2000). Women's preference for a transformational leadership style (Rosener, 1990) may also influence boardroom dynamics in a positive, inclusive and constructive way, with positive spillover on leadership and organizational practice. From a meta-analysis of research findings on leadership styles, Eagly et al. (2003) reported that women leaders inspire extra effort from subordinates and are seen as more effective as leaders than their male peers.

In addition, women directors play an important part as role models for younger women and symbolize career possibilities to prospective recruits (Bilimoria, 2000). New research by Bilimoria (in press) found that the number of women corporate directors on *Fortune* 500 boards was positively related to the number of women officers, the number of women holding line management jobs, a critical mass of women officers, the number of women holding high-ranking titles and the number of women in the top earners of the company. The UK's Institute of Management (2001) reported that in companies with female directors, 54 per cent of women managers perceived increased promotion opportunities in the past five years, compared to only 37 per cent in companies where there were no women on the board. Furthermore, 23 per cent of women aspired to become board members in their present organization, and a third were aiming for external directorships, belying the myth that women lack ambition to become directors. Women directors provide mentoring and networking opportunities for more junior women to develop their careers (Bilimoria, in press). The presence of women directors also contributes to increased retention of women – important when the economic cost of losing a well-qualified woman is estimated as at least one and a half times her salary (ABA, 2000).

A further part of the business case for proactively managing gender diversity and appointing women to the senior tiers of the organization is the reduction of sex discrimination cases. Many high-profile cases are reported in the national press of the USA and the UK, for pay and rewards discrimination, sexual harassment and sackings after pregnancy. Women now appear to be less willing to give up and go quietly, and such cases have a very negative impact on the reputation of the company as a desirable employer for the best female talent.

Companies with women directors have visibly demonstrated that women can get to the top. They gain legitimacy as 'female-friendly employers' with career tracks that advance women as well as men. Institutional theory would suggest that when a sufficient proportion of companies demonstrate this practice, other companies will feel obliged to copy (Powell and DiMaggio, 1991). The corporate perception of the importance of gender diversity in terms of corporate reputation and image is shown in the highlighting of awards for diversity management and membership of equality organizations in corporate promotion material and websites.

Female representation and corporate financial performance

A number of scholars have called for further research on the link to corporate financial performance. For example, Bilimoria (2000: 25) states: 'The overall corporate bottom-line impact of women directors needs to be investigated specifically. Are firms with women directors indeed more profitable than firms without women on their boards? Do companies with multiple women directors show a healthier return than companies with only one woman director?' Indeed, an emerging body of research explores the relationship between the presence of women on boards and measures of corporate financial performance.[1] In general, the findings are mixed and are reported separately below.

Earlier studies have identified a strong relationship between company market capitalization[2] and gender diversity of the board (Catalyst, 1999, 2004b; Singh and Vinnicombe, 2003). In a study of FTSE 100 firms in 2004, market capitalization was found to be strongly correlated with board size ($p = 0.000$), the presence of women directors ($p = 0.013$), and the number of women on the board ($p = 0.000$) (Singh and Vinnicombe, 2004b).

This finding indicates that the larger the company's market capitalization, the more likely the company is to have multiple women directors, and is consistent with other research in the USA, Canada and Australia.

The results are mixed in terms of the relationship between Return on Equity (ROE), a measure of the company's efficiency and profitability given the resources provided by investors, and the presence of women on the boards. In a study of 200 *Fortune* 500 firms, Shrader et al. (1997) found a negative relationship between the percentage of females on the board and ROE. Catalyst (2004b) found that ROE was 35.1 per cent higher in the top quartile of firms with women on the boards, than the bottom quartile of firms by gender diversity.

The Cranfield FTSE 100 2004 study found that firms with women on their boards had a slightly higher average ROE than those boards without women (see Table 14.2). The results for ROE over the last three years indicate that the 69 companies with women directors had an average ROE of 13.8 compared to a ROE of 9.9 for the 31 companies with all-male boards.

Table 14.2   Gender diversity on the board and Return on Equity

Gender diversity on the board	Average ROE 3yr[*] (2002–2004)
Firms with women on the board (n=69)	13.8
Firms without women on the board (n=31)	9.9
Gender diversity on the board	**Average ROE 3yr**
Firms with 3 and 4 women on the board	13.6
Firms with 2 women on the board	10.4
Firms with 1 women on the board	15.6
Firms with 0 women on the board	9.9

Note: Based on data stream calculation for ROE = (Earned for ordinary – tax)/[(equity capital & reserves) – (total intangibles)+(total deferred tax)].

Source: Singh and Vinnicombe (2004b).

Carter et al. (2003) reported a significant correlation between percentage of females on the board and firm value measured by Tobin's Q, using a sample of almost 800 *Fortune* 1000 firms. However, in a study of 200 *Fortune* 500 firms, Shrader et al. (1997) identified a negative relationship between the percentage of females on the board and Return on Assets (ROA).[3] Another study of 127 large US companies highlighted a positive link between board gender diversity and ROA (Erhardt et al., 2003). Results on this indicator are mixed and therefore uncertain.

A consistent finding in the literature is a link between the presence of women on the boards and revenue.[4] For example, in the USA, a 1997 Catalyst study found that the top 100 firms by revenue were more than twice as likely to have multiple female directors as the bottom 100 firms in the *Fortune* 500 list. In Canada, there is a significant correlation between the number of women directors and the revenues, as well as assets and number of employees (Burke, 2000). Canadian companies with at least three women directors had more components of recommended good governance compared to companies with all-male boards (Brown et al., 2002). The companies with women on the board showed significantly higher use of non-financial performance measures in terms of board performance and were also more likely to measure innovation, corporate social responsibility, employee and customer satisfaction, communication and strategy implementation, all contributing to corporate performance (Brown et al., 2002).

The link between firm profit and board gender diversity has been found in a number of studies. The number of female directors and firm profit was correlated in the UK (Singh et al., 2001), Canada (Burke, 2000) and in the USA where the top ten most profitable *Fortune* 500 firms had at least one female director, as did 44 of the top 50 most profitable firms (Chin and Lee, 2002). The relationship was also found at the industry level, with companies with a high percentage of female directors outperforming other firms in their industry (Adler, 2001). However, profit is a measure of performance that can be adjusted within a given year and hence does not provide a consistent measure of performance at a single data point.

The Catalyst (2004b) study found that firms in the highest quartile of percentage of women board members had a total shareholder return[5] which was 34 per cent higher than those firms in the lowest quartile of board gender diversity. A study of Singapore firms found a positive 2.3 per cent return increase over two days following the appointment of a female director (Ding and Charoenwong, 2004).

Following on from this link with the appointment of women directors, an interesting question is raised by Ryan and Haslam (2005), following further work on the published results of the Cranfield Female FTSE 100 studies. Using the 2003 data, when 17 companies had appointed new women directors, their analysis suggested that poor financial performance in the previous five months and the subsequent appointment of female directors might result in women facing a 'glass cliff'. For companies that appointed men, company performance was relatively stable prior to the appointment, regardless of the state of the stock market. In contrast, for those that appointed women directors when the stock market was declining, the companies generally had poor performance preceding the woman's appointment. Women were more likely than male directors to be placed in precarious situations (that is onto boards of poorly performing companies in periods of decline). When in executive positions, the new women directors were highly visible and in danger of being criticized for their leadership style and individual abilities, which could leave them with a tarnished reputation if the downturn continued, whilst the context of their appointment at an unpropitious time was overlooked.

Although the studies indicate no consistently significant relationship between the proportion of women on boards and financial performance, we cannot conclude that gender diversity in the board is not beneficial to shareholder value. Ultimately, diversity is always part of exemplary corporate governance that enhances long-term shareholder value (Robinson and Dechant, 1997; Brown et al., 2002).

Female representation and corporate governance

Increasing attention is being paid to the need for better governance of companies. Following a number of accounting and reporting scandals in large corporations, major reviews have been undertaken of corporate governance practices. The Higgs Report (2003) reviewed the role and effectiveness of non-executive directors in UK-listed companies. New regulations and codes of practice have been implemented; in the USA, the Sarbanes-Oxley Act 2002 and in the UK, the new Combined Code (Financial Reporting Council, 2003). Increased diversity of directors by expansion of the talent pool is recommended as a means of improvement of decision-making and representation (Tyson, 2003). If companies heed the message, then the climate should be fruitful for aspiring women directors in the UK.

Singh and Vinnicombe (2004b) examined the links between gender diversity on FTSE 100 boards and compliance with the recommendations of the Higgs Review. They identified 13 relevant indicators, and found that companies with women directors, especially those with multiple women on the board, had significantly higher scores overall than those with all-male boards. Companies with women on the board were very significantly more likely to report having an annual evaluation of director and board performance. Other differences were that companies with females in the boardroom were more likely to have induction for new directors, training for existing directors, regular reviews of the balance of board skills, experience and knowledge, a succession plan in position and approval for the use of search consultants for director appointments.

Strategies for change in the USA, Scandinavia and UK

The liberal approach in the USA

It is interesting that different countries have adopted radically different strategies for change. In the USA, there is very much a liberal and entrepreneurial approach to the issue of increasing access of women into corporate boardrooms. Catalyst has undertaken a regular census of *Fortune* 500 companies for over a decade, and more recently extended their biennial analysis to include *Fortune* 1000 companies. In addition to providing regular statistics on companies with women directors, Catalyst identifies best practice, gives awards to companies making most progress, and undertakes research on important areas such as the progress of women of colour, and the need for policies to facilitate better work–life balance. They also undertake census studies of other countries, such as Canada, and international research studies such as the survey of career barriers for senior women in the UK in collaboration with Opportunity Now (Catalyst and Opportunity Now, 2000). However, the approach is entrepreneurial, and the government does not appear to promote a concerted effort to achieve change.

The coercive approach in Norway

A very different approach is evident in some Nordic countries. The Norwegian government identified that whilst women had achieved significant representation on the boards of public sector bodies, the private sector was very slow and even resistant to change. As reported earlier in this chapter, in 2002 an agreement was reached across political divides that more stringent measures to address the issue were necessary. Unless 40 per cent representation of women on corporate boards was achieved within three years, legislation would enforce this. The results have been encouraging, but few companies had achieved even half of the target. The number of women holding multiple seats increased, and many women were appointed to supervisory board seats as employee or union representatives.

The consensus approach in the UK

The stakeholders
A different approach has been made in the UK, alongside the efforts to modernize and improve the effectiveness of the top corporate boardrooms following the Higgs Review and the Tyson Report (2003). The UK government is trying to do this without recourse to enabling legislation or quotas, but rather to engage the stakeholders of this issue and get them to work together in energetic and innovative ways to create momentum. Stakeholder theory views stakeholders as the people who can affect or are affected by the activities of a company in reaching its objectives, and they can be grouped by whether or not they have a contractual relationship with the firm (Frooman and Murrell, 2005). Other stakeholders include the press, government and community members (Huse, 1998). Stakeholders hold varying degrees of influence, and firms and stakeholders may be dependent

or independent of each other for survival. Frooman and Murrell (2005) suggest that stakeholder influence may be coercive or cooperative, and the influence can be enacted either directly or indirectly. In contrast to some Scandinavian governments' coercive approaches, UK policies can be seen as more cooperative.

In the UK, policy is discussed and developed with many other parties, including the companies, their chairmen and chief executives, search consultants, various lobby groups, women directors, HR directors, academics and the press. Before the Female FTSE Index produced annual evidence of the slow pace of change, the issue of women directors was rarely discussed, except for the occasional flurry of press interest when a new woman director was appointed. The Higgs Review (2003) highlighted that the lack of diversity on boards was a real business issue, and the UK government held a series of consultation activities engaging the wider stakeholders in the debate on the way forward. We describe one such outcome below.

The chairmen's mentoring scheme
In 2004, Women Directors on Boards, a consortium of five senior women from industry, academia and government who came together to offer their expertise and time as a catalyst for change, established the Cross-Company Mentoring (CCM) programme. The CCM programme was limited to the FTSE 100 firms, and designed to address the need to broaden the gene pool from which directors are drawn and specifically to increase the number of women on FTSE 100 boards. Each participating FTSE 100 chairman nominates a senior executive woman from the layer below main board level of his or her company to be mentored by another FTSE 100 chairman/CEO. At the same time the chairman agrees to mentor a woman from another, non-competing FTSE 100 company. The programme provides the mentees with the benefit of access to top-level insights and experience, and facilitates the introduction of 'new' women candidates to chairmen who are in a position to nominate candidates for their own and other boards. By 2006, almost a third of FTSE 100 company leaders (mainly chairmen but also some chief executives) are actively participating in this innovative scheme.

Future directions

There is still much to be examined and understood in this field. Extant research into women directors on corporate boards is based upon publicly available data in annual reports and proxy statements. The field would benefit from more direct involvement of the subjects of the research, the women directors themselves. Further research is needed into the dynamics of the appointment process, from a 360-degree perspective to capture the reasons for successful applications and the experience of the applicants and decision-makers. The involvement of search consulting firms in board recruitment and increasingly, in board skills assessments and reviews, should be explored to see what role gender diversity plays in the process. Do the search consultants take action to find diverse candidates, do the chairmen and nominations committees suggest that they are open to diverse appointments, and how do they deal with all-male shortlists? Some of these firms are introducing coaching and mentoring for would-be directors, particularly targeted at women, and again, this area is under-researched.

Bilimoria (2000) highlighted that four areas needed further research. First is the link between gender diversity on boards and overall corporate financial status and reputation. Second is the strategic input of women directors. Third is the impact of women on effective boardroom behaviours, and fourth is the contribution to corporate women employees. It is useful to review progress on these issues six years later.

Catalyst (2004b) sought to address the first by examining companies with women and without on the board and return on investment and total return to shareholders, finding a positive relationship with board gender diversity in four of five industries. However, the authors acknowledge that these findings do not prove causality. Whilst attempts will no doubt continue to seek to demonstrate the added value to the bottom line of female diversity on the board, it is unreasonable to expect that one female director will bring about a financial contribution soon after appointment. However, studies of a longitudinal nature could explore the links between multiple female representation on the board and corporate performance in sectors where gender diversity would be expected to be particularly beneficial, such as retailing, over time. In addition, it would be useful to ascertain just how much influence board gender diversity has on ethical investment decisions by the stakeholders of these companies. Do ethical fund managers invest in companies simply because there is a woman on the board, or are more stringent criteria applied? Who is driving such requirements – is it pension fund managers of female-dominated professions such as nursing, or trade union funds? Are companies aware of this apparent trend, and if so, are they adapting the demographic profile of the board to include more diversity, more females? There is increasing awareness; some leading companies in Europe are starting to use their corporate websites to promote the link between good diversity management, diversity in leadership and the need to be attractive to all stakeholders including investors (Singh and Point, 2004).

More is now known about the contribution of female directors to corporate women employees. Bilimoria (in press) has examined the importance of the relationship between women directors and women corporate officers. Women directors are engaging in networking and mentoring of women through corporate networks (Singh and Vinnicombe, 2005; Singh, Vinnicombe and Kumra, 2006 in press) and new research is being carried out at Cranfield into the symbolic value of women directors as role models for senior and middle level women.

Bilimoria (2000) also suggested more research into the strategic input of women directors on services and products designed to appeal to women. New research in the UK has highlighted that senior women managers and members of corporate women's networks are getting involved in business development with female clients as well as product design to provide a female perspective (Singh et al., 2006 in press), but more needs to be known about women directors' contribution in this regard.

Bilimoria (2000) commented that more needs to be understood about how women directors actually contribute to their boards, and what helps them to make an effective contribution. Do women directors have a voice? Do they feel comfortable in taking up issues to do with women in the organization, leading on the more feminine, 'softer' issues, or do they run the risk of being stereotyped as 'whingeing women' or as ardent feminists not to be taken seriously? Bradshaw and Wicks (2000) found that Canadian women directors, who were mainly from upper class backgrounds, did not appear to have a feminist change agenda, but rather saw themselves in stewardship roles, and hence were not proactive in facilitating the situation for more women to reach the boardroom. Is this still the case, as more women from a variety of backgrounds reach the boardroom? More research is also needed into boardroom dynamics, when women are new members of the team, playing new roles in directing and governing their companies. How effective is their induction, and how do they start to make effective contributions?

Furthermore, whilst it is important to continue to track progress of women into the boardroom, many studies of women directors lack a strong theoretical base, making it difficult to extend the theoretical understanding of the field. New insights could be gained from reviewing the phenomenon from different theoretical perspectives.

Finally, as Bilimoria (2000) commented, more efforts need to be made to disseminate research findings so that a stronger business case can be established. There has been considerable progress in terms of benchmarking across an increasing number of countries. Governments are monitoring the implementation and effectiveness of diversity policies and practices across countries, using robust research results to design interventions. Research into women on corporate boards is an important tool, not only for making an academic contribution, but to provide the basis for change, not just for a more equitable but also for a more effective gender representation at the decision-making levels of the corporate world.

Notes

1. Firm financial performance can be measured using accounting-based or market-based indicators, and both have been criticized. Accounting-based financial measures (such as Return on Equity) are not standardized across firms, have the potential to undervalue assets and can be subject to manipulation and distortion by the firm. In general, accounting measures are considered to be within management's control. Market-based returns (such as Market Capitalization) reflect risk-adjusted performance, but are believed to be beyond management's control.
2. Market capitalization is a measure of a public company's size, as measured by the total dollar value of all outstanding shares. Market capitalization is calculated by multiplying the number of a firm's shares by their current market price.
3. Return on Assets is a measure of net income divided by total assets.
4. Revenue is the amount of money which a firm receives for its activities, before expenses.
5. Total Shareholder Return (TRS) is a measure of firm stock and share performance over time, including price appreciation and dividends paid.

References

ABA (2000), *Balanced Lives: Changing the Culture of Legal Practice*, Chicago, IL: American Bar Association Commission on Women in the Profession.

Adler, R.D. (2001), 'Women in the executive suite correlate to high profits', *Harvard Business Review*, **79**(3), 30–32.

BBC (2006), *The Money Programme*, London, 26 February.

Becker, Gary (1964), *Human Capital*, Chicago, IL: University of Chicago Press.

Bilimoria, Diana (2000), 'Building the business case for women corporate directors', in Ronald Burke and Mary Mattis (eds), *Women on Corporate Boards of Directors: International Challenges and Opportunities*, Dordrecht: Kluwer, pp. 25–40.

Bilimoria, Diana (in press), 'The relationship between women corporate directors and women corporate officers', *Journal of Managerial Issues*.

Bilimoria, Diana and Sandy Piderit (1994), 'Board committee membership: effects of sex-based bias', *Academy of Management Journal*, **37**(6), 1453–77.

Bilimoria, Diana and Jane Wheeler (2000), 'Women corporate directors: current research and future directions', in Marilyn Davidson and Ronald Burke (eds), *Women in Management: Current Research Issues, Volume II*, London: Paul Chapman, pp. 138–63.

Bradshaw, Patricia and David Wicks (2000), 'The experiences of white women on corporate boards in Canada', in Ronald Burke and Mary Mattis (eds), *Women on Corporate Boards of Directors: International Challenges and Opportunities*, Dordrecht: Kluwer, pp. 197–212.

Brown, David, Debra Brown and Vanessa Anastasopoulos (2002), 'Women on boards: not just the right thing…but the "bright" thing', Report 341-02, Ottawa: The Conference Board of Canada.

Burgess, Zena and Phyllis Tharenou (2002), 'Women board directors: Characteristics of the few', *Journal of Business Ethics*, **37**(1), 39–49.

Burke, Ronald (2000), 'Company size, board size and the numbers of women corporate directors', in Ronald Burke and Mary Mattis (eds), *Women on Corporate Boards of Directors: International Challenges and Opportunities*, Dordrecht: Kluwer, pp. 118–25.

Burke, Ronald and Debra Nelson (2002), 'Advancing women in management: progress and prospects', in Ronald Burke and Debra Nelson (eds) *Advancing Women's Careers*, Oxford: Blackwell, pp. 3–14.

Carter, David, Betty Simkins and Gary Simpson (2003), 'Corporate governance, board diversity & firm value', *Financial Review*, **38**, 33–53.

Catalyst (1993), *Women on Corporate Boards: The Challenge of Change*, New York: Catalyst.

Catalyst (1997), *Census of Women Board Directors of the Fortune 500*, New York: Catalyst.

Catalyst (1999), *The 1999 Census of Women Board Directors of the Fortune 1000*, New York: Catalyst.

Catalyst (2003), *The 2003 Census of Women Board Directors of the Fortune 1000*, New York: Catalyst.

Catalyst (2004a), *The 2003 Catalyst Census of Women Board Directors of Canada*, New York: Catalyst.

Catalyst (2004b), *The Bottom Line: Connecting Corporate Performance and Gender Diversity*, New York: Catalyst.

Catalyst and Opportunity Now (2000), *Breaking the Barriers: Women in Senior Management in the UK*, New York: Catalyst and London: Business in the Community.

Center for Corporate Diversity (2004), *The Nordic 500 Index*, Oslo: Center for Corporate Diversity.

Chin, E.A., and J. Lee (2002), 'Get women on board', *The Business Times* (Singapore), 30 January.

Corporate Women Directors International (2004), *Women Board Directors of the Fortune Global 200 Companies*, Report, Washington: Corporate Women Directors International.

Daily, Catherine, Trevis Certo and Dan Dalton (1999), 'A decade of corporate women: some progress in the boardroom, none in the executive suite', *Strategic Management Journal*, **20**, 93–99.

Daily, Catherine, Trevis Certo and Dan Dalton (2000), 'International experience in the executive suite: The path to prosperity?', *Strategic Management Journal*, **21**(4), 515–23.

Ding, David and Charlie Charoenwong (2004), 'Women on board: is it boon or bane?', Working Paper presented at 2004 *FMA European Conference*, Zürich, June.

Eagly, Alice, Mary Johannesen-Schmidt and Marloes van Engen (2003), 'Transformational, transactional and laissez-faire leadership styles: a meta-analysis comparing women and men', *Psychological Bulletin*, **129**(4), 569–92.

Erhardt, Niclas, James Werbel and Charles Shrader (2003), 'Board of director diversity and firm financial performance', *Corporate Governance*, **11**(2), 102–11.

European Commission (2005), *Women and Men in Decision-Making*, Luxembourg: Employment and Social Affairs Directorate, http://europa.eu.int/comm/employment_social/women_men_stats/out/measures_out438_en.htm, 24 November.

Financial Reporting Council (2003), *The Combined Code on Corporate Governance*, London: FCA.

Fondas, Nancy and Susan Sassalos (2000), 'A different voice in the boardroom: how the presence of women directors affects board influence over management', *Global Focus*, **12**, 13–22.

Frooman, Jeff and Audrey Murrell (2005), 'Stakeholder influence strategies: The role of structural and demographic determinants', *Business and Society*, **44**(1), 3–31.

Higgs, Derek (2003), *Review of the Role and Effectiveness of Non-Executive Directors*, London: Department of Trade & Industry.

Hillman, Amy, Albert Cannella and Ramona Paetzold (2000), 'The resource dependence role of corporate directors: adaptation of board composition in response to environmental change', *Journal of Management Studies*, **37**(2), 235–55.

Howe, Elspeth and Susan McRae (1991), *Women on the Board*, London: Hansard Society.

Huse, Morten (1998), 'Researching the dynamics of board-stakeholder relations', *Long Range Planning*, **31**(2), 218–26.

Huse, Morten (2005), 'Accountability and creating accountability: a framework for exploring behavioural perspectives of corporate governance', *British Journal of Management*, **16**, S65–S79.

Ibrahim, Nabil and John Angelidis (1995), 'The corporate social responsiveness orientation of board members: are there differences between inside and outside directors?', *Journal of Business Ethics*, **14**(5), 405–10.

Institute of Management (2001), *A Woman's Place*, London: Institute of Management.

Izraeli, Dafna (2000), 'Women directors in Israel', in Ronald Burke and Mary Mattis (eds), *Women on Corporate Boards of Directors: International Challenges and Opportunities*, Dordrecht: Kluwer, pp. 75–96.

Kanter, Rosabeth Moss (1977), *Men and Women of the Corporation*, New York: Basic Books.

Kesner, Idalene (1988), 'Directors' characteristics and committee membership: an investigation of type, occupation, tenure and gender', *Academy of Management Journal*, **31**, 66–84.

Mattis, Mary (2000), 'Women corporate directors in the United States', in Ronald Burke and Mary Mattis (eds), *Women on Corporate Boards of Directors: International Challenges and Opportunities*, Dordrecht: Kluwer, pp. 43–55.

Norburn, David (1989), 'The chief executive: a breed apart', *Strategic Management Journal*, **10**(1), 1–15.

Oakley, Judith (2000), 'Gender-based barriers to senior management positions: understanding the scarcity of female CEOs', *Journal of Business Ethics*, **27**, 321–34.

Pfeffer, Jeffrey and Gerald Salancik (1978), *The External Control of Organizations: A Resource-Dependence Perspective*, New York: Harper & Row.

Powell, Walter and Paul DiMaggio (eds) (1991), *The New Institutionalism in Organizational Analysis*, Chicago, IL: University of Chicago Press.

Ragins, Belle Rose and Erik Sundstrom (1989), 'Gender and power in organizations: a longitudinal perspective', *Psychological Bulletin*, **105**(1), 51–88.

Robinson, Gail and Kathleen Dechant (1997), 'Building a business case for diversity', *Academy of Management Executive*, **11**, 21–30.

Rosener, Judy (1990), 'Ways women lead', *Harvard Business Review*, November–December, 119–25.

Russell Reynolds & Associates (2002), *What makes an Effective Board? Views from FTSE 100 Chairmen*, London: Russell Reynolds.

Ryan, Michelle and Alex Haslam (2005), 'The glass cliff: evidence that women are over-represented in precarious leadership positions', *British Journal of Management*, **16**, 81–90.

Shrader, Charles, Virginia Blackburn and Paul Iles (1997), 'Women in management and firm value: an exploratory study', *Journal of Managerial Issues*, **9**, 355–72.

Singh, Val and Sébastien Point (2004), 'Strategic responses by European companies to the diversity challenge: an on-line comparison', *Long Range Planning*, **37**(4), 295–318.

Singh, Val and Susan Vinnicombe (2003), *The Female FTSE Report 2003*, Cranfield: Cranfield University.

Singh, Val and Susan Vinnicombe (2004a), 'Why so few women directors in top UK boardrooms? Evidence and theoretical explanations', *Corporate Governance: An International Review*, **12**(4), 479–88.

Singh, Val and Susan Vinnicombe (2004b), *The Female FTSE Report 2004*, Cranfield: Cranfield University.

Singh, Val and Susan Vinnicombe (2005), *The Female FTSE Report 2005*, Cranfield: Cranfield University.

Singh, Val, Susan Vinnicombe and Phyllis Johnson (2001), 'Women directors on top UK boards', *Corporate Governance: An International Review*, **9**(3), 206–16.

Singh, Val, Susan Vinnicombe and Savita Kumra (2006 in press), 'Women in formal corporate networks – An organisational citizenship perspective', *Women in Management Review*.

Tajfel, Henri and J.C. Turner (1986), 'The social identity theory of intergroup behaviour', in S.Worchel and W.G. Austin (eds), *Psychology of Intergroup Relations*, Chicago, IL: Nelson-Hall.

Tharenou, Phyllis, S.Latimer and Denise Conroy (1994), 'How to make it to the top? An examination of influences on women's and men's managerial advancement', *Academy of Management Journal*, **37**, 899–931.

Tyson, Laura (2003), *The Tyson Report on the Recruitment and Development of Non-Executive Directors*, London: London Business School.

Westphal, James and Edward Zajac (1995), 'Who shall govern? CEO/Board power, demographic similarity and new director selection', *Administrative Science Quarterly*, **40**(1), 60–83.

Windolf, Paul (1998), 'Elite networks in Germany and Britain', *Sociology*, **32**, 321–53.

Women & Equality Unit (2002), *Key Indicators of Women's Position in Britain*, London: Department of Trade & Industry.

Zelechowski, Deborah and Diana Bilimoria (2004), 'Characteristics of women and men corporate inside directors in the US', *Corporate Governance*, **12**(3), 337–42.

15 One world: women leading and managing worldwide

Nancy J. Adler

'The best reason for believing that more women will be in charge before long is that in a ferociously competitive global economy, no company can afford to waste valuable brainpower simply because it's wearing a skirt.'

A. Fisher, *Fortune Magazine* (1992)

'For all practical purposes, all business today is global' (Mitroff, 1987: ix). Whereas the twentieth century began the transition to a global economy, the twenty-first century's worldwide interconnectivity of societies and economies is unprecedented. *New York Times* editorial columnist Thomas Friedman (2005a, 2005b) now baldly states that 'the world is flat'. Management scholar Ian Mitroff (1987: x) warns leaders from all sectors that 'Those individual businesses, firms, industries, and whole societies that clearly understand the new rules of doing business in a world economy will prosper; those that do not will perish.' Global competition is forcing executives to realize 'that if they and their organizations are to survive, let alone prosper, they will have to learn to manage and to think very differently'; they will have to learn to manage and to think globally (Mitroff (1987: x).

While companies craft increasingly integrated global business strategies, individuals are being forced to reassess their career possibilities and trajectories from a worldwide perspective. Skills, standards of excellence, opportunities and competitive threats are no longer relative to the firm next door or neighboring communities; they too have become irrefutably global. Being the best performer locally no longer guarantees a promotion, nor even that one's job or company will exist a year from now. Economically-advantaged managers and professionals from historically prosperous regions readily perceive such increases in global competition as threats. Those from transitional and developing economies – such as China and India – often perceive the same increase in worldwide competitiveness as offering unprecedented economic opportunities (see Friedman, 2005a, 2005b). What will the world's global interconnectedness and competitiveness mean for women seeking to manage and to lead worldwide?

This chapter will explain the reasons for the increasing numbers of women executives and leaders worldwide. It will place the characteristics of women managers and leaders, often labeled as 'feminine' in the North American literature, within a broader cross-cultural context. It will then explore a series of myths and facts about women who are working across borders. It will close by raising questions about what women and men need to bring to twenty-first century leadership.

A scarcity of women: no longer an option

Throughout history, including in the most recent century, women have been underrepresented in business and societal leadership everywhere in the world. At the close of the twentieth century, women held less than 3 per cent of the most senior management positions in major corporations in the United States (Wellington, 1996) and less than 2 per cent of senior management positions in Europe (Dwyer et al., 1996). In many countries, the proportion of women executives never made it above 1 per cent. In Italy, for example, only 0.1 per cent of senior managers were women (Dwyer et al., 1996; see also International Labor Office, 1997). Such scarcity is no longer an option for societies and companies hoping to prosper in the twenty-first century. As global competition intensifies, the opportunity cost of limiting executive talent to men is just too high (see Elron and Kark, 2000; Linehan and Walsh, 2001; and Adler 2002a, among others).

Not surprisingly, careful observation reveals that historic patterns are changing, with increasing numbers of companies and countries moving away from their traditional men-only patterns for senior leadership. As shown in Table 15.1, for example, of the 68 women who have served in their country's highest political leadership position – either as president or prime minister – half have come into office in just the last decade. As shown in Table 15.2, more than 80 per cent (57 of the 68) are the first woman their country has ever selected.[1] Similarly, among the women CEOs currently leading major companies, almost all are the first woman their particular company has ever selected (see Adler 1997a, 1997b, 1999a, 1999b, 1999c, 2002a, 2003a and 2005).[2]

Larger candidate pools guarantee better executives

Increases in the number of women executives are due primarily to the imperatives of global competition, often accompanied by an overwhelming desire for change, not to a worldwide upsurge in societal commitment to either equity or equality. Legislation mandating equitable treatment of women has been passed in some countries, including affirmative-action

Table 15.1   Women leading countries: a chronology

Country	Name	Office	Date
Sri Lanka	(Sirimavo Bandaranaike)	Prime Minister	1960–65, 70–77, 94–2000
India	(Indira Gandhi)	Prime Minister	1966–1977, 1980–1984
Israel	(Golda Meir)	Prime Minister	1969–1975
Argentina	(Maria Estela [Isabel] Martínez de Perón)	President	1974–1976
Central African Rep.	Elizabeth Domitien	Prime Minister	1975–1976
Netherlands Antilles	Lucinda da Costa Gomez-Matheeuws	Prime Minister	1977
Portugal	Maria de Lourdes Pintasilgo	Prime Minister	1979 (5 mths)
Bolivia	Lidia Gueiler Tejada	Interim President, Prime Minister	1979–1980
Great Britain	Margaret Thatcher	Prime Minister	1979–1990
Dominica	Mary Eugenia Charles	Prime Minister	1980–1995
Iceland	Vigdís Finnbógadottir	President	1980–1996
Norway	Gro Harlem Brundtland	Prime Minister	1981;1986–89;1990–1996
Yugoslavia	Milka Planinc	Prime Minister	1982–1986
Malta	Agatha Barbara	President	1982–1987
Guinea Bissau	Carmen Pereira	Acting President	1984 (3 days)
Netherlands Antilles	Maria Liberia-Peters	Prime Minister	1984–1986; 1989–1994
The Philippines	Corazon Aquino	President	1986–1992
Pakistan	Benazir Bhutto	Prime Minister	1988–1990; 1993–1996
Lithuania	Kazimiera-Danute Prunskiene	Prime Minister	1990–1991
Haiti	Ertha Pascal-Trouillot	President	1990–1991
Burma (Myanmar)	Aung San Suu Kyi	Opposition Leader**	1990–**
German Democratic Republic	Sabine Bergmann-Pohl	Chairman of the Volksammer (Staatspräsident)	1990 (6 mths)

Ireland	Mary Robinson	President	1990–1997
Nicaragua	Violeta Barrios de Chamorro	President	1990–1996
Bangladesh	*Khaleda Zia	Prime Minister	1991–1996; 2001-*
France	Edith Cresson	Prime Minister	1991–1992
Poland	Hanna Suchocka	Prime Minister	1992–1993
Canada	Kim Campbell	Prime Minister	1993
Burundi	Sylvia Kinigi	Prime Minister	1993–1994 (4 mths)
Faeroe Islands	Marita Peterson	Prime Minister	1993–1994
Rwanda	(Agatha Uwilingiyimana)	Prime Minister	1993–1994
Turkey	Tansu Çiller	Prime Minister	1993–1996
Netherlands Antilles	Susanne Camelia-Romer	Prime Minister	1993; 1998–1999
Bulgaria	Reneta Indzhova	Interim Prime Minister	1994–1995 (3 mths)
Sri Lanka	*Chandrika Bandaranaike Kumaratunga	President & former Prime Minister	1994-*
Haiti	Claudette Werleigh	Prime Minister	1995–1996
Bangladesh	Hasina Wajed	Prime Minister	1996–2001
Liberia	Ruth Perry	Chair, Ruling Council	1996–97
Ecuador	Rosalia Arteaga	President	1997 (3 days)
Bermuda	Pamela Gordon	Premier	1997–1998
Bosnian Serb Republic	Biliana Plavsic	President	1997–1998
Ireland	*Mary McAleese	President	1997-*
New Zealand	Jenny Shipley	Prime Minister	1997–1999
Guyana	Janet Jagan	Prime Minister, President	1997–1999
Bermuda	Jennifer Smith	Premier	1998–2003
Lithuania	Irene Degutienë	Acting Prime Minister	1999 (22 days)
Mongolia	Nyam-Osorily Tuyaa	Acting Prime Minister	July 1999 (9 days)
Switzerland	Ruth Dreifuss	President	1999
Latvia	*Vaira Vike-Freiberga	President	1999-*

Table 15.1 continued

Country	Name	Office	Date
Panama	Mireya Moscoso	President	1999–2004
New Zealand	*Helen Clark	Prime Minister	1999–*
Finland	*Tarja Halonen	President	2000–*
Philippines	*Gloria Macapagal-Arroyo	President	2001–*
Senegal	Madior Boye	Prime Minister	2001–2002
Indonesia	Megawati Sukarnoputri	President	2001–2004
South Korea	Chang Sang	Prime Minister	July 2002 (20 days)
Serbia	Natasa Micic	Acting President	Dec. 2002–Feb. 2004
São Tome & Principe	Maria das Neves de Souse	Prime Minister	2002–2004
Finland	Anneli Jäätteenmäki	Prime Minister	April–June 2003 (2 mths)
Peru	Beatriz Merino	Prime Minister	2003 (6 mths)
Netherlands Antilles	Mirna Louise-Godett	Prime Minister	2003–2004
Georgia	Nino Burdzhanadze	Acting President	2003–2004
Macedonia	Radmila Sekerinska	Acting Prime Minister	2004
Austria	Barbara Prammer	Acting Joint Head of State	July–August 2004
New Caledonia	*Maria-Noëlle Thérmereau	President	2004–*
Mozambique	*Luisa Dias Diogo	Prime Minister	2004–*
Ukraine	*Yuliya Tymoshenko	Prime Minister	2005–*

Notes:
( ) = No longer living.
* = Currently in office.
** = Party won 1990 election but prevented by military from taking office; Nobel Prize laureate.

Table 15.2 *Countries having selected two or more women as president or prime minister*

Country	Name	Office
Bangladesh	Khaleda Zia	Prime Minister
	Hasina Wajid	Prime Minister
Bermuda	Pamela Gordon	Premier
	Jennifer Smith	Premier
Finland	Tarja Halonen	President
	Anneli Jäätteenmäki	Prime Minister
Haiti	Bertha Pascal-Trouillot	President
	Claudette Werleigh	Prime Minister
Ireland	Mary Robinson	President
	Mary McAleese	President
Lithuania	Kazimiera-Danute Prunskiene	Prime Minister
	Irene Degutienë	Prime Minister
Liberia	Ruth Perry	Chair, Ruling Council
	Ellen Johnson-Sirleaf	President
Netherlands-	Lucinda de Costa	
Antilles	Gomez-Matheeuws	Prime Minister
	Maria Liberia-Peters	Prime Minister
	Suzanne Camelia-Romer	Prime Minister
	Mirna Louise-Godett	Prime Minister
New Zealand	Jenny Shipley	Prime Minister
	Helen Clark	Prime Minister
Philippines	Corazon Aquino	President
	Gloria Arroyo	President
Sri Lanka	Sirimavo Bandaranaike	Prime Minister
	Chandrika Kumaratunga	President

initiatives, but is strictly enforced in only a subset of those countries. Such legislative initiatives, however, neither explain the worldwide trends, nor the changes at the top of the hierarchy. Bangladesh, for example, a country not known for its commitment to women's rights, has had two women serve as prime minister. Countries often lauded for having some of the most progressive legislation supporting the equal treatment of women, such as Sweden and the United States, have had, to date, no women presidents or prime ministers. As years of glass-ceiling research reveals, senior executive and leadership positions are much less subject to legislative pressures than are positions at lower levels (see, among others, Strachan et al. (2004) for a broad overview and Vilkinas (1991) for an Australian perspective). As Powell

(1999b, p. 334) explains, 'women's presence in top management positions violates the societal norm of men's higher status and superiority to a greater extent than women's presence in lower-level management positions.'

Adding women to the executive ranks increases competitiveness, and is therefore particularly important today. One need not rely on ideological or values-based arguments to understand why. Basic statistics reveal the inevitable dynamic. Including both women and men doubles the pool of potential talent. Statistically, if you draw from a larger population, on average, you select better leaders. Placed within the context of economic competitiveness, companies and countries that do not discriminate against women for professional positions are therefore likely to outperform those that do. As long as competition was neither global nor intense, the impact of such discrimination was, to a large extent, muted. Borders protected countries from being threatened by higher levels of competitiveness in other countries and regions. Given the competitive nature of the twenty-first century's global economy, the impact of discrimination can no longer be hidden. As summarized by Harvard Business School professor Rosabeth Moss-Kanter,

> Meritocracy – letting talent rise to the top regardless of where it is found and whether it is male or female – is essential to business success in free-market economies. Within this context, the equality of women in the work force is no longer a political luxury. It has become a competitive necessity.[3]

It is not surprising that banking and finance – one of the first industries to go global – was also one of the first industries to expand its expatriate-manager candidate pool (already in the 1980s) to include women (Adler, 1987; Adler and Izraeli, 1988 and 1994).

Women's unique and complementary contributions

Statistics-based explanations for the increase in women managers and executives worldwide do not rely on the assumption that women are either similar to or different from men. However, other common explanations for why organizations worldwide are including more women assume that women bring unique skills and approaches to managing and leading. They suggest that organizations and societies can benefit from the unique and complementary contributions women can make.[4] Based on research, some scholars have concluded that the ways in which women differ from men endow them with the very skills that twenty-first century organizations most need (see, among others, Aburdene and Naisbitt, 1992; Eisler, 1987; Grant, 1988; Helgesen, 1990; Peters, 1989 and Rosener, 1990). Calas and Smirchich (1993), for example, succinctly state that 'the economic exigenc[ies] of global competition...[make] feminine characteristics admirable in both men and women.' At the very least, this perspective views women's and men's differentiated approaches as complementary.

The benefits of synergy

Beyond capturing the unique contributions of women, some scholars suggest that increasing the number of women executives offers the potential to achieve synergies. Synergy occurs when the combination of women's and men's approaches leads to creativity and composite benefits that would be unlikely, or completely impossible, within homogeneous (male-only) populations (see Adler, 2002b: Chapter 4). Similar to the complementary-contribution perspective, synergy relies on the assumption that women differ from men in ways that are relevant to twenty-first century management and leadership.

As described above, statistics-based benefits hold true whether or not women differ from their male counterparts. By contrast, complementary-contribution and synergistic benefits depend on women differing from men in their approaches to managing and leading. Not surprisingly, this crucial similar-versus-different dilemma surfaces frequently within multinational enterprises, with American managers often asserting that relevant differences do not exist, while managers from non-English speaking countries frequently contend the opposite – that women are inherently different from men.[5] Given the paucity of research on global women leaders, existing studies cannot, as yet, resolve this controversy (see, among others, Osland et al., 1998; Powell, 1999a; Yeager, 1999).[6]

In considering women's roles as global leaders and managers, one of the greatest traps is the belief that assumptions are facts, rather than assumptions. Another common trap is the belief that people from around the world are similar, if not identical. They are not. Because such assumptions are frequently held subconsciously, rather than expressed explicitly, opportunities for dysfunctional disagreement are high. Denying that significant differences exist, for example, has a long history in countries such as the United States in which fairness is most frequently implicitly defined as treating women and men identically (rather than equivalently). Rarely does it occur to Americans that other equally fair, but different approaches exist.

Understanding how global organizations view difference

When viewing differences between women's and men's approaches to leadership from a global perspective, one needs to proceed with caution (Adler, 2002c). Leadership approaches that have frequently been labeled as feminine in the

North American management literature – including seeing women as more cooperative, participative, interactional, and as using a more relational style – reflect patterns of male/female differences specific to the United States, rather than reflecting broader, more universal patterns. Male managers in many parts of the world, including in the fastest growing economies of Asia, exhibit a more supposedly feminine style than do many American men.[7] Cambridge management scholar Charles Hampden-Turner (1993:1) notes:

> America's ultra-masculine corporate value system has been losing touch progressively with the wider world. It needs a change of values, desperately, or it will continue to under-perform, continue to lose touch with the value systems of foreigners, which ironically are much closer to the values in which American women are raised.... American women, who are socialized to display values antithetical yet complementary to American men, have within their culture vitally important cures for American economic decline.

Many of the distinctions describing domestic American women and men have been over-generalized, and, as such, offer poor guidance to those leading global organizations or working in other parts of the world.

Taking a global perspective, Hampden-Turner (1993) describes some of the changes in values orientations as the economy shifts from the twentieth century's emphasis on mass production to the twenty-first century's emphasis on mass-customization. With such shifts, styles based more on interaction and relationship become more important. Whereas the typical American male's universalistic approach of treating everyone the same according to codified rules worked well for mass production of products such as jeans, Coke, and hamburgers sold to a mass domestic market, a more typically feminine (from a North American perspective) particularist approach works best for developing products and services – such as software – which must be tailored to individual clients and their particular needs (Hampden-Turner, 1993:6). To understand specific markets and specific clients well enough to fashion suitable products and services to their needs, one must develop deep relationships (Hampden-Turner, 1993:6). Not surprisingly, relational skills (labeled by anthropologists as particularism and by North Americans as typically feminine) outperform the seemingly more objective approach of everyone following the same rules (labeled as universalism by anthropologists and as typically male by North Americans). The distinction is not strictly male/female, but rather a difference between the approach of most American male managers and that of most other managers around the world.[8]

According to research, American women display a relational style of communicating that more closely resembles the style of most non-American managers than that of most American male managers. Given American women managers' concurrence with the relational styles of their non-

American clients and colleagues, it is not surprising that, on average, women expatriate managers from the United States outperform their American male counterparts (Adler, 1994, 1987). It is not that the distinction between women and men identified in the US-based managerial literature is either incorrect or inconsequential; it is simply incomplete. Without appreciating American male managers as outliers relative to their colleagues from around the world, it is impossible to begin to appreciate what women's and men's approaches can bring to global organizations in the twenty-first century.

Women managing across borders

Whereas the proportion of women managers working domestically within such countries as the United States has increased markedly over the last few decades, the number of women working outside their home country has not increased to the same degree. Given the globalization of the economy, this paucity of international experience among women managers is particularly concerning, as no person, male or female, will be prepared to assume significant leadership in the twenty-first century without having developed a global worldview based on substantial multi-country experience (Adler, 2003b).[9]

Reality: numbers increasing

How many women are sent by their companies on assignments abroad? In the 1980s, only 3 per cent of North American expatriate managers were women (Adler, 1984c). At that time, no higher percentage existed anywhere else in the world. By the early 1990s, a survey of Asian, European and North American expatriate managers revealed that the proportion of women had risen to 5 per cent (ORC, 1992). A few years later, a 1995 UK survey (UMIST, CBI and CIB, 1995) documented that just under 9 per cent of expatriates were women. At about the same time, a 1996 US survey found that 14 per cent of American expatriate managers were women (Windham, NFTC, 1997). By 2002, data from Asia, Europe and the United States revealed that the proportion of women among expatriate managers in all three regions was 14 per cent (ORC, 2002). Although these surveys cannot be meaningfully compared due to varying methodologies, the proportion of women expatriates has clearly risen and can be expected to continue to do so. Selmer and Leung (2003d), among others, attribute this increase to the escalating intensity of worldwide economic competition, along with changes in corporate business strategies and changes in the women professionals themselves.

During the same period that the proportion of women expatriates was increasing, the work performed by expatriates and their role within multinational companies' overall business strategy also evolved. Through most of the twentieth century, most companies viewed expatriates, as well as the international operations within which they worked, as marginal to their overall business strategies (see Adler, 2002b). By the end of the twentieth century, however, most companies recognized that their industries and companies had gone global, and, for the first time, expatriates were viewed as central to business success (Adler, 2002b). Moreover, by the close of the twentieth century, the success of global operations was no longer seen as primarily the concern of expatriates, but rather, it was viewed as part of almost every manager's responsibility. As historic patterns of domestic and multi-domestic management became a relic of the past, virtual and co-located global teams, international business travel, international commuting, and both shorter- and longer-term global assignments emerged as part of most successful managers' business careers (see, among others, Adler, 2000; Adler and Ghadar, 1990, 1993; Mayerhofer et al., 2004). For women, this means that what had been a nice-to-have international experience that was often denied to them became a must-have career experience that was becoming somewhat more open to them, but which was still more frequently offered to men.

Why have multinational and global companies sent so few women on expatriate assignments? The most commonly believed reasons are that (1) women don't want to go abroad, (2) companies do not want to send women abroad, (3) foreigners are so prejudiced that women would not succeed even if sent, and (4) dual-career marriages make expatriation impossible for most women (Adler, 1994; also see Harris, 1995).

Myth: women don't want international careers
The longstanding belief that women don't want international careers, widely held by men and women alike, was first disproved in a study in the 1980s. Women were shown to be just as interested in international careers and expatriate assignments as their male counterparts, and slightly more prepared (Adler, 1984b, 1994). More than a decade later, Chusmir and Frontczak (1990) reconfirmed women's and men's equal interest, and in some cases equal disinterest, in international careers. Hill and Tillery (1992), basing their conclusions on a study of university students, demonstrated that women were more interested than men in working abroad. Not surprisingly, the level of women's interest varies, as does that of their male colleagues, depending on the region of the world in which the foreign assignment is located (see Lowe et al., 1999; Adler, 1984b).

Although research existed earlier, it was not until 2000 that many companies began to realize that women were as interested as their male colleagues in international careers (Stroh et al., 2000b; Caligiuri and

Tung, 1999). Many women, however, continue to doubt their companies' commitment to act on such changed beliefs (Stroh et al., 2000a, 2000b).

Unlike attitudes prominently expressed during the 1980s, when being a woman was perceived to be a disadvantage vis-à-vis getting selected for and performing well on an international assignment, by the 1990s women began realizing that being a woman could be an advantage (Adler and Izraeli, 1994; Taylor and Napier, 1996b). Interestingly, some of the advantages of being a woman that the female expatriates recognized when working abroad are also now cited by women country presidents and prime ministers as they assume the highest political leadership of their country. The advantages these prominent women see include being visible and memorable as well as symbolizing the potential for closer relationships and for the types of positive change that were previously unimaginable (see Adler, 1987, 1996, 1998a, 2003a). In the context of what is needed for the twenty-first century, most people would consider these to be important advantages.

One demonstration of women's interest in working internationally was already reflected in the earlier studies: most women expatriates, unlike their male counterparts, asked to be sent abroad (Adler, 1987).[10] By contrast, up through the 1980s, most men waited for their company to ask them to consider a foreign assignment. Most women in the same era who were successful in being sent abroad initiated their assignments by going to their boss or other relevant decision-maker within the company and expressing interest in a foreign posting. If the woman failed to initiate a conversation in which she expressed interest in expatriation, it would often not occur to her company that they could consider her as a potential candidate. A recent study conducted in Hong Kong found that women who take the initiative to secure global assignments usually succeed in being sent (Selmer and Leung, 2003b). Given that the historical expatriate literature shows that the desire to go abroad is one of the best predictors of success on an expatriate assignment, it is particularly encouraging to learn that most women who are selected for international assignments desire to go. Historically, this has never been the case for the majority of male expatriates (see Adler, 2002b).

Reality: companies hesitate to send women abroad
Research in the late 1970s first confirmed that companies do, in fact, hesitate to send women abroad (Thal and Cateora, 1979; Izraeli et al, 1980). This hesitation was reconfirmed by Adler (1984a) in the early 1980s. More than half the international human resource managers surveyed in the early 1980s expressed hesitation, if not outright resistance, to selecting women as expatriate managers (Adler, 1984a). The primary reasons companies gave for their hesitancy, as expressed by three-quarters of the surveyed

international HR managers, were that they believed that foreigners would not accept or sufficiently respect women expatriate managers for them to succeed abroad and that dual-career marriages would make it impossible for married women to move abroad (Adler, 1984a). Both concerns will be discussed in the following sections.

In the 1990s, further research confirmed similar results: companies continued to discriminate against women in their selection of expatriate managers (see Stone, 1991 and Punnett et al., 1992, among others). Some companies claimed that there were insufficient women available to send abroad (Izraeli and Zeira, 1993). Other companies required higher quali- fications for women than for men before they would consider selecting a woman for an international assignment, including requiring women to have a higher level of education, greater technical competency, and more senior experience than their male colleagues prior to being sent abroad (Linehan and Walsh, 1999; 2000). Vague selection criteria gave still other companies the leeway to deselect women for a variety of unspecified reasons (see Harris, 1999; 2002). By contrast, companies using transparent and formal selection processes for men and women, based on job-specific criteria, select more women for international assignments (see Harris, 1999; 2002). Other research identified the scarcity of women mentors, coaches and role models as organizational factors reducing women's ability to take expatriate assignments and to follow international careers (Linehan and Scullion, 2001a; see also Linehan and Scullion, 2001b).[11] Given the nature of the twenty-first century's global economy, difficulty obtaining international assignments not only reduces the number of women expatriates, it also contributes to the glass ceiling inhibiting women's promotion into companies' most senior executive positions (see Linehan and Walsh, 1999; Foster, 1999; Haines and Saba, 1999).

In addition to reviewing selection processes, scholars have begun to investigate corporate career-development activities offered to male and female expatriates (see Culpan and Wright, 2002, among others). Based on their research, Selmer and Leung (2003a) doubt that the support given to today's female and male expatriates is equivalent. Not surprisingly, they concluded that it is unreasonable to expect male and female expatriates to perform at equivalent levels until they receive equivalent developmental support (Selmer and Leung, 2003a).

One particularly forward-thinking developmental strategy was used by Bestfoods, an 8.5 billion dollar global company, based out of the United States. The then CEO of Bestfoods, Dick Shoemate, understood the need to change the perceptions of Bestfoods' mostly-male senior leadership, as well as that of the highest potential women managers from around the world, if he was to reach his goal for Bestfoods: increasing business competitiveness by increasing the number of women from around the world in the company's most senior leadership positions. Shoemate convened a Women's Global Leadership Forum after instituting a corporate-wide process to identify the highest potential and most senior women in the company worldwide, the perceptual and systemic barriers to women's career success, and the potential advantages to the company's business strategy that could be derived from promoting more women. The pre-Forum and post-Forum process, along with the Forum itself, led to marked changes in the number of women from around the world in senior positions as well as to increases in the recognition and support the women received. One of the aspects that made Bestfoods' Women's Global Leadership Forum unique – as compared with many seemingly similar events held at other companies – was that it was global. Neither an American perspective nor people from the United States were allowed to dominate the Forum or the process. Cultural variations among the women in how they saw themselves, their careers, and their roles within the company were allowed to surface and be discussed. There was no attempt to construct a monolithic women's perspective and juxtapose it against an equally artificial unitary men's perspective (see Osland et al., 2002, and Adler et al., 2001a, 2001b, 2000).

Myth: foreigners' prejudice makes it impossible for women to succeed abroad

One of the most common reasons companies give for hesitating to send women abroad on expatriate assignments is that foreigners are so prejudiced against women that it would be impossible for female expatriate managers to succeed abroad. The evidence, however, reveals that their fears are unwarranted (and are often, unfortunately, a naïve projection of their own belief systems onto foreigners). The first study of women expatriate managers' ability to succeed abroad was conducted in the 1980s and showed that North American women were slightly more successful than their male counterparts when working in Asia on expatriate assignments for North American multinational companies (Adler, 1987). In the 1990s, Caligiuri and Tung (1999) found that performance on expatriate assignments, as assessed by supervisors and as reflected in the proportion of expatriates who wanted to return home early, was equivalent for men and women.[12] More recent studies have confirmed that expatriate women, although facing varying challenges, have succeeded in countries such as China, Japan and, Turkey (Napier and Taylor, 2002; Taylor and Napier, 2001; 1996a). Similar to their North American counterparts, European women have also succeeded when sent abroad as expatriate managers (Linehan and Scullion, 2004; Van der Boon, 2003) as have female Japanese expatriates (Thang et al., 2002).

Paik and Vance's research (2002) established that American women expatriates sent abroad by US multinationals were perceived more negatively by their American colleagues than by their Mexican, Korean and German colleagues; thus strongly suggesting that the problem is much more an issue of home-country prejudice and stereotyping than one of prejudicial behavior on the part of host-country nationals. For years, anecdotal evidence has suggested that the problem of discrimination and prejudice resides at home, but is attributed to foreigners living abroad. As a number of North American women expatriates have stated, 'The hardest job on an international assignment is getting sent, not succeeding once sent' (Adler, 1987; 1994). Paik and Vance's 2002 research was the first to confirm the truth of such anecdotes (also see Van der Boon, 2003).

Many managers, male and female alike, often erroneously assume that foreigners will treat women expatriates in the same way they treat local women. Given that many cultures fail to give their local women adequate respect to allow them to succeed as business and societal leaders, there appeared to be reason for multinational companies to be concerned.[13] The basis for comparison, however, is faulty. Local nationals, wherever they are in the world, differentiate between foreign and local women, and almost always accord the foreign women sent in expatriate status by major multinational companies the respect and status the women need to succeed (see Adler, 1987; Adler and Izraeli, 1994).

Myth: dual-career marriages create insurmountable obstacles for women working abroad

Do dual-career marriages still create insurmountable obstacles for companies considering sending women abroad? According to a Catalyst survey of human resource managers from the United States, dual-career marriages render many women unable or unwilling to accept expatriate assignments (as reported in Moore, 2002). Concerns about dual-career marriages were cited as a major factor inhibiting companies' ability to send women abroad by three-quarters of the international human resource managers in the companies surveyed by Adler (1987 and 2002b).

The reality is that most dual-career challenges can be addressed. Many problems, however, are created by companies using international human resource paradigms and policies that were designed for another era – an era dominated by single-career couples in which the man was sent abroad as the expatriate manager and his wife either did not work outside the home or was assumed not to work (see Adler, 2002b: Chapter 9). The dynamics of dual-career marriages, therefore, need to be re-examined vis-à-vis global careers, both from the company's and from the woman manager's perspective.[14]

Few dual-career obstacles remain insurmountable when companies exhibit a commitment to resolve them.

Companies and potential women expatriates often assume that living abroad will be more difficult than living in one's home country, and even more difficult for women in dual-career marriages with families. However, when expatriate women from economically developed countries, such as the United States, describe their experiences living abroad with children, many report that it is easier to maintain their three primary roles – those of mother, wife and manager – while abroad than at home (see Adler, 2002b: 280–90). Why? This is because expatriates on most international assignments have access to servants who take care of many of the tasks that the women expatriates were personally responsible for while living in their home country. Moving abroad often offers women more of their scarcest resource: time. Whereas it is easier to move abroad when children are young than when they are teenagers, the influence of children's ages does not differ for female versus male expatriates.

Most, although not all, challenges facing dual-career expatriate couples are either caused or exacerbated by companies using traditional single-career paradigms rather than approaches designed for dual-career couples. Historically, when most companies' expatriate policies were developed, they assumed that the husband was the expatriate manager and that his wife would accompany him, but would not work outside the home. Such companies traditionally offered expatriates extra money – so, among other things, the wife could enjoy the international club while not working. When the topic of employment for the wife came up, companies usually pointed out that the foreign country did not offer working permits to spouses. In some cases, companies attempted to secure low-level positions for the wife at a partner company (thus implicitly assuming that the wife neither had nor wanted a higher level position). In other cases, companies suggested that the wife forgo employment and involve herself in volunteer activities. Other companies offered to replace the salary of wives who had worked at home but couldn't work abroad. In almost all such cases, however, the company assumed that the wife's replacement salary would be insignificant when compared with that of her expatriate manager husband. None of these solutions are a good fit for today's dual-career couples. Each assumes that the wife was either not previously employed, did not previously hold a high-ranked professional position, had a job (not a career), was willing to give up her job, did not want to work abroad, or could not work abroad (see Adler, 2002b).

The first experience most companies had with dual-career couples was with male expatriates who wanted their wives to accompany them abroad. In most of these cases, the companies initially attempted to continue using their single-career-couple paradigms; that is, they told the accompanying wives that they could not work (usually attributing the barrier to the lack of working permits). Whereas this solution seemed appropriate to most companies as long as the expatriate managers they were sending abroad were men and the trailing spouses being asked to give up their jobs and careers were women, the same approach suddenly seemed inappropriate when the same companies began considering sending female expatriate managers abroad whose husbands planned to accompany them. Most companies did not feel comfortable in asking a man to give up either his job or his career. Only when faced with trailing spouses who were men did most companies begin to invent more creative ways to address dual-career obstacles.

Today, whether trailing spouses are male or female, what dual-career couples need from the companies that wish to send them abroad are: (1) career counseling so that the trailing spouse (whether husband or wife) can think through the options that might work at his or her particular career stage and in the part of the world where the potential expatriate assignment is to be located; (2) international executive search services to help the trailing spouse locate appropriate professional positions abroad and learn to present themselves in ways that are attractive to potential foreign-based employers; and (3) flexible benefits packages.

Different couples make different decisions about what will work for them. Many expatriate couples choose to commute, rather than both co-locating in the same foreign city. In such cases, couples need their expatriate package to cover 'staying connected' costs (primarily airline tickets and phone bills). Other couples choose to both move into the same region, but are unable to co-locate in the same city. They too need staying-connected costs reimbursed. Still other couples prefer to have the trailing spouse take primary responsibility for the children, the home and social functions rather than taking paid employment. Whereas this choice has been the conventional choice when the trailing spouse was a woman, it becomes a more challenging choice when the trailing spouse is a man. Few societies readily respect men who take primary responsibility for the home and children and who are financially supported by their wife. If such culturally generated stresses are not explicitly addressed, they can easily damage both the marriage and the expatriate manager's productivity.

Company support is critical for female expatriate managers, no matter what the family situation (see Caligiuri et al., 1999; Selmer and Leung 2003c; Westwood and Leung, 1994, among others). It should be noted that single women who go abroad as expatriate managers, similar to men who find themselves in the role of a trailing spouse, face challenges that most of their predecessors never considered. The issue is not that such problems are insoluble, but rather that reality-based creativity is needed to solve them.

The future

In the decades to come, it is highly likely that companies will increasingly draw on their most talented men and women for global leadership and careers. Women will therefore have more opportunities to succeed on global assignments and as global leaders in the twenty-first century than in any prior era (see, among others, Caliguiuri and Cascio, 1998). Some scholars are even predicting that women will be more in demand than men (among others, see Guthrie et al, 2003). Among other reasons given are that women are model global managers (Tung, 2004), women have more experience working as outsiders (Altman and Shortland, 2001), and as relative remuneration decreases for expatriation – as is currently the case – the proportion of women working abroad will rise (Selmer, 2001).

As scholars seek to understand better the role of women managers and leaders in the twenty-first century, it will be important to go beyond the twentieth-century models based on the personal and professional lifestyles of men. Equally, it will be important to go beyond models based primarily on the experiences of multinational companies headquartered in traditionally prosperous countries. We need to understand better the experience of women from economically developing and transitional economies who seek international careers. More broadly, we need to understand the global business and human resource strategies of companies headquartered outside of North America, Europe and Japan. As our global understanding increases, it will become easier to provide nuanced descriptions of women's managerial and leadership styles, rather than continue to assume that women's contexts and experiences are similar worldwide. Lastly, given the competitive intensity of the global economy, we should strive to learn more about the complementary and synergistic possibilities inherent in women and men working together.

The most important question for the future is not simply how we can increase the proportion of women leaders, executives and managers. Rather, the crucial twenty-first century question is how we can create a society worthy of being bequeathed to future generations (see Adler, 1998b). To create such a society, we need corporations worldwide to understand that the most effective leadership comes from women and men. The world will not benefit if we simply substitute ineffective, greedy women for similarly ineffective, greedy men. The goal is not to have the next Enron led to its demise by Katrina Lay rather than Ken Lay. Equity is only sustainable within a larger system of purpose and meaning.

Notes

1. For a more in-depth discussion of the trends influencing women moving into positions of political leadership, see Adler (1996), (1997a) and (1998a).

2. In the early years of the twenty-first century, the world's media turned their focus on women leaders, including CEOs. See, for example, the Special Issue of the *FT Magazine* on Women in Business (15–16 October, 2005) and *Newsweek*'s special issue on How Women Lead (see Kantrowitz, 2005; Kantrowitz et al., 2005; and McGinn, 2005). In particular, see the articles about women CEOs, including on Shelly Lazarus (Silverman, 2005), on Europe's top 25 women business leaders (Hill et al., 2005), on Spain's Ana Patricia Botin (Crawford, 2005), on what keeps the most senior women leaders on the job (Maitland, 2005), and on Norway's top down strategy increasing the number of women in senior leadership (Clark, 2005).

3. Rosabeth Moss-Kanter's comment on Nancy A. Nichols' *Reach for the Top: Women and the Changing Facts of Work Life* (Nichols, 1994), as cited in the book review by John R. Hook (1994: p. 89).

4. For a discussion of the complementary contribution model, see Adler (1994).

5. For a discussion of Americans' bias toward seeing men and women as similar in the ways they approach organizational issues versus the bias of most non-English speaking cultures to see women and men as clearly differentiated, see Adler et al., (2000, 2001a, 2001b) discussion on the intercultural dynamics within one global company. For a review of the research on the similarities and differences between women and men managers in the United States, see Eagly and Johnson (1990); Eagly et al. (1995); Fondas (1997); Gilligan (1982), Iannello (1992); Lipman-Blumen (1983); Marshall (1984); and Tannen (1990) and (1994).

6. While few studies have focused on women leaders from a cross-cultural perspective, researchers have documented differences between women and men in general, and between female and male managers (primarily in the United States). Although unanimity on specific differences and their effects has yet to be reached, scholars do agree that female and male managers are perceived differently (Maccoby and Jacklin, 1974). Most US research contends that both men and women describe successful managers as more like men than women (see Schein, 1975, among others), with the exception of Schein et al.'s, 1989 study in which men, but not women, persisted in sex-typing managers. Women in countries such as Japan and Thailand are seen as having different characteristics from men in general and from successful managers (Schein et al., 1996).

7. For an example of American men using a more 'masculine' style (as perceived by the Americans) while Malaysian men use a more feminine style (again, as perceived by the Americans), see Adler (2002b: 209–11).

8. Results of research by Trompenaars (1993) and Hampden-Turner (1993) show that American male managers strongly prefer universalism (the less relational style), whereas executives from many very strong economies, such as Hong Kong, Japan and South Korea, emphasize more relational values that are opposite to those of their American male colleagues (Hampden-Turner, 1993). As Hampden-Turner (1993: 6) summarized, at the close of the twentieth century: 'Most American male executives suddenly find themselves ill-suited to the wider world, trying to codify the uncodifiable, flanked by a huge surplus of lawyers using cumbersome rules where other nations enter trusting relationships with subtle communications.'

9. Whereas the focus of this section is on expatriation, there are many approaches that companies use for developing an international perspective in their hi-potential managers and for getting business conducted effectively around the world, including business travel, global project teams, short term assignments abroad, and traditional multi-year expatriate assignments. For a discussion of what has been labeled as *flexpatriation,* see Mayerhofer et al. (2004).

10. Few studies have been conducted to study women's own reluctance to go abroad as expatriate manages. Fischlmayr (2002), for example, investigated the possible impact of women's lack of self confidence and use of negative stereotypes.

11. For a discussion on coaching for women considering international careers and expatriate assignments, see Adler (2003b). For a discussion of the role of mentors for repatriating women expatriate managers, see Linehan and Scullion (2002).

12. See Linehan and Scullion (2002) for a discussion of re-entry issues for women expatriates.

13. See the discussions of local women managers in Canada (Andrew et al., 1994), Finland (Hännien-Salmelin and Petäjäniemi, 1994), France (Serdjenian, 1994), Germany (Antal and Krebsback-Gnath, 1994), Great Britain (Hammond and Holton, 1994), Hong Kong (de Leon and Ho, 1994), Indonesia (Wright and Crockett-Tellei, 1994), Japan (Steinhoff and Tanaka, 1994), Malaysia (Mansor, 1994), the People's Republic of China (Korabik, 1994), Poland (Siemienska, 1994), Singapore (Chan and Lee, 1994), South Africa (Erwee, 1994), the former Soviet Union (Puffer, 1994), Taiwan (Cheng and Liao, 1994), Tanzania (Hollway & Mukurasi, 1994), Thailand (Siengthai and Leelakulthanit, 1994), former Yugoslavia (Kavčič, 1994), and Zimbabwe (Muller, 1994), among others.

14. See Mathur-Helm (2002) for a discussion of the success factors for women selected for international assignments, accepting the assignment, and succeeding once sent.

References

Aburdene, P. and J. Naisbitt (1992), *Megatrends for Women,* New York: Villard Books.

Adler, N.J. (1984a), 'Expecting international success: female managers overseas', *Columbia Journal of World Business*, **19**(3), 79–85.

Adler, N.J. (1984b), 'Women do not want international careers: and other myths about international management', *Organizational Dynamics*, **13**(2), 66–79.

Adler, N.J. (1984c), 'Women in international management: where are they?', *California Management Review*, **26**(4), 78–89.

Adler, N.J. (1987), 'Pacific Basin managers: a gaijin, not a woman', *Human Resource Management*, **26**(2), 169–92.

Adler, N.J. (1994), 'Competitive frontiers: women managing across borders', in N.J. Adler and D.N. Izraeli (eds), *Competitive Frontiers: Women Managers in a Global Economy*, Cambridge, MA: Blackwell, pp. 22–40.

Adler, N.J. (1996), 'Global women political leaders: an invisible history, an increasingly important future', *Leadership Quarterly*, **7**(1), 133–61.

Adler, N.J. (1997a), 'Global leaders: a dialogue with future history', *International Management*, **1**(2), 21–33.

Adler, N.J. (1997b), 'Global leadership: women leaders', *Management International Review*, **37** (Special Issue 1), 135–43.

Adler, N.J. (1998a), 'Did you hear? Global leadership in charity's world', *Journal of Management Inquiry*, **7**(2), 21–33.

Adler, N.J. (1998b), 'Societal leadership: the wisdom of peace', in S. Srivastva (ed.), *Executive Wisdom and Organizational Change*, San Francisco, CA: Jossey-Bass, pp. 243–337.

Adler, N.J. (1999a), 'Global entrepreneurs: women, myths, and history', *Global Focus*, **1**(4), 125–34.

Adler, N.J. (1999b), 'Global leaders: women of influence', in G.N. Powell (ed.), *Handbook of Gender in Organizations*, Thousand Oaks, CA: Sage, pp. 239–61.

Adler, N.J. (1999c), 'Twenty-first century leadership: reality beyond the myths', in A.M. Rugman (series ed.) and Richard Wright (volume ed.), *Research in Global Strategic Management, Volume 7: International Entrepreneurship: Globalization of Emerging Business*, Greenwich, CT: JAI Press, pp. 173–90.

Adler, N.J. (2000), 'Coaching global executives: women succeeding in a world beyond here', in M. Goldsmith, L. Lyons and A. Freas (eds), *Coaching for leadership*, San Francisco, CA: Jossey-Bass, pp. 359–68.

Adler, N.J. (2002a), 'Global managers: no longer men alone', *International Journal of Human Resource Management*, **13**(5), 743–60.

Adler, N.J. (2002b), *International Dimensions of Organizational Behavior*, 4th edn, Cincinnati, OH: South Western.

Adler, N.J. (2002c), 'Women joining men as global leaders in the new economy', in M. Gannon and K. Newman (eds), *Handbook of Cross-Cultural Management*, Oxford: Basil Blackwell, pp. 236–49.

Adler, N.J. (2003a), 'Shaping history: global leadership in the twenty-first century', in R.J. Burke and C.L. Cooper (eds), *Leading in Turbulent Times: Managing in the New World of Work*, Oxford: Blackwell , pp. 302–18.

Adler, N.J. (2003b), 'The art of leadership: coaching in the 21st century', in H. Morgan, P. Harkins and M. Goldsmith (eds), *Profiles in Coaching: The 2004 Handbook of Best Practices in Leadership Coaching*, Burlington, MA: Linkage, pp. 113–17.

Adler, N.J. (2005), 'Leading beyond boundaries: the courage to enrich the world', in L. Coughlin, E. Wingard and K. Hollihan (eds), *Enlightened Power: How Women Are Transforming the Practice of Leadership*, San Francisco, CA: Jossey-Bass, pp. 350–66 and 505–507.

Adler, N.J. and F. Ghadar (1990), 'Strategic human resource management: a global perspective', in R. Pieper (ed.), *Human Resource Management in International Comparison*, Berlin: deGruyter, pp. 235–60.

Adler, N.J. and F. Ghadar (1993), 'A strategic phase approach to international human resource management', in D. Wong-Rieger and F. Rieger (eds), *International Management Research: Looking to the Future*, Berlin: deGruyter, pp. 55–77.

Adler, N.J. and D.N. Izraeli (eds) (1988), *Women in Management Worldwide*, Armonk, New York: M.E. Sharpe.

Adler, N.J. and D.N. Izraeli (eds) (1994), *Competitive Frontiers: Women Managers in a Global Economy*, Oxford: Blackwell .

Adler, N.J.; L.W. Brody and J.S. Osland (2000), 'The women's global leadership forum: enhancing one company's global leadership capability', *Human Resource Management*, **39**(2–3), 209–25.

Adler, N.J., L.W. Brody and J.S. Osland (2001a), 'Advances in global leadership: the women's global leadership forum', in W.H. Mobley (ed.), *Advances in Global Research*, Volume 2, Greenwich, CT: JAI Press, pp. 351–83.

Adler, N.J., L.W. Brody and J.S. Osland (2001b), 'Going beyond twentieth century leadership: a CEO develops his company's global competitiveness', *Cross-Cultural Management: An International Journal*, **8**(3–4), 11–34.

Altman, Y. and S. Shortland (2001), 'Women, aliens and international assignments', *Women in Management Review*, **16**(3), 141–5.

Andrew, C., C. Coderre and A. Denis (1994), 'Women in management: the Canadian Experience', in N.J. Adler and D.N. Izraeli (eds), *Competitive Frontiers: Women Managers in a Global Economy*, Cambridge, MA: Blackwell, pp. 377–87.

Antal, A.B. and C. Krebsbach-Gnath (1994), 'Women in management in Germany: East, West, and Reunited', in N.J. Adler and D.N. Izraeli (eds), *Competitive Frontiers: Women Managers in a Global Economy*, Cambridge, MA: Blackwell, pp. 208–23.

Calas, M.B. and L. Smircich (1993), 'Dangerous liaisons: The "feminine-in-management" meets "globalization"', *Business Horizons*, **36**(2), 71–81.

Caligiuri, P.M. and W.F. Cascio (1998), 'Can we send her there? Maximizing the success of western women on global assignments', *Journal of World Business*, **33**(4), 394–416.

Caligiuri, P.M. and R.L. Tung (1999), 'Comparing the success of male and female expatriates from a US-based multinational company', *International Journal of Human Resource Management*, **10**(5), 763–82.

Caligiuri, P.M., A. Joshi and M. Lazarova (1999), 'Factors influencing the adjustment of women on global assignments', *International Journal of Human Resource Management*, **10**(2), 163–79.

Chan, A. and J. Lee (1994), 'Women executives in a newly industrialized economy: the singapore scenario', in N.J. Adler and D.N. Izraeli (eds), *Competitive Frontiers: Women Managers in a Global Economy*, Cambridge, MA: Blackwell, pp. 127–42.

Cheng, W. and L. Liao (1994), 'Women managers in Taiwan', in N.J. Adler and D.N. Izraeli (eds), *Competitive Frontiers: Women Managers in a Global Economy*, Cambridge, MA: Blackwell, pp. 143–59.

Chusmir, L.H. and N.T. Frontczak (1990), 'International management opportunities for women: women and men paint different pictures', *International Journal of Management*, **7**(3), 295–301.

Clark, P. (2005), 'The accidental feminist', *FT Magazine*, 15–16 October (127), 38–43.

Crawford, L. (2005), 'More than a name', *FT Magazine*, 15–16 October (127), 20–21.

Culpan, O. and G.H. Wright (2002), 'Women abroad: getting the best results from women managers', *International Journal of Human Resource Management*, **13**(5), 784–801.

De Leon, C.T. and S. Ho (1994), 'The third identity of modern chinese women: women managers in Hong Kong', in N.J. Adler and D.N. Izraeli (eds), *Competitive Frontiers: Women Managers in a Global Economy*, Cambridge, MA: Blackwell, pp. 43–56.

Dwyer, P., M. Johnston and K. Lowry (1996), 'Europe's corporate women', *Business Week*, 15 April, pp. 40–42.

Eagly, A.H. and B. Johnson (1990), 'Gender and leadership style: a meta-analysis', *Psychological Bulletin*, **108**, 233–56.

Eagly, A.H., S.J. Karau and M.G. Makhijani (1995), 'Gender and the effectiveness of leadership: a meta-analysis', *Psychological Bulletin*, **117**, 125–45.

Eisler, R. (1987), *The Chalice and The Blade*, San Francisco, CA: HarperSanFrancisco.

Elron, E. and R. Kark (2000), 'Women managers and international assignments: some recommendations for bridging the gap', in M. Mendenhall and G. Oddou (eds), *Readings and Cases in International Human Resource Management*, Cincinnati, OH: South-Western, pp. 144–54.

Erwee, R. (1994), 'South African women: changing career patterns', in N.J. Adler and D.N. Izraeli (eds), *Competitive Frontiers: Women Managers in a Global Economy*, Cambridge, MA: Blackwell, pp. 325–42.

Fischlmayr, I.C. (2002), 'Female self perception as barrier to international careers?', *International Journal of Human Resource Management*, **13**(5), 773–83.

Fisher, A.B. (1992), 'When will women get to the top?', *Fortune*, 21 September, pp. 44–56.

Fondas, N. (1997), 'The origins of feminization', *Academy of Management Review*, **22**(1), 257–82.

Foster, N. (1999), 'Another "Glass Ceiling"?: The experiences of women professionals and managers on international assignments', *Gender, Work and Organization*, **6**(2), 79–90.

Friedman, T.L. (2005a), 'The World is flat', *New York Times*, 3 April.

Friedman T.L. (2005b), *The World is Flat: A Brief History of the Twenty-First Century*, New York: Farrar, Straus and Giroux.

FT Magazine (2005), 'Women in business: Europe's Top 25', Special Issue, 15–16 October, (127).

Gilligan, C. (1982), *In a Different Voice: Psychological Theory and Women's Development*, Cambridge, MA: Harvard University Press.

Grant, J. (1988), 'Women as managers: what can they offer organizations?', *Organizational Dynamics*, **16**(1), 56–63.

Guthrie, J.P., R.A. Ash and C.D. Stevens (2003), 'Are women better than men? Personality differences and expatriate selection', *Journal of Managerial Psychology*, **18**(3), 229–43.

Haines, V.Y. III and T. Saba (1999), 'International mobility policies and practices: are there gender differences in importance ratings?', *Career Development International*, **4**(4), 206–11.

Hammond, V. and V. Holton (1994), 'The scenario for women managers in Britain in the 1990s', in N.J. Adler and D.N. Izraeli (eds), *Competitive Frontiers: Women Managers in a Global Economy*, Cambridge, MA: Blackwell, pp. 224–42.

Hampden-Turner, C. (1993), 'The structure of entrapment: dilemmas standing in the way of women managers and strategies to resolve these', New York City, Global Business Network Meeting, 9–10 December.

Hänninen-Salmelin, E. and T. Petäjäniemi (1994), 'Women managers, the challenge to management?', in N.J. Adler and D.N. Izraeli (eds), *Competitive Frontiers: Women Managers in a Global Economy*, Cambridge, MA: Blackwell, pp. 175–89.

Harris, H. (1995), 'Women's role in (international) management', in A.-W. Harzig and J. Van Ruysseveldt (eds), *International Human Resource Management*, London: Sage, pp. 229–51.

Harris, H. (1999), 'Women in international management – Why are they not selected?', in C. Brewster and H. Harris (eds), *International HRM – Contemporary Issues in Europe*, London: Routledge, pp. 258–76.

Harris, H. (2002), 'Think international manager, think male: why are women not selected for international management assignments?', *Thunderbird International Business Review*, **44**(2), 175–203.

Helgesen, S. (1990), *The Female Advantage: Women's Ways of Leadership*, New York: Doubleday Currency.

Hill, A., H. Ehren and A. Maitland (2005), 'Breaking ranks', *FT Magazine*, 15–16 October, Issue 127, pp. 18, 22–34.

Hill, C.J. and K.R. Tillery (1992), 'What do male/female perceptions of an international business career suggest about recruitment policies', *SAM Advanced Management Journal*, Autumn, pp. 10–14.

Hollway, W. and L. Mukurasi (1994), 'Women managers in the Tanzanian civil service', in N.J. Adler and D.N. Izraeli (eds), *Competitive Frontiers: Women Managers in a Global Economy*, Cambridge, MA: Blackwell, pp. 343–57.

Hook, J.R. (1994), 'Review of N.A. Nichols' Reach for the Top: women and the changing facts of work life', *Academy of Management Executive*, **8**(2), 87–9.

Iannello, K.P. (1992), *Decisions Without Hierarchy: Feminist Interventions in Organization Theory and Practice*, New York: Routledge.

International Labor Office (1997), *Breaking Through the Glass Ceiling: Women in Management*, Geneva: International Labor Office.

Izraeli, D.N. (1994), 'Outsiders in the promised land: women managers in Israel', in N.J. Adler and D.N. Izraeli (eds), *Competitive Frontiers: Women Managers in a Global Economy*, Cambridge, MA: Blackwell, pp. 301–24.

Izraeli, D.N. and Y. Zeira (1993), 'Women managers in international business: a research review and appraisal', *Business and the Contemporary World*, **5**(3), 35–46.

Izraeli, D.N., M. Banai and Y. Zeira (1980), 'Women executives in MNC subsidiaries', *California Management Review*, **23**(1), 53–63.

Kantrowitz, B. (2005), 'When women lead', *Newsweek*, 24 October, pp. 46–7.

Kantrowitz, B., H. Peterson and P. Wingert (2005), *Newsweek*, 24 October, pp. 48–62.

Kavčič, B. (1994), 'Women in management: the case of the former Yugoslavia', in N.J. Adler and D.N. Izraeli (eds), *Competitive Frontiers: Women Managers in a Global Economy*, Cambridge, MA: Blackwell, pp. 286–98.

Korabik, K. (1994), 'Managerial women in the People's Republic of China: the long march continues' in N.J. Adler and D.N. Izraeli (eds), *Competitive Frontiers: Women Managers in a Global Economy*, Cambridge, MA: Blackwell, pp. 114–26.

Linehan, M. and H. Scullion (2001a), 'Challenges for female international managers: evidence from Europe', *Journal of Managerial Psychology*, **16**(3), 215–28.

Linehan, M. and H. Scullion (2001b), 'European female expatriates careers: critical success factors', *Journal of European Industrial Training*, **25**(8), 392–418.

Linehan, M. and H. Scullion (2002), 'Repatriation of European female corporate executives: an empirical study', *International Journal of Human Resource Management*, **13**(2), 254–67.

Linehan, M. and H. Scullion (2004), 'Towards an understanding of the female expatriate experience in Europe', *Human Resource Management Review*, **14**, 433–48.

Linehan, M. and J.S. Walsh (1999), 'Senior female international managers: breaking the glass border', *Women in Management Review*, **14**(7), 264–72.

Linehan, M. and J.S. Walsh (2000), 'Beyond the traditional linear view of international managerial careers: a new model of the senior female career in an international context', *Journal of European Industrial Training*, **24**(2–4), 178–89.

Linehan, M. and J.S. Walsh (2001), 'Key issues in the senior female international career move: A qualitative study in a European context', *British Journal of Management*, **12**(1), 85–95.

Lipman-Blumen, J. (1983), 'Emerging patterns of female leadership in formal organizations', in M. Horner, C.C. Nadelson, and M.T. Notman (eds), *The Challenge of Change*, New York: Plenum Press, pp. 61–91.

Lowe, K.B., M. Downes and K.G. Kroeck (1999), 'The impact of gender and location on the willingness to accept overseas assignments', *International Journal of Human Resource Management*, **10**(2), 223–34.

Maccoby, E. and C. Jacklin (1974), *The Psychology of Sex Differences*, Stanford, CA: Stanford University Press.

Maitland, A. (2005), 'When push comes to shove', *FT Magazine*, 15–16 October, (127), 36–7.

Mansor, N. (1994), 'Women managers in Malaysia: their mobility and challenges', in N.J. Adler and D.N. Izraeli (eds), *Competitive Frontiers: Women Managers in a Global Economy*, Cambridge, MA: Blackwell, pp. 101–13.

Marshall, J. (1984), *Women Managers: Travellers in a Male World*, New York: Wiley.

Mathur-Helm, B. (2002), 'Expatriate women managers: at the crossroads of success, challenges and career goals', *Women in Management Review*, **17**(1), 18–28.

Mayerhofer, H., L.C. Hartmann and A. Herbert (2004), 'Career management issues for flexpatriate international staff', *Thunderbird International Business Review*, **46**(6), 647–66.

McGinn, D. (2005), 'In good company', *Newsweek*, 24 October, pp. 68–9.

Mitroff, I. (1987), *Business Not As Usual*, San Francisco, CA: Jossey-Bass.

Moore, M.J. (2002), 'Same ticket, different trip: supporting dual-career couples on global assignments', *Women in Management Review*, **17**(2), 61–7.

Muller, H.J. (1994), 'The legacy and opportunities for women managers in Zimbabwe', in N.J. Adler and D.N. Izraeli (eds), *Competitive Frontiers: Women Managers in a Global Economy*, Cambridge, MA: Blackwell, pp. 358–73.

Napier, N.K. and S. Taylor (2002), 'Experiences of women professionals abroad comparisons across Japan, China and Turkey', *International Journal of Human Resource Management*, **15**(2), 837–85.

Nichols, N.A. (1994), *Reach for the Top: Women and the Changing Facts of Work Life*, Boston, MA: Harvard Business School Press.

ORC (Organization Resources Counselors)/CBI (1992), *Update on Survey on Spouses/Partners and International Assignments*, London: ORC Europe and CBI Employee Relocation Council.

ORC (Organization Resources Counselors) (2002), *Dual Careers and International Assignments Survey*, London: Organization Resources Counselors, Inc.

Osland, J.S., N.J. Adler and L.W. Brody (2002), 'Developing women as global leaders: lessons and sense making from an organizational change effort', in R.J. Burke and D.L. Nelson (eds), *Advancing Women's Careers*, Oxford, UK: Blackwell, pp. 15–36.

Osland, J.S., M.M. Snyder and L. Hunter (1998), 'A comparative study of managerial styles among female executives in Nicaragua and Costa Rica', *International Studies of Management and Organization*, **28**(2), 54–73.

Paik, Y. and Vance, C.M. (2002), 'Evidence of back-home selection bias against American female expatriates', *Women in Management Review*, **17**(2), 68–79.

Peters, T. (1989), 'Listen up, guys: women fit profile of execs of future', *Seattle Post-Intelligencer*, 11 April, p. B6.

Powell, G.N. (ed.) (1999a), *Handbook of Gender in Organizations*, Thousand Oaks, CA: Sage.

Powell, G.N. (1999b), 'Reflections on the glass ceiling: recent trends and future prospects', in G.N. Powell (ed.), *Handbook of Gender in Organizations*, Thousand Oaks, CA: Sage, pp. 325–45.

Puffer, S.M. (1994), 'Women managers in the former USSR: a case of "too much equality"?', in N.J. Adler and D.N. Izraeli (eds), *Competitive Frontiers: Women Managers in a Global Economy*, Cambridge, MA: Blackwell, pp. 263–85.

Punnett, B.J., O. Crocker and M.A. Stevens (1992), 'The challenge for women expatriates and spouses: some empirical evidence', *International Journal of Human Resource Management*, **3**(3), 585–92.

Rosener, J. (1990), 'Ways women lead', *Harvard Business Review*, **68**(6), 119–25.

Schein, V. (1975), 'The relationship between sex role stereotypes and requisite management characteristics', *Journal of Applied Psychology*, **60**(3), 340–44.

Schein, V., R. Mueller and C. Jacobson (1989), 'The relationship between structured and requisite management characteristics among college students', *Sex Roles*, **20**(1–2), 103–10.

Schein, V., R. Mueller, T. Lituchy, T and J. Liu (1996), 'Think manager – think male: a global phenomenon?', *Journal of Organizational Behavior*, **17**, 33–41.

Selmer, J. (2001), 'Expatriate selection: back to basics?', *International Journal of Human Resource Management*, **12**(8), 1219–33.

Selmer, J. and A.S.M. Leung (2003a), 'Are corporate career development activities less available to female than to male expatriates?', *Journal of Business Ethics*, **43**(1–2), 125–36.

Selmer, J. and A.S.M. Leung (2003b), 'Expatriate career intentions of women on foreign assignments and their adjustment', *Journal of Managerial Psychology*, **18**(3), 244–58.

Selmer, J. and A.S.M. Leung (2003c), 'International adjustment of female vs. male business expatriates', *The International Journal of Human Resource Management*, **14**(7), 1117–31.

Selmer, J. and A.S.M. Leung (2003d), 'Personal characteristics of female vs male business expatriates', *International Journal of Cross Cultural Management*, **3**(2), 195–212.

Serdjenian, E. (1994), 'Women managers in France', in N.J. Adler and D.N. Izraeli (eds), *Competitive Frontiers: Women Managers in a Global Economy*, Cambridge, MA: Blackwell, pp. 190–205.

Siemienska, R. (1994), 'Women managers in Poland: in transition from Communism', in N.J. Adler and D.N. Izraeli (eds), *Competitive Frontiers: Women Managers in a Global Economy*, Cambridge, MA: Blackwell, pp. 243–62.

Siengthai, S. and O. Leelakulthanit (1994), 'Women in management in Thailand', in N.J. Adler and D.N. Izraeli (eds), *Competitive Frontiers: Women Managers in a Global Economy*, Cambridge, MA: Blackwell, pp. 160–71.

Silverman, G. (2005), 'Accidents will happen', *FT Magazine*, 15–16 October, (127), 16–17.

Steinhoff, P.G. and K. Tanaka (1994), 'Women managers in Japan', in N.J. Adler and D.N. Izraeli (eds), *Competitive Frontiers: Women Managers in a Global Economy*, Cambridge, MA: Blackwell, pp. 79–100.

Stone, R.J. (1991), 'Expatriate selection and failure', *Human Resource Planning*, **14**, 9–18.

Strachan, G., J. Burgess and A. Sullivan (2004), 'Affirmative action or managing diversity: what is the future of equal opportunity policies in organizations?', *Women in Management Review*, **19**(4), 196–204.

Stroh, L.K., A. Varma and S.J. Valy-Durbin (2000a), 'Why are women left at home: Are they unwilling to go on international assignments?', *Journal of World Business*, **35**(3), 241–55.

Stroh, L.K., A. Varma and S.J. Valy-Durbin (2000b), 'Women and expatriation: revisiting Adler's findings', in M.J. Davidson and R.J. Burke (eds), *Women in Management*, London: Sage.

Tannen, D. (1990), *You Just Don't Understand: Women and Men in Conversation*, New York: Ballantine Books.

Tannen, D. (1994), *Talking from 9 to 5: How Women's and Men's Conversational Styles Affect Who Gets Heard, Who Gets Credit, and What Gets Done at Work*, New York: Morrow.

Taylor, S. and N. Napier (1996a), 'Successful women expatriates: the case of Japan', *Journal of International Management*, **2**(1), 51–78.

Taylor, S. and N. Napier (1996b), 'Working in Japan: lessons for women expatriates', *Sloan Management Review*, **37**(Spring), 76–84.

Taylor, S. and N. Napier (2001), 'An American woman in Turkey: adventures unexpected and knowledge unplanned', *Human Resource Management*, **40**(4), 347–64.

Thal, N.L. and P. Cateora (1979), 'Opportunities for women in international business', *Business Horizons*, **22**(6), 21–7.

Thang, L.L., E. MacLachlan and M. Goda (2002), 'Expatriates on the margin – a study of Japanese women working in Singapore', *Geoforum*, **33**(4), 539–51.

Trompenaars, F. (1993), *Riding the Waves of Culture: Understanding Cultural Diversity in Business*, London: The Economist Books.

Tung, R.L. (2004), 'Female expatriates: the model global manager?', *Organizational Dynamics*, **33**(3), 243–53.

UMIST, CBI and CIB (1995), *Assessment, Selection and Preparation for Expatriate Assignments*, London: University of Manchester Institute of Science and Technology, CBI Employee Relocation Council, and the Centre for International Briefing.

Van der Boon, M. (2003), 'Women in international management: An international perspective on women's ways of leadership', *Women in Management Review*, **18**(3), 132–46.

Varma, V., L.K. Stroh and L.B. Schmitt (2001), 'Women and international assignments: the impact of supervisor-subordinate relationships', *Journal of World Business*, **36**(4), 380–88.

Vilkinas, T. (1991), 'Australian women in management', *Women in Management Review and Abstracts*, **6**(1) 17–25.

Wellington, S.W. (1996), *Women in Corporate Leadership: Progress and Prospects*, New York: Catalyst.

Westwood, R.I. and S.M. Leung (1994), 'The female expatriate manager experience', *International Studies of Management and Organization*, **24**(3), 64–85.

Windham and NFTC (1997), *Global Relocation Trends 1996 Survey Report*, New York: Windham International and the National Foreign Trade Council.

Wright, L. and V. Crockett-Tellei (1994), 'Women in management in Indonesia', in N.J. Adler and D.N. Izraeli (eds), *Competitive Frontiers: Women Managers in a Global Economy*, Cambridge, MA: Blackwell, pp. 57–78.

Yeager, M.A. (1999), *Women in Business*, Volumes 1, 2, and 3, Cheltenham, UK and Northampton, MA, USA: Edward Elgar.

Index